STUDIES IN BUSINESS, UNIVERSITY OF CHICAGO

The Management of

CORPORATE CAPITAL

FIRST SERIES (1916 - 1938)

Materials for the Study of Business

EDITED BY DEAN LEON CARROLL MARSHALL AND
DEAN WILLIAM HOMER SPENCER

SECOND SERIES (1938 - 1956)

Business and Economic Publications

EDITED BY DEAN WILLIAM HOMER SPENCER

THIRD SERIES (1959 -)

Studies in Business

EDITED BY DEAN W. ALLEN WALLIS

The Management of CORPORATE CAPITAL

Edited by

EZRA SOLOMON

PROFESSOR OF FINANCE, UNIVERSITY OF CHICAGO

A PUBLICATION OF

Graduate School of Business, The University of Chicago

THIRD SERIES

PUBLISHED BY

The Free Press of Glencoe

A DIVISION OF THE CROWELL-COLLIER PUBLISHING COMPANY

Printed in the United States of America

For information, address:

THE FREE PRESS OF GLENCOE
A DIVISION OF THE CROWELL-COLLIER PUBLISHING COMPANY
640 Fifth Avenue, New York 19, N. Y.

Second Printing May 1961

Library of Congress Catalog Card Number 59-13868

LITHOGRAPHED FOR THE PUBLISHERS BY
NOBLE OFFSET PRINTERS, INC., NEW YORK

Foreword

The present series continues a publication program which the Graduate School of Business inaugurated in 1916. During World War I, the School (then known as the School of Commerce and Administration) sponsored a series called *Materials for the Study of Business,* designed for the purpose of "organizing the business curriculum into a coherent whole." Under the editorship of Dean Leon Carroll Marshall and Dean William Homer Spencer, over fifty titles were published through the University of Chicago Press, many of which have become classics in the field. Among these are:

John Maurice Clark, *Social Control of Business,* 1926. *Studies in the Economics of Overhead Costs,* 1923.

Paul H. Douglas et al., *The Worker in Modern Economic Society,* 1923.

Charles O. Hardy, *Risk and Risk-Bearing,* 1923.

James O. McKinsey, *Managerial Accounting,* 1924.

Harold G. Moulton, *The Financial Organization of Society,* 1921.

Theodore O. Yntema, *A Mathematical Reformation of the General Theory of International Trade,* 1932.

In 1938 the name of the series was changed to *Business and Economic Publications,* and under the editorship of Dean Spencer thirteen volumes were published through the McGraw-Hill Book Company, the last in 1953. They included:

Harry A. Millis and Royal F. Montgomery, *The Economics of Labor* (3 vols.), 1938.

Edward A. Duddy and David Revzan, *Marketing: An Institutional Approach,* 1947.

Billy E. Goetz, *Management Planning and Control,* 1949.

Concurrently with its series of books, the School published a monograph series, *Studies in Business Administration,* in which some seventy works appeared between 1929 and 1948, when the monograph series was discontinued.

The present series is in part a new venture in that it will differ from its predecessors both in scope and in content. In part, it simply continues the older tradition of publishing fundamental and applied research which contributes new knowledge and ideas important for the practice of business.

W. ALLEN WALLIS
DEAN
GRADUATE SCHOOL OF BUSINESS
UNIVERSITY OF CHICAGO

Acknowledgments

The editor and the Graduate School of Business would like to thank the following authors and publications for their courtesy in permitting reproduction of the essays contained in this volume.

A. A. Alchian, "The Rate of Interest, Fisher's Rate of Return over Cost, and Keynes' Internal Rate of Return," *The American Economic Review,* December, 1955, copyright 1955, The American Economic Association.

A. Charnes, W. W. Cooper, and M. H. Miller, "Application of Linear Programming to Financial Budgeting and The Costing of Funds," *Journal of Business,* January, 1959, copyright 1959, University of Chicago.

Joel Dean, "Measuring the Productivity of Capital," *Harvard Business Review,* January-February, 1954, copyright 1954, Harvard College.

Joel Dean and Winfield Smith, "Has MAPI a Place in a Comprehensive System of Capital Control?" *Journal of Business,* October, 1955, copyright 1955, University of Chicago.

D. Durand, "The Cost of Debt and Equity Funds for Business," and discussions by Clay J. Anderson and Martin W. Davenport, *National Bureau of Economic Research,* 1952, copyright 1952, National Bureau of Economic research.

D. Durand, "The Cost of Capital in an Imperfect Market: A Reply to Modigliani and Miller," *The American Economic Review,* June, 1959, copyright 1959, The American Economic Association.

M. J. Gordon, "The Payoff Period and the Rate of Profit," *Journal of Business,* October, 1955, copyright 1955, University of Chicago.

M. J. Gordon and Eli Shapiro, "Capital Equipment Analysis: The Required Rate of Profit," *Management Science,* October, 1956, copyright 1956, The Institute of Management Science.

Horace Hill, Jr., "A New Method of Computing the Rate of Return on Capital Expenditures," *Philadelphia Society of Business Budgeting,* 1953, copyright 1953, Horace Hill, Jr.

Horace Hill, Jr., "Capital Expenditure Management," *Journal of Business,* October, 1955, copyright 1955, University of Chicago.

J. Hirshleifer, "On the Theory of Optimal Investment Decision," *Journal of Political Economy,* August, 1958, copyright 1958, University of Chicago.

J. Lorie and L. J. Savage, "Three Problems in Capital Rationing," *Journal of Business,* October, 1955, copyright 1955, University of Chicago.

F. Modigliani and M. H. Miller, "The Cost of Capital, Corporation Finance, and The Theory of Investment," *The American Economic Review,* June, 1958, copyright 1958, The American Economic Association.

F. E. Norton, "Administrative Organization in Capital Budgeting," *Journal of Business,* October, 1955, copyright 1955, University of Chicago.

E. Renshaw, "A Note on The Arithmetic of Capital Budgeting Decisions," *Journal of Business,* July, 1957, copyright 1957, University of Chicago.

H. V. Roberts, "Current Problems in the Economics of Capital Budgeting," *Journal of Business,* January, 1957, copyright 1957, University of Chicago.

Romney Robinson, "Interest—Return over Costs or Internal Rate: Comment," *The American Economic Review,* December, 1956, copyright 1956, The American Economic Association.

G. Shillinglaw, "Profit Analysis for Abandonment Decisions," *Journal of Business,* January, 1957, copyright 1957, University of Chicago.

G. Shillinglaw, "Residual Values in Investment Analysis," *Journal of Business,* October, 1955, copyright 1955, University of Chicago.

Ezra Solomon, "Measuring a Company's Cost of Capital," *Journal of Business,* October, 1955, copyright, 1955, University of Chicago.

Ezra Solomon, "The Arithmetic of Capital Budgeting Decisions," *Journal of Business,* April, 1956, copyright 1956, University of Chicago.

George Terborgh, "Some Comments on the Dean-Smith Article on the MAPI Formula," *Journal of Business,* April, 1956, copyright 1956, University of Chicago.

In addition, the editor wishes to acknowledge his debt to Professor James H. Lorie for his help in selecting the present essays and in developing an earlier collection, *Capital Budgeting,* (Journal of Business, October, 1955) from which the present volume is an outgrowth, and to thank the staff of the Applied Mathematics Section, Monsanto Chemical Company, who prepared the compound discount tables reproduced here.

Contents

I
Introduction

Introduction

BY EZRA SOLOMON*

The twenty-two essays in this volume have three features in common. All of them deal with the management of corporate capital; all of them are concerned with how problems should be solved rather than with how they are resolved in practice; and all of them are reprinted from the journal literature of the past seven years.

The problem of capital management is not, by any means, new. Business firms have always had to make decisions about how much capital to invest; what assets to acquire; and the composition of financing. But these decisions have been made in a wide variety of ways, and on the basis of a diversity of implicit principles. Interest in the formulation of an explicit and defensible approach to capital allocation decisions is a relatively recent phenomenon. As the essays in this volume indicate, the problem of developing such an approach is not easy and requires the settlement of a broad range of hitherto unresolved issues. They also indicate the considerable progress which has been made, due, in part, to an interchange of ideas among previously isolated disciplines. In spite of differences of opinion, there is today a much better understanding of the basic problems of capital management and of their solution.

A systematic approach to corporate capital decisions has three prerequisites: (1) a correct formulation of long-run goals; (2) a suitable framework within which relevant information on all available courses of investment and financing action can be assembled; and (3) a set of decision processes for the selection of actions which will lead to the chosen goals. The essays in this volume deal mainly with the last of these three problems because it is in this area that most conceptual difficulties lie and unresolved issues persist. The first two issues are also important, and the second issue in particular presents difficult problems of estimation, forecasting, and administration. But neither of the first two issues involves conceptual difficulties or serious differences of opinion with respect to the logical approach required.

All of the essays in this volume assume that the goal of capital management is the maximization of long-run earnings to present stockholders. This is not to deny that companies may have other goals, e.g., size, product line, market share, production methods, or employee relations—but each of these specific sub-goals is a means to an end rather than an end in itself. The all-encompassing end is service to the economic community as a whole. There is general agreement, dating from Adam Smith, that this end can best be served if individual companies act, within the law, to maximize future long-run earnings to owners. In a broad sense, the function of capital management is the direction of funds into and through a business so as to achieve this end.

The essays also assume that syste-

* Professor of Finance, Graduate School of Business, University of Chicago.

matic capital decisions require a central review and selection of all proposals using company funds. Although the use of a central capital budget as the formal framework within which management makes and expresses its decisions is not yet universal, it has grown considerably in importance relative to the alternative procedure of item-by-item decisions made at separate points within a company and at separate times. At the same time, there has been a growing use of explicit estimates of costs and benefits associated with each alternative use of company funds.

The third aspect—and the one which has received the most attention in the literature since 1950—is concerned with the following problem: Given the goal of long-run profit maximization, given specific and agreed upon estimates of benefits and costs for various uses of company funds, and given certain conditions in the capital markets, how should these be translated into optimal investment and financing decisions? This optimum solution requires three inter-related decisions. These are: (1) the total volume of gross investment to be made; (2) the composition of expenditures; and (3) the composition of financing. Because each decision affects the other two, all three must be solved simultaneously.

A necessary first step toward establishing a total system for these three decisions is to establish a correct procedure for arriving at each of them under the artificial assumption that the remaining two are given. By and large, this has been the procedure used in the literature. But even when the problems are viewed in isolation, differences of opinion exist on how they should be solved and thus far no single, clear-cut solution for the overall problem has emerged, even in theory. However, the differences which do exist among the alternative solutions suggested in this volume are relatively small when compared with the much broader difference which exists between the range of suggested solutions, and the range of solutions used in practice.

Areas of Agreement

The essays show a broad measure of agreement on several issues.

It is generally agreed that two sets of relevant facts are required for evaluating a proposal. The first fact required is an estimate of a company's "cost-of-capital." The second set consists of estimates of the *incremental cash-flows* expected from a proposal over time, and estimates of the *incremental cash-outlays* required to implement it. As opposed to the more conventional division of project costs into direct or indirect, prime or overhead, the *incremental* concept refers to the difference between what costs are expected to be if the proposal is accepted, and what they are expected to be if it is not. Similarly, incremental revenues are measured in terms of the difference between two estimated streams—with the proposal and without. Unlike conventional measures of income which separate the "return *on* capital" from the "return *of* capital" represented by depreciation and other non-cash charges, the concept of cash-flow counts all receipts.

It is also generally agreed that the correct technique for measuring the estimated rate of return offered by a proposal is to find that rate of compound discount (or interest) which equates the value of all expected cash inflows and cash outlays attributable to a proposal when these flows are discounted (or compounded) to a common point of time. This is the method used in financial circles to compute the "yield to maturity" of a bond which is purchased at a price different than its redemption value. The method has been referred to in the literature under a variety of names—among these are: "discounted-cash-flow approach," "scientific method," "the investor's method," "the interest-rate-of-return," "the internal rate of return," and the "marginal efficiency of capital." Other approaches are frequently used in business circles to measure profitability, e.g., the pay-out period, the ratio of net conventional income to gross investment, and the ratio of net conventional income to average book-value of capital tied up in a proposal. It is generally agreed that the use of these approaches does not provide an accurate solution to the capital allocation problem.

There is broad agreement that funds supplied by owners—whether from retained earnings or new issues of common stock—have a cost, and that the market price of outstanding stock should be an important element in measuring this "cost," and hence, that a company's cost of equity capital changes over time with changes in the market value of its shares. Although the ideas underlying this approach are not exactly new, either in business or academic circles,[1] explicit formulations of the cost of equity capital are fairly recent.

Finally, there is agreement that a correct decision to accept a proposal must satisfy the condition that the expected rate of return it offers exceeds the company's cost of capital. Alternatively, a proposal is acceptable if the present value of the net cash inflow it promises, discounted at the cost of capital, exceeds the present value of net cash outlays it requires. Other approaches to investment evaluation may not maximize long-run earnings to present owners.

Problem Areas

The examination of principles underlying optimum capital allocation has uncovered problems as well as answers.

One problem is that the technique of measuring the rate of return on an investment through equating the discounted cash-flows cannot be literally applied for certain patterns of incremental cash-flows. When an investment produces incremental benefits early in its life, but involves incremental costs later, the technique of equating discounted-cash-flows does not yield a meaningful measure of its profitability. In fact, it may yield several answers, none of which is correct. A correct answer can be found in all such cases, but it is far simpler to make these decisions by comparing the present value of benefits (discounted at the cost of capital) against the present value of outlays. Unlike the rate-of-return formulation, the latter approach always yields a correct and unambiguous answer.

A second problem is that the two criteria for judging investment worth (the rate-of-return, and the net present value per dollar of outlay), although they always give the same answer with respect to an accept-or-reject decision, do not always *rank* proposals in the same order. When several mutually-exclusive proposals are under consider-

[1] See for example, J. M. Keynes, *A Treatise on Money*: Harcourt Brace & Co., New York, 1930, Vol. II, p. 195.

ation, and only one can be selected, relative ranking is crucial, and the question arises regarding which of the two systems of ranking is correct. Such conflicts in relative ranking occur particularly frequently when the time-pattern of benefits offered by alternative proposals differ.

The "answer" appears to lie in the fact that the rate-of-return criterion implicitly assumes that funds generated by a proposal can be reinvested at the same rate-of-return as the proposal itself offers, whereas the net present value per dollar of outlay criterion assumes that they can be reinvested at a rate equal to the company's cost of capital. The solution to such a conflict of rankings can be resolved either by selecting the method which makes the reinvestment assumption that appears to be most reasonable, or if the investment is an important one, by making an explicit assumption about this rate.

Unsettled Issues

The important issues of capital theory which are still unsettled concern the influence of issuing senior capital—preferred stocks and debt securities—on a company's cost of capital. Several broad differences of opinion exist on this subject.

One set of differences is about whether the use of borrowed funds, at some nominal cost which is below the cost of equity capital, actually reduces a company's overall cost of capital, or whether the investment market reacts to keep the overall cost at some given level regardless of the amount of debt used in the financial structure. In operational terms, some would measure the cost of capital (including borrowed funds) as some average of the cost of the individual varieties of funds available—others would measure it simply as the cost of equity capital regardless of the proportion of non-equity financing employed.

A second set of differences—among those who assume that the wise use of debt can lower the overall cost of capital—concerns the precise way in which the overall costs of capital should be measured.

Because of these differences, the measurement of the cost of mixtures of capital must be regarded as a controversial and unsettled issue. Nonetheless, there is agreement that the concept itself is vital to correct capital allocation within a company.

Applications and Techniques

Apart from progress that can be expected in settling the "cost of capital" problem, there are a number of areas in which development in the theory of capital management can be foreseen. One of these areas is the use of newer techniques, such as linear programming, for the solution of capital budgeting questions. A second area is the systematic application of basic principles to specialized problems which involve the evaluation of cost and revenue estimates. Examples of these—not all of which are covered in this volume—are: (a) buy or lease decisions; (b) make or buy decisions; (c) equipment replacement decisions; and (d) decisions with respect to alternative methods of debt financing such as sale and lease-back vs. debt. With these developments, the recent trend toward systematic rather than implicit approaches to the problems of capital management is likely to move even faster in the decade ahead than it has moved since the end of World War II.

Compound Discount Tables

Most modern approaches to the evaluation of investment worth require the use of compound discount (or present value) tables. However tables covering the range of interest rates relevant for business investment proposals are not generally available.

Two sets of tables are useful for capital allocation decisions: (1) the present value of $1.00 of cost or revenue at various points of time, and at various rates of discount; and (2) the present value of $1.00 per annum for various time periods at various rates of discount.

The preparation of tables requires an assumption about the compounding interval to be used. Financial analysis uses that compounding interval—annual, semi-annual, or quarterly—which is appropriate to the frequency of interest requirements. The question of which interval is appropriate for capital investment analysis has not been explicitly settled. Most economists would choose continuous compounding on the grounds that earnings flow continuously. However, the major financial variables used by capital management—earnings, dividends, and taxes—are generally measured in terms of rates based on discrete intervals.

The tables presented at the end of this volume have been computed on an annual compounding basis. Table 1 gives present values of $1.00 and Table 2 present values of $1.00 per annum. Each table covers rates ranging from one to forty percent per annum and periods from one to twenty-five years.

The difference between continuous vs. annual discounting intervals is shown in Table 3 for a sample of rates and time periods. For low rates and short time spans, these differences are relatively minor. As rates and periods are increased, the *relative* differences become significant. However, because the present value of distant sums falls very sharply at high rates of discount, the *absolute* difference in results brought about by different compounding intervals is minor.

II
Measuring Investment Worth

MEASURING THE PRODUCTIVITY OF CAPITAL

JOEL DEAN

THE PRESIDENT of one of our largest oil companies, who was pushing through a program of drastic decentralization of management, stated recently that the last thing he would delegate would be decisions about capital expenditures. This is understandable because capital-expenditure decisions form the framework for a company's future development and are a major determinant of efficiency and competitive power. The wisdom of these corporate investment decisions, therefore, has a profound effect upon a company's future earnings and growth.

From the standpoint of the stockholder and of the consumer, capital expenditures are the principal bulwark against the seemingly endless progression of wage increases. From the standpoint of labor, capital expenditures are the basic economic source of future wage advances since they embody the creative forward strides of advancing technology. Finally, capital expenditures, both by their aggregate size and by their cyclical timing, have a great deal to do with the character of the economy as a whole, and thus with the government's role in maintaining stability.

MANAGEMENT PROGRAM

Farsighted judgment is an essential requisite for wise decisions about capital expenditures. But such judgment, to be sound, must be based on analysis of all the facts, many of them extremely technical and complex. In particular, top management needs an objective means of measuring the economic worth of individual investment proposals in order to have a realistic basis for choosing among them and selecting those which will mean the most to the company's long-run prosperity. The basic measure of economic worth is the productivity of capital, which means its power to produce profits. The purpose of this article is to suggest better ways of making that measurement.

Need for Specialized Skills

Unfortunately, the problem of managing capital expenditure has not generally been attacked with the kind of thorough and objective analysis that has paid such big dividends in other management areas. I have made a study of the capital-expenditure methods of some 50 large companies. These are all well-managed companies so far as production, engineering, and marketing methods are concerned, and I have a great deal of admiration for their executives. But on capital expenditures they show widespread failure to measure the investment worth of individual proposals directly, lack of defensible objective standards of an acceptable investment, and distorted dedication to procedures and paper work, with inadequate understanding of the economic content of the concepts used. In other words, when it comes to capital expenditures, they are still forced to play by ear to a distressing extent.

The development of an effective system for managing capital expendi-

AUTHOR'S NOTES: I want to express my gratitude to Phyllis van Dyk Dean of Joel Dean Associates for assistance in preparing this article.

tures requires a complex combination of disciplines: (a) application of economic theory at several vital points; (b) knowledge of financial mathematics, which most of us acquired in our apprenticeship days but have inevitably forgotten long since; (c) economic forecasting; (d) techniques for projecting the amount and timing of outlays and receipts; and (e) techniques of control through comparison of actualities with projections. Top management clearly needs technical help. No executive, even if he had the time to analyze each capital proposal personally, could be expected to have all the necessary disciplines at his command; they can only be gathered together in a team of specialists.

Ten Elements

This article concentrates on the measurement of the economic worth of individual investment proposals. But we must remember that, though this is likely to be the critical element, it is only one of many components in a well-rounded program of capital management. Exhibit I, describing the ten components of a complete management program for capital expenditures, may serve to put this particular element (No. 4 in the exhibit) in its operational setting.

Are Profits Controlling?

As we turn, now, to the phase of capital-expenditure management that is our main concern here—measurement of capital productivity—we must face an underlying question: To what degree are investment decisions actually controlled by profit considerations?

Concern with capital productivity of course implies that the company's goal is profits. But actually in many cases money making is a secondary objective. Often the primary goal is strategic—to maintain or increase the company's share of the market, to achieve growth in sales volume or number of employees, or simply to build reputation and status. Often capital expenditures capture and embody this kind of motivation in the form of corporate monuments made "just to become the kind of company we want to be." I am thinking of welfare and prestige investments like gymnasiums, country clubs, and palatial offices.

A corporation is not single-minded. It is composed of groups and individuals whose interests conflict. The concept of management as arbiter among employees, customers, and stockholders can lead to capital-expenditure policies and commitments that stray from the directional beam of capital productivity. Not that this is necessarily wrong. But, at least, when a company does let such goals as welfare or prestige govern, it ought to know the cost of such a policy. The only way to find out this cost is to determine the profitability of capital projects and see how much profit is being passed up in order to build such corporate monuments. The cost of prestige, then, is the amount of earnings foregone by departing from a pattern of investment ruthlessly directed at profit maximization.

Even where money making does dominate, the theory that a company tries to maximize its profits needs some qualification. Much more prevalent is what can be described as the doctrine of *adequate profits*. Of course, when profits performance or outlook is inadequate, the stockholder's power does come into play and capital expenditures are likely to be oriented toward profit maximization. But so long as the company is making adequate profits, the drive to have all capital expenditures selected on the basis of profit maximization is blunted.

Thus, I am well aware that making maximum profits is often not the sole or even the dominant goal in managing capital expenditures. But that does not lessen the importance of being able to measure the productivity of capital (i.e., its power to produce profits). Moreover, my viewpoint here remains that of the missionary rather than the anthropologist. As in other applications of managerial economics, the objective is to help executives improve policies, not simply to report practice (or malpractice).

YARDSTICKS OF INVESTMENT WORTH

The heart of good capital-expenditure management, then, is the measurement of the investment worth of individual proposals. But in order to measure how good a project is, we must have the right kind of yardstick. Just what should a good yardstick do?

The productivity of capital can be indicated in several ways, but the central requirement of a good yardstick is that it should measure what the proposed outlay will do to net earnings, and do this in a way that permits realistic

EXHIBIT I

TEN COMPONENTS OF A CAPITAL-EXPENDITURE MANAGEMENT PROGRAM

A realistic way to see how these elements tie together is to trace the biography of a single project, such as a proposal to invest $10,000 in a fork-lift truck and pallets for mechanizing materials handling in a warehouse.

1. *Creative Search for Profitable Opportunities.* The first stage is conception of the underlying profit-making idea which is to be embodied in the capital facility, in this case the fork-lift truck. Turning up profitable opportunities for investing the company's capital is in part a by-product of good management. But this cannot be depended on to provide the plethora of enticing capital proposals that constitute the raw material for good management of capital expenditures. Inadvertent opportunities should be supplemented by an active program of seeking out and investigating such opportunities.

Competition is a great creator of investment opportunities, as when equipment manufacturers vie with one another to make facilities obsolete. Comparisons of costs, earnings, and facilities with those of rivals often suggest productive avenues for investment. One company has for several years been going over its entire product line with a comprehensive survey of product design and product components pointed at reducing costs by changing design, substituting materials and processes, and reconsidering past buy-or-make decisions.

2. *Long-Range Capital Plans.* The second stage in the life cycle of our fork-lift truck proposal is to see whether it conforms with long-range dreams of company development as embodied in future facilities plans.

Because today's capital expenditures make the bed that the company must lie in tomorrow, today's decisions must be based on definite assumptions as to what tomorrow will be like. For example, decisions on warehouse facilities need to be made in the light of an over-all long-range plan for the number and general location of distribution facilities needed for the future. Based on projections of future economic conditions, some companies have prepared detailed plant and equipment targets, toward which their entire capital-expenditure program is oriented. Others have been content to draw up their future facilities plans in broad brush strokes, leaving the details to be worked out and adapted as the program is implemented.

To provide consistent bench marks for proposals originating in all parts of the organization, it is necessary to have *some kind of plan* sketched out for the future, no matter how tentative.

3. *Short-Range Capital Budget.* The next hurdle our fork-lift truck project must take is that of getting onto the one-year capital budget. Listing a project in this budget should not mean that the expenditure is authorized but only that it is approved—such *approval* indicating that the project is considered sufficiently timely and promising to warrant careful study for the coming year.

The short-run budget has several purposes. One is to force operating management to submit the bulk of its capital proposals early enough to give top management an indication of the company's aggregate demand for funds. A comparison of the capital requested with the available supply of funds will help management in weighing the desirability of outside financing or the need for cutbacks. Another purpose is to stimulate creative thinking about the capital-facilities program early in the game, so that there will be a reasonable amount of time for analysis.

4. *Measurement of Project Worth.* The next stage is *justification* of the fork-lift project on the basis of a financial and economic analysis of its investment worth to the company. In order to permit an objective ranking of projects, this analysis needs to be summarized in a single measure of the productivity of the proposed outlay. This is the critical component of capital management and, as our central concern, will be discussed fully below.

5. *Screening and Selection.* Next, our project must pass the screening tests set up by the company to compare this fork-lift truck proposal with rival projects. Screening standards should be set in the light of the supply of cash available for capital expenditures, the cost of money to the company, and the attractiveness of alternative investment opportunities. If our project survives these rejection tests, the capital expenditure is *authorized.*

6. *Control of Authorized Outlays.* The next stage is *control* of the outlays authorized for acquisition (or construction). Controls are needed by top management at this life stage in order to assure that the facility conforms to specifications and that the outlay does not exceed the amount authorized. A system for the prevention of overages will keep estimates of investment amount "honest."

7. *Post-Mortems.* Capital-expenditure management cannot stop when our facility goes into operation. In order to preserve the integrity of the estimates of projected earnings and to provide an experience base for improving such estimates in the future, a post-completion audit of the earnings performance of our fork-lift truck is needed.

One company recently instituted a profit audit of all major projects that had been put into service in the preceding year. On a third of these projects it was found that the earnings had been overestimated by an average of 25%, including one new product investment aggregating several hundred thousands of dollars which was rendered obsolete by a competitive development two weeks after it went into production. On another one-third of the audited projects, the available data were found to be inadequate to the task of checking on the original estimates. This points up the need for a system of record keeping which will permit competent post-completion audits.

A sound program of post-mortems can do much to make earnings estimates more conscientious and realistic. Without some comparison of projections with actual performance, estimates might be inflated to the point of making a joke of the entire capital-rationing system.

8. *Retirement and Disposal.* Management's responsibility for an investment project ceases only when the facilities have been disposed of. The usual expectation is that the asset will be retained throughout its economic life so that it will be virtually worthless at the time of disposal. In a dynamic economy, however, economic life projections are necessarily imprecise. One impact of change is that the specialized assets may come to have more value to others than to the company itself. To find out and take proper action when the future earnings' value falls below the asset's market value requires an investment analysis focused on the desirability of disposal.

9. *Forms and Procedures.* At many stages in our project's life it will have to tangle with forms and procedures. An effective system of capital-expenditure control must in any large company be implemented by specialized forms, written project analyses, and routines of approval, which are tailored to the company's needs. This paper work, though a nuisance, is essential to smooth operation.

10. *Economics of Capital Budgeting.* Good estimates of the rate of return on capital-expenditure projects require an understanding of the economic concepts that underlie sound investment decisions, as well as ability in estimating techniques. Such understanding can be achieved only through special training. To assure a good job and to underscore the importance of education for capital expenditures, the financial vice president of one company personally conducted a training course for head-office executives and then took the show on the road to all plants.

---

comparison of one investment proposal with another. What we seek is a measuring rod which will help decide, for example, whether a $5,000 project that will earn $2,000 a year for three years is more attractive than a $60,000 project that will earn $10,000 a year for ten years.

A good yardstick of investment worth should summarize in a single figure all the information that is relevant to the decision whether or not to make the particular investment, and none that is irrelevant. It should be applicable to all types of proposals and should permit appraisal in terms of a single set of standards. Also, it should provide an index that is relatively simple to compute; once the basic data on the proposal have been assembled, the operating people should be able to measure the project's worth easily and without any need to explain how they do it. Finally, the yardstick should permit simple adjustments to allow for ranges of uncertainty in the earnings estimates, since one of the facts to be taken into account is man's inability to see very far into the future with any great precision.

How do the three most commonly used yardsticks—(a) degree of necessity, (b) payback period, and (c) rate of return–stack up against those criteria?

Degree of Necessity

The degree of urgency of the proposed project—that is, the extent to which it cannot be postponed to later years—is one kind of yardstick for assigning priority to investment proposals. For example, a railroad might put a power crane replacement proposal ahead of a repair shop modernization request because the old crane had broken down and something had to be done about it immediately, whereas the repair shop project could wait.

Degree of necessity has a place in the capital budgeting scheme. Some investments must be made to meet requirements imposed by a government agency. Grade-crossing eliminations for railroads, sanitary facilities in food-processing plants, and mandatory smoke-control installations are examples. Other investments clearly must be made if the company is to remain in business, e.g., replacement of a washed-out section of a railroad's main line. In these cases the alternative is such that its adoption would have a catastrophic effect on the firm's profits. Projects of this nature seldom bulk large in a company's over-all capital-expenditure program.

A serious defect of degree of urgency is that it fails to measure the capital productivity of a proposal—that is, the effect it will have on the company's earnings. A plant-modernization project may be highly postponable; but if it can produce annual savings which will yield 30% on the added capital tied up, it is to be preferred to a less postponable but less profitable project. Or, replacement of a shop destroyed by fire may seem completely unpostponable, whereas actually the company might find its over-all profits enhanced by subcontracting the operations formerly performed in the destroyed facilities.

Moreover, the degree of urgency is not a measurable quantity. Proposed projects cannot be assembled and arranged in a single priority ladder; acceptance standards cannot be set up to choose wisely among projects submitted on a necessity basis.

The most serious result of accepting or rejecting proposals primarily on the basis of how urgent they seem to be is that the capital budgeting program is likely to degenerate into a contest of personalities. The biggest share of the capital-expenditure money will go to the division heads who are the most eloquent or most persistent in presenting their requests, rather than to those who have taken the time and effort necessary to make an objective appraisal of the project's economic worth. The result is that all projects come up for review in an atmosphere of haste and emergency, with full scope allowed for the arts of persuasion and exhortation. Not only will projects whose economic desirability is dubious be pushed through to acceptance, but also a large proportion of investments that would yield big savings and high profits may be put off almost indefinitely.

Payback Period

The yardstick of payback period—that is, the number of years required for the earnings on the project to pay back the original outlay with no allowance for capital wastage—is unquestionably the most widely used measure of investment worth. Payback is superior to postponability since it takes into consideration the projected gross earnings, and it does have certain uses in capital-expenditure management:

Payback can serve as a coarse screen to pick out high-profit projects that are so clearly desirable as to require no refined rate-of-return estimates and to reject quickly those projects which show such poor promise that they do not merit thorough economic analysis. In addition, it may be adequate as a measure of investment worth for companies with a high outside cost of capital and severely limited internal cash-generating ability in comparison with the volume of highly profitable internal investment opportunities. If a shortage of funds forces the company to accept only proposals which promise a payback period after taxes of two years or less, the use of a more refined measure might not affect the list of accepted projects.

It also can be useful for appraising risky investments where the rate of capital wastage is particularly hard to predict. Since payback weights near-year earnings heavily and distant earnings not at all, it contains a sort of built-in hedge against the possibility of a short economic life.

For most corporations, however, payback is an inadequate measure of investment worth. It is a cash concept, designed to answer the single question of how soon the cash outlay can be returned to the company's treasury. As such it fails in three important respects to provide a satisfactory yardstick for appraising all the profit-producing investments of a firm:

(1) Payback tends to overweight the importance of liquidity as a goal of the capital-expenditure program. No firm can ignore needed liquidity. But most can achieve it by means that are more direct and less costly than sacrificing profits by allowing payback to govern the selection of capital projects.

(2) It ignores capital wastage. By confining analysis to the project's gross earnings (before depreciation) it takes no cognizance of its probable economic life.

(3) It fails to consider the earnings of a project after the initial outlay has been paid back. By concentrating on liquidity, it ignores the vital matter of what the life pattern of the earnings will be. Up to the end of the payback period the company has just got its bait back. How much longer the earnings will last is what determines the profitability of the investment. A three-year payback project may yield a 30% return on average investment if it has a long life, but only 12% if its life is four years, and no return at all if just three years.

In short, because payback does not measure or reflect all the dimensions of profitability which are relevant to capital expenditure decisions, it is neither inclusive enough nor sensitive enough to be used as the company's over-all measure of investment worth.

Rate of Return

Measurement of the economic worth of an investment proposal by means of rate of return relates the project's anticipated earnings to the amount of funds which will be tied up during the investment life of the facility. Rate of return embodies the concept of *net* earnings after allowing for capital wastage.

Neither degree of necessity nor payback period uses this concept, since payback is measured in terms of gross earnings, and urgency does not consider earnings at all.

Rate of return has its shortcomings. A sound rate-of-return system is more complex than most of the methods of rationing a corporation's capital that are in current use. It costs more to install and put into operation. Also it may run into obstacles because it is unfamiliar and possibly because it will block privileged channels from access to capital funds.

But such limitations should not be decisive. Good management of capital expenditures is too vital to be blocked by ignorance, caution, or smugness. Overcoming the old organization's natural resistance to learning new tricks and training it in a new pattern of thought about capital expenditures is a one-shot affair. Once the system is installed, very little effort and cost are needed to keep it going.

Superiorities of This Yardstick. The positive superiorities of a rate-of-return measure of investment worth are imposing. It takes account of the full lifetime of a capital-expenditure proposal. Two projects, each of which shows a three-year payback, may differ greatly in the length of time for which they will produce earnings for the company. Take this experience which one company had:

> Certain refinery equipment that showed a three-year payback actually became obsolete and was replaced in less than three years. This project's rate of return, therefore, was less than zero, despite what appeared to be a very satisfactory payback. In contrast, a pipeline that had the same three-year payback kept on earning (and promises to continue for twenty years more). Clearly its rate of return was much higher.

Capital wastage—that is, the gradual loss of the economic value of the facility over a period of time—is of vital importance in the appraisal of an investment proposal. Capital productivity should be measured by earnings over the whole life of the investment, even though estimates of the distant future may be subject to wide margins of error.

Because rate of return considers the full life of an investment proposal, correct comparisons of the degree of value of projects can be made. Proposals can therefore be arranged in a ladder of priority even where they seem to be of the same degree of urgency or to have the same payback period. Moreover, the fact that the projects themselves may differ widely in their characteristics does not impede the comparison. New-product investments can thus be compared with cost-reducing projects; or a proposal this year can be compared with one which will not be ready until next year.

Better standards of rejection are made possible by rate of return. A company's combined cost of capital—say, 15%—can be used to determine the proper rate of cutoff on the capital-demand ladder just discussed; i.e., the minimum acceptable profitability of a proposal. This not only provides an objective, defensible basis for acceptance or rejection; it also aids top management in delegating authority by providing sound bench marks for personnel down the line to use in killing off the worst propositions before they have gone far up the chain of command.

Finally, rate-of-return rationing is likely to produce more earnings for stockholders, since it directs the flow of funds to their most profitable use by measuring the productivity of capital correctly and comparing it with a relevant standard of acceptable profitability.

MAKING THE ESTIMATES

We have seen that for most companies rate of return is the best yardstick of economic worth. Two problems arise in the practical application of this yardstick. The first concerns the concept for making the empirical projections that are needed to get the three basic determinants of project worth: (a) earnings, (b) economic life, and (c) amount of capital tied up. The second problem (discussed later) is how to combine these determinants in an index of profitability.

Ten Fallacies

The part of this measurement problem which is most often muffed is the job of getting a clear idea of just what needs to be estimated. Why should there be any problem in clarifying the concepts for rate-of-return measurement? The nature of the difficulties and their importance for good measurement can be seen by looking at ten common fallacies:

1. *"No Alternatives."* Perhaps the most common mistake in analyzing a capital proposal is the failure to consider any alternatives. There are always alternatives to an investment proposal, and a systematic analysis of the alternatives is the bench mark for estimating both the investment and the earnings of a capital project. What will happen if the requested investment is not made measures what the company will get out of it if the investment is made. If, as usual, there are several alternatives differing in the amount of investment required, earnings estimates should logically be built upon the smallest investment alternative which is acceptably profitable. Alternatives which require greater investment are preferable to this one only if the *added* investment over this amount produces enough *added* earnings to yield a satisfactory rate of return.

2. *" 'Must' Investment."* Closely related is the "must" investment fallacy. The common conviction that certain equipment replacements are indispensable for continuing operations implies that top management has no alternatives. True, the alternative is sometimes so catastrophic that it is academic. But even in such a case the reason for making the investment should not be that it is urgent or indispensable, but that its profitability is terrific measured against the catastrophic alternative. Thus the rate of return from replacing a burnt-out pump in an oil pipeline may be astronomical; the investment is small and its earnings are the profits from the whole line, since the only alternative is a complete shutdown.

High-profit investments of this special nature are rarer than realized. Skeptical study of supposed "must" investments will reveal alternatives to many of them and will show that some of them are neither necessary nor even acceptably profitable.

3. *"High Strategy."* Another fallacy is the notion that some projects are so pivotal for the long-run welfare of the enterprise that they possess high strategic value which overrides mere economic considerations and lifts their evaluation into a mystic realm beyond the ken of economic and financial analysis. For example, the dogma that an integrated oil company should own 75% of its crude oil sometimes precludes economic analysis of integration investments.

It is true that some capital expenditures do have benefits which are hard to measure because they are diffused over a wide area of company activity or because they stretch over a protracted time period. And there are some investments which must be made on almost pure faith (e.g., a new research center). Nevertheless, the idea that there is such a thing as strategic value not ultimately rooted in economic worth is demonstrably wrong. If a contemplated investment produces results that do not have any economic value, then directors and stockholders should question its wisdom.

4. *"Routine Replacement."* This fallacy maintains that scheduled periodic replacement of capital facilities is a practical and inexpensive substitute for an investment analysis of the economic desirability of individual replacements. For example, many fleet owners

replace motor trucks on a routine basis (i.e., after a certain number of years or a certain number of miles), without determining whether the added net earnings from replacing this or that old truck with a new one will produce an adequate return on the specific added investment. Routine replacement has the virtues of simplicity, orderliness, and predictability. But vintage retirement will not produce as profitable a pattern of investment as will a capital-earnings plan.

5. *"Prediction is Impossible."* Scoffers maintain that since the future cannot be predicted with accuracy, it is futile to try to guess the useful life of a proposed facility or to project its earnings beyond the first year. The consequence of this fallacy is an unwillingness to define concepts in a way that will force explicit projection. People try to duck out by proclaiming that "with a four-year payback, it doesn't matter" or by embracing "unfair" Bureau of Internal Revenue depreciation rates.

The basic mistake is refusing to recognize that forecasting, though difficult and subject to error, is nevertheless necessary in appraising the worth of capital projects. Prediction, whether or not it is done consciously, lies at the heart of any executive judgment about a proposed investment. Usually it is better to *know* what is being done.

6. *"Fair Share of Overhead."* A common error in project analysis is to use allocations of current overhead instead of estimating the added costs that will be caused by the project. This cost-proration fallacy confuses problems of equity with problems of economic consequences. This is illustrated by a question frequently raised: Should a new product line, acquisition of which is being contemplated, carry its full share of the overhead now borne by mature products, or should it get a free ride? Neither of these suggested solutions is correct, at least for estimating project earnings. Old overheads do not matter—only new overheads. What is needed is not a reallocation of past overheads but a forecast of how future overheads will increase by acceptance as opposed to rejection of the project. This cost increment is wholly unaffected by the conventions of apportionment of common costs.

7. *"Free Ride."* A related fallacy that frequently misguides analysis of capital proposals errs in the opposite direction. It holds that new products or added volume are "plus business" in the sense of incurring negligible additional costs. This "free ride" fallacy leads to the conclusion that earnings from expansion investments are almost equivalent to their revenue. There is something to this notion; long-run incremental costs are often smaller than fully allocated average costs. But they are larger than short-run marginal costs and never negligible.

While short-run marginal costs are relevant for operating decisions, long-run added costs must be used for investment decisions. Herein lies the peril of the "free ride" fallacy. What, for instance, are the earnings from an added gasoline service station when pipeline and bulk plant capacities will just take that added volume? If only the marginal cost of using this bulk-movement capacity is included, rate of return is high. But continued normal growth will soon force expansion of the bulk-movement capacity; the new service station brings this time that much closer. If the full cost of this expansion is included in estimating lifetime earnings, the return of course shows up as much lower.

8. *"Carrying Charge."* The practice of charging the earnings of all projects with an interest cost might be called the "carrying charge" fallacy. Usually this charge is computed by applying the company's short-term borrowing rate to the capitalized portion of the original investment. This approach has the virtue of recognizing that money is not costless, even though no entry is made in the accounts. It has, however, two defects: (a) it uses the wrong cost of money, since high-cost equity capital is left out, and (b) it introduces cost of money into the capital-management program in the wrong way. Instead of subtracting carrying costs from individual projects, it is better to use cost of capital as a cutoff rate to select acceptably profitable projects.

9. *"Book Value."* Determination of the investment amount looks so easy that it is often done wrong. Bookkeeping is the root of error here. Accounting conventions that are indispensable for financial reporting give the wrong steer for estimating a project's investment base. The test of what should be included in the investment amount is not how it is handled on the books, which bears only on the tax effects of the proposal, an important but quite

separate issue. The test is whether or not the outlay is necessary to produce the stream of earnings contemplated in the proposal.

The "book value" concept would exclude outlays that are expensed (rather than capitalized) from the amount of investment serving as the base for the rate-of-return estimate. Take a proposal to convert an unused portion of a building into a sausage factory requiring $100,000 of capitalizable machinery plus $150,000 of expensed repairs. The pretax investment amount is the whole $250,000; after deflating the expensed portion for 50% income tax rates ($150,000 minus $75,000), the after-tax investment amount is seen to be $175,000. But the book value is only $100,000.

Book value also gives bad investment guidance in propping up, transferring, or abandoning existing assets. The book value of an existing asset is based on recorded historical cost less accumulated depreciation. For investment decisions, its value should be determined by what the company can get for the asset or what the company can do with it in its next best internal use, rather than by the figures that happen to be on the books.

10. *"Taxes Don't Matter."* There is a surprisingly widespread conviction that adjustment for corporate income taxes is academic. This "taxes don't matter" fallacy assumes that the underlying worth of a project is obscured (rather than revealed) by allowing for tax effects, and that the ranking of capital products will be the same whether or not they are deflated for taxes. This beguiling notion is wrong in two respects: (a) In order to apply tenable acceptance standards such as the company's outside cost of capital, it is necessary to measure rate of return after taxes, rather than before taxes. (b) The impact of taxes differs depending on the time shape of the project; and the after-tax ranking of proposals will differ significantly from their before-tax ranking if taxes are correctly taken into account in computing rate of return. For example, the tax effects of accelerated amortization can convert a border-line project into a highly profitable investment opportunity.

Positive Concepts

Having looked at these ten fallacies, we are in a better position to formulate positive concepts of what needs to be estimated in measuring project earnings and project investment.

A correct estimate of earnings must be based on the simple principle that the earnings from a proposal are measured by the total *added* earnings or savings from making the investment as opposed to not making it. The proper bench mark for computing earnings on a project is the *best alternative* way of doing the job; comparison therewith will indicate the source and amount of the added earnings. Project costs should be unaffected by allocations of existing overheads but should cover all the changes in total overhead (and other) costs that are forecasted to result from the investment, but nothing else—nothing that will be the same regardless of whether the proposal is accepted or rejected.

The value of a proposed investment depends on its future earnings. Hence, the earnings estimate should be based on the best available projections of future volume, wage rates, and price levels. Earnings should be estimated over the economic life of the proposed facilities. Because project earnings vary in time shape, and because this will affect the rate of return, the earnings estimates should reflect the variations in the time trend of earnings.

In estimating economic life of an investment, consideration must be given to (a) physical deterioration, (b) obsolescence, and (c) the possibility that the source of earnings will dry up before either of the first two factors becomes operative.

Interest on investment should not be deducted from project earnings. Charging interest increases the complexity of the rate-of-return computation without adding to the information it provides. Earnings should be stated after corporate income taxes, for only in such form are they relevant for capital attraction and for dividend payment.

The appropriate investment base for calculating rate of return is the added outlay which is occasioned by the adoption of the project as opposed to rejecting it and adopting an alternative which requires less investment. The entire amount of the original added outlay should be included in the investment amount, regardless of how it is treated in the books. Any tax benefit which results from expensing certain items rather than capitalizing them should be reflected. Those repairs which would be made whether or not the proposal is adopted should be excluded from the investment amount, because they are not caused by it.

If the proposal involves a transfer of facilities from another part of the company, the opportunity cost of these facilities (the amount foregone by using them this way rather than another) should be added to the amount of investment. If the opportunity foregone is merely to sell the facilities for scrap, then this will indicate the value to set on the transferred assets.

The amount of the investment should also include the amount of any additional necessary investment in working capital or other auxiliary facilities. Research and promotional expenses to get new products rolling or to develop new methods or to expand business are no less investments than plant and equipment.

CALCULATING RATE OF RETURN

Once the basic estimates of project earnings and investment have been made, there are two major ways of combining them into a rate-of-return measurement. One way—which can be called the "accounting method" because it is closely related to many of the concepts used in conventional accounting procedure—computes rate of return as the ratio of (a) the project's earnings averaged over the life of the proposition to (b) the average lifetime investment. The other—which can be called "discounted cash flow"—computes rate of return as the maximum interest rate which could be paid on the capital tied up over the life of the investment without dipping into earnings produced elsewhere in the company.

Accounting Method

A characteristic of the accounting method is that it has many variants, each of which produces a different rate-of-return figure for any one investment proposal. One set of variants comes from diverse concepts of the investment amount (e.g., the original outlay, $100,000, versus the average amount tied up in the facility over its life, $50,000). Another source of variants is the diverse concepts of the project earnings. Earnings can be either gross or net of depreciation, either before or after taxes. They can be the average for several years or for the first year only. This variety of alternatives produces a tremendous range of rate-of-return results. But they all fall into the category of accounting method, provided the final result is a ratio of earnings to investment.

This shortcoming can be minimized only by arbitrarily standardizing on one variant of the method and making all computations according to this standard.

A more serious drawback to the use of the accounting method is that it is insensitive to variations in the time pattern of investment outlays and earnings. By taking an annual average of earnings over the life of a project this method ignores the earning trends, which may be quite important.

The economic worth of an investment will be affected by the time shape of its lifetime earnings, because near money has greater economic value than distant money. For example, an oil well has a strikingly different time shape than a service station. A well which comes in as a gusher trails off to a pumper. In contrast, a service station in a new area has a rising curve of earnings and is likely to show post-operative losses in the first year or so. Failure to reflect these time-shape disparities in the index of investment worth leads to unprofitable capital-expenditure decisions.

The effect of time shape on economic worth is especially great when the company's cost of capital is high or when the foregone earnings on projects that are passed up are high. Only a company whose investment projects are roughly similar in time shape and in economic life can ignore this feature. For such a firm the added accuracy of the discounted-cash-flow method probably does not justify the transitional pain and effort required to install the system. But any company which has projects that vary significantly in either time shape or longevity has an important stake in using the most sensitive rate-of-return method available.

Discounted Cash Flow

The mechanics of the cash-flow method consist essentially of finding the interest rate that discounts future earnings of a project down to a present value equal to the project cost. This interest rate is the rate of return on that investment. Exhibit II illustrates the way in which rate of return can be determined under the cash-flow method for a cost-reducing machine which costs $2,200 and has an anticipated life of five years with no salvage value at the end of that time. In this case, an interest rate of 20% is found to make the present value of the future earnings stream equal to the present cost of the machine, so this is the rate of return.

EXHIBIT II

CASH-FLOW METHOD OF COMPUTING RATE OF RETURN ILLUSTRATED

(Machine costing $2,200 with anticipated life of five years and no salvage value at the end of that time)

Year	*Gross earnings before depreciation*	*Present value of earnings discounted at* 18%	20%	22%
1	$200	$184	$182	$180
2	600	458	446	432
3	800	510	486	462
4	1,200	640	596	556
5	1,200	534	488	448
Total	$4,000	$2,326	$2,198	$2,078

Conceptually, this method is based on the principle that in making an investment outlay we are actually buying a series of future annual incomes—ranging in the example in the exhibit from $200 the first year to $1,200 by the fourth and fifth years. We have an investment in each of those incomes, an investment which compounds in value through time until its own year arrives and it materializes in cash earnings. Thus, for example, the $596 present value of the fourth year's earnings at 20% is the amount that would have to be invested at 20% now to yield $1,200 gross earnings during the fourth year ($596 compounded at 20% for 3½ years–since the $1,200 would begin to come in at the beginning of the fourth year).

The basic simplicity of this method is brought out by this illustration. Earnings are stated as gross cash receipts (not figuring depreciation). Therefore, it is not necessary to allocate the cost of the machine over its life before computing return. Depreciation is allowed for automatically because the interest rate that discounts the sum of present values to zero is the rate of return on the investment after annual provisions for repaying the principal amount. We are not, as in the accounting method, watching the write-off of original cost; we are watching instead the growth of our investment outlay as we compound it through time.

The method is simplified by the fact that there is no need to make a decision as to which earnings base to use (e.g., original outlay, average investment, and so on), nor is there any need to enter interest as a direct cost of the project. Once the data are gathered and set up, there is only one rate-of-return answer possible, and it can be arrived at by straightforward working of charts and interest tables.

Net Superiority of Discounted Cash Flow. The accounting method does have the advantage of familiarity and transparency. Although education would be necessary to get everyone to standardize on one method of averaging earnings and investment, the idea of computing a simple ratio by dividing one number by another is familiar to anyone who went beyond the second grade.

The discounted-cash-flow method admittedly is less familiar. While a method essentially similar to this has been widely used throughout the financial community for computing bond yields, insurance premiums, and rates on leased facilities where accuracy is important and even small errors may cause serious loss, it is new in its application to the measurement of productivity of individual capital-expenditure projects in industry. Hence the job of explaining it to the bookkeeper and the clerk will require time and effort. But its appearance of complexity is deceptive. Once the basic method is understood, it is actually simpler and quicker to use than the accounting method.

Another deterrent to its use is the fact that it does not correspond to accounting concepts about the recording of costs and revenues, so that special analysis is necessary to compute a postmortem on an investment made in the past. But this seems minor in comparison with its imposing superiorities:

(1) The discounted-cash-flow method is economically realistic in confining the analysis to cash flows and forgetting about customary book allocations. The books, although very valuable for other purposes, are irrelevant for the task of measuring investment worth.

(2) The use of this method forces guided thinking about the whole life of the project and concentration on the lifetime earnings.

(3) It weights the time pattern of the investment outlay and the cash earnings from that outlay in such a way as to reflect real and important differences in the value of near and distant cash flows.

(4) It reflects accurately and without ambiguity the timing of tax savings, either from expensing part of the investment outlay or from writing off capitalized costs over the life of the investment—something quite difficult to do by the accounting method.

(5) It permits simple allowances for risks and uncertainties and can be adapted readily to increasing the risk allowance over time.

(6) It is strictly comparable to cost-of-capital ratios so that decisions can be made quickly and safely on the basis of the relationship between indicated rate of return and the value of money to the company.

CONCLUSION

Examination of the capital-expenditure policies and procedures of some 50 well-managed companies shows that top management is forced to a distressing degree to rely on intuition and authority. Management lacks the skilled analysis and the scientific control needed for sound judgment on these intricate, vital capital decisions. The pivotal problem of capital-expenditure management is the measurement of the investment worth of individual proposals. Project evaluation needs to be integrated into a comprehensive program of capital management composed of the ten elements listed in EXHIBIT I.

Systematic exploration to assure that investment opportunities are ferreted out and objectively analyzed is a prerequisite for the measurement of investment worth. Long-range capital plans and projections enable management to appraise projects in better perspective and to fit them into broader patterns. The comprehensive short-range capital budget which forecasts the timing of probable cash outlays for investment and the timing of cash inflows is essential for determining cut-off points by cash-generation criteria.

For orderly operation of rate-of-return rationing, management needs not only good management of capital productivity but also objective and defensible standards of minimum acceptability. These should generally be based on the company's cost of capital. Candid and economically realistic post-completion audits are indispensable incentives for measuring project profitability accurately; they also provide the systematized experience for improving project measurement in the future.

Special forms and procedures to implement these capital-expenditure management principles also need to be tailored to the particular conditions of the individual company. Above all, good capital-expenditure management must operate in an enlightened intellectual environment throughout the company; all the personnel concerned should understand the economics of capital expenditures and of the measurements and controls which a sound program entails.

For most companies, productivity of capital should be measured by rate of return, rather than by payback or degree of necessity. Estimates of a project's rate of return should be based on concepts of capital investment and project earnings, which are indicated by what would happen if the company were to go ahead on the project instead of selecting some alternative which requires a smaller investment.

Prediction is essential; project worth depends solely on future earnings—the added earnings that will result from the added investment. These future earnings need to be forecasted over the whole economic life of the facility. Project costs should be unaffected by allocations of existing overhead, but should include all increases in overhead (and in other costs) that will be caused by the project. Earnings should be deflated for taxes. The investment base should be the entire added outlay regardless of bookkeeping—adjusted for corporate income taxes.

The discounted-cash-flow method of computing rate of return is demonstrably superior to existing alternatives in accuracy, realism, relevance, and sensitivity. Acceptance of rate-of-return capital budgeting should not hinge on willingness or reluctance to go this far in breaking with traditional methods.

A NEW METHOD OF COMPUTING RATE OF RETURN ON CAPITAL EXPENDITURES

HORACE G. HILL, JR.

THE RESEARCH COMMITTEE of the Philadelphia Chapter believed that it would be rendering a real service to management in its planning efforts if it could discover the correct answer to the much debated problem of how a capital expenditure should be appraised, in both a relative and an absolute way. The Committee was aware of the absence of any uniformity throughout industry in the handling of this subject, and it was afraid that this implied that no known method could qualify as being generally satisfactory. However, it determined to make a cursory examination of local practices in order to become acquainted with the difficulties already recognized. The Committee believed that this background would enable it to avoid many mistakes in its intended search for the method which would be always reliable.

CURRENT PRACTICE

Some hasty exploration in the local field developed the following:

The Payout Period was most often referred to as the measure of profitability of a capital investment. It has many forms, depending upon particular definitions of what constitutes the initial investment and what constitutes the revenue through which it is paid back. It makes a statement such as, "This investment will be paid out in three years." In many companies this is considered as equivalent to a 33% rate of return, either by direct calculation or by implication, but most companies admit that the method is superficial although better than nothing. Its admitted weakness is in the absence of any attention to the period following the payout when the profit will be shown if it exists. The Committee recognized that the Payout Period might be a useful tool in comparing operations of identical characteristics, but it could not furnish a rate of return on any investment. For this reason the Committee laid it aside as holding no possibility of serving its purpose.

The First Year Profit, in relation to the initial investment, was occasionally offered as the means of measuring the desirability of an investment and was referred to as a rate of return. The Committee recognized that this method was even more inadequate than the Payout Period, in that it paid attention to only one year of operation, and it was also laid aside as being of no help.

The MAPI (or Terborgh) formula was found in use in some plants as a guide to a proper capital expenditure program. This system was developed by the Machinery and Allied Products Institute as an indicator of whether the current year was the right time to make a replacement. It has a limited field of application and it is not designed to show the expected rate of return on the proposed investment. For these reasons the Committee considered it to be a special tool for particular circumstances, but not a factor in the basic problem which the Committee had undertaken.

The Average Book Method was the name given to a system, used by many of the larger companies and employing forecasts of what the books will show during the life of the project. The general principle, common to all such systems, was the relating of average annual profit to the average book investment in plant. This method was much more comprehensive, in that it covered the whole active life of the investment, and it was based on data as they would later appear on the books. The Committee believed that the Average Book Method should be more fully explored in the hope of evolving a system which would merit general acceptance.

The Investor's Method was the name given to a plan of investment valuation by one company which had performed some research work on the problem of rate of return and had developed a method which it was finding helpful. The method uses only a listing of net cash expenditures or receipts in time table form. The discount rate which can be applied to this table of figures, so that the algebraic sum of the extensions is zero, is the rate of return on the investment. The Committee examined this method with interest and agreed that it should be considered along with the Average Book Method in the search for the one best method which would be satisfactory under any conditions.

The Committee found that a surprising number of companies had no system of evaluating or justifying a capital expenditure, but depended entirely on the judgment of their executives. This was merely an added incentive to develop something which could be offered to industry as a reliable measure to encourage the best use of capital funds.

BASIC ASSUMPTIONS

In the course of its preliminary inquiries, the Committee was confronted with the usual objections to trying to govern capital expenditures by the single rule of "Rate of Return." The reasons most frequently given by companies which had no current interest in a systematized approach to the problem were:

a. It is impossible to look ten or twenty years ahead with sufficient accuracy to give the forecast any value.
b. There are intangible factors, other than profit, which can justify many projects.
c. Most capital expenditures are matters of necessity, and project justifications are superfluous.
d. There is no recognized method of computing a rate of return which is generally accepted.

The Committee weighed these objections, discussed them with companies where they were being apparently overcome, and agreed upon the following assumptions:

1. When the applicant for an appropriation is ready to be judged by the success of his venture throughout its life, and when his forecasts of volumes and prices and expenses have been checked by management's representatives, the long-range look should be the best available and the only basis for an approval decision.
2. Basically the only excuse for appropriating funds is to make a profit, and the applicant can make a reasonable estimate of his "intangible" advantages if management so directs.
3. There is always an alternative to every request which claims priority as being mandatory, and the

money value can be stated in at least rough terms.

4. The Committee hopes that its study will provide a method of computing a rate of return which will appeal to industry as being realistic and dependable, so that its gradual acceptance will result.

METHOD OF WORKING

The Committee made use of the ideas of companies contacted and the data employed in company studies wherever these could be made available. This gave the work a good start and avoided duplication of much effort. The readiness to permit the findings of individual companies to be used as a springboard for a broader study was much appreciated and made some real progress possible. For this reason, the Committee does not claim that the work described in the subsequent paragraphs is entirely original.

The Committee reviewed some experiments which were made in order to determine whether the inclusion or exclusion of income tax, as a charge and a subsequent payment in the basic data, would change the relative attractiveness of a random assortment of capital investments. In the great majority of projects it made no appreciable difference whether they were evaluated before tax and the computed rate of return halved before using, or computed after including the tax as one of the basic annual expenses, but the safest course would be to treat income tax as just another expense from the beginning. Accelerated depreciation, statutory depletion, excess profits brackets, foreign operations, portion immediately chargeable to expense, are some of the factors which might make the income tax a significant element in a specific rate of return. However, the research work was primarily to select the best method and it was agreed that this would be expedited by avoiding the income tax complication until the fundamental principles had been settled.

The Committee then concentrated on the critical study of the two methods which had appeared logical on the surface—the Average Book Method and the Investor's Method. The Average Book Method, as previously mentioned, was used in various forms to suit the ideas of the particular company which was depending on it, but the principles were all the same. After some preliminary tests had been made of many of these various forms, it was found that they all reacted in similar manner to change in the basic data, even though the degree of the reaction might vary. The Committee selected the form in most common use for the purpose of its detailed study. The two methods to be compared were then defined as follows:

The Average Book Method relates the average profit to the average net fixed asset remaining on the books, both averages being taken over the span of active operation of the project.

The Investor's Method relates the average profit to the average unreturned obligation, including interest at the highest rate which could be paid without producing a final deficit, both averages being taken over the span of utilization of funds in the project.

The Committee constructed the foregoing definition of the Investor's Method in an attempt to show the similarities and the divergences when compared to the Average Book Method. However, a clearer view may result from a completely independent statement, such as

The Investor's Method indicates the maximum rate of interest at which funds could be borrowed to finance the project without causing it to show an ultimate loss; or

The Investor's Method indicates the maximum discount rate which could be applied to all future net receipts so as to make their sum equal to the initial expenditure.

The Committee selected its test problems with a desire to be as realistic as possible. As a basic example it picked a project which would cost $40,000, operate for ten years, produce net receipts of $100,000 during its operation, and have a $60,000 profit to its credit when it retired. At first glance this would seem to portray all that is needed to compute a rate of return, but the Committee wanted to see how the different methods would react to various factors which are being met in actual practice. For instance, two projects might be presented by different departments in the same company, both meeting the above specifications and being similar in every other financial or accounting way except that:

1. One would charge the whole $40,000 to Plant while the other would see some way of charging half of it to expense.
2. One would depreciate the $40,000 by the straight line policy while the other would depreciate on a basis of production.
3. One would produce its net receipts uniformly while the other would produce heavily at the start and taper off to nothing.
4. One would completely exhaust its $40,000 investment while the other would have substantial salvage value remaining.
5. One would make its investment of $40,000 by instantaneous purchase while the other would laboriously construct over a period before operation.

These factors were selected for testing the methods because the relative merits of the alternatives were apparent in each case on a basis of common financial sense. The Committee's first aim was to find or develop a method which would always give a sensible answer, at least in a relative way. The factors were injected in varying degrees and both methods of computing the rate of return were applied to every case.

RESULTS

After performing all the experiments which might throw any light on the problem, the results were brought together to see what findings were indicated. These were grouped according to the five factors mentioned above and the indications are shown on the following pages.

BORROWING AT INDICATED RATES

The Refinery project, shown in Exhibit #1, is described as:

An initial expenditure of $40,000—50% chargeable to Expense;

An annual net cash receipt of $10,000 each year;

A life of 10 years with no salvage.

The *Average Book Method* rates this project at 60%.

The *Investor's Method* rates this project at 22% (actually 22.32%). If money were actually borrowed at these rates to finance the project, what would be the status of the account at the end of the 10-year period?

Case	PIPE LINE PROJECT Booster Pump Authorized for $40,000 Net Receipts $10,000/yr. Life - 10 years Salvage - None Capitalized - 100% Depr. Rate - 10%				REFINERY PROJECT Still Rebuilding Authorized for $40,000 Net Receipts $10,000/yr. Life - 10 years Salvage - None Capitalized - 50% Depr. Rate - 10%				EITHER PROJECT Authorized for $40,000 Net Receipts $10,000/yr. Life - 10 years Salvage - None	
Method	AVERAGE BOOK				AVERAGE BOOK				INVESTOR'S	
Time Table	Net Cash Rec.	Book Write-off	Book Profit	Aver. Book Invest	Net Cash Rec.	Book Write-off	Book Profit	Aver. Book Invest	Net Cash Rec.	
0	(-40)				(-40)	20	(-20)		(-40)	→ Initial Investment
0- 1	10	4	6	38	10	2	8	19	10	is
1- 2	10	4	6	34	10	2	8	17	10	Roughly
2- 3	10	4	6	30	10	2	8	15	10	Balanced
3- 4	10	4	6	26	10	2	8	13	10	by
4- 5	10	4	6	22	10	2	8	11	10	Receipts
5- 6	10	4	6	18	10	2	8	9	10	Discounted
6- 7	10	4	6	14	10	2	8	7	10	to
7- 8	10	4	6	10	10	2	8	5	10	Zero Date
8- 9	10	4	6	6	10	2	8	3	10	at
9-10	10	4	6	2	10	2	8	1	10	22%
	60	40	60	200	60	40	60	100	60	
	Aver. Profit 6 Aver. Invest. 20				Aver. Profit 6 Aver. Invest. 10				Aver. Profit 6	
	RETURN 30%				RETURN 60%				RETURN 22%	

A-1 A-2

Total or Average Profit is the same in each case.
Rates of Return vary inversely with Investment.
Book Values Reflect Accounting Policies.
Graphical Presentation shows why rates vary.

A-3

Unreturned Balance is Cash Position after 22% Interest Payments. It need not be calculated to find the Rate of Return.

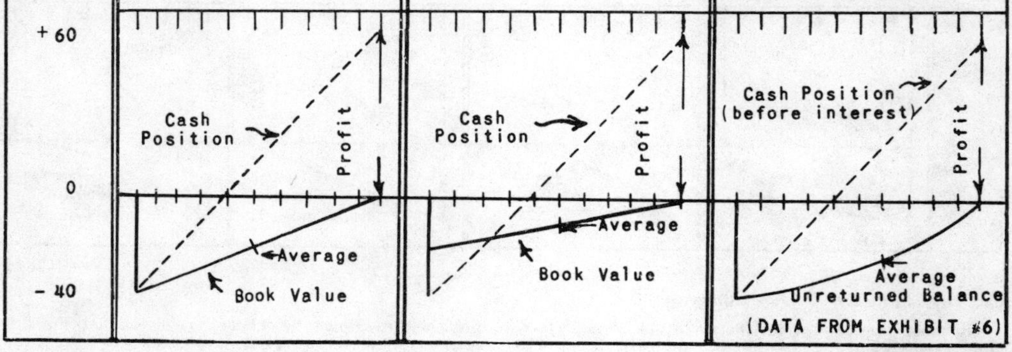

EXHIBIT #1

1. Varying Policy of Capitalization

There is always a twilight zone from which charges may be made with propriety to either Plant or Expense. The *Average Book Method* makes use of these decisions, which may even be based on a fluctuating policy, and the resulting rate of return on the project is affected inversely by the proportion of the outlay which is charged to Plant.

The *Investor's Method* pays no attention to accounting distinctions but deals solely with dollars required to make the project operative and dollars received from its operation. It, therefore, showed the same rate of return for all the test cases where the only difference was the policy of capitalization.

EXHIBIT #1 shows a pair of the examples used.

The Committee believed that the Investor's Method reflected the correct comparison between the two cases, and that it should not be assumed that a project could be made more attractive by charging part of its required outlay to Expense, except for the slight advantage of some tax deferment which is beside the point.

Case	PIPE LINE PROJECT	PRODUCING PROJECT	REFINERY PROJECT	ANYONE OF THE THREE
	Branch Line	Lease Development	Vacuum Still	
	Authorized for $40	Authorized for $40	Authorized for $40	Authorized for $40
	Declining Rec – Totaling $100	Declining Rec – Totaling $100	Declining Rec – Totaling $100	Declining Rec – Totaling $100
	Life – 10 years	Life – 10 years	Life – 10 years	Life – 10 years
	Salvage – None	Salvage – None	Salvage – None	Salvage – None
	Capitalized – 100%	Capitalized – 100%	Capitalized – 100%	
	Depr. Rate – 5%	Depr. Rate – variable	Depr. Rate – 10%	
Method	AVERAGE BOOK	AVERAGE BOOK	AVERAGE BOOK	INVESTORS

Time Table	Net Cash Rec.	Book Write-off	Book Profit	Aver. Book Invest.	Net Cash Rec.	Book Write-off	Book Profit	Aver. Book Invest.	Net Cash Rec.	Book Write-off	Book Profit	Aver. Book Invest.	Net Cash Rec.	
0	(–40)				(–40)				(–40)				(–40)	→ Initial Investment
0– 1	19	2	17	39	19	7.6	11.4	36.2	19	4	15	38	19	is
1– 2	17	2	15	37	17	6.8	10.2	29.0	17	4	13	34	17	roughly
2– 3	15	2	13	35	15	6.0	9.0	22.6	15	4	11	30	15	Balanced
3– 4	13	2	11	33	13	5.2	7.8	17.0	13	4	9	26	13	by
4– 5	11	2	9	31	11	4.4	6.6	12.2	11	4	7	22	11	Receipts
5– 6	9	2	7	29	9	3.6	5.4	8.2	9	4	5	18	9	Discounted
6– 7	7	2	5	27	7	2.8	4.2	5.0	7	4	3	14	7	to
7– 8	5	2	3	25	5	2.0	3.0	2.6	5	4	1	10	5	Zero Date
8– 9	3	2	1	23	3	1.2	1.8	1.0	3	4	(–1)	6	3	at
9–10	1	2	(–1)	21	1	.4	.6	.2	1	4	(–3)	2	1	36%
	60	20	80	300	60	40.0	60.0	134.0	60	40	60	200	60	

	PIPE LINE PROJECT	PRODUCING PROJECT	REFINERY PROJECT	INVESTORS
	Aver. Profit 8	Aver. Profit 6	Aver. Profit 6	Aver. Profit 6
	Aver. Invest. 30	Aver. Invest. 13.4	Aver. Invest. 20	Aver. Invest. 16.5
	RETURN 27%	RETURN 45%	RETURN 30%	RETURN 36%

The Total Cash Profit is the same in each case.
Rates of Return vary with the speed of depreciation.
Book Values reflect Accounting Policies.
Graphical Presentation shows why rates vary.

Unreturned Balance is cash position after 36% interest payments. It need not be calculated to find the rate of return.

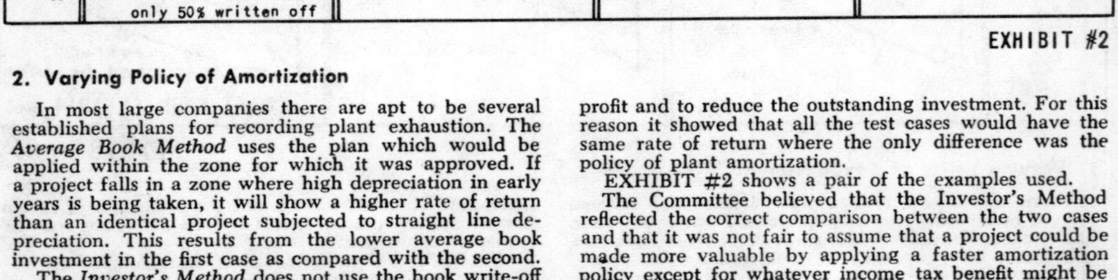

EXHIBIT #2

2. Varying Policy of Amortization

In most large companies there are apt to be several established plans for recording plant exhaustion. The *Average Book Method* uses the plan which would be applied within the zone for which it was approved. If a project falls in a zone where high depreciation in early years is being taken, it will show a higher rate of return than an identical project subjected to straight line depreciation. This results from the lower average book investment in the first case as compared with the second.

The *Investor's Method* does not use the book write-off as an indication of return of invested funds, but depends entirely on the net cash receipts to provide the claimed profit and to reduce the outstanding investment. For this reason it showed that all the test cases would have the same rate of return where the only difference was the policy of plant amortization.

EXHIBIT #2 shows a pair of the examples used.

The Committee believed that the Investor's Method reflected the correct comparison between the two cases and that it was not fair to assume that a project could be made more valuable by applying a faster amortization policy except for whatever income tax benefit might be involved.

Case	REFINERY PROJECT Vacuum Still Authorized for $40 Declining Receipts Totaling $100 Life – 10 years Salvage – None Capitalized – 100% Depr. Rate – 10%						SALES PROJECT Product Terminal Authorized for $40 increasing Receipts – Totaling $100 Life – 10 years Salvage – None Capitalized – 100% Depr. Rate – 10%					
Method	AVERAGE BOOK				INVESTOR'S		AVERAGE BOOK				INVESTOR'S	
Time Table	Net Cash Rec.	Book Write-off	Book Profit	Aver. Book Invest	Net Cash Rec.		Net Cash Rec.	Book Write-off	Book Profit	Aver. Book Invest	Net Cash Rec.	
0	(-40)				(-40)	→ Initial Investment	(-40)				(-40)	→ Initial Investment
0- 1	19	4	15	38	19	is	1	4	(-3)	38	1	is
1- 2	17	4	13	34	17	roughly	3	4	(-1)	34	3	roughly
2- 3	15	4	11	30	15	balanced	5	4	1	30	5	balanced
3- 4	13	4	9	26	13	by	7	4	3	26	7	by
4- 5	11	4	7	22	11	Receipts	9	4	5	22	9	Receipts
5- 6	9	4	5	18	9	discounted	11	4	7	18	11	discounted
6- 7	7	4	3	14	7	to	13	4	9	14	13	to
7- 8	5	4	1	10	5	Zero Date	15	4	11	10	15	Zero Date
8- 9	3	4	(-1)	6	3	at	17	4	13	6	17	at
9-10	1	4	(-3)	2	1	36%	19	4	15	2	19	15%
	60	40	60	200	60		60	40	60	200	60	
	Aver. Profit 6 Aver. Invest. 20				Aver. Profit 6 Aver. Invest. 16.5		Aver. Profit 6 Aver. Invest. 20				Aver. Profit 6 Aver. Invest. 40.5	
	RETURN 30%				RETURN 36%		RETURN 30%				RETURN 15%	
	A-1 2 Yr. Payout no better than 6 year.				A-2 Quick Payout gives higher rate.		B-1 6 Yr. Payout as good as 2 year.				B-2 Slow Payout gives lower rate.	

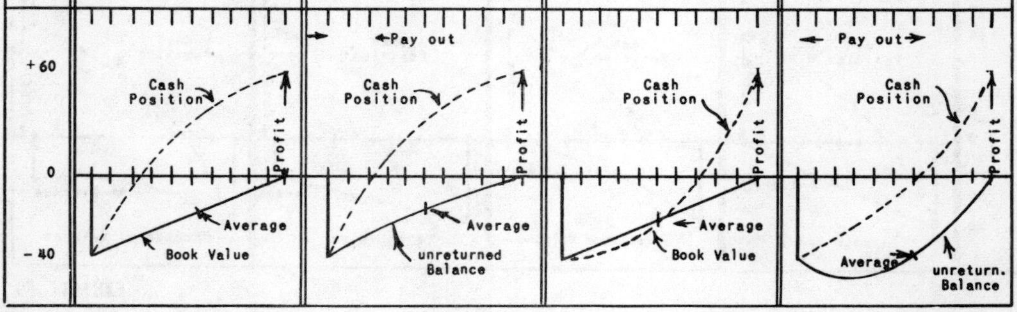

EXHIBIT #3

3. Varying Patterns of Cash Receipts

Some projects will perform with great uniformity throughout their life, but others will have their major advantages in early years before competition forces them down and eventually out.

The *Average Book Method* is based on the average annual profit in which the receipts in the final year have the same weight as those in the first year. This resulted in giving the same rate of return to all test cases in this group because they all had the same total profit.

The *Investor's Method* attaches considerable importance to the time factor and indicates that an early receipt is more valuable than a later one. For this reason it showed that all test cases in which the net receipts were higher in the first few years provided better rates of return, even though the total profit was unchanged for the life span.

EXHIBIT #3 shows a pair of the examples used.

The Committee believed that the Investor's Method reflected the correct comparison btween the two cases because the speed at which the cash outlay would be recovered is a real factor in any financial evaluation. This is equivalent to saying that the Investor's Method gave a higher rate of return to the project with the shortest payout period when the total profit was the same in both cases.

Case	SALES PROJECT Service Station on Leased Land Authorized for $40 Declining Operating Receipts - Totaling $100 Life - 10 years Salvage - None Capitalized - 100% Depr. Rate - 10%						SALES PROJECT Service Station on Owned Land Authorized for $40 total (incl. $20 Land) Declining Operating Receipts - Totaling $100 Life - 10 years Salvage - $20 (Land Value) in addition to Oper. Rec. Capitalized - 100% Depr. Rate - 10% on $20					
Method	**AVERAGE BOOK**				**INVESTOR'S**		**AVERAGE BOOK**				**INVESTOR'S**	
Time Table	Net Cash Rec.	Book Write-off	Book Profit	Aver. Book Invest	Net Cash Rec.		Net Cash Rec.	Book Write-off	Book Profit	Aver. Book Invest	Net Cash Rec.	
0	(-40)				(-40)	→ Initial Investment	(-40)				(-40)	→ Initial Investment
0- 1	19	4	15	38	19	is	19	2	17	39	19	is
1- 2	17	4	13	34	17	roughly	17	2	15	37	17	roughly
2- 3	15	4	11	30	15	balanced	15	2	13	35	15	balanced
3- 4	13	4	9	26	13	by	13	2	11	33	13	by
4- 5	11	4	7	22	11	Receipts	11	2	9	31	11	Receipts
5- 6	9	4	5	18	9	discounted	9	2	7	29	9	discounted
6- 7	7	4	3	14	7	to	7	2	5	27	7	to
7- 8	5	4	1	10	5	Zero Date	5	2	3	25	5	Zero Date
8- 9	3	4	(-1)	6	3	at	3	2	1	23	3	at
9-10	1	4	(-3)	2	1	36%	1	2	(-1)	21	1	37%
10-Salv.	---	---	---	---	---		20	20	--	--	20	
	60	40	60	200	60		80	40	80	300	80	

	Average Book	Investor's	Average Book	Investor's
	Aver. Profit 6 Aver. Invest. 20	Aver. Profit 6 Aver. Invest. 16.5	Aver. Profit 8 Aver. Invest. 30	Aver. Profit 8 Aver. Invest. 21.5
	RETURN 30%	**RETURN 36%**	**RETURN 27%**	**RETURN 37%**
	A-1 Same Rate of Return as Exhibit 1-(A-1) but pays off twice as fast.	A-2 Unreturned Balance is Cash Position after 36% Interest Payments. It need not be calculated to find the Rate of Return.	B-1 Addition of Salvage Profit can result in Lower Rate of Return, by increasing book investment.	B-2 Addition of Salvage Profit results in higher rate of return.

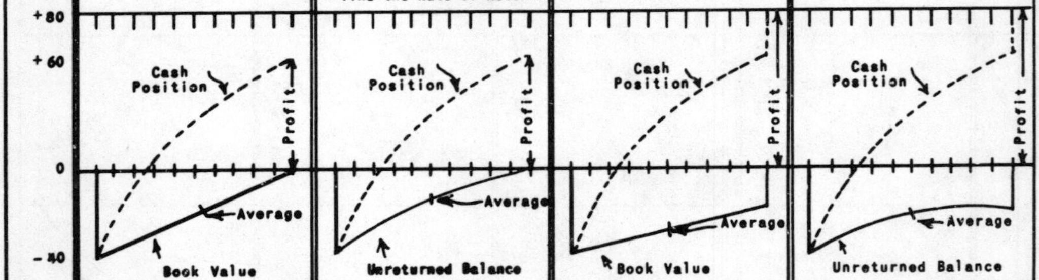

EXHIBIT #4

4. Varying Salvage Value

This group of test cases was designed to test the reaction of each method to the inclusion of a superimposed salvage value at the close of the project life. This frequently occurs as the only difference between two projects and was a realistic test.

The *Average Book Method* generally showed a lower rate of return for the project which claimed residual salvage value. This was due to the fact that the average book investment would be increased more sharply than the average profit unless the profit were at a very low level.

The *Investor's Method* showed a higher rate of return in every case to which an expected salvage value had been added as the final cash receipt.

EXHIBIT #4 shows a pair of the examples used.

The Committee believed that the Investor's Method gave the logical answer in this comparison, because the future receipt at the time of salvage would always have some positive value even though it might be small when discounted at a high rate over the life span of the project.

TERMINAL PUMP ADDITION

ACQUIRED FINISHED

Method:	AVERAGE BOOK				INVESTOR'S	
Time Table	Net Cash Rec.	Book Write-off	Book Profit	Aver. Book Invest.	Net Cash Rec.	
0	(−40)				(−40)	Initial Investment is roughly balanced by Receipts discounted to Zero Date at 22%
0– 1	10	4	6	38	10	
1– 2	10	4	6	34	10	
2– 3	10	4	6	30	10	
3– 4	10	4	6	26	10	
4– 5	10	4	6	22	10	
5– 6	10	4	6	18	10	
6– 7	10	4	6	14	10	
7– 8	10	4	6	10	10	
8– 9	10	4	6	6	10	
9–10	10	4	6	2	10	
	60	40	60	200	60	

ACQUIRED SEMI-FINISHED

Method:	AVERAGE BOOK				INVESTOR'S	
Time Table	Net Cash Rec.	Book Write-off	Book Profit	Aver. Book Invest.	Net Cash Rec.	
0	(−20)				(−20)	Initial Investment is roughly balanced by Receipts discounted to Zero Date at 15%
0– 1	--	Not recognized as Project Investment		20	--	
1– 2	--			20		
2– 3	(−20)			30	(−20)	
3– 4	10	4	6	38	10	
4– 5	10	4	6	34	10	
5– 6	10	4	6	30	10	
6– 7	10	4	6	26	10	
7– 8	10	4	6	22	10	
8– 9	10	4	6	18	10	
9–10	10	4	6	14	10	
10–11	10	4	6	10	10	
11–12	10	4	6	6	10	
12–13	10	4	6	2	10	
	60	40	60	200	60	

	Acquired Finished — Average Book	Acquired Finished — Investor's	Acquired Semi-Finished — Average Book	Acquired Semi-Finished — Investor's
	Aver. Profit 6 Aver. Invest. 20	Aver. Profit 6 Aver. Invest 26.9	Aver. Profit 6 Aver. Invest. 20	Aver. Profit 4.6 Aver. Invest. 31.6
	RETURN 30%	RETURN 22%	RETURN 30%	RETURN 15%
	Same case as Exhibit #1.	Unreturned Balance is cash position after 22% interest payments. It need not be calculated to find rate of return.	Total profit same as before. Rate of return claimed as equal. 3 yrs. @ 0 % are ignored.	Unreturned Balance is cash position after 22% interest payments. It need not be calculated to find rate of return.

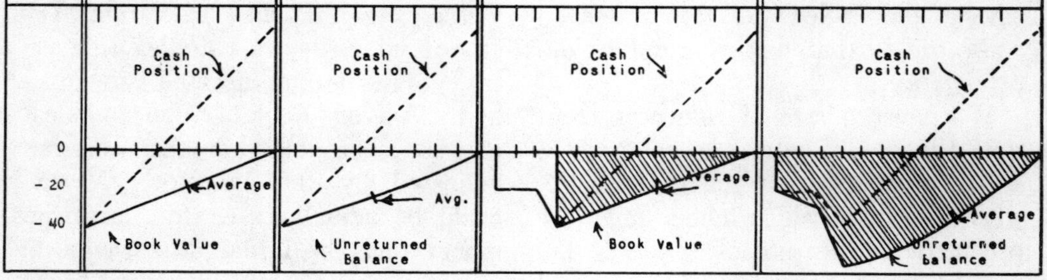

EXHIBIT #5

5. Pre-Operating Investment

Most capital expenditures involve a substantial outlay of funds before the earning power of the project can come into play. This may be normal construction time, necessary prior acquisition of property, or any other good reason.

The *Average Book Method*, as applied by all the companies contacted, ignores all such pre-operating investment on the grounds that it is not capital even though the outlays have been inseparably linked with the project under review. On this basis the same rate of return was indicated for all the test cases in this group, whether the project started immediate operation of an instantaneous purchase or was forced to build up its investment gradually. The Committee recognized that a book method could be devised which would cover the pre-operating period when invested funds were not earning profit, but that it was not an accepted method.

The *Investor's Method*, which deals with only what goes into or out of the cash box, does not confine itself to the period of operation but considers all cash transactions as equally pertinent. It showed that a project, starting off from an instantaneous acquisition, had a real advantage and a higher rate of return than one which had to carry idle investment for any appreciable period.

EXHIBIT #5 shows a pair of the examples used.

The Committee believed that the Investor's Method properly reflected this difference in the rate of return as reported to management, which the prevalent Average Book Method failed to do.

EXHIBIT #6

		Opening Balance of Debt	*Continuously Compounded at Claimed Rate*	*Credit for Compounding of $10,000 Receipts*	*Closing Balance of Debt*
@ 22%–	1st Year	40,000	50,000	11,200	38,800
	2	38,800	48,500	11,200	37,300
	3	37,300	46,600	11,200	35,400
	4	35,400	44,300	11,200	33,100
	5	33,100	41,400	11,200	30,200
	6	30,200	37,700	11,200	26,500
	7	26,500	33,100	11,200	21,900
	8	21,900	27,400	11,200	16,200
	9	16,200	20,200	11,200	9,000
	10	9,000	11,200	11,200	—
@ 60%–	1st Year	40,000	72,900	13,700	59,200
	2	59,200	107,800	13,700	94,100
	3	94,100	171,500	13,700	157,800
	4	157,800	287,600	13,700	273,900
	5	273,900	499,000	13,700	485,300
	6	485,300	884,300	13,700	870,600
	7	870,600	1,586,200	13,700	1,572,500
	8	1,572,500	2,865,300	13,700	2,851,600
	9	2,851,600	5,195,900	13,700	5,182,200
	10	5,182,200	9,442,500	13,700	9,428,800

Borrowing at any rate less than 22% for this project will show profit. Borrowing at any rate more than 22% for this project will show loss. 22% is the absolute evaluation as a financial transaction.

In all of the foregoing studies the Committee was viewing the methods as to their *relative* dependability to produce the logical answer. In every problem it found that the Average Book Method could give misleading information but that the Investor's Method always appeared to go in the right direction. This was an encouraging discovery and it led the Committee to make the further test of *absolute* dependability.

Whenever a rate of return is mentioned it is only natural to compare it, either mentally or conversationally, with the rate at which money might be procured. If the rate of return is believed to result from complete and sound basic data, if it has picked up income taxes and overhead expenses, if it has included probable growth in assets other than plant in its cash outlay, and if it shows a return which is substantially higher than the market cost of money, then the project is looked upon with favor and it is presented for an expected approval. But management must have faith in the method of computing the rate of return, which claims that money might be borrowed at any lower rate and still show some profit. The Committee tested the methods by assuming that money would be borrowed at the rate indicated by each method when applied to various test cases used in the prior studies. In every case it was found that the rate given by the Average Book Method could lead to serious trouble, but that the rate indicated by the Investor's Method could be actually used for borrowing money and the initial debt would be repaid at the end of the project's life.

EXHIBIT #6 shows one of these comparisons, taken from the test cases used in Group #1.

The Committee believed that the Investor's Method had demonstrated its ability to show a rate of return which was dependable in an absolute way, as well as being dependable in the relative sense of giving more reasonable answers than other methods.

The Committee was interested in knowing why one method seemed so eminently satisfactory while the other was not trustworthy, although the basic data for both would be taken from the same anticipated books of account. A little analysis showed two fundamental reasons. In the first place, a rate of return on a proposed outlay is a pure financial matter involving only the cash accounts, and any injection of non-cash book transactions tends only to confuse the picture and distort the result. In the second place, the time element is an essential factor in financial matters, and its omission leads to erroneous results.

The Investor's Method made the best showing because it used only the cash transactions and it gave full weight to the time factor on each such transaction. The Average Book Method showed its inferiority because it supplemented the cash transactions by the inclusion of regular book charges and it gave no heed to the time factor.

At the risk of offering a caution which may be superfluous, the Committee realizes that dependability of a computed rate of return can be no greater than the accuracy of the submitted basic data. These data should include all risk factors and should indicate the reasonable expectancy against which the project's sponsor is willing to be judged.

The Committee was gratified to find that a special interest table had been constructed by the company which was employing the Investor's Method. Such a tool facilitates the practical application of the method, which is quite cumbersome if published interest tables must be used. This particular special table was compiled on a principle of continuous compounding instead of the usual procedure of compounding annually, semi-annually or quarterly. This is not an essential feature but it has some mechanical advantages of greater flexibility in using the table, and it seems reasonable when the dollar movements will be daily throughout the life of the project.

EXHIBIT #7 shows a specimen sheet from the interest table and its application to a preceding problem.

The Committee learned, in the course of its study, that Dr. Joel Dean had come out in favor of a method which appeared to parallel the Investor's Method. Dr. Dean was contacted and it was found that the two systems were identical, although they had been developed independently. His wholehearted endorsement gave added impetus to the Committee's growing conviction that it should make a specific recommendation even though it might appear to be radical.

The Committee, with the assistance of Dr. Dean, gave the Philadelphia Chapter a brief introduction to the Investor's Method and recommended that it be endorsed by the Chapter for presentation to the National Society as Philadelphia's contribution. The Chapter members were sufficiently interested to set a time for a special meeting when they could concentrate on the one subject, have their questions answered as to theory and practice, and make up their individual minds as to whether they wished to support their Research Committee in recommending the method to the National Society. At that special meeting the Philadelphia Chapter adopted the report of its committee with

CONTINUOUS INTEREST TABLE

COMPOUNDING PERFORMANCE BEFORE-REFERENCE POINT WHICH OCCURS:	21%	22%	23%	24%	25%	26%	27%	28%	29%	30%
A. IN AN INSTANT										
1 MONTH BEFORE	1.0177	1.0185	1.0194	1.0202	1.0211	1.0219	1.0228	1.0236	1.0245	1.0253
2 MONTHS "	1.0356	1.0373	1.0391	1.0408	1.0425	1.0443	1.0460	1.0478	1.0495	1.0513
3 " "	1.0539	1.0565	1.0592	1.0618	1.0645	1.0672	1.0698	1.0725	1.0752	1.0779
6 MONTHS BEFORE	1.1107	1.1163	1.1219	1.1275	1.1331	1.1388	1.1445	1.1503	1.1560	1.1618
9 " "	1.1706	1.1794	1.1883	1.1972	1.2062	1.2153	1.2245	1.2337	1.2430	1.2523
12 " "	1.2337	1.2461	1.2586	1.2712	1.2840	1.2969	1.3100	1.3231	1.3364	1.3499
1½ YEARS BEFORE	1.3703	1.3910	1.4120	1.4333	1.4550	1.4770	1.4993	1.5220	1.5450	1.5683
2 " "	1.5220	1.5527	1.5841	1.6161	1.6487	1.6820	1.7160	1.7507	1.7860	1.8221
2½ " "	1.6905	1.7333	1.7771	1.8221	1.8682	1.9155	1.9640	2.0138	2.0647	2.1170
3 " "	1.8776	1.9348	1.9937	2.0544	2.1170	2.1815	2.2479	2.3164	2.3869	2.4596
B. UNIFORMLY UNTIL REFERENCE POINT										
FROM 3 MONTHS BEFORE TO 0	1.0267	1.0280	1.0293	1.0306	1.0319	1.0332	1.0345	1.0358	1.0371	1.0385
" 6 " " " 0	1.0544	1.0571	1.0598	1.0625	1.0652	1.0679	1.0706	1.0734	1.0761	1.0789
" 9 " " " 0	1.0831	1.0872	1.0914	1.0957	1.0999	1.1042	1.1084	1.1128	1.1171	1.1214
" 12 " " " 0	1.1128	1.1185	1.1244	1.1302	1.1361	1.1420	1.1480	1.1540	1.1601	1.1662
FROM 2 YEARS BEFORE TO 0	1.2428	1.2562	1.2697	1.2835	1.2974	1.3116	1.3259	1.3405	1.3552	1.3702
" 3 " " " 0	1.3930	1.4164	1.4402	1.4645	1.4893	1.5147	1.5406	1.5671	1.5942	1.6218
DISCOUNTING PERFORMANCE AFTER REFERENCE POINT WHICH OCCURS:										
C. IN AN INSTANT										
1 YEAR LATER	.8106	.8025	.7945	.7866	.7788	.7711	.7634	.7558	.7483	.7408
2 YEARS "	.6570	.6440	.6313	.6188	.6065	.5945	.5827	.5712	.5599	.5488
3 " "	.5326	.5169	.5016	.4868	.4724	.4584	.4449	.4317	.4190	.4066
4 " "	.4317	.4148	.3985	.3829	.3679	.3535	.3396	.3263	.3135	.3012
5 " "	.3499	.3329	.3166	.3012	.2865	.2725	.2592	.2466	.2346	.2231
10 YEARS LATER	.1225	.1108	.1003	.0907	.0821	.0743	.0672	.0608	.0550	.0498
15 " "	.0429	.0369	.0317	.0273	.0235	.0202	.0174	.0150	.0129	.0111
20 " "	.0150	.0123	.0101	.0082	.0067	.0055	.0045	.0037	.0030	.0025
25 " "	.0052	.0041	.0032	.0025	.0019	.0015	.0012	.0009	.0007	.0006
30 " "	.0018	.0014	.0010	.0007	.0006	.0004	.0003	.0002	.0002	.0001
35 YEARS LATER	.0006	.0005	.0003	.0002	.0002	.0001	.0001	.0001	-	-
40 " "	.0002	.0002	.0001	.0001	-	-	-	-	-	
45 " "	.0001	.0001	-	-	-	-	-	-	-	
50 " "	-	-	-	-	-	-	-	-	-	
D. UNIFORMLY OVER INDIVIDUAL YEARS										
FROM 0 TO 1 YEAR	.9020	.8976	.8933	.8890	.8848	.8806	.8764	.8722	.8681	.8640
" 1 " 2 YEARS	.7311	.7204	.7098	.6993	.6891	.6790	.6690	.6592	.6495	.6400
" 2 " 3 "	.5926	.5781	.5639	.5501	.5367	.5235	.5107	.4982	.4860	.4741
" 3 " 4 "	.4804	.4639	.4481	.4327	.4179	.4037	.3899	.3765	.3637	.3513
" 4 " 5 "	.3894	.3723	.3560	.3404	.3255	.3112	.2976	.2846	.2721	.2602
FROM 5 TO 6 YEARS	.3156	.2988	.2829	.2678	.2535	.2400	.2272	.2151	.2036	1928
" 6 " 7 "	.2558	.2398	.2247	.2106	.1974	.1850	.1734	.1626	.1524	.1428
" 7 " 8 "	.2074	.1924	.1786	.1657	.1538	1427	.1324	.1229	.1140	.1058
" 8 " 9 "	.1681	.1544	.1419	.1303	.1197	.1100	.1011	.0929	.0853	.0784
" 9 " 10 "	.1363	.1239	.1127	.1025	.0933	.0848	.0772	.0702	0638	.0581
FROM 10 TO 11 YEARS	.1105	.0995	.0896	.0807	.0726	.0654	0589	.0530	.0478	.0430
" 11 " 12 "	.0895	.0798	.0711	.0634	.0566	.0504	.0450	.0401	.0357	.0319
" 12 " 13 "	.0726	.0641	.0565	.0499	.0441	.0389	.0343	.0303	.0267	.0236
" 13 " 14 "	.0588	.0514	.0449	.0393	.0343	.0300	0262	.0229	.0200	.0175
" 14 " 15 "	.0477	.0413	.0357	.0309	.0267	.0231	.0200	.0173	.0150	.0130
E. UNIFORMLY OVER 5 YEAR PERIODS										
FROM 0 TO 5 YEARS	.6191	.6065	.5942	.5823	.5708	.5596	.5487	.5381	.5279	.5179
" 5 " 10 "	.2166	.2019	.1882	.1754	.1635	.1525	.1422	.1327	.1238	.1156
" 10 " 15 "	.0758	.0672	.0596	.0528	.0469	.0416	.0369	.0327	.0290	.0258
" 15 " 20 "	.0265	.0224	.0189	.0159	.0134	.0113	.0096	.0081	.0068	.0058
" 20 " 25 "	.0093	.0074	.0060	.0048	.0038	.0031	.0025	.0020	.0016	.0013
FROM 25 TO 30 YEARS	.0032	.0025	.0019	.0014	.0011	.0008	.0006	.0005	.0004	.0003
" 30 " 35 "	.0011	.0008	.0006	.0004	.0003	.0002	.0002	.0001	.0001	.0001
" 35 " 40 "	.0004	.0003	.0002	.0001	.0001	.0001	-	-	-	-
" 40 " 45 "	.0001	.0001	.0001	-	-	-	-	-	-	-
" 45 " 50 "	.0000		-	-	-	-	-	-	-	-
F. DECLINING TO NOTHING AT CONSTANT RATE										
FROM 0 TO 5 YEARS	.7255	.7155	.7057	.6961	.6867	.6776	.6686	.6598	.6512	.6428
" 0 " 10 "	.5544	.5417	.5294	.5176	.5063	.4953	.4848	.4747	.4649	.4555
" 0 " 15 "	.4420	.4292	.4170	.4055	.3945	.3840	.3740	.3645	.3554	.3468
" 0 " 20 "	.3645	.3525	.3412	.3306	.3205	.3111	.3020	.2936	.2856	.2779
" 0 " 25 "	.3088	.2978	.2875	.2779	.2689	.2604	.2525	.2449	.2378	.2311
FROM 0 TO 30 YEARS	.2672	.2572	.2479	.2392	.2311	.2235	.2166	.2098	.2036	.1975
" 0 " 35 "	.2351	.2260	.2177	.2098	.2026	.1957	.1893	.1834	.1776	.1723

EXHIBIT #7

its recommendations. It is now offering the Investor's Method, for computing the rate of return on a proposed outlay of funds, to this National Convention and to industry.

THE INTEREST TABLES

In constructing the tables, it was recognized that operators would vary in their selection of the zero date or reference point, and this selection does not change the result. The date of spending the first dollar, the date of starting operation, or any other date which might seem logical, could be adopted to suit personal preference. To provide for transactions which would occur before the selected zero date, it was necessary to use the principle of compounding, while all subsequent transactions would be subject to discount. It was also realized that some transactions would occur instantaneously while others would be spread over a period with some degree of probable uniformity.

Section A indicates factors to be applied to a transaction which will occur instantly and prior to zero date. Section B provides factors to be applied when the transaction is spread over the period before the zero date. Section C is the reciprocal of Section A and provides factors for discounting instantaneous transactions back to the zero date. Sections D and E apply to transactions which are uniformly spread over the stated periods. Section F is designed for a quick overall appraisal of a project from which the net cash receipts are expected to decline by an arithmetic progression from a maximum in the first year to zero at the end of its life. The use of the tables, a specimen sheet of which is shown as Exhibit #7, is illustrated by the following simple example:

SPECIMEN CALCULATION

Using the example in Exhibit #1, the annual receipts are uniform and the time table may be stated in the simple terms below (Column A). Factors are taken from Table E in the Interest Tables at the trial rates selected (Columns B and D).

With a problem as simple as the above, an experienced operator would not have to go through even the few steps described. He would note that the ratio of initial outlay to a five-year receipt was .80. He would then scan his interest table to see where the first two factors in Table E added up to .80. He would locate it at approximately 22%.

Trial Rates of Interest

	0%	22%		23%	
		Factor	Value	Factor	Value
	A	B	C	D	E
0	(−40)	1.0000	(−40)	1.0000	(−40)
0 to 5	50	.6065	30.3	.5942	29.7
5 to 10	50	.2019	10.1	.1882	9.4
	60		.4		(− .9)

At 0% there is an excess of $60,000
At 22% there is an excess of $ 400
At 23% there is a deficit of $ 900
The project rates at 22% plus.
By interpolation it is 22.32%.

THE PAYOFF PERIOD AND THE RATE OF PROFIT

MYRON J. GORDON*

I. INTRODUCTION

AN ELEMENT of the capital budgeting process is the selection and use of a formula for evaluating the profitability of the available investment opportunities. The formula used reduces the attributes of an investment proposal (cost, savings or earnings, life, etc.) to a single number, and it thereby provides a comparative and an absolute measure of the profitability of the proposal. As a comparative measure, the formula aids in selecting among alternative proposals; and as an absolute measure, the formula aids in determining the size of the capital budget.

While the selection of a formula is not the most important of the problems connected with capital budgeting, the use of an accurate and efficient formula contributes to effective capital budgeting. Furthermore, there has been considerable controversy over the merits of alternative formulas, particularly the payoff period, the average investment formula, and the Terborgh formula, and it would seem desirable to have the question resolved. This is the purpose of the present paper.

The major conclusions reached by the analysis may be summarized as follows: First, the reciprocal of the payoff period is in fact an estimate of a proposal's rate of profit. Second, when a proposal's life is *greater than its posttax payoff period*, the reciprocal of the payoff period provides the best short-cut estimate of its rate of profit; and, when a proposal's life is *less than its posttax payoff period*, the average investment formula provides the better short-cut estimate of its rate of profit. The error in the two formulas is found by comparing them with the present-value formula, which provides a proposal's true rate of profit. The third conclusion is that the Terborgh formula provides an index of the profitability of an investment proposal that has serious limitations in the purpose for which it is intended.

* Associate professor, Massachusetts Institute of Technology.

II. THE TRUE RATE OF PROFIT

An equipment proposal, like any other investment opportunity, involves a current outlay and the expectation of a series of receipts in the future; and the proposal's rate of profit is the rate of interest or discount that equates the future receipts with the outlay. To elaborate, let

C = the cost of a proposal,
S_t = the earnings or savings before depreciation that the proposal is expected to provide in the year t,
n = the number of years the equipment is expected to last,
J_n = the scrap value of the equipment at $t = n$,
k = the proposal's expected rate of profit.

Then, if all the other quantities are known, a proposal's rate of profit is the value of k that satisfies the equation

$$C = \frac{S_1}{1+k} + \frac{S_2}{(1+k)^2} + \dots + \frac{S_t}{(1+k)^t} + \dots + \frac{S_n + J_n}{(1+k)^n}. \quad (1)$$

It is commonly assumed for simplicity and for lack of better information that the savings in each year will be the same, so that $S_t = S$. It is also common to ignore the equipment's scrap value on the grounds that J_n is small and its present value is even smaller in relation to C. Making these two assumptions, Eq. (1) reduces to

$$C = \sum_{t=1}^{n} \frac{S}{(1+k)^t} = \frac{S}{k} - \frac{S}{k}\left(\frac{1}{1+k}\right)^n. \qquad (2)$$

Eq. (2) is simply the well-known formula for the present value of an annuity.[1]

The value of k that satisfies Eq. (2), given C, S, and n, provides a proposal's true rate of profit.[2] Nonetheless, the formula is rarely if ever used to evaluate equipment proposals for two complementary reasons. First, solving the equation for k involves tedious trial-and-error calculations,[3] and, second, the range of error in the estimate of the future receipts is considerable. The limitations of the basic data appear, therefore, to make it unwise to spend any considerable effort in using a correct but difficult formula.

III. THE PAYOFF ESTIMATE

A proposal's payoff period is the ratio of its cost to its annual earnings before depreciation, and our definition of the payoff reciprocal estimate of the rate of profit is

$$k_p = \frac{S}{C}. \qquad (3)$$

The relation between it and the rate of profit can be seen by rewriting Eq. (2) as follows:[4]

$$k = \frac{S}{C} - \frac{S}{C}\left(\frac{1}{1+k}\right)^n \qquad (4)$$

Examination of Eq. (4) reveals that a proposal's rate of profit is *equal to the reciprocal of its payoff minus the same quantity multiplied by* $[1/(1+k)]^n$. Since $[1/(1+k)]^n$ is a fraction, the second term on the right-hand side of Eq. (4) approaches zero as n, the life of the proposal, becomes infinitely large. Therefore, we can make the following interesting statements with regard to the payoff period.

1. If an equipment proposal will earn or save the same amount *forever*, its rate of profit is simply the reciprocal of its payoff. To illustrate, if the payoff is 5 years, the rate of profit is 20 per cent; if the payoff is 3 years, the rate of profit is $33\frac{1}{3}$ per cent.

2. If, as is generally the case, the equipment will last a finite number of years, the rate of profit is *at most the reciprocal of the payoff* and smaller than this by the quantity $S/C(1+k)^n$.

Consequently, subject to some margin of error, a firm may take the reciprocal of a proposal's payoff period as an estimate of its rate of profit. The margin of error is $S/C(1+k)^n$, and it falls as the life of the proposal increases. We will see shortly that the error is negligible over a wide and important range of values for n.

[1] Cf. John A. Northcutt, *Mathematics of Finance* (New York: Rinehart, 1946), pp. 53–54, or Eugene L. Grant, *Principles of Engineering Economy* (3d ed.; New York: Ronald, 1950), pp. 42–45.

[2] See Grant, *op. cit.*, pp. 132–49. The formula is advocated by Joel Dean, "Controls for Capital Expenditures," in *Modern Management of Capital Expenditures* (Financial Management Series, No. 105 [New York: American Management Association, 1953]), pp. 6–7, and by John M. Schultz, "The Investor's Method of Computing Rate of Return as Applied to Replacement Valuation," in *Capital Equipment Replacement* (Special Report No. 1 [New York: American Management Association, 1954]).

[3] Tables exist which can be used for values of k up to 10 per cent, but few firms would even give formal consideration to a proposal that did not earn more than 10 per cent before taxes.

[4] Jay N. Fues and Thomas E. Bastis, two of the writer's former students, used the formula in this form to estimate the true rate of profit in a case assigned to them. The equation and their solution to the problem suggested the possibility of using the payoff period as an approximation of the rate of profit.

IV. THE AVERAGE INVESTMENT ESTIMATE

The average investment formula estimate of the rate of profit is the annual earnings after depreciation, D, divided by one-half of the cost of the investment, or

$$k_a = \frac{S - D}{\frac{1}{2}C}. \tag{5}$$

Notice, here as in the previous formulas, the savings are assumed to be the same in each year, and the salvage value is ignored. Since the annual depreciation is equal to the cost divided by the life, we can substitute C/n for D in Eq. (5). Doing so and simplifying, we find that it becomes

$$k_a = \frac{2S}{C} - \frac{2}{n}. \tag{6}$$

As a proposal's life reaches infinity, the second term on the right-hand side of Eq. (6) disappears, and k_a approaches twice the reciprocal of the payoff period. Consequently, while the error in the payoff reciprocal disappears as n becomes large, the error in the average investment formula approaches 100 per cent, i.e., k_a approaches twice k. A more detailed comparison of the formulas is presented below.

V. COMPARATIVE ANALYSIS OF THE FORMULAS

By setting the right-hand sides of Eqs. (3) and (5) equal to each other and solving for n, we find that k_p, the payoff reciprocal, and k_a, the average investment formula, are equal when

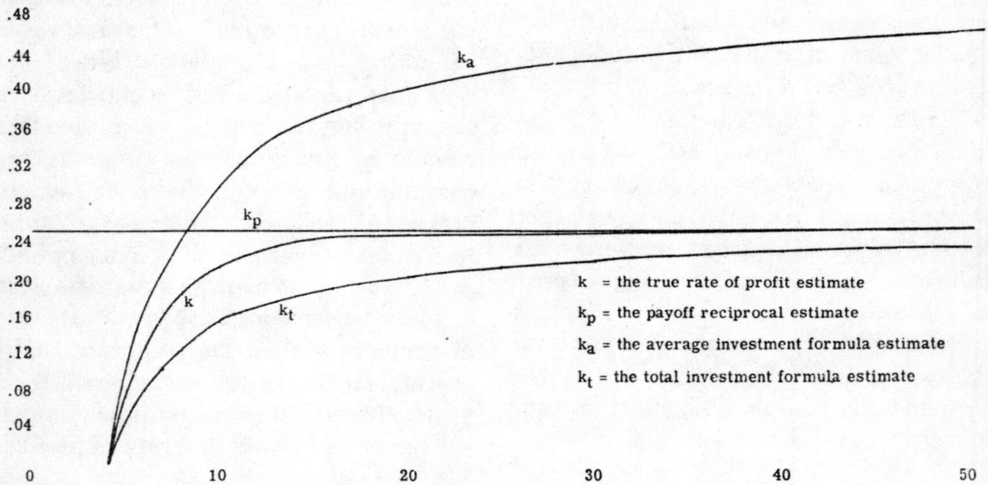

FIG. 1.—Rate of profit under various formulas for a proposal with a four-year payoff

$$n = \frac{2C}{S}. \tag{7}$$

It also can be shown that when n, the life in years, is greater than twice the payoff period, k_a is above k_p, and, when n is below this quantity, k_a is below k_p. Since the true rate of profit is always below k_p, it is the better estimate of k when n is above $2C/S$, and k_a is the better estimate when n is below $2C/S$.

The above propositions are clearly illustrated in Figure 1, where the curves for the three formulas are drawn for a payoff of four years. The payoff reciprocal is equal to 25 per cent for all values of n. The average investment estimate is equal to zero when $n = 4$, equal to 25 per cent (the payoff reciprocal) when $n = 8$, and approaches 50 per cent as n becomes large. The true rate of profit is also equal to zero when $n = 4$ and approaches 25 per cent as n becomes large. It should be noted that k rises sharply between $n = 4$ and $n = 10$, so that the difference between k and k_p is negligible for n greater than ten years.

TABLE 1

TRUE AND ESTIMATED BEFORE-TAX RATES OF PROFIT FOR SELECTED PAYOFFS AND LIVES

Payoff C/S	Life in Years n	Payoff Estimate* (Percentage)	True Value† (Percentage)	Average Investment Estimate‡ (Percentage)
1	4	100	93.0	150
2	6	50	44.5	66.7
3	9	33.3	30.0	44.5
4	10	25	22.5	30
5	13	20	17.5	24.6

* Equal to reciprocal of payoff.

† The value of k, stated as a percentage, that satisfies eq. (4) to the nearest one-half of 1 per cent.

‡ The value of k that satisfies eq. (6).

It should also be noted that the three rates of profit for any n will vary depending on the payoff period, but the general relations among the curves described in the previous paragraphs and illustrated in Figure 1 will always hold.

As a means of compensating for the error in the average investment formula, it has been suggested that the savings after depreciation be divided by the full cost. The formula is

$$k_t = \frac{S - D}{C} = \frac{S}{C} - \frac{1}{n}. \quad (8)$$

This curve is also drawn in Figure 1, where it can be seen that k_t will always lie below the true rate of profit. In general for n greater than $2C/S$, the payoff reciprocal remains the best short-cut estimate of the true rate of profit. For n smaller than $2C/S$, k_t may be more or less accurate than k_a. The formula's chief recommendation is that it is conservative, since k_t is always below k_p.

As stated earlier, the difference between the payoff reciprocal and the true rate of profit rapidly becomes negligible. This is more fully demonstrated in Table 1, where the rates of profit under the three formulas are shown for various values of C/S and n. The payoffs selected are one through five years, and the lives selected are those which result in an error in the payoff reciprocal of about 10 per cent in each case. The life that satisfies this condition for each payoff period is only two or three years greater than twice the payoff.[5] Beyond these lives the error in k_p becomes extremely small, and, hence, over a wide and important range of investment proposals, the payoff reciprocal provides a highly accurate estimate of a proposal's rate of profit.

In contrast, the average investment estimate involves a considerable error for the values of n shown, and the error increases as the proposal's life is increased.

VI. THE AFTER-TAX RATE OF PROFIT

In selecting among alternative investment proposals, and in setting the over-all capital budget, a firm is probably more interested in the after-tax rate of profit than in the pretax rate. The two need not bear the same relation for all formulas, and our purpose in this section is to es-

[5] For payoffs greater than five years, the difference is larger absolutely but not relatively. Also a proposal that requires more than five years to pay for itself cannot earn 20 per cent, and a firm is not likely to consider a proposal that earns less than 20 per cent before taxes. This may explain in part the insistence on short payoff periods.

tablish the error in the formulas on an after-tax basis.

Assuming straight-line depreciation[6] and letting r equal the income tax rate, the amount of annual receipts before depreciation and after the tax is the depreciation charge plus the income after depreciation and tax, or

$$D + (S - D)(1 - r) = S(1 - r) + \frac{rC}{n}. \tag{9}$$

The analysis is simplified without loss of generality by assuming a specific tax rate. We will use 50 per cent. Setting $r = 0.5$, Eq. (9) becomes

$$\frac{S}{2} + \frac{C}{2n}. \tag{10}$$

Substituting the above expression for S in Eq. (4) yields the true rate of profit after taxes,

$$k' = \frac{S}{2C} + \frac{1}{2n} - \left(\frac{S}{2C} + \frac{1}{2n}\right) \times \left(\frac{1}{1+k'}\right)^n. \tag{11}$$

Notice, the after-tax rate of profit approaches one-half the pretax rate as n becomes large, but for n not large, its behavior is not immediately evident from inspection of Eq. (11).

The payoff estimate of the rate of profit may be obtained by substituting expression (10) for S in Eq. (3). However, a common practice and, in fact, a more desirable estimate is obtained by using one-half the pretax value. Hence, the estimate we will use is

$$k'_p = \frac{S}{2C}. \tag{12}$$

Finally, the average investment formula for the posttax rate of profit is one-half of the pretax rate, Eq. (5), or

$$k'_a = \frac{\frac{1}{2}(S - D)}{\frac{1}{2}C} = \frac{S}{C} - \frac{1}{n}. \tag{13}$$

The same result is obtained by substituting expression (10) in Eq. (5).

The relations among the three formulas are best described in conjunction with Figure 2, where the relations are illustrated for a posttax payoff period of eight years. The relations established, however, are valid for all combinations of payoff period and life. First, k'_p, the payoff reciprocal, is 12.5 per cent for all values of n. Second, for $n = 4$, or one-half the posttax payoff, k'_a is zero; for $n = 8$, the posttax payoff, $k'_a = k'_p =$ 12.5 per cent; and as n becomes large k'_a approaches 25 per cent, or twice the payoff reciprocal rate of profit. Hence, the relation between k'_p and k'_a remains similar to the relation between their pretax values.

However, the true rate of profit behaves somewhat differently. Initially k' is slightly above k'_a; k' rises rapidly up to $n = 8$, the payoff period: and beyond $n = 8$ the true rate of profit is slightly below and then slightly above the payoff reciprocal rate, approaching it as n becomes large. The conclusion to be reached from this analysis is similar to the conclusion reached for the pretax rate of profit. *For a life less than the posttax payoff; k'_a is the best short-cut estimate, and, for*

[6] The federal tax law now allows a declining depreciation charge. However, it has been shown that the difference in the rate of profit under straight-line depreciation and any of the newly allowed methods is negligible. See E. Cary Brown, "The New Depreciation Policy under the Income Tax: An Economic Analysis," *National Tax Journal*, VIII (March, 1955), 93.

a life above the posttax payoff, k'_p is the best short-cut estimate.[7]

The magnitude of the error in using the payoff reciprocal to estimate the true rate of profit is indicated by the data of Table 2. There, the payoff reciprocal and true rates of profit are shown for posttax payoffs of 2, 4, 6, 8, and 10 years and for lives equal to the payoffs and 50 per cent longer than the payoffs. We see that for *n* equal to the payoff period the error in the payoff reciprocal is not small, but for *n* 50 per cent greater, the error is negligible. The error remains negligible for all values of *n* greater than this value.

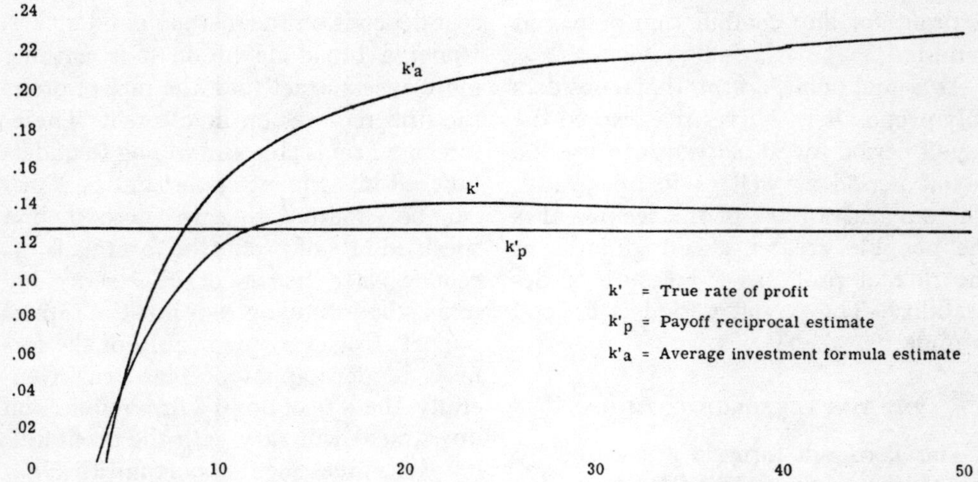

FIG. 2.—After-tax rates of profit under various formulas for an after-tax payoff of eight years

TABLE 2

PAYOFF RECIPROCAL AND TRUE POST-TAX RATES OF PROFIT FOR SELECTED PAYOFFS AND LIVES

After-Tax Payoff	Life in Years	Payoff Estimate (Percentage)	True Value (Percentage)
2	2	50.0	31.9
	3	50.0	44.6
4	4	25.0	18.5
	6	25.0	24.2
6	6	16.7	13.0
	9	16.7	16.8
8	8	12.5	10.0
	12	12.5	12.7
10	10	10.0	8.0
	15	10.0	10.2

The data of Table 2 show that a firm with a policy of considering only proposals with lives that exceed the payoff period by 50 per cent or more would find the payoff reciprocal a perfectly satisfactory short-cut estimate of the rate of profit. It might appear that this cut-off point would lead to the rejection of profitable proposals. However, a small error in a proposal with an estimated life that does not satisfy the above condition involves a large error in the rate of profit estimate.[8] Hence, there is some wisdom in avoiding such borderline proposals.

A firm that wishes to consider pro-

[7] This conclusion must be qualified by the fact that the life for which the payoff reciprocal becomes the best estimate depends on the tax rate. The conclusion is valid for a 50 per cent corporate tax rate.

[8] For instance, a proposal with a three-year payoff and a fifteen-year life will earn only a slightly lower rate of profit if it lasts only ten years. On the other hand, if the estimated life were four years and it proved to be three years, the rate of profit would be drastically reduced.

posals which fall in the interval between the payoff period and 50 per cent above it must accept a margin of error in its estimate of the rate of profit or compute the true rate by trial-and-error methods. However, if the data are considered useful, it is possible to construct a simple one-page table which gives the true rate of profit for any combination of payoff and life.

As a final point, a firm that considers only proposals with lives that exceed the payoff period by 50 per cent can use the payoff period as well as its reciprocal. The only advantage of the reciprocal is the possible greater meaningfulness of the rate of profit as a measure of desirability. The payoff period is a good formula.

VII. THE TERBORGH FORMULA

The Terborgh formula advocated by the Machinery and Allied Products Institute differs from those previously considered in a number of ways. While these differences are material to the relative usefulness of the formulas, fortunately examining them does not require a detailed review of Terborgh's formula.

The foremost difference stems from the fact that Terborgh's formula does not provide a measure of a proposal's rate of profit. Rather, it decides whether an investment should be made by comparing the cost of the existing and proposed equipment with interest on the investment included in the cost. "More precisely, we should replace when the lowest combined average of operating inferiority and capital cost obtainable from the best new unit is below the lowest average obtainable from further use of the old one."[9] The desirability of replacement is determined under the formula, given certain information *which includes an interest rate that represents the cost of money.*

In his major work on the subject, Terborgh devotes a chapter to the cost of money[10] where it is evident that under a narrow definition of "cost of money" the cost depends on the method of financing. Under a broad definition it is nothing more or less exact than the rate of profit the firm requires on investment. Therefore, if a firm is able and willing to undertake *all* investment opportunities which can be expected to earn more than a specified rate of profit, the formula is excellent. Once the rate of profit is decided upon, the formula grinds out the capital budget. However, the beauty of the formula is more apparent than real. Generally, the rate of profit a firm requires on investment will vary with the profitability of the investment opportunities available to it and inversely with the availability of funds. For instance, when retained earnings are large or when the expected rate of profit on available projects is low, a firm will require a lower rate of profit than it otherwise would. Therefore, Terborgh's formula for evaluating the desirability of investment proposals assumes that the firm knows what it will find out only after the opportunities have been evaluated, viz., the required rate of profit.

The formula can be used in a more modest manner than that described above. If the new equipment's "operating inferiority and capital cost" is below that of the old equipment, we can say that it will earn a higher rate of profit than the rate used in the formula. It is also true that the higher the ratio of the

[9] *MAPI Replacement Manual*, Machinery and Allied Products Institute, 1950, p. 11.

[10] George Terborgh, *Dynamic Equipment Policy: A MAPI Study* (New York: McGraw-Hill, 1949), chap. x.

costs with the old equipment to the costs with the new equipment, the higher the rate of profit on the proposal. However, to tell those responsible for investment decisions that a proposal has a 1.4 cost ratio using a 10 per cent rate of interest[11] does not provide them with a meaningful piece of information. The great virtue and probably the prime reason for the popularity of the payoff period is that the payoff and life ring a bell as an index of the profitability of a proposal.

The chief advantage of the Terborgh formula is that it assumes, quite realistically and contrary to the formulas discussed previously, that the expected savings or earnings on an investment will decline over its life. In formulas where the savings are assumed to be constant, the error is compensated for roughly by using a shorter life than expected or by requiring a higher rate of profit than is really required. Another advantage of the formula is that tables have been computed and made available in graphic form which make the computations involved in the use of the formula negligible.

With respect to these advantages, first, the graphs only reduce the computations to those required for the short-cut formulas. Second, if the accuracy of declining savings is desired, the true rate of profit formula can be formulated to recognize a declining stream of savings. The short-cut formulas cannot be so modified without introducing a considerable margin of error in the estimates they provide, but it is possible to compute the data for a table which provides the true rate of profit for all required combinations of life and ratio of first-year savings to cost.

[11] The ratio will yary depending on the rate of interest used. A similar procedure is the use of the present value formula, Eq. (2) with k known, to determine the *value* of a proposal. The ratio of the value to the cost given the rate of interest used is a measure of profitability.

THREE PROBLEMS IN RATIONING CAPITAL*

JAMES H. LORIE† AND LEONARD J. SAVAGE‡

I. INTRODUCTION

CORPORATE executives face three tasks in achieving good financial management. The first is largely administrative and consists in finding an efficient procedure for preparing and reviewing capital budgets, for delegating authority and fixing responsibility for expenditures, and for finding some means for ultimate evaluation of completed investments. The second task is to forecast correctly the cash flows that can be expected to result from specified investment proposals, as well as the liquid resources that will be available for investment. The third task is to ration available capital or liquid resources among competing investment opportunities. This article is concerned with only this last task; it discusses three problems in the rationing of capital, in the sense of liquid resources.

1. Given a firm's cost of capital and a management policy of using this cost to identify acceptable investment proposals, which group of "independent" investment proposals should the firm accept? In other words, how should the firm's cost of capital be used to distinguish between acceptable and unacceptable investments? This is a problem that is typically faced by top management whenever it reviews and approves a capital budget.

* This work was supported in part by the Office of Naval Research and in part by Joel Dean Associates.

† Associate professor of marketing, University of Chicago, and senior consultant, Joel Dean Associates.

‡ Professor of statistics, University of Chicago.

Before presenting the second problem with which this paper deals, the use of the word "independent" in the preceding paragraph should be explained. Investment proposals are termed "independent"—although not completely accurately—when the worth of the individual investment proposal is not profoundly affected by the acceptance of others. For example, a proposal to invest in materials-handling equipment at location A may not profoundly affect the value of a proposal to build a new warehouse in location B. It is clear that the independence is never complete, but the degree of independence is markedly greater than for sets of so-called "mutually exclusive" investment proposals. Acceptance of one proposal in such a set renders all others in the same set clearly unacceptable—or even unthinkable. An example of mutually exclusive proposals would be alternative makes of automotive equipment for the same fleet or alternative warehouse designs for the same site. The choice among mutually exclusive proposals is usually faced later in the process of financial management than is the initial approval of a capital budget. That is, the decision as to which make automotive equipment to purchase, for example, typically comes later than the decision to purchase some make of equipment.

2. Given a fixed sum of money to be used for capital investment, what group of investment proposals should be undertaken? If a firm pursues a policy of fixing the size of its capital budget in dollars, without explicit cognizance of, or refer-

ence to, its cost of capital, how can it best allocate that sum among competing investment proposals? This problem will be considered both for proposals which require net outlays in only one accounting period and for those which require outlays in more than one accounting period. In the latter case, special difficulties arise.

3. How should a firm select the best among mutually exclusive alternatives? That is, when the management of an enterprise, in attempting to make concrete and explicit proposals for expenditures of a type which is included in an approved capital budget, develops more than one plausible way of investing money in conformance with the budget, how can it select the "best" way?

After presenting our solutions to these three problems, we shall discuss the solutions implied by the rate-of-return method of capital budgeting.[1] These solutions are worthy of special attention, since they are based on a different principle from the solutions that we propose and since the rate-of-return method is the most defensible method heretofore proposed in the business literature for maximizing corporate profits and net worth.

II. THE THREE PROBLEMS

A. GIVEN THE COST OF CAPITAL, WHAT GROUP OF INVESTMENTS SHOULD BE SELECTED?

The question of determining the cost of capital is difficult, and we, happily, shall not discuss it. Although there may be disagreement about methods of calculating a firm's cost of capital, there is substantial agreement that the cost of capital is the rate at which a firm should discount future cash flows in order to determine their present value.[2] The first problem is to determine how selection should be made among "independent" investment proposals, given this cost or rate.

Assume that the firm's objective is to maximize the value of its net worth—not necessarily as measured by the accountant but rather as measured by the present value of its expected cash flows. This assumption is commonly made by economists and even business practitioners who have spoken on the subject. It is equivalent to asserting that the corporate management's objective is to maximize the value of the owner's equity or, alternatively, the value of the owner's income from the business. Given this objective and agreement about the significance of the firm's cost of capital, the problem of selecting investment proposals becomes trivial in those situations where there is a well-defined cost of capital; namely, proposals should be selected that have positive present values when discounted at the firm's cost of capital. The things to discount are the net cash flows resulting from the investments, and these cash flows should take taxes into account.

There is nothing unusual or original about this proposed solution. It is identical with that proposed by Lutz and Lutz[3] and is an economic commonplace. Joel Dean in his writings has developed

[1] This method was developed by Joel Dean, who has probably done more than anyone else in applying the formal apparatus of economics to the solution of capital budgeting problems in their business context.

[2] One of the difficulties with the concept of cost of capital is that in complicated circumstances there may be no one rate that plays this role. Still worse, the very concept of present value may be obscure.

[3] Friederich and Vera Lutz, *The Theory of Investment of the Firm* (Princeton: Princeton University Press, 1951). The solution proposed here is identical with the maximization of $V - C$, where V is the present value of future inflows and C is the present value of future outflows. This is discussed in chap. ii of the Lutz book.

and recommended a method which typically yields the same results for this problem, although the principle of solution is somewhat different, as is discussed later in this article.

The principle of accepting all proposals having positive present value at the firm's cost of capital is obvious, since the failure to do so would clearly mean foregoing an available increment in the present value of the firm's net worth. The principle is discussed here only because it seems a useful introduction to the somewhat more complicated problems that follow. An interesting property of this principle is that adherence to it will result in the present value of the firm's net worth being at a maximum at all points in time.

B. GIVEN A FIXED SUM FOR CAPITAL INVESTMENT, WHAT GROUP OF INVESTMENT PROPOSALS SHOULD BE UNDERTAKEN?

Some business firms—perhaps most—do not use the firm's cost of capital to distinguish between acceptable and unacceptable investments but, instead, determine the magnitude of their capital budget in some other way that results in fixing an absolute dollar limit on capital expenditures. Perhaps, for example, a corporate management may determine for any one year that the capital budget shall not exceed estimated income after taxes plus depreciation allowances, after specified dividend payments. It is probable that the sum fixed as the limit is not radically different from the sum that would be expended if correct and explicit use were made of the firm's cost of capital, since most business firms presumably do not long persist in policies antithetical to the objective of making money. (The profit-maximizing principle is the one that makes use of the firm's cost of capital, as described previously.) Nevertheless, there are probably some differences in the amount that would be invested by a firm if it made correct use of the firm's cost of capital and the amount that would be invested if it fixed its capital budget by other means, expressing the constraint on expenditures as being a maximum outlay. At the very least, the differences in the ways of thinking suggest the usefulness to some firms of a principle that indicates the "best" group of investments that can be made with a fixed sum of money.

The problem is trivial when there are net outlays in only one accounting period—typically, one year. In such cases, investment proposals should be ranked according to their present value—at the firm's cost of capital—per dollar of outlay required. Once investment proposals have been ranked according to this criterion, it is easy to select the best group by starting with the investment proposal having the highest present value per dollar of outlay and proceeding down the list until the fixed sum is exhausted.[4]

The problem can become more difficult when discontinuities are taken into account. For large firms, the vast majority of investment proposals constitute such a small proportion of their total capital budget that the problems created by discontinuities can be disregarded at only insignificant cost, especially when the imprecision of the estimates of incomes is taken into account. When a project constitutes a large proportion of the capi-

[4] We mention, for completeness, that the outlay or the present value or both for a proposal can be negative. Proposals for which the outlay alone is negative—something for nothing—are always desirable but almost never available. Proposals for which both the outlay and present value are negative can sometimes be acceptable if something sufficiently profitable can be done with ready cash expressed by the negative outlay. The rules which we shall develop can be extended to cover such cases.

tal budget, the problem of discontinuities may become serious, though not necessarily difficult to deal with. This problem can become serious because of the obvious fact that accepting the large proposal because it is "richer" than smaller proposals may preclude the possibility of accepting two or more smaller and less rich proposals which, in combination, have a greater value than the larger proposal. For example, suppose that the total amount available for investment were $1,000 and that only three investment proposals had been made: one requiring a net outlay of $600 and creating an increment in present value of $1,000 and two others, each requiring a net outlay of $500 and each creating an increment in present value of $600. Under these circumstances, the adoption of the richest alternative, the first, would mean foregoing the other two alternatives, even though in combination they would create an increment in present value of $1,200 as compared with the increment of $1,000 resulting from the adoption of the richest investment alternative. Such discontinuities deserve special attention, but the general principles dealing with them will not be worked out here, primarily because we do not know them.

We shall, however, deal with the more serious difficulties created by the necessity to choose among investment proposals some of which require net cash outlays in more than one accounting period. In such cases a constraint is imposed not only by the fixed sum available for capital investment in the first period but also by the fixed sums available to carry out present commitments in subsequent time periods. Each such investment requires, so to speak, the use of two or more kinds of money—money from the first period and money from each subsequent period in which net outlays are required. We shall discuss only the case of investments requiring net outlays in two periods, for simplicity of exposition and because the principle—although not the mechanics—is the same as for investments requiring net outlays in more than two periods.

Let us start with a very simple case. Suppose that all the available opportunities for investment that yield a positive income can be adopted without exceeding the maximum permitted outlay in either time period one or time period two. Clearly, no better solution can be found, because all desirable opportunities have been exhausted. This simple case is mentioned not because of its practical importance, which is admittedly slight, but because it may clarify the more complicated cases that follow.

Next, consider a slightly more complicated case. Suppose that the opportunities available require more funds from either time period one or two than are permitted by the imposed constraints. Under these circumstances the problem becomes somewhat more complicated, but it still may not be very complicated. It is still relatively simple if (*a*) the best use of money available in period one does not exhaust the money available in period two or (*b*) the best use of money available in period two does not exhaust the money available in period one. In either case the optimum solution—that is, the solution which results in the greatest increment in the net worth of the firm, subject to the two stated constraints—is the one that makes the best possible use of the funds available for investment in one of the two time periods.

This statement is justified by the following reasoning. The imposition of additional restrictions upon the freedom of action of any agency can obviously never increase the value of the best opportunity available to that agency. In the problem at hand, this means that the imposition of an absolute dollar constraint or restriction in time period two can never make it possible to make better use of dollars available in time period one than would have been possible in the absence of that constraint. Thus, if the best possible use is made of the dollars available in time period one, the imposition of a restriction relating to time period two can never mean increased possibilities of profit from the use of funds available in time period one. Therefore, the maximization of the productivity of dollars available in time period one will constitute a maximization of productivity subject to the two constraints as well as to the one constraint. The reasoning is equally valid if we start with the constraint referring to time period two and maximize productivity of money available in that time period and then think of the effect of the additional constraint imposed for time period one.

Unfortunately, typical circumstances will probably make the relatively simple solutions unavailable. The solution to the relatively complex problem will—abstracting from discontinuities—require expending the full amount available for investment in each period. To illustrate how the solution is to be reached, consider the average actual net outlay of the two periods as being an outlay in a single "virtual" period and consider the average net outlay that is permitted by the constraints as being the average permitted outlay for the "virtual" period. Plan a budget for this "virtual" period according to the method of the one-period problem with which this section begins. That is, ration the capital available in the "virtual" period among the available investment opportunities so as to maximize the firm's net worth according to the principles stated in the discussion of the one-period problem. If, by accident, this budget happens to require precisely those outlays which are permitted for the first and second periods, it is easy to see that the problem has been solved. No other budget with a higher present value can be devised within the stated constraints for periods one and two.

Typically, the happy accident referred to in the preceding paragraph will not occur. The optimum use of the average amount available for investment in the two periods will typically result in expending too much in one period and not so much as is permitted in the other. Indeed, the happy accident was mentioned only as a step in explaining one method that will work. Though a simple average will almost never work, there is always some weighted average that will, and it can be found by trial and error. We shall describe in some detail a method that is mathematically equivalent to this method of weighted averages. In this method the solution is found by choosing, for suitable positive constants p_1 and p_2, those, and only those, proposals for which the following quantity is positive: $y - p_1c_1 - p_2c_2$. Here y is the present value of the proposal; c_1 and c_2 are the present values of the net outlays required in the first and second periods, respectively; and the multipliers p_1 and p_2 are auxiliary quantities for which there does not seem to be an immediate interpretation but that nonetheless help in solving the problem.[5]

Initially, the values of p_1 and p_2 will be determined by judgment. Subsequently, they will be altered by trial and error until the amounts to be expended in the first and second periods, according to the

[5] The multipliers, p_1 and p_2, are closely related to what are known in mathematics and in economics as "Lagrange multipliers."

rule just enunciated, are precisely the amounts permitted by the constraints. The initial choice of values for p_1 and p_2 is not very important, since a graphical process can usually lead rapidly to the correct values.

TABLE 1

Investment	Outlay—Period 1 (c_1)	Outlay—Period 2 (c_2)	Present Value of Investment
a	$12	$ 3	$14
b	54	7	17
c	6	6	17
d	6	2	15
e	30	35	40
f	6	6	12
g	48	4	14
h	36	3	10
i	18	3	12

Certain special possibilities are worth noting. Proposals of positive present value may have negative cost, that is, release cash, for either period. Some proposals of zero or negative present value may be acceptable because they release cash for one period or both. All such possibilities are automatically covered by the rule as stated and by the rules to be given for later problems.

Finding the correct values for p_1 and p_2 is sometimes not easy—especially when combined with the problem of selecting among mutually exclusive alternatives—but the task is usually as nothing compared to the interests involved or compared to many everyday engineering problems.[6] The following example may clarify the process.

Nine investments have been proposed. The present value of the net outlays required in the first and second time periods and the present values of the investments are as shown in Table 1. The finance committee has stated that $50 and $22 will be available for capital investment in the first and second periods, respectively. We shall consider these amounts to have present values of $50 and $20, respectively. According to the principle stated above, we must now find appropriate multipliers, p_1 and p_2.

Multipliers p_1 and p_2 were initially set at 1 and 3, respectively. With these values, only for investment *d* was the expression $(y - p_1c_1 - p_2c_2)$ positive and therefore acceptable. This would have resulted in net outlays of only $6 and $2 in periods one and two, respectively. Clearly, the values initially chosen for p_1 and p_2 were too great. On the other hand, values of 0.1 and 0.5 for p_1 and p_2, respectively, are too low, resulting in a positive value of $(y - p_1c_1 - p_2c_2)$ for all investments and required outlays in periods one and two far exceeding the permitted outlays.

Values of 0.33 and 1 for p_1 and p_2 result in a near-perfect fit. The expression $(y - p_1c_1 - p_2c_2)$ is positive for investments *a*, *c*, *d*, *f*, and *i*. These investments require outlays of $48 and $20 in the first and second periods, as near the permitted outlays of $50 and $20 as discontinuities permit. No other group of investments that is possible within the stated constraints has a greater present value than $70, the present value of this group.[7]

C. SELECTING THE BEST AMONG MUTUALLY EXCLUSIVE ALTERNATIVES

Before moneys are actually expended in fulfilment of an approved capital budget, the firm usually considers mutually exclusive alternative ways of making the generally described capital investment. When the firm is operating without an absolute limit on the dollars

[6] It is true, however, that the numbers in engineering problems are less conjectural; hence the cost of calculation is more likely to be considered worth while.

[7] For the three-period problem, the relevant quantity is $(y - p_1c_1 - p_2c_2 - p_3c_3)$ rather than $(y - p_1c_1 - p_2c_2)$.

to be invested, the solution to the problem of selecting the best alternative is obvious. (Throughout this article, it is assumed that decisions regarding individual investment proposals do not significantly affect the firm's cost of capital.) The best alternative is the one with the greatest present value at the firm's cost of capital.

When the firm is operating subject to the constraint of an absolute dollar limit on capital expenditures, the problem is more difficult. Consider, first, the case in which there are net outlays in only one time period. The solution is found by the following process:

1. From each set of mutually exclusive alternatives, select that alternative for which the following quantity is a maximum: $y - pc$. Here y is the present value of the alternative; c is the net outlay required; and p is a constant of a magnitude chosen initially according to the judgment of the analyst. (Remember that the alternative of making no investment—that is, accepting $y = 0$ and $c = 0$—is always available, so that the maximum in question is never negative.)

2. Compute the total outlays required to adopt all the investment proposals selected according to the principle just specified.

3. If the total outlay required exceeds the total amount available, p should be increased; if the total amount required is less than the amount available for investment, p should be reduced. By trial and error, a value for p can be found that will equate the amount required for investment with that available for investment.

It should be clear that, as the value of p is increased, the importance of the product, pc, increases, with a consequent increase in the probability that in each set of mutually exclusive alternatives, an alternative will be selected that requires a smaller net outlay than is required with a smaller value for p. Thus increasing p tends to reduce the total amount required to adopt the investment proposals selected according to the principle indicated in (1) above. Conversely, reducing p tends to increase the outlay required to adopt the investment proposals selected according to this principle.

When there are net outlays in more than one period, the principle of solution is the same. Instead of maximizing the quantity $(y - pc)$, it is necessary to maximize the quantity $(y - p_1c_1 - p_2c_2)$, where again c_1 and c_2 are the net outlays in the first and second periods and p_1 and p_2 are auxiliary multipliers.

Up to this point, we have not discussed the problem of rationing capital among both independent investment proposals and sets of mutually exclusive investment proposals. Superficially, this problem seems different from the one of rationing among mutually exclusive proposals only, but in fact the problems are the same. The identity rests upon the fact that each so-called "independent" proposal is and should be considered a member of the set of proposals consisting of the independent proposal and of the always present proposal to do nothing. When independent proposals are viewed in this way, it can be seen that the case of rationing simultaneously among independent proposals and sets of mutually exclusive proposals is really just a special case of rationing among mutually exclusive proposals according to the principles outlined in the preceding paragraph.

The mechanics of solution are easily worked out. All that is required in order to make the solution the same as the solution for what we have called "mutually exclusive" sets of alternatives is that each so-called "independent" proposal be treated as a member of a mutually exclusive set consisting of itself and of the alternative of doing nothing. Once this is done, it is possible to go into the familiar routine of selecting from each set that proposal for which the expression $(y - pc)$, or its appropriate modification to take account of constraints existing in more than one time period, is a maximum. Again, of course, that value of p will have to be found which results in matching as nearly as discontinuities permit the outlays required by the accepted proposals with the outlays permitted by the stated budgetary constraints.

III. SOME COMPARISONS WITH THE RATE-OF-RETURN METHOD OF CAPITAL RATIONING[8]

Since the rate-of-return method of capital rationing is fully described elsewhere, we shall describe it only briefly.[9] As in the methods described previously, attention is focused exclusively on net cash flows rather than on the data produced by conventional accounting practices. Investment proposals are ranked according to their "rate of return," defined as that rate of discounting which reduces a stream of cash flows to zero, and selected from this ranking, starting with the highest rate of return.

The rate-of-return solution to the three problems that are the subject of this paper is discussed below.

A. GIVEN THE COST OF CAPITAL, WHAT GROUP OF INVESTMENTS SHOULD BE SELECTED?

The rate-of-return solution to the problem of selecting a group of independent proposals, given the firm's cost of capital, is to accept all investment proposals having a rate of return greater than the firm's cost of capital. This solution is necessarily identical with the solution proposed previously, except when the present value of some of the proposals is other than a steadily decreasing function of the cost of capital. An intuitive substantiation of this statement is achieved by an understanding of Figure 1. In Figure 1, *I–I* indicates the present value of an investment at different rates of interest; *Oa* is the firm's cost of capital; *Ob* is the rate of return on the investment; and *aa′* is the present value of the investment at the firm's cost of capital. It should be clear from the diagram that any proposal that has a positive ordinate (present value) at the firm's cost of capital will also have a rate of return (x-intercept) greater than the cost of capital. (However, it usually takes a little longer to find an intercept than to determine the value of an ordinate at one point.)

Under what circumstances can the present value of an investment proposal be something other than a steadily decreasing function of the cost of capital? Some investment proposals can intersect the x-axis at more than one point. In particular, investment proposals having initial cash outlays, subsequent net cash inflows, and final net cash outlays can intersect the x-axis more than once and have, therefore, more than one rate of return. Investments of this nature are rare, but they do occur, especially in the extractive industries. For example, an investment proposal might consist of an investment in an oil pump that gets a fixed quantity of oil out of the ground more rapidly than

[8] Joel Dean has pioneered in the development of methods of capital rationing that have an understandable relationship to profit maximization, in contrast to methods still quite widely used in business that rely on such criteria as pay-back, average return on book investment, etc. The method that he advocates is called the "rate-of-return" method.

[9] See Joel Dean, *Capital Budgeting* (New York: Columbia University Press, 1951); "Measuring the Productivity of Capital," *Harvard Business Review*, January–February, 1954.

the pump currently in use. Making this investment would require an initial net outlay (for the new pump), subsequent net incremental cash inflow (larger oil production), and final net incremental cash outlay (the absence of oil production, because of its earlier exhaustion with the use of the higher-capacity new pump).[10] The present value of an invest-

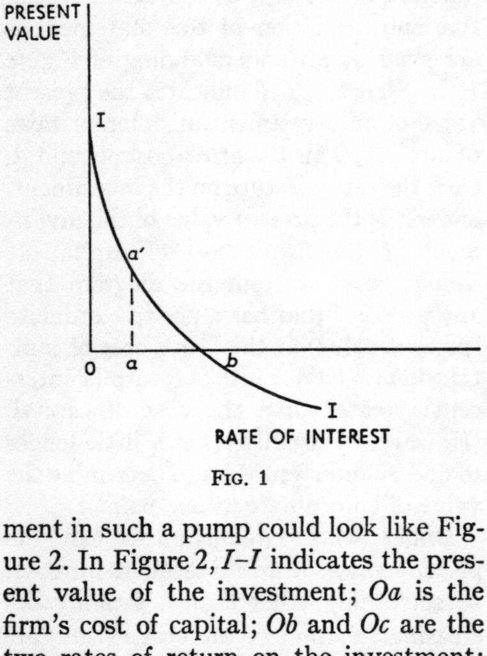

FIG. 1

ment in such a pump could look like Figure 2. In Figure 2, *I–I* indicates the present value of the investment; *Oa* is the firm's cost of capital; *Ob* and *Oc* are the two rates of return on the investment; and *aa′* is the present value of the investment at the firm's cost of capital.

The reasoning behind this apparent paradox of the double rate of return is as follows:

a) As the cost of capital of the firm approaches zero, the present value of the investment proposal approaches the algebraic sum of net cash flows and will be negative if this sum is negative.

b) As the cost of capital increases, the present value of the final net cash outflow diminishes in importance relative to the earlier flows, and this diminution can cause the present value of the entire proposal to become positive.

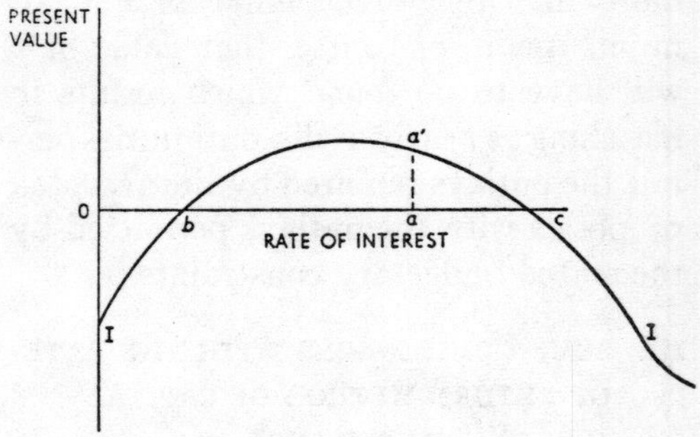

FIG. 2

c) If the cost of capital continues to increase, the significance of all future cash flows tends to diminish, causing the present value of the proposal to approach the initial outlay as a limit.

The rate-of-return criterion for judging the acceptability of investment proposals, as it has been presented in published works, is then ambiguous or anomalous. This is in contrast to the clarity and uniform accuracy of the decisions indicated by the principle proposed earlier, which relates to the present value of an investment at the cost of capital rather than to a comparison between the cost of capital and the rate of return.[11]

B. GIVEN A FIXED SUM FOR CAPITAL INVESTMENT, WHAT GROUP OF INVESTMENT PROPOSALS SHOULD BE UNDERTAKEN?

The rate-of-return solution to the problem of allocating a fixed sum of money—

[10] These incremental flows are measured with reference to the flows that would have resulted from the use of the smaller pump. Thus the final net outlay is not absolute but rather by comparison with oil (money) that would have been produced had the smaller pump been in use.

[11] The rate-of-return rule could be easily modified to remove this ambiguity or anomaly by specifying that the relevant rate of return is the one at which the investment is a decreasing function of the rate of interest.

without reference to cost of capital—among competing proposals is to order the proposals according to their rate of return and to proceed down the ladder

TABLE 2

Period	Net Cash Flows Investment A	Investment B
0– year......	−$ 85	−$ 90
0–1 year......	+ 17	+ 21
1–2 years.....	+ 35	+ 33
2–3 years.....	+ 68	+ 57
3–4 years.....	+ 131	+ 94
4–5 years.....	+ 216	+ 155
5–6 years.....	+ 357	+ 255
6–7 years.....	+ 546	+ 420
7–8 years.....	+ 555	+ 695
8–9 years.....	+ 345	+ 1,150
Present value at 20%....	+ 606	+ 853
Rate of return......	66%	62%

thus created until the available funds are exhausted. The group of investment proposals selected by the use of this principle can be different, and probably would usually be different, from the group selected when the criterion is present value rather than rate of return. A difference between the two groups would not exist if the available capital funds were just equal to that amount which would permit investment in all those proposals having a rate of return at least equal to the firm's cost of capital and only those proposals, and if the anomalies mentioned under Section A were not present.

The preceding statements are equivalent to saying that the groups of investments that would be chosen by the use of the two principles or criteria would necessarily be the same only if the fixed sum to be invested happened to be the optimum sum and that investment of any other sum could result in selection of different groups of proposals by use of the two principles. This difference would result from the fact that the different principles can result in a different ranking of proposals within the group that would be accepted if the optimum amount were invested. Table 2 indicates the validity of the statement that the ordering of two investment proposals according to their rate of return can be contrary to their ordering according to their present value per dollar of outlay.

The example of Table 2 illustrates that a proposal with a higher rate of return can have a lower present value and that, therefore, the two rules can conflict. The present-value rule maximizes the present value of the firm's net worth—by definition—and the rate-of-return rule therefore may not.

This discrepancy is undoubtedly of small practical significance. In the first place, firms that ration their capital rationally use the firm's cost of capital as the constraint rather than an absolute dollar sum, and under such rational behavior the two rules yield the same results, with the exception noted previously. (Undoubtedly, no firms long persist in setting absolute dollar constraints that differ significantly in their effects from the cost of capital constraint.) In the second place, the present values of investment proposals, expressed as functions of the cost of capital, are often thoughtful enough not to intersect above the x-axis (the rate-of-interest axis), a necessary condition for a conflict between the rate-of-return and present-value principles

C. SELECTING THE BEST AMONG MUTUALLY EXCLUSIVE ALTERNATIVES

The rate-of-return solution to the problem of selecting the "best" among mutually exclusive investment alternatives, although occasionally tricky in practice, is simply explained as follows:

1. Compute the rate of return for that investment proposal, among the set of

mutually exclusive proposals, requiring the least initial net outlay.

2. If the rate of return on the investment requiring the smallest outlay exceeds the firm's cost of capital (or other cutoff rate), tentatively accept that investment. Next compute the rate of return on the incremental outlay needed for the investment requiring the second lowest outlay. If that rate exceeds the firm's cutoff rate, accept the investment requiring the greater outlay in preference to that requiring the lesser. Proceed by such paired comparisons (based on rates of return on incremental outlay) to eliminate all but one investment.

3. If the rate of return on the proposal requiring the least outlay does not exceed the firm's cutoff rate, drop it from further consideration, and compute the rate of return for the proposal requiring the next least outlay. If that rate exceeds the firm's cutoff rate, that investment proposal becomes the bench mark for the first paired comparison. If that rate does not exceed the firm's cutoff rate, drop that proposal from further consideration. The process just described is to be repeated until either a proposal is found with a rate of return exceeding the cost of capital or until all proposals have been eliminated because their rates of return do not exceed the cutoff rate.

The rate-of-return solution to the problem of selecting the best among mutually exclusive investment alternatives is especially subject to the ambiguities and anomalies mentioned under Section A, because the costs and revenues associated with incremental investments required for proposals included in mutually exclusive sets are much more likely to have unusual time shapes and reversals than are the costs and revenues associated with independent investments.

SUMMARY

We have given solutions to three problems in budgeting capital so as to maximize the net worth of the firm. The solutions that we have given differ in principle from those implied by the rate-of-return method of capital rationing. The difference in principle can lead to differences in behavior. Differences in behavior will be rare in coping with problems of the first and third sorts and will be relatively frequent for problems of the second sort. When differences do exist, the rate-of-return solution does not result in maximizing the present value of the firm's net worth.

THE RATE OF INTEREST, FISHER'S RATE OF RETURN OVER COSTS AND KEYNES' INTERNAL RATE OF RETURN

ARMEN A. ALCHIAN†

REPUBLICATION of Irving Fisher's *The Theory of Interest*[1] will enable economists to correct an error propagated by a careless statement in Keynes' *General Theory*. Keynes erroneously alleged that his marginal efficiency of capital is identical with Fisher's marginal rate of return over cost, and that it is used for exactly the same purpose. Unfortunately Keynes was wrong; they are not the same and they were not used for the same purpose.

1. *Keynes' Marginal Efficiency of Capital.* Keynes' marginal efficiency of capital is the rate of discount which equates the present worth of the receipt stream to the present worth of the expense stream.[2] If $R\ (t)$ denotes the rereceipt stream and $E\ (t)$ denotes the outlay stream, both as functions of time, and if e^{-rt} be the discount factor for t, then $\int_0^t [R(t) - E(t)]\, e^{-rt}dt$ is the net present worth of an investment option. The rate r which sets this present worth equal to zero is the marginal efficiency of capital, or the internal rate of return, but it is not Fisher's rate of return over cost.[3]

However, it is interesting to note that Keynes did believe he was really following Fisher, for he wrote, "Professor Fisher uses his 'rate of return over cost' in the same sense and for precisely the same purposes as I employ the 'marginal efficiency of capital.' "[4]

2. *Fisher's Rate of Return over Cost.* Fisher's rate of return over cost concept, developed in order to rank investment alternatives by the universally correct criterion of maximum present value, can be defined only by reference to at least two alternative investment options. Letting subscripts denote investment options,

$$\int_0^t \Big([R_1(t) - E_1(t)] - [R_2(t) - E_2(t)] \Big) e^{-rt}dt$$

is the difference in present worths of the two investment options when each is discounted at the rate r. The rate r which sets this *difference* equal to zero is Fisher's marginal rate of return over cost.[5] Fisher always meant by the expression "opportunity" a choice between two alternative investments.[6] Therefore he could say that for this opportunity (between the two options) the advantage of 1 over 2 at any moment t, is $(R_1 - E_1) - (R_2 - E_2)$, or upon rearranging terms, is $(R_1 - R_2) - (E_1 - E_2)$. Fisher called this latter expression the surplus of advantages over disadvantages.[7] The rate of dis-

† The author is associate professor of economics at the University of California, Los Angeles.

[1] Irving Fisher, *The Theory of Interest* (New York, 1930) and reissued by Kelley and Millman, New York, 1954.

[2] J. M. Keynes, *The General Theory of Employment Interest and Money* (New York, 1936), p. 140. The distinction between the marginal internal rate of return and the average internal rate of return, provided that the reader thinks in terms of either an incremental unit or a lump-sum nondivisible investment, while important for some problems, is not critical for the present discussion.

[3] Fisher, *op. cit.*, pp. 151-55.

[4] Keynes, *op. cit.*, p. 141.

[5] Fisher, *op. cit.*, p. 155.

[6] *Ibid.*, p. 151.

[7] *Ibid.*, p. 153.

count which equates the present worth of the advantages, $(R_1 - R_2)$, to the present worth of the disadvantages, $(E_1 - E_2)$ is the rate of return over cost.[8] If one makes the careless step of thinking of the advantages as a simple receipt stream and the disadvantage as a simple cost stream for a *single* investment he will then be able to think that the internal rate of return is the rate of return over cost. Fisher's rate of return over cost *always* involved a comparison of two options, not a discounting of merely one option.

A numerical example might sharpen the difference. Suppose that each of two alternative investment options requires an immediate outlay of $25. Suppose that one, *A*, yields a receipt stream of $5 per year for ten years, and the other, *B*, yields $1 in the first year, $2 in the second, etc., up to ten years. The internal rate of return of *A* is about 17 per cent while *B*'s is about 12.5 per cent. Yet the Fisherian rate of return over cost of *B* compared with *A* is 6 per cent. Figure 1 shows the present value of the net receipt streams of *A* and of *B* for different discount rates. The discount rate at which line *AA* cuts the horizontal line for $25 is 17 per cent. Line *BB* cuts the $25 line at 12.5 per cent. But notice that *BB* intersects *AA* at 6 per cent; under 6 per cent *B* is superior because it has the larger present value, while at rates over 6 per cent *A* is superior. The distance between the lines *AA* (or *BB*) and the $25 cost line, at any rate of interest, measures the net present worth of opportunity *A* (or *B*).

According to their internal rates of return *A* would be preferred to *B* (17 per cent as compared to 12.5 per cent); yet *B* will be the preferred investment

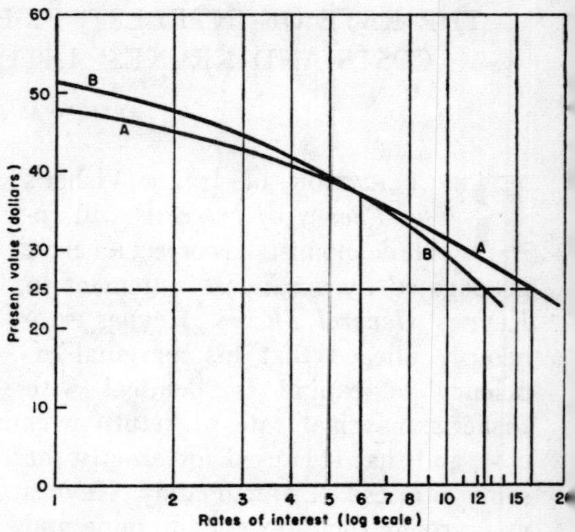

FIGURE 1. RATE OF RETURN OVER COST AND INTERNAL RATE OF RETURN

at interest rates below 6 per cent according to the maximum present wealth criterion. Before the reader interjects that both investments will be profitable and hence both will be undertaken let him assume that the two investments, *A* and *B*, are mutually exclusive alternatives, *e.g.*, a wood bridge or a steel bridge, an electric bus system vs. a gasoline one, a brick house vs. a wood house. Hence both cannot be undertaken. A ranking of substitutable investments by the Keynesian internal rate of return is not consistent with the maximizing of net present wealth.

Fisher wanted to show that the ranking of alternatives according to the maximum wealth criterion would depend upon the market rate of interest. To emphasize this, he developed the rate of return over cost concept as a means of determining at what rate of interest the reversal of preference would occur.[9] Fisher's rate of return over cost

[8] *Ibid.*, p. 155.

[9] "To induce him o make a change, the *rate of return over cost musi exceed the rate of interest.*"

serves merely as a device to determine all the rates of interest at which investment 1 would be preferred to 2. It does not give a rate of return over cost with which to rank investments once and for all, for the simple reason that the rankings change as the rate of interest changes. Now, ranking on the basis of internal rates of return is correlated with present-worth rankings if the only investment options compared are a particular investment and an option to invest at the market rate. But if there are two investment options alternative to market lending, the internal rates of return of the two options will *not* rank them consistently with their present values.

3. *Sources of Confusion.* A plausible source of the confusion is Fisher's sentence which Keynes quoted in his *General Theory*. "The rate of return over cost is that rate which, employed in computing the present worth of all the costs and the present worth of all the returns, will make these two equal."[10] But Keynes did not quote the next sentence which reads, "Or, as a mathematician would prefer to put it, the rate which, employed in computing the present worth of the whole series of differences between the two income streams (some differences being positive and others negative) will make the total zero."[11] And the next sentence, "If the rate, so computed, were taken for every possible pair of income streams compared as to their advantages and disadvantages, it would authentically decide in each case which of the pair is to be preferred."

Or possibly Keynes had read the section in Fisher's book just preceding the quoted sentence—a section titled "The Case of Perpetual Returns," which discusses investment options that generate constant net receipt streams to perpetuity. In that case, the ranking provided by Keynes' internal rate of return will conform to Fisher's ranking by the present value at the market rate. This means that Keynes' and Fisher's ranking will agree in the event that two special conditions (which are not usually fulfilled) are fulfilled: (1) the net receipt stream generated by the nonconstant nonperpetual investment option can immediately upon its generation be reinvested in new investment options with the same Keynesian internal rate of return, and that (2) this reinvestment of the generated net receipts can be continued in this way at this same internal rate *forever*. Any net receipt stream can be converted in the market to a constant net receipt stream to perpetuity, but this does not mean that the Keynesian internal rate of return for the nonconstant nonperpetuity investment prior to conversion to a constant income perpetuity will be the same as the internal rate of return on the purchase after conversion to a constant perpetuity in the market; this latter rate will equal the market rate.[12]

But Fisher attaches the following generalizing footnote to this sentence: "In case the advantages (returns) precede the disadvantages (costs), . . . the proposition must be reversed, as follows: The earlier advantage will be chosen only in case the rate of future costs over present returns is *less* than the rate of interest." *Ibid.*, p. 159.

[10] Keynes, *op. cit.*, p. 140. This sentence quoted by Keynes is the only one I can find in Fisher's *Theory of Interest* which referred to equating costs and returns, without also referring to *two* investment options.

[11] Fisher, *op. cit.*, pp. 168-69.

[12] For example in the earlier examples, investment option *B*, had an internal rate of return of 12.5 per cent. If it were sold in the market at $42 (with the market rate at 4 per cent), the $42 would buy a constant 4 per cent perpetuity of $1.68 per year, equivalent to 6.7 per cent of $25. If the market

If the time paths of the net receipts of the compared options are identical (except for a proportionality factor) the Keynesian internal rate of return ranking will agree with the Fisherian maximum wealth criterion. In other words, in order to have the Keynesian ranking agree with Fisher's either we must assume exactly similar time paths, or we must assume the net receipts from the two alternatives can be *immediately* and perpetually reinvested at their own internal rates of return.

4. *Significance of Confusion.* Many economists agree with Keynes in attributing the internal rate of return to Fisher, but they seem to have overlooked the fact that Keynes' internal rate of return did not give an investment demand function according to the maximum present wealth criterion of choice by investors.[13] Consequently their rationale for explaining why the rate of investment increases as the rate of interest falls has been logically defective (inconsistent with wealth maximizing) and may be empirically inconsistent.

In so far as Keynes' *General Theory* is concerned, the error is completely harmless. Keynes sought a proposition about the slope of the aggregate investment function. Whether one uses the internal rate of return or the Fisherian rate of return over cost to rank investment options according to present net wealth, lower market rates of interest imply larger rates of investment. The fact that his derivation of the negative slope did not correspond to Fisher's led to no difficulty in Keynes' *General Theory*. How one derives a proposition is irrelevant if one is interested only in the empirical validity of the proposition. Keynes might aptly have said, "Merely another example of the advantage of practical knowledge over logical analysis."

Fisher's theory is a model for deriving propositions about how the economic system operates, and how it reacts to changed circumstances. He asserted that the kinds of investment that will be characteristic of a low-interest-rate economy are so-and-so as compared with those in a high-interest-rate economy. Or that certain kinds of cultural attitudes or technological changes will lead to lower interest rates, etc. And these theorems are valid even when uncertainty prevails for the individual economic participants—uncertainty which destroys the prescriptive and descriptive content of the postulates of individual behavior which Fisher used to derive his economy-wide theorems.

From the methodological point of

---

rate had been 2 per cent, *i.e.,* if the present value of option *B* turned out to be $48, it could have been converted into an annual perpetuity of 2 per cent on the $48, equivalent to 3.87 per cent on the $25 cost. Of course, the ratio of the converted perpetuity rate of return on the cost to the market rate, 3.87/2.00, always equals the ratio of present value to cost $48/$25.

[13] See, as typical examples: D. Dillard, *The Economics of John Maynard Keynes* (New York, 1948), pp. 135-42; S. Enke, *Intermediate Economic Theory* (New York, 1948), pp. 141-48 (*e.g.,* compare the statements on p. 141 with those on pp. 146-47); A. Hart, *Money, Debt and Economic Activity* (New York, 1948), p. 180; A. Hansen, *Monetary Theory and Fiscal Policy* (New York, 1949), pp. 57-58; R. Ruggles, *National Income and Income Analysis* (New York, 1949), pp. 262-65; E. Schneider, *Pricing and Equilibrium* (London, 1952), p. 166; T. Scitovsky, *Welfare and Competition* (Chicago, 1951), p. 210.

Many others without using the concept of the marginal efficiency of capital (the internal rate of return) reach essentially correct formulations, although they do not indicate that there is a conflict in the literature. J. Bain, *Pricing, Distribution and Employment,* rev. ed. (New York, 1953), pp. 695-96. P. A. Samuelson, *Economics,* 3rd ed. (New York, 1955); but see his footnote 1, p. 578.

view, the interesting feature is the way in which Fisher derived his theorems. He assumed certainty and he built up the investment demand schedule by changing the rate of interest and for each rate computing the implied present value of different actions. This opens him to a charge of logical inconsistency—one that can be levied against the internal rate of return also. The internal rate of return depends upon present and future prices; present prices reflect future use values through the market place's discounting process, which depends upon the rate of interest. As the interest rate changes, the structure of prices changes, especially the ratio of present prices to future prices. This in turn will affect the internal rate of return. Thus the internal rate of return cannot be measured independently of the existing rate of interest, and therefore a schedule of investment demand at different market rates of interest requires that one compute the internal rates of return in terms of the prices that would prevail at each potential market rate of interest. Hence in addition to its inconsistency with wealth maximizing, it has an inherent logical inconsistency as a basis for deriving the demand curve of investment, *i.e.*, it is dependent upon the rate of interest.

In a nutshell, we cannot in full logical consistency draw up a demand curve for investment by varying only the rate of interest (holding all other prices in the impound of *ceteris paribus*).[14] Fisher, despite his exposition which is based on the supposition that one merely changes the rate of interest and holds other prices fixed, understood this. He said that interest rate changes were part and parcel of changes in the structure of price ratios.[15] For example, he discussed how low rates of interest mean that steel bridges, which have relatively higher present worths than at higher rates, will be able to bid away land sites.[16] He could have gone even farther and indicated that changed tastes, new inventions, increased supplies of resources (discovery of new ores, etc.) all lead to revised demand and supply relations among present resources as well as between present and future resource availabilities. A discussion of the effects of changes in the rate of interest in the context of a given price structure is likely to be misleading.[17] Fisher illustrated the process of change via changes in the price structure. The proximate Fisherian analysis of interest rate effects via a fixed price structure is not adequate for deeper understanding of the significance of interest rate changes. However, these logical inconsistencies or shortcuts enable a simpler analysis which has led to valid theorems about observable investment events and characteristics.

[14] This is exactly analogous to the distinction between the Marshallian partial equilibrium demand and the Walrasian general equilibrium demand discussed by Milton Friedman, "The Marshallian Demand Curve," *Jour. Pol. Econ.*, Dec. 1949, LVII, 463-95. In the present context the partial analysis curve misses the essence of capital theory, the relationship between interest rates and the price structure.

[15] Fisher, *op. cit.*, footnote, p. 131.

[16] *Ibid.*, *pp.* 178-205.

[17] It might be that standard textbook discussions are vulnerable on this count. See for example, J. Bain, *op. cit.*, pp. 695-96; A. Hansen, *Business Cycles and National Income*, (New York, 1951), pp. 131-35.

THE RATE OF INTEREST, FISHER'S RATE OF RETURN OVER COSTS AND KEYNES' INTERNAL RATE OF RETURN: COMMENT

ROMNEY ROBINSON†

IN THE DECEMBER 1955 issue of the *American Economic Review,* A. A. Alchian draws attention to the fact that Irving Fisher's "rate of return over cost" differs from the Keynesian "marginal efficiency of capital." Fisher's rate of return over cost is properly used only to compare two investment projects; it draws attention to the fact that, given the cost and revenue streams of such projects, their ranking according to the present discounted value criterion may vary according to the interest rate used to discount them. The rate of return over cost is the critical or turning-point interest rate, at which the two have the *same* present value.

Rankings of investment projects according to their internal rates of return (*i.e.,* to their marginal efficiency) do *not* vary with any external interest rate. Is there a conflict between the internal rate criterion for profit-maximization and the present discounted value criterion?

To illustrate: Either of two investments, A and B, may be purchased for $100, payable immediately. Investment A promises (with certainty) $179 in 10 years; investment B, $147 in 5 years. The internal rate of return (with annual compounding) is 6 per cent on A, and 8 per cent on B.

At market rates of interest above 4 per cent, B has the higher present discounted value and would be the preferred investment (assuming that for some reason a choice between A and B is necessary) regardless of the criterion used. At 4 per cent, the two investments have equal present worths of $121. Below 4 per cent, A acquires the higher present value. At 3 per cent, for instance, A's present worth is $133, whereas B's is only $127.

With matters so presented, it seems as though there can be a real conflict between the two criteria. If so, it is not immediately obvious or clear why present discounted value should be "universally correct" (Alchian's phrase) or why in some circumstances a 6 per cent rate of return should be chosen over an 8 per cent rate.

Actually, the two rules are not in conflict. The trouble is that descriptions of investment opportunities such as those supplied for A and B above are insufficient for rational choice. When the missing information is forthcoming, the two criteria become one and the same.

If the market interest rate is 3 per cent, the mere existence of two projects such as A and B means that adjustment to a competitive equilibrium is incomplete. In equilibrium, such opportunities would not exist. The cost figure would be bid up or the revenue figure would be driven down through competition until both yielded an internal rate of 3 per cent, thus eliminating any need for comparison.

Direct comparison of two projects is impossible when they cover different time-periods. One or both must be re-

† The author is associate professor of economics at Brandeis University.

	Earnings During:		
	First 5 Years	Second 5 Years	All Subsequent Years
Project A	6% (internal rate)	6% (internal rate)	3% (market rate)
Project B	8% (internal rate)	3% (market rate)	3% (market rate)

newed until both cover a common multiple of the original time-spans. But for this purpose, it is necessary to know whether or not renewals can be made on the same terms. In the absence of this information, some assumption about renewal must be made. To compare A and B on the basis of discounted present worth is to assume that these "disequilibrium opportunities" can last no longer than the stated time-periods. At the close of the 5-year or 10-year period, competition (or some other unspecified factor) will have removed the opportunity for renewal at a better-than-market rate. On the other hand, to compare A and B on the basis of their respective internal rates of return is to assume an opportunity for renewal on the same terms as before.

Alternative B (the 8 per cent internal rate project) should be rejected if, at the end of its 5-year term, the proceeds can only be reinvested at a market rate of 3 per cent. The present worth criterion sets matters up per table. The present worth criterion rejects B since 8 per cent over the first half of the 10-year period and 3 per cent over the second half do not average out so well as 6 per cent over the full period.

Alchian takes account of the need to consider the return on renewals in noting (p. 941) that the two criteria will agree in the case where continual renewals to perpetuity at the same internal rate are possible. But to confine agreement to the perpetuity case seems unduly limiting. They should agree whenever the two investments are extended to any equal finite period. Even if B can be renewed for only one further period at its 8 per cent rate,[1] it acquires the same time-span as A, and either measure will then pronounce it superior to A.

Without information as to the opportunities for renewal, neither formula can necessarily be expected to furnish a meaningful answer. To assume that the particular opportunity lasts for no longer than the time explicitly stated may be in keeping with the conventional assumptions of certainty and pure competition. Yet however convenient these latter assumptions may be, they are thoroughly inappropriate for many capital-involving problems.[2] Where uncertainty exists, where knowledge is imperfect and where market competition cannot always be relied upon to iron out profit opportunities, the assumption implicit in the internal rate criterion may be preferable in so far as the circumstances make either concept a usable one.

[1] This conclusion will hold even if B can be renewed for its original amount of $100 only. But such a limited renewal opportunity is clearly a factor which may have to be taken into account.

[2] In particular, it is sometimes difficult to accept the assumption that a better-than-market or "disequilibrium" opportunity is available with complete certainty of revenue.

THE ARITHMETIC OF CAPITAL-BUDGETING DECISIONS

EZRA SOLOMON*

In order to make correct capital-expenditure decisions, corporate management needs at least three sets of information. Estimates must be made of net capital outlays required and future cash earnings promised by each proposed project. This is a problem in engineering valuation and market forecasting. Estimates must also be made of the availability and cost of capital to the company. This is a problem in financial analysis. Finally, management needs a correct set of standards by which to select projects for execution so that long-run economic benefits to present owners will be maximized. This is a problem in logic and arithmetic. This paper is concerned exclusively with the last of these three problems.[1]

With respect to the question "Should this investment proposal be accepted or rejected?" the problem of arriving at a correct decision is uncomplicated. Either one of two approaches to measuring the investment worth of a proposal will provide a correct answer.[2] In the usual form in which these approaches are used as capital-rationing criteria, they are:

The rate-of-return approach.—This approach expresses each project's estimated value as a single over-all "rate of return per annum." This rate is equal to the rate of interest at which the present value of expected capital outlays is exactly equal to the present value of expected cash earnings on that project. The concept is identical with the "effective yield to maturity" on a bond that is purchased at some price other than its par value. It has also been called the "internal rate of profit"[3] or the "marginal efficiency of capital."[4]

If the rate of return on a project is greater than the company's cost of capital (also expressed as a percentage per annum rate), then the project should be accepted.

The present-value approach.—For each project, find the present value of the expected capital outlays, using the cost of capital as a discount rate. Likewise, find the present value of the expected cash earnings. If the present value of earnings is greater than the present value of outlays, the project should be accepted.

These two approaches give the same results for "accept or reject" decisions. This is so because the computed rate of return on a project will be higher than the cost of capital in all cases for which

* Associate professor of finance, School of Business, University of Chicago.

[1] For a discussion of the first two problems see Joel Dean, *Capital Budgeting* (New York: Columbia University Press, 1951), and Ezra Solomon, "Measuring a Company's Cost of Capital," *Journal of Business*, XXVIII (October, 1955), 240–52.

[2] There are other criteria in use, e.g., determining capital budgets by size of department, by pay-out periods, or by the postponability of projects. It has already been shown that these are at best crude approximations to a correct solution (see Dean, *op. cit.*, chap. ii, and M. J. Gordon, "The Payoff Period and the Rate of Profit," *Journal of Business*, XXVIII [October, 1955], 253–60).

[3] See Kenneth L. Boulding, *Economic Analysis* (rev. ed.; New York: Harper & Bros., 1948), chaps. xxxv and xxxvi.

[4] See J. M. Keynes, *The General Theory of Employment, Interest, and Money* (New York: Macmillan Co., 1936), pp. 140 ff.

the present value of earnings, discounted at the cost of capital, is greater than the present value of outlays. Or, conversely, if a project promises a rate of return greater than the company's cost of capital, then the present value of its earnings, discounted at the cost of capital, will be greater than the present value of its outlays.

For problems which involve more than a simple "accept or reject" decision, the application of these two criteria, as they are generally defined, often yield contradictory or ambiguous results. The purpose of this paper is to explore the reasons for these contradictions or ambiguities and to reformulate this general approach to measuring investment worth so that it always provides a unique and correct basis for decision making.

MUTUALLY EXCLUSIVE PROPOSALS

It is often necessary for management to ask not only "Is this project worth undertaking?" but also "which of two projects is the better one?" This latter question is crucial whenever two or more projects or proposals are mutually exclusive. For example, the proposals may be alternative ways of doing the same thing. Both might be profitable in an absolute sense. But since only one of the two can be undertaken, the problem is to decide which alternative is the better one.

When the *relative* merit of alternative proposals is at issue, the rate-of-return criterion, as defined earlier, and the present-value criterion, as defined, can yield contradictory results. With the increased interest in applying rational approaches to the solution of capital-investment decisions, this possible conflict between the two generally acceptable criteria has received renewed attention. Several recent papers have shown that when projects are ranked by the rate-of-return standard, the results may differ from a ranking of the same projects based on the present-value standard.[5] For analytical purposes, the simplest example of such a conflict will suffice: Assume that there are two investment opportunities available. Both are profitable in an absolute sense, but only one can be undertaken because the two are mutually exclusive.

Project X requires an outlay of $100 now, at time t_0, and promises to return $120 exactly 1 year hence at time t_1. Project Y also requires an outlay of $100 now and promises to return $174.90 exactly 4 years hence at time t_4. Assume also that the degree of certainty attaching to each project is identical and that the investor's present "cost of capital" is 10 per cent.

The "rate of return" on project X is 20 per cent, and on project Y it is 15 per cent. The present value of project X, discounted at the cost of capital, is $109.09. For project Y, the present value, discounted at the cost of capital, is $119.46. If the two projects are ranked by their rate of return, project X is the better one. If, on the other hand, they are ranked in terms of present value, project Y is the better one. Which should the investor choose?

In order to resolve the problem correctly, it is necessary to isolate the source of the conflict between the two approaches. The easiest way to do this is to compare the two investment proposals in terms of their relative value as of the

[5] See James H. Lorie and Leonard J. Savage, "Three Problems in Rationing Capital," *Journal of Business*, XXVIII (October, 1955), 229–39; George Terborgh, "Some Comments on the Dean-Smith Article on the MAPI Formula," *Journal of Business*, XXIX (April, 1956), 138–40; and A. A. Alchian, "The Rate of Interest, Fisher's Rate of Return over Costs, and Keynes' Internal Rate of Return," *American Economic Review*, XLV (December, 1955), 938–42.

terminal date (t_4) of the longer-lived project.[6]

According to the data given, proposal Y will provide the investor with $174.90 at time t_4. All we know about proposal X is that it provides $120.00 at time t_1. What happens to these funds between time t_1 and t_4 is obviously an important piece of necessary information. Neither the rate-of-return approach nor the present-value approach answers this question *explicitly*. But they both answer it *implicitly* and in different ways. This is the source of the conflicting results that they yield.

Those who use the rate-of-return approach, as it is usually defined, would choose project X over project Y. Hence they must assume that this choice will yield a larger terminal value than that promised by project Y, i.e., $174.90. This, in turn, implies that the $120 obtained from project X at time t_1 can be reinvested between time t_1 and t_4 at a rate lucrative enough to accumulate to more than $174.90 by time t_4. *In general*, the implicit assumption made by the rate-of-return approach is that the reinvestment rate is at least equal to the rate promised by the longer-lived of the two projects, in this case, 15 per cent.[7]

The present-value approach, as usually defined, assumes that the funds obtained from either project can be reinvested at a rate equal to the company's present cost of capital, i.e., 10 per cent. Using this assumption, the investor will end up at time t_4 with only $159.72 if he chooses project X. With project Y, he would have $174.90. Thus, according to this approach, project Y is the better choice.

The question of which assumption is likely to be the more justified one is important, but it is not relevant to the argument being made in this paper, namely, that the apparent conflict between the two approaches results only from differing assumptions that each makes about the future. If a common assumption is adopted, both approaches will always rank projects identically.

Let us assume, for example, that the investor can put money to use between time t_1 and time t_4 at an average return of 12 per cent. The following computations and results would ensue:

Terminal value.—For project Y this is $174.90. For project X we have $120 at time t_1, plus interest at 12 per cent per annum for 3 years. This would accumulate to $168.47.

Rate of return.—For project Y this averages 15 per cent up to the terminal date at time t_4. For project X the rate would be 20 per cent for 1 year and 12 per cent for 3 years—an over-all rate equal to 13.9 per cent.

Present value.—For project Y this would be $174.90, discounted from time t_4 back to time t_1 at 12 per cent[8] and back from time t_1 to t_0 at 10 per cent. This gives $113.17. For project X the present value would be $120 discounted from time t_1 to time t_0 at 10 per cent, or $109.09.

All three criteria rank the two projects in the same order. With the particular assumption we used, project Y is the better one by any standard. Using some other assumption, the ranking might be

[6] The "terminal date" refers to the date at which cash earnings from the longer-lived of the two competing projects cease.

[7] For example, if project Z, a third alternative, yielded 15 per cent in perpetuity and project X yielded 20 per cent, the rate-of-return approach would choose project X over project Z. Hence the approach must assume that funds received from project X can be reinvested at least at 15 per cent.

[8] This is the relevant rate because we are assuming that the investor can earn 12 per cent on his funds between time t_1 and time t_4.

reversed, but the alternative approaches would still yield identical results.

Our conclusion is that correct and consistent ranking of the investment worth of competing proposals can be obtained only if the following factors are taken into account:

1. The valid comparison is not simply between two projects but between two alternative courses of action. The ultimate criterion is the total wealth that the investor can expect from each alternative by the terminal date of the longer-lived project. In order to make a fair comparison, an explicit and common assumption must be made regarding the rate at which funds released by either project can be reinvested up to the terminal date.

2. If the rate of return is to be used as an index of relative profitability, then the relevant rate is the per annum yield promised by each alternative course of action from its inception to a common terminal date in the future (usually the terminal date of the longer-lived project).

3. If the present value is to be used as an index of relative profitability, the expected reinvestment rate or set of rates should be used as the discounting factor. These rates will be equal to the company's present cost of capital only by coincidence. When comparing two projects requiring different outlays, it is necessary to compare "present value per dollar of outlay" rather than the absolute present value of the projects.

THE PROBLEM OF "DUAL RATES OF RETURN"

In a recent paper Lorie and Savage[9] have drawn attention to a second problem involving the arithmetic of capital budgeting. In this paper the authors attempt to show that certain rare and complex investment situations exist which cannot be expressed in terms of a single, unique "rate of return." In such situations the application of the usual prescription for finding *the* rate of return yields two solutions, and thus "the rate-of-return criterion for judging the acceptability of investment proposals, as it has been presented in published works, is ambiguous or anomalous."[10]

In order to understand the problem involved, it is helpful to recognize two basic types of investment situation, classified according to the pattern of estimated cash flows that are projected. In the usual type of situation, which we will call "pattern A," the stream of net cash inflows promised by a project ends either before or when it reaches that point in time beyond which the value of *net future flows* is negative. In other words, the project is assumed to terminate before the stage beyond which its continuation yields a net loss to the investor. The second situation, which we call "pattern B," is a much rarer one. Projects which fall into this category continue beyond the point defined previously, i.e., the terminal section contains a net cash outflow (a net loss). Such a pattern obviously exists only if there are contractual or other compelling reasons which make it impossible for the investor to avoid the terminal losses.

As far as pattern A projects are concerned, it is always possible to express the investment worth of the project as a single, meaningful "rate of return" and hence to make a clear-cut decision on the basis of such a criterion. For pattern B projects the application of the usually prescribed method of finding the appro-

[9] *Op. cit.*

[10] *Ibid.*, p. 237.

priate "rate of return" can yield more than one answer.[11]

Let us take a specific example of a pattern B investment project. The proposal being considered is the installation of a larger oil pump that would get a fixed quantity of oil out of the ground more rapidly than the pump that is already in use. Let us assume that, by operating the existing pump, the investor can expect $10,000 a year hence and $10,000 two years hence. Let us assume that, by installing the larger pump at a net cost of $1,600 now, he can expect $20,000 a year hence and nothing the second year. The installation of the larger pump can be viewed as a project having the cash-flow characteristics shown in Table 1.

TABLE 1

Time Period	Incremental Cash Flow Due to Investment
t_0..........	− $1,600
t_1..........	+ 10,000
t_2..........	− 10,000

The usual prescription for finding the rate of return of a project is to find that rate which makes the discounted value of net cash flows equal to the discounted value of capital outlays. Alternatively—and this amounts to the same thing—find that rate which makes the algebraic sum of the discounted cash outflows and inflows equal to zero. The application of this method to our example will yield two answers, namely, 25 and 400 per cent. In other words, using a 25 per cent rate, the discounted value of the cash flows is exactly equal to the outlay of $1,600. However, a rate of 400 per cent also equates cash flows with capital outlay. Which of the two "rates" is the correct measure of the investment worth of the project, 25 or 400 per cent?

The answer is that neither of these rates is a measure of investment worth, neither has relevance to the profitability of the project under consideration, and neither, therefore, is correct. The fault lies in the incorrect application of the "usual prescription" for finding the rate of return. A closer look at the implications of defining the rate of return in this context as that rate (or rates) which reduce the discounted cash flows to zero reveals the gross error that such a process entails. In order to find this error, let us vary the net outlay required to instal the larger pump (keeping all other cash flows constant) and solve for the "rate of return," using the usual prescription. We get the following absurd results:

1. If the larger pump costs nothing, then the project is worth 0 per cent, i.e., at 0 per cent, the discounted value of the net cash flows is equal to the value of the outlay.[12]

2. If the larger pump costs $827, the project, according to this method, suddenly becomes quite profitable and is rated at 10 per cent, i.e., at a rate of 10 per cent, the discounted value of the net cash flows is equal to $827.

3. The more the pump costs, the more "profitable" the project becomes! At a cost of $1,600 the rate of return is 25 per cent; at a cost of $2,500 it yields 100 per cent. The method would have us believe that the engineer who first thought of the idea of installing the larger pump could have a gold mine if only he could persuade the pump manufacturer to charge him enough for the installation![13]

Needless to say, any definition of "profitability" that leads to these absurd

[11] Lorie and Savage explain the general basis for dual rates (*ibid.*, p. 237).

[12] Alternatively, one could say that the rate is infinitely large.

[13] This increase in the "rate," as the cost of the pump increases, reaches a maximum level, after which the relationship is reversed.

results must itself be in error.

The correct solution for the investment worth of the project is simple and straightforward. But it requires an explicit answer to a relevant question: "What is it worth to the investor to receive \$10,000 one year earlier than he would have otherwise received it?" This is actually all that the installation of the larger pump achieves. If the investor expects to be able to put the \$10,000 to work at a yield of x per cent per annum, then getting the money a year earlier is worth \$100x. If x is 23 per cent, for example, getting \$10,000 a year earlier is worth \$2,300. In other words, if he spent \$1,600 on the larger pump now (at time t_0), he would end up at time t_2 having \$2,300 more than he otherwise would have had. This can be stated as an equivalent "rate of return," which in this case would be about 20 per cent (\$1,600 at 20 per cent per annum would amount to \$2,304 at the end of two years). Using this approach, a unique and meaningful rate of return can always be found for any set of cash inflows and outflows.

SUMMARY

The rate of return is a useful concept that enables us to express the profitability of an investment proposal as a single explicit value. This value automatically adjusts for differences in the time pattern of expected cash outflows and inflows. It is also independent of the absolute size of the project. Thus it provides a useful standard by which all types of projects—large and small, long-run and short-run—can be ranked against each other in relative terms and also against the company's cost of capital, in order to judge their absolute worth. The arithmetic involved in rate-of-return computations is generally straightforward. However, there are two situations in which such computations require a careful consideration of the logic that is involved.

1. When mutually exclusive proposals are being compared, it is necessary to compute the rate on each alternative course of action up to the terminal date of the longer-lived alternative. This requires an explicit estimate of the yield to be derived from the cash flows generated by each of the alternatives being considered.

2. When a rate is being computed for complex proposals that have negative terminal values, the usual mechanistic prescription for solving for rates does not apply. This situation also requires an explicit estimate of the yield to be derived from incremental cash flows generated by a project. Given this estimate, the equivalent dollar value of the incremental cash flows can be computed explicitly. A comparison of this value with the outlays required for the project will give a correct and unambiguous measure of the project's rate of return.

If these concepts and methods are used in defining and computing rates of return, this criterion will always provide an unambiguous investment standard, the use of which will lead to a maximization of the investor's net present worth, in so far as the estimates used are accurate.

A NOTE ON THE ARITHMETIC OF CAPITAL BUDGETING DECISIONS

ED RENSHAW*

IN TWO recent articles Professors Lorie and Savage and Solomon[1] have examined some of the logical problems involved in choosing between investment alternatives, given the expected income and expenditure flows from each alternative and the availability and cost of capital to the firm. In this paper an attempt is made to clarify and extend some of the points raised by these authors. Attention is focused upon the conflict existing between ranking investment alternatives by rates of return as opposed to ranking by present values, upon problems involved in making the concept of reinvestment rates operational and upon the possibility of dual rates of return.

I. CHOICE OF A RANKING PROCEDURE

A contribution of the Lorie-Savage article was to emphasize a possible inconsistency in the ranking of alternative investments using the internal rate-of-return[2] approach as opposed to the present-value approach.[3] A necessary, but not a sufficient, condition for the two approaches to yield contradictory rankings of investment alternatives is that income and expenditure flows from individual projects differ with respect to their relative occurrence in time.[4] This follows from the fact that changes in the discount rate have the greatest impact (measured in terms of changes in present values) on the most distant income and expenditure flows under consideration.

The contribution of the Solomon article was to point out that the apparent conflict between these two ranking procedures was due to differing implicit assumptions about reinvestment rates (the present-value approach assumes reinvestment of intermediate cash receipts at the discounting rate, while the internal rate-of-return approach assumes reinvestment at the internal rate)

* Mr. Renshaw is an instructor and research assistant in the Department of Economics of the University of Chicago.

[1] James H. Lorie and Leonard J. Savage, "Three Problems in Rationing Capital," *Journal of Business*, XXVIII (October, 1955), 229–39; Ezra Solomon, "The Arithmetic of Capital Budgeting Decisions," *Journal of Business*, XXIX (April, 1956), 124–29.

[2] The internal rate of return is usually defined as that rate which makes the discounted value of net cash flows for a single alternative equal to the discounted value of capital outlays. In the economic literature, this rate is often identified with Keynes's marginal efficiency of capital. A difficulty of this concept, to be discussed shortly, is the fact that the rate may not be unique.

[3] The present value of an investment alternative is determined by discounting all the associated cash outlays back to the present and finding the net present sum.

[4] The inconsistency in rankings can be illustrated with reference to Chart 1, which appears in the last section of this paper. Chart 1 plots the present values of two investment alternatives as a function of the discounting interest rate. In this chart the internal rate is the interest rate for which present value is zero (see definition in preceding footnote). The rate-of-return approach would have us choose alternative *B* over alternative *A*, since the curves are so constructed that *B* has an infinite rate of return (never comes to the axis), while *A* has an internal rate of 1,150 per cent. For any discount rate between 25 and 400 per cent, however, the present value of alternative *A* is greater than the present value of alternative *B*.

and to suggest that the conflict could be eliminated by making an explicit assumption about the expected return from reinvestment. This rate or set of rates could then be used to reduce income and expenditure flows to present values or, equivalently, to compound the flows to terminal values of a common date. It should be emphasized that the consistency which Solomon has established is for methods of investment comparison which are, in fact, of only approximal[5] use in obtaining an economic maximum. The use of an explicit assumption about a common terminal date establishes an equivalency between a ranking of investment alternatives in terms of the ratio of net cash inflows to investment expenditures (sometimes referred to as a "benefit-cost ratio") and a ranking of investment alternatives in terms of what Solomon calls the "over-all rate of return on capital." The ratio of discounted cash inflow can be interpreted as a capital gains ratio, whereas Solomon's over-all rate of return should be interpreted as an average rate of return on funds investment to the common terminal date.

From an economic point of view, a ranking of investment alternatives according to the difference between discounted cash inflows and outflows would appear to be a more acceptable ranking procedure than any comparative procedure based upon either a simple or a complicated ratio of receipts to expenditures, whether in the form of a capital gains ratio or a ratio which yields a rate of return.[6] An exact maximization of present value will always be obtained by the difference method unless there exists a fixed budget restraint such that some projects yielding a positive present value must be rejected for reasons other than mutual exclusiveness. In the case of a fixed capital budget, it may be necessary to make iterative substitutions until, for a given capital expenditure, present value is maximized.

In general, the ratio of cash inflow to expenditure approach and the over-all rate-of-return approach can be relied upon only to maximize the present value of the firm or the over-all return on a firm's own capital, if the alternatives to choose from have expenditure bases of roughly the same size. These two approaches should not be used to compare projects varying in scale, since one has no way of knowing at what scale the incremental return from a larger project equals the incremental cost.

The limited usefulness of the over-all rate of return, even though it is superior to the internal rate of return, as a maximizing tool, should be stressed. The present-value approach in its refined discounted inflow minus outflow form, on the other hand, is so completely general that it is difficult to imagine an investment or disinvestment alternative that could not be included and made comparable to any other investment alternative. So long as an investment or combination of investments (whether made in the past, to be made in the present, or to be deferred to some future date) can be looked upon as generating an independent series of net future cash

[5] Approximal, owing to investment indivisibilities. Given a fixed investment budget, it may be desirable on the margin to accept a smaller ratio of receipts to expenditures or a smaller over-all rate of return in order to keep more of the capital budget employed. In the case of mutually exclusive investments, it may be desirable to accept a smaller ratio/rate of return if greater amounts of capital can be employed.

[6] A. Samuelson, "Some Aspects of the Pure Theory of Capital," *Quarterly Journal of Economics*, LI (1936–37), 469.

flows, discounting procedures can be used to make the investment comparable to other alternatives.

II. THE CONCEPT OF REINVESTMENT RATES

The concept of reinvestment rates raises the fundamental question as to how a firm should price or value the opportunity to make investments which can reasonably be expected to yield a higher rate or return than need be paid on borrowed funds. The position of those in favor of discounting by reinvestment rates is that this special advantage should be priced in terms of the future cost of capital rather than the present cost of capital.

The usefulness of Solomon's suggestion to discount future cash flows by means of expected reinvestment rates rather than by the current cost of capital rests essentially on a firm's ability to make the concept of reinvestment rates operational. The idea of discounting by reinvestment rates is appealing, since, in committing investment funds, one cannot afford to ignore reinvestment opportunities. In adopting the reinvestment approach to capital investment decisions, one is essentially taking the position that any positive present value accruing from a firm's current opportunity to make investment decisions should be priced or valued in terms of interest rates that are expected to prevail at the time that net cash flows actually accrue. Both the positive and the normative questions as to whether firms *do* and *should* price current investment advantage in terms of the expected future cost of capital rather than the present cost of capital are unsettled.

The problem of accepting one philosophy of discounting as opposed to the other, of course, exists only if the firm has some grounds for distinguishing between the current cost of capital and future reinvestment rates. Any current set or pattern of term interest rates must, among other things, reflect to some extent the general expectations of the market with regard to future investment possibilities.[7] In the final analysis, the adoption of a set of reinvestment rates by the firm which is different from the current cost of capital essentially implies one or more of two things. First, it may imply that the firm's expectations with regard to the future differ from general market expectations and that management is willing to gamble that the market, in pricing capital to the firm, is making a mistake.[8] Second, it may imply that the firm's preference for current, as opposed to future, income differs from time preferences implied in prevailing market rates of interest.

III. THE RELATION OF REINVESTMENT RATES TO INFLOWS AND OUTFLOWS

A distinction should be made between the reinvestment rates used to discount cash outflows as opposed to cash inflows, since optimal financial behavior

[7] Considerable doubt exists, at least in the short run, as to whether interest rates do in fact reflect only the marginal productivity of capital. Risk premiums, time preferences, and rate policies imposed by monetary and government authorities may tend to obscure allowances made in the existing rate structure for expected changes in reinvestment opportunities.

[8] From a resource-allocation point of view, the mistake may be either an aggregate mistake in the current price of capital which affects all firms alike and which can be expected to correct itself in terms of a change in market rates or a mistake which fixes the quantity of capital that a firm may borrow without regard to the marginal internal rate of return that management expects to be able to earn on increments of investment.

on the part of the firm may be different in the two cases.

On the outflow or expenditure side, the concept of reinvestment rates presumably refers to rates of return obtainable on funds between the time of their availability for investment and actual investment. Discounting on the outflow side, of course, is necessary only if investment is to be deferred or is to take place in more than one year. On the inflow or cash return side, the concept presumably refers to rates of return obtainable on funds reinvested to a common terminal date. The notion of a common terminal date less than infinity is arbitrary. Assuming a life for the firm or its investors beyond the agreed-upon terminal date, one might well wish to consider, for purposes of discounting, reinvestment rates obtainable on funds invested beyond the terminal date, since long-term rates are generally higher than short-term rates and obviously constitute relevant reinvestment alternatives.

On general economic grounds one would expect the rates used to discount cash outflows to present values to be lower than the rates used to discount net inflows, since investment funds must be kept intact and can be used elsewhere only for specified intervals. Various circumstances might serve to lessen and in the extreme case make the differential between the two sets of rates negative. One circumstance would be very good short-term investment possibilities within the firm as opposed to long-term investment possibilities. A second circumstance might be created by monetary authorities acting to suppress inflation by raising short-term interest rates in the hope that long-term rates will follow. Other things being equal, a reduction of the differential between short- and long-term reinvestment rates will tend to favor investment deferral.

IV. PROJECTING REINVESTMENT RATES

This section is essentially concerned with stating the conditions under which a firm should look to reinvestment opportunities outside the firm as opposed to opportunities inside the firm when projecting discount rates. If external reinvestment rates are used, a choice must be made between lending rates and borrowing rates. If internal reinvestment rates are used, it may be necesary to resolve an interdependency between discount rates and investment alternatives selected.

A. APPLICABILITY OF EXTERNAL REINVESTMENT RATES

In the absence of non-price rationing of investment capital,[9] reinvestment rates should be looked upon as being determined outside the firm. Roberts[10] and others have distinguished between two external sets of rates—lending rates and borrowing rates. From a theoretical point of view, lending rates have certain advantages over borrowing rates. They are of particular relevance when investments are being financed out of retained earnings and depreciation allowances rather than by net borrowing. Further, the lending rate can be considered the correct rate of discount to use, when selecting, from a set of alternatives that are mutually exclusive, the one alter-

[9] A situation in which the size of the capital budget is fixed independently of expected rate of return.

[10] Harry V. Roberts, "Current Problems in the Economics of Capital Budgeting," *Journal of Business*, XXX (January, 1957), 12–17.

native which maximizes a firm's net worth.[11]

In the absence of alternatives with mutually exclusive characteristics, the use of either lending or borrowing rates will lead to similar investment selections. Choice of lending rates as opposed to borrowing rates will then essentially rest on whether it is more convenient to treat the incremental cost of borrowing in terms of a reduction of net cash inflows (as an expense) or in terms of a higher discount rate.[12] The discrepancy between the two procedures for treating borrowing costs diminishes toward zero as the ratio of net discounted cash inflows to discounted expenditures approaches unity. By assumption, the absence of capital rationing or a budgetary restraint makes it in the interest of the firm to accept all non-mutually exclusive investments with a ratio greater than unity, so the precise ordering or ranking of accepted investments does not matter.

When reinvestment rates are determined outside the firm, the financial problem associated with the capital budgeting process resolves itself primarily into a problem of forecasting changes in external interest rates and returns on equity capital outside the firm. While the problem of financial forecast is really the subject of another paper, presumably one would want to look very closely at the Federal Reserve's monetary policy and the state of the general economy, which tends to govern interest rate policy in particular.

B. APPLICABILITY OF INTERNAL REINVESTMENT RATES

Given a fixed capital budget restraint within the firm, which implies, from an economic point of view, that at the budget margin internal investment opportunities are expected to be so "good" that higher rates of return could be earned on incremental investment within the firm than can be earned on investment outside the firm, the appropriate reinvestment rate to discount by is an internal rate rather than an external rate. In this connection it should be emphasized that the only internal reinvestment rate by which it makes sense to discount current alternatives is the expected rate or set of rates marginal to future investment budgets of the firm;[13] average rates of return on future investment budgets are inappropriate.

The notion of fixed budget restraints raises a general question as to whether future reinvestment rates can ever be considered to be independent of contemporary project selection. To some extent the size of future investment budgets must be a function of net cash inflows from current investments, in which case the marginal reinvestment rate within the firm for every future budget will also be a function of contemporary project selection. The possi-

[11] The lending rate is presumed to reflect the opportunity return available to a firm's stockholders on investments outside the firm. The firm would not be acting in the interest of its stockholders if it accepted a lower rate of return on internal investments than could be earned elsewhere. On the other hand, to forego an opportunity to make investments yielding a net return in excess of prevailing lending (capitalization) rates would be denying stockholders capital gains.

[12] An alternative approach to the problem of investment selection might be to treat all borrowing costs as though they were annual expenses. Projects would then be chosen on the basis of the discounted special advantage associated with being able to make investments yielding a higher rate of return than is paid on borrowed funds.

[13] An assumption implicit in conventional discounting practice is that the marginal reinvestment rate can be treated as a constant within the relevant range of flows to be discounted.

ble interdependency between current investment alternatives, the size of future investment budgets, and reinvestment rates can perhaps best be visualized within a general decision-making context which involves two specific categories of investment alternatives—research and development alternatives and deferred investment alternatives.

A primary objective of research and development may be to better future investment alternatives. The act of accepting or rejecting current research and development alternatives may therefore influence reinvestment rates. A somewhat different interdependency may arise when a firm considers the possibility of deferring investment to a later period. Assuming that the magnitudes of cash flows will not be affected, the wisdom of deferral will not be independent of the return that funds can earn in the interim between availability and deferred investment. Given a fixed investment budget, this interim return may depend to a large degree upon which short-term investment alternatives are actually chosen.[14]

The problem of the simultaneous interdependence of investment alternatives and reinvestment rates must be either met or begged by management. A general procedure for meeting the problem of interdependence might be to rediscount in an iterative manner[15] all investment alternatives until the set actually chosen is the set implied when all alternatives are discounted by the marginal reinvestment rate implied by all included investments.

An operational device for begging the problem of an interdependency between current investment selection and reinvestment rates might be to take the position that future reinvestment opportunities are so uncertain that the best we can do with regard to predicting future opportunities is to project historical rates of return which have been realized at the margin of past investment budgets. Allowances might, in an explicit way, then be made for expected technological break-throughs and other events that can reasonably be expected to alter historical trends. The projective approach has an added operational advantage, in that, as time goes along, one can perhaps take advantage of historical mistakes in such a way as to firm up projections of future reinvestment rates.

An important by-product of making cash flow estimates and discount rates explicit rather than subjective is that explicit estimates can become a part of a firm's records and can be subjected to the test of an ex post appraisal.

Discounting techniques are useful tools of investment analysis in so far as they provide a means for comparing cash flows which accrue unevenly with respect to time. A final word of caution should be addressed against taking too seriously any mechanical procedure for ranking and comparing income and expenditure flows which accrue unevenly throughout time however. It is doubtful whether individual firms can afford to

[14] A very easy way around this latter interdependency would be to combine short-term investment alternatives with deferred investment alternatives and then select, by means of conventional discounting procedure, the best mutually exclusive combination.

[15] As a first approximation, discount all investment alternatives by the reinvestment rates implied by the set of alternatives you intuitively feel will be chosen; rank the alternatives; and run down the list until the budget is exhausted. If the set which exhausts the budget implies the same rediscount rates used initially, your intuition was a success; if not, rediscount by the rates implied by the latest ranking. Continue until either reaching a consistency or an indifference between sets of alternatives.

be mathematically indifferent with respect to the timing of income and investment flows. In the complex and uncertain world we live in, ability to meet interest and dividend commitments, retain earnings, and borrow funds are inextricably interwoven with the patterns of historical flows. Any set of investment alternatives chosen by mechanical means must always be checked in terms of specific flow considerations and restrictions imposed by finance, since it will usually be convenient to assume a great deal more independence between discount rates and investment selections than in fact exists.

V. DUAL RATES OF RETURN

In this section the possibility of dual rates of return is discussed within the context of the example presented by Solomon. A distinction is drawn between what is regarded in the economic literature as a conventional internal rate of return and a Fisherian rate of return over cost. The possibility of dual rates of return again serves to emphasize the limited usefulness of the internal rate-of-return approach as a maximizing tool in investment selection. In general, Solomon's over-all rate of return, which does not suffer from the possibility of duality, is a better maximizing tool, but is still inferior to a ranking of investment alternatives in terms of present values.

A dramatic contribution of the Lorie-Savage article was to point out that investment alternatives with terminal costs can conceivably have more than one internal rate of return. The example that was used to illustrate this possibility, however, cannot truly be classified as a case involving terminal costs or actual cash outlays. Further, the dual rates which make the algebraic sum of the discounted cash outflows and inflows equal to zero should properly be classified as Fisherian rates of return over cost[16] rather than conventional internal rates of return—the latter usually refer to rates of return on a single investment alternative rather than rates of return on the cash flow difference between two alternatives.[17]

The foregoing can perhaps be better understood if we break the example of dual rates of return appearing in the Solomon article into its component parts. This breakdown is shown in Table 1. Essentially, the example is concerned with determining the conditions under which it would pay to replace the existing pump in an oil well with a larger pump. Investment in a larger pump (alternative A), which is expected to cost \$1,600 in t_0 and yield \$20,000 in t_1, can be viewed as an alternative to making no investment or continuing to use the existing pump (alternative B), which is expected to cost nothing in t_0 and yield \$10,000 in both t_1 and t_2. Broken down

TABLE 1

CASH FLOWS

Time Period	Alternative A (Investment in a Larger Pump)	Alternative B (No Additional Investment)	Incremental Cash Flow Due to Investment in Larger Pump
t_0.......	− 1,600	0	− 1,600
t_1.......	20,000	10,000	10,000
t_2.......	0	10,000	−10,000

16 For a clarification and example of the Fisherian rate of return involving a single rate see A. A. Alchian, "The Rate of Interest, Fisher's Rate of Return over Costs and Keynes' Internal Rate of Return," *American Economic Review*, XLV (December, 1955), 938.

17 The distinction between the Fisherian rate of return over cost and the conventional internal rate of return, in the final analysis, is a matter of deciding what constitutes an investment alternative and not a matter of discounting technique. Actual discounting procedure is essentially the same in both cases.

into its component parts, each part can be viewed as yielding a separate internal rate of return. The internal rate of return on alternative A (investment in a larger pump) is 1,150 per cent; see Table 2 for the rate of return which makes

TABLE 2

PRESENT VALUE OF CASH FLOWS IN TIME PERIOD t_0

Interest Rate	Alternative A (Investment in a Larger Pump)	Alternative B (No Additional Investment)	Incremental Cash Flow Due to Investment in Larger Pump
0....	18,400	20,000	−1,600
20....	15,067	15,278	− 211
25....	14,400	14,400	0
50....	11,733	11,111	622
100....	8,400	7,500	900
200....	5,067	4,444	623
300....	3,400	3,125	275
400....	2,400	2,400	0
500....	1,733	1,944	− 211
1,150....	0	1,440	−1,440
Infinity..	− 1,600	0	−1,600

the present value of cash flows in time period t_0 equal to zero. The internal rate of return on alternative B (no additional investment) is infinite; it would still be infinite if future cash flows only amounted to one dollar or a penny, since, by assumption, outlays are zero.

Obviously, in comparing mutually exclusive investment alternatives, one or more of which involve zero outlays, a ranking in terms of individual rates of return breaks down. A way out of this dilemma is to subtract the cash flows generated by a zero outlay investment from the cash flows generated by an investment which in the process of subtraction will leave a real or spurious outlay base. Subtracting alternative B from alternative A and obtaining an incremental cash flow due to investment in the larger pump is equivalent to isolating a Fisherian rate of return over cost which sets the difference in net cash flows between two alternatives equal to zero. Fisher's view was that the true cost of accepting a given alternative is the opportunities foregone (opportunity cost).

In the example used by Solomon, there are in fact two Fisherian rates of return over cost, 25 and 400 per cent. They bracket a region of possible discount rates in which investment in a larger pump is preferable to no investment (see Chart I, which displays in graphic form the data of Table 2). At all discount or reinvestment rates between 25 and 400 per cent, investment

CHART I

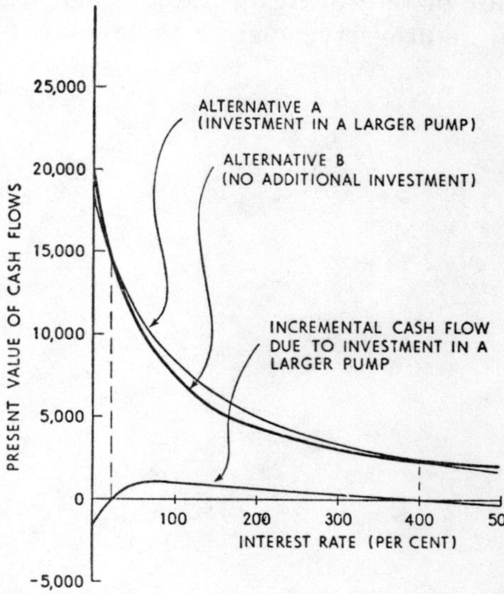

in the large pump has a greater present value in t_0 than alternative B and hence is the preferred alternative.

The point which should be made is that the Fisherian prescription for finding the rate of return from a complex investment proposal is as applicable as the conventional prescription for finding the internal rate of return on a simple proposal. The only usefulness of such rates is to aid one in identifying regions of profitableness with respect to changes in the discount rate—they need not give any clue as to average profitability over a common time period.

A word should perhaps be said with respect to simple proposals involving terminal costs in the form of net cash outlays exceeding cash inflows. It is not inconceivable that a firm might wish to consider entering into a contractual agreement involving *actual* cash flows equivalent to the differential cash flows discussed in the example above. Net initial and terminal expenditure flows as demonstrated by this example can sometimes result in more than one internal rate of return. Again the internal rates of return serve merely to bracket regions with respect to changes in the reinvestment rate which are profitable in the sense that the net worth or present value of the firm can be expected to increase by accepting the proposal. Solomon's general prescription for finding the over-all rate of return up to a fixed terminal date will hold. Given the expected reinvestment rates, Solomon's over-all rate of return on either complex proposals or proposals involving terminal costs will always be a unique and unambiguous rate of return. It should not be compared, however, with over-all rates of return from projects having different outlay bases, if one wishes to be confident of obtaining an economic maximum.

III
The Cost of Debt and Equity Funds

COSTS OF DEBT AND EQUITY FUNDS FOR BUSINESS: TRENDS AND PROBLEMS OF MEASUREMENT

DAVID DURAND†

IT DOES NOT seem feasible at this time to present a paper that will do justice to the title, "Costs of Debt and Equity Funds for Business: Trends and Problems of Measurement." To me this title implies a critical analysis of available data, and concrete proposals for research. The need for such research is great. We have heard a great deal recently about an alleged shortage of equity capital, and we have actually observed that many corporations finance expansion with cash retained from operations or by borrowing. This may mean, as some have argued, that the usual sources of equity capital have dried up, but it may also mean that corporations find selling stock much less attractive, or perhaps more costly, than other methods of financing. How, therefore, do the costs of stock financing compare with the costs of borrowing, or the costs of retentions? When, if ever, do the costs of financing discourage business expansion? And finally, does the tax structure have any effect on the costs of financing?

I shall deal solely with conceptual problems and, in doing this, ruthlessly brush aside the practical details in hope of clarifying the basic issues. Although we have, I believe, a rather rough notion of what we mean by the cost of raising capital, this notion needs to be sharpened before it is applicable for use in actual measurement. Furthermore, the sharpening process indicates that our conceptual groundwork is inadequate to deal with many questions of investment and capital cost. Hence, the formulation of a working definition of capital cost necessitates reformulating a good deal of basic and generally accepted economic theory. But even if we achieve a satisfactory definition of cost and a sound basic theory, the practical problems of actual measurement are going to be tremendous. However, a good theory should enable us to understand these problems much better, even if it does not diminish them appreciably.

That these problems of measuring capital costs are much the same as the problems that arise in trying to appraise the going concern value of a business enterprise is the general theme of this paper. Almost any method of estimating costs will, I believe, at least imply an evaluation of the common stock of a corporation or the proprietor's interest in an unincorporated business. That is, we can measure the costs of capital about as accurately as we can measure the value of common stock, and any of us who think that stock appraisal is a form of crystal gazing should prepare to include research on the cost of capital in the same category.

Before going on with this argument, I wish to offer a general disclaimer. During the past three months of intermittent work on this paper, I have repeatedly had to revise my opinions, and I expect to have to revise them further in the ensuing three months. I do, of course, expect to stand by two general

† The author is professor of industrial management at The Massachusetts Institute of Technology.

principles: 1) *Our basic economic theory needs revisions;* 2) *Security appraisal is the key to measuring the cost of capital.* But the details of the argument are, like a timetable, subject to change without notice. This paper is therefore a historical statement of the development of my ideas to date.

Finally, I wish to thank Martin W. Davenport and Wilson F. Payne for contributing a large number of ideas, some of them basic, and for aid in formulating the argument.

I BASIC CONSIDERATIONS

A great deal of our economic thinking is derived from a few fundamental notions concerning self-interest. The businessman is supposed to know what is best for him and to act accordingly. From analyzing these self-seeking actions, we hope to derive a theory of economic behavior. This paper is conventional in accepting the principle of self-interest and applying it to the problems of capital cost. If the businessman raises capital to finance a venture, it must be in furtherance of his interests; and any definition of the costs of raising this capital must be consistent with this principle.

This paper is unorthodox, however, in its conception of what actually constitutes a businessman's best interest. Instead of accepting the common dictum that the businessman's interest is to maximize his income, this paper counters with the alternative proposal that the businessman should try to maximize his wealth. This alternative has the advantage of greater flexibility, and for this reason it avoids errors that may result from forcing the principle of maximizing income on situations to which it is strictly inapplicable.

1 *Maximizing Income vs. Maximizing Investment Value*

One can attack the principle of maximizing income simply on the grounds that mankind's motives transcend the pecuniary, and that these motives affect his behavior, even in the market place. But leaving these nonpecuniary motives aside, one can also attack the principle of maximizing income on the ground that it is totally meaningless in any world in which income is expected to change. Suppose, for example, that a businessman has two possible ways to operate his business. Operation A promises him an annual return of \$6,500 in perpetuity, and Operation B promises him \$10,000 in perpetuity. The principle of maximizing income works well in this example. The businessman will certainly choose Operation B with its higher income (since nonpecuniary motives are ruled out).

But suppose this businessman has another alternative — Operation C — which gets under way slowly and thus promises him \$7,000 the first year, \$9,000 the second year, and \$10,500 thereafter. The principle of maximizing income tells us that Operation C is preferable to Operation A because the income from Operation C is certainly larger than that from Operation A. But the principle cannot tell us whether Operation C is also preferable to Operation B. Is the combination of \$7,000, \$9,000, and \$10,500 thereafter greater or less than \$10,000 in perpetuity? This difficulty can be readily resolved provided a discount rate or other index of time preference is available, and provided, further, that the principle of maximizing income is appropriately modified.

The table below shows the discounted, or present, value of income under Operations B and C at four arbitrary rates of discount (standard compound interest tables were used). Thus, Operation B is preferable for rates of 10 percent and above, whereas Operation C is preferable for rates of 9 percent and below.

DISCOUNTED VALUE

Discount Rate	*Operation B*	*Operation C*	*Difference (Op. C — Op. B)*
7%	$142,857	$144,514	$1,657
8	125,000	125,832	832
9	111,111	111,314	203
10	100,000	99,711	—289

To effect this simple solution, it was necessary to modify the principle of maximizing income. The statement, "The businessman tries to maximize his income," was changed to read, "The businessman tries to maximize the *discounted value of his future income.*" Of course, some variations in terminology are possible within the revised statement; and, in fact, this paper will henceforth use the term "investment value" to mean the discounted value of an expected income stream.[1]

This revision is more than mere verbiage. The shift from maximation of income to maximation of discounted value has important implications for the measurement of costs and the analysis of investment problems. It emphasizes the basic importance of appraisal and security analysis in molding business decisions. How can the businessman go about maximizing investment value without developing a system of appraisal that is suitable, to him at least?

Economic theory has used the principle of maximizing income to demonstrate that business expansion will proceed until the marginal return on capital equals the rate of interest. A brief resumé of the argument is illustrated in Chart 1. Here the marginal return

CHART 1

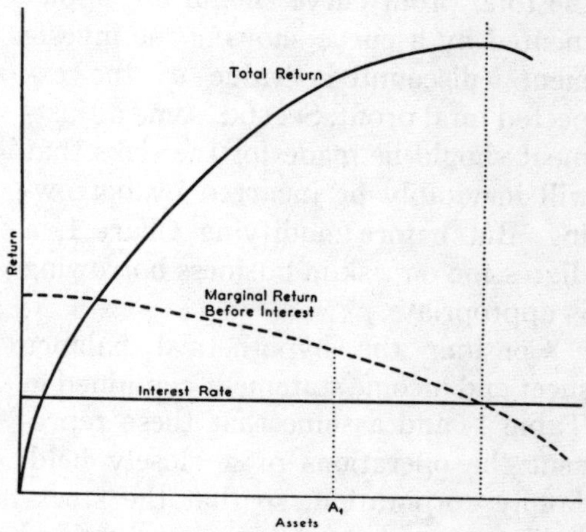

curve represents the rate of return on successive small increments to a businessman's assets. The curve always slopes downward because the businessman is supposed to make his successive small investments in order of profitability. Since the marginal return represents the net return before interest, the distance between this curve and the horizontal line representing the interest rate is the marginal net return after interest. Thus, if the businessman expands his assets to the point A_1, his total profit is represented by the area between the marginal return curve, the interest line, the vertical axis, and a vertical line through A_1. The maximum possible total profit is attained when assets are expanded to the point where marginal return crosses the interest line.

This demonstration is valid if the returns attributable to the successive investment increments (represented by

[1] Among the possible alternatives are "going-concern value" and "intrinsic value." Some security analysts specifically think of intrinsic value as a sum of discounted future income payments; others are less specific.

the curve for marginal return) can be assumed to remain constant and certain over time. But if these returns vary from year to year, and if there is an element of uncertainty as well, the treatment must be reformulated. First, the total profit curve should be supplemented by a curve showing the investment (discounted) value of the expected total profit. Second, some adjustment should be made for the risks that will inevitably be incurred by borrowing. But before modifying Chart 1, a digression on risk in business borrowing is appropriate.

Consider the hypothetical balance sheet and income statement contained in Table 1, and assume that these represent the operations of a closely held, family corporation, so that the stockholders can exert an active and unified influence on the management.[2]

Could such a corporation profitably finance additional plant by issuing $10 million of 4 percent bonds, provided the expansion were expected to earn $800,000 annually, or 8 percent? The estimated income statement after the proposed expansion is shown below.

TABLE 1

BALANCE SHEET OF THE ABC MANUFACTURING COMPANY

Assets		
Cash	$ 2,000,000	
Accounts receivable	5,000,000	
Inventory	7,000,000	
Total Current	14,000,000	
Plant and equipment, less depreciation	16,000,000	
TOTAL		$30,000,000
Liabilities		
Accrued items	$ 1,000,000	
Accounts payable	5,000,000	
Total Current	6,000,000	
Common stock, 1,000,000 shares at $15 per share	15,000,000	
Surplus	9,000,000	
	24,000,000	
TOTAL		$30,000,000

INCOME STATEMENT OF THE ABC MANUFACTURING COMPANY

Sales	$30,000,000	
Cost of goods sold	27,500,000	
Net operating income		2,500,000
Dividends paid		2,000,000
Transferred to Surplus		500,000
Earnings per share		$2.50
Dividends per share		$2.00
Net operating income, current operations	$ 2,500,000	
Net operating income, proposed operations	800,000	
	3,300,000	
Interest	400,000	
Net income		$ 2,900,000
Dividends (old rate)		2,000,000
Available for surplus		$ 900,000

As a practical matter, the current position of this corporation might discourage the investment bankers from handling the issue—even though net operating income would cover interest twice on the new plant alone and over eight times on the entire corporation. Ordinarily, the net current assets are supposed to be sufficient to cover the long-term debt; but the net current assets in this case are only $8 million—a deficiency of $2 million. Of course, an arrangement might be worked out by requiring that the bonds be paid serially, or that dividends should not be paid as long as the net current assets failed to cover the bond issue. Either of these arrangements might curtail dividends for two or three years.

But if the bond issue could be ar-

[2]I have a special reason for specifying such a corporation. The stockholders, who are few in number and relatively well acquainted, are apt to take a more active interest in the corporate affairs; and often the stockholders and the management are the same individuals. This gives the family corporation a peculiar degree of unity. In many ways it is like a proprietorship or partnership except for the legal organization in corporate form. In a widely held corporation, however, the stockholders have no such unity, and the management may represent the interests of a small group of stockholders, probably including the managers themselves.

ranged, would the stockholders consider the transaction attractive? The expansion has the advantage of increasing the prospective earnings from $2.50 a share to $2.90. It also has the disadvantage of increasing the risk because the proposed bond issue is so large that dividends might be curtailed for several years—even if the expected earnings were realized; and the entire financial position of the company might be jeopardized if earnings fell off sharply. Somehow the stockholders must balance the greater return against the greater risk, and they can do this by estimating the investment value of their stock. Will the shares be worth more or less following the expansion?

In practice such appraisals are usually difficult and often involve highly complex intangibles. But if the uncomfortable details are left aside, the principle of the appraisal can be very simply illustrated. Suppose, for example, that 12½ percent, or eight times earnings, is considered a fair capitalization rate as long as the company remains debt free, and that an increase to 15 percent, or six and two-thirds times earnings, is considered an adequate adjustment to compensate for the risk of carrying $10 million in debt. These assumed rates are completely arbitrary. Although several bases for adjusting capitalization rates to borrowing risks will be discussed in Section II, it is sufficient for the present argument merely to assume that the stockholders consider the rates satisfactory. The necessary stock appraisals can then be made easily, as shown below. These calculations imply that the proposed expansion is inadvisable.

Earnings per share from current operations	$ 2.50
Multiplier	8
Investment value per share	$20.00
Projected earnings after expansion	$ 2.90
Multiplier	6⅔
Investment value	$19.33

Because the stockholders suffer a decline in the investment value of their holdings, the small increase in earnings is not sufficient to compensate for the additional risk.[3]

2 *Required Return*

The preceding example showed that the risks incurred in borrowing may discourage investment, even though the rate of return on the new investment exceeds the interest cost of borrowed money. Specifically, the possibility of earning 8 percent in this example did not justify borrowing at only half that rate. But a still higher rate of return would have justified the investment. The following calculations show how to ascertain a rate that is just high enough to offset the risk. It is assumed that the risk will be just offset if the prospective per share earnings capitalized at 15 percent maintain the value of the common stock at $20.00.

Required value of stock per share	$20.00
Capitalization rate	.15
Required earnings, per share	3.00
Required earnings, 1,000,000 shares	3,000,000
Earnings previously available	2,500,000
Additional earnings required	500,000
Interest charges	400,000
Required earnings before interest	900,000
Rate of required earnings	9%

The required rate of earnings—9 percent for this example—is in a sense the cost to this corporation of borrowing the needed money. Of course, it is not an out-of-pocket cost, but a sort of opportunity cost—the minimum rate that the

[3] Of course, a somewhat smaller increase in the capitalization rate would not depreciate the stock. At 13⅓ percent, for example, the stock would be worth seven and one-half times $2.90 or $21.75.

new investment must earn without being actually disadvantageous to the stockholders. But perhaps this is too broad an interpretation of cost, and the reader is, therefore, free to choose for himself. Regardless of his decision, he will find the required rate of earnings an important entity because of the emphasis economists currently place on the determinants of investment. If we can ascertain what new investment has to earn in order to be profitable, we will be much wiser, whether we think this constitutes the cost of capital or something else. For the remainder of this paper the required rate of earnings will be referred to as the *required return* and will be abbreviated, *RR*.

Although the *RR* discussed above refers to bond financing, there is also an *RR* when a corporation sells stock, and sometimes even when it finances expansion with cash retained from operations. If the stockholders in the previous example had been deterred from authorizing the proposed expansion because the expected returns were inadequate to justify the inherent risk incurred by bond financing, they might have considered preferred stock, common stock, and perhaps a judicious combination of common stock and bonds. Would the expected return have been sufficient to justify any of these alternatives? And if not, what rate of return would have been sufficient?

Although this subject will be explored more fully in Section III, a single example may be helpful here. When capital is raised by a common stock issue, the old stockholders will suffer a dilution of earning power and hence a dilution of investment value unless the new investment is capable of earning enough to maintain per share earnings at the old level. The *RR* depends upon the old level of earnings and the price at which the new shares must be sold. If the stockholders of the ABC Company wanted to raise $10 million by selling 500,000 shares on the market at $20.00, the new investment would have to earn $1,250,000 or 12½ percent to avoid dilution of earnings. Hence 12½ percent is the *RR*.

3 *Reformulation of Basic Theory*

A more realistic presentation of Chart 1 is now in order. Like its predecessor, Chart 2 contains curves repre-

CHART 2

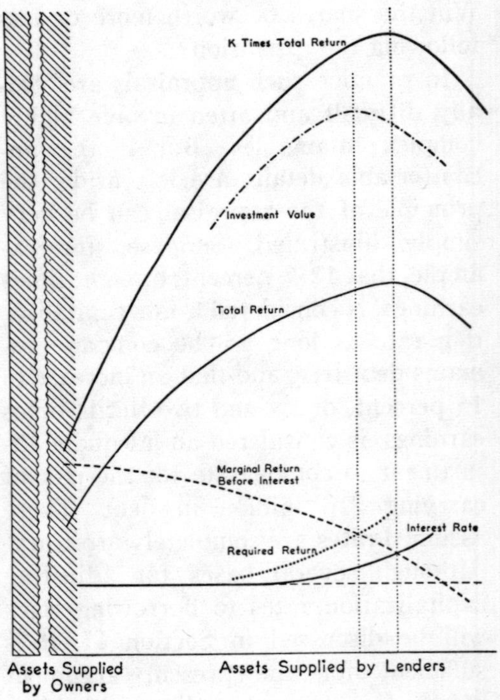

senting the marginal return on capital, the interest rate, and the total return. But Chart 2 differs in a number of important respects. First, at the left of the chart is a shaded area representing the assets supplied by the owners themselves, which are assumed to remain constant while additional assets are supplied by lenders. Since the owners' assets earn a return, the total return curve is substantially above zero at the point where borrowed assets are zero.

Second, the interest curve is not level, but slopes upward, because a business that borrows heavily will have to pay a higher rate of interest to compensate lenders for bearing additional risk. As drawn, this curve is actually level for a while before turning up, but some readers will undoubtedly prefer a curve that slopes upward at all points, even if only slightly. The interest curve shown in Chart 2 might be called a "marginal interest curve." This implies that the rate for each successive borrowing does not affect the rate on previous borrowings. The marginal interest curve is of such character that the maximum total return occurs when the interest rate equals the marginal return. However, a "total interest curve" is also possible. This implies that all debt must pay the same rate, which increases as the total amount of the debt increases. With the total interest curve, unlike the marginal curve, the maximum total return will occur before the point where the interest rate is equal to the marginal return.[4]

[4] From the viewpoint of practical finance the total interest curve is probably more accurately descriptive than the marginal curve. The best example is the type of business, like some sales finance companies, that raises large amounts of money through short-term bank loans. Although the first loan may carry a lower rate than the second, and this in turn may carry a lower rate than the third, these early loans will eventually have to be renewed, after which they will no longer enjoy their preferential status; hence, in the long run, all debt will carry the same rate. Probably the nearest approach to the marginal curve occurs when a company issues first mortgage bonds at a low rate, later issues second mortgage bonds at a somewhat higher rate, and finally issues debentures at a still higher rate.

Third, at the very top of the chart is a curve representing the value of the total return when capitalized at a constant rate *K*. This curve—which would represent investment value if borrowing entailed no risk to the owners of the business—naturally reaches its maximum at the same point where total return reaches its maximum. Somewhat below this *K*-times-total-return curve is the assumed actual investment value. When there is no borrowing, investment value is *K* times total return, and the two curves coincide. But as the volume of the borrowing and the attendant risks increase, total return has to be capitalized at a higher and higher rate; therefore investment value falls farther and farther below *K* times total return. Naturally, investment value reaches its maximum before total return (or *K* times total return). This is the point of optimum operation. If a business expands beyond this point, it may attain a higher expected future income, but it will have to incur unjustified risks in the process, which means that the market value of the stock will suffer.

The fourth and final feature of the chart is a curve for the *RR*. As drawn the curve is a marginal curve, that is, it expresses the minimum rate that must be earned by successive small investments financed by bonds in order to maintain the investment value of the common stock. By definition, this curve must cross the marginal return curve at the point of optimum operations; to the left of this point, successive investments earn more than the *RR* and the investment value is therefore enhanced; to the right, successive investments earn less than the *RR*, and the investment value is depreciated. On this particular chart, only a small section of the RR curve is shown. The reason for this is that the shape of the RR curve depends upon the method used for capitalizing earnings. With one method, the RR curve coincides with the interest curve at the point of zero borrowing; but with another method, the RR curve is always above the interest curve. This interesting dilemma will be elaborated in the next section.

For those with a mathematical turn of mind, it may be interesting to note that the RR is expressible in the following equation[5]

$$RR = I + V\frac{dC}{dX}$$

where (I) is the marginal rate of interest, (V) is the investment value, and $\frac{dC}{dX}$ is the rate of change in the capitalization rate (percent) as the debt burden increases. This means that the RR is equal to the rate of interest as long as the capitalization rate remains constant; but as soon as the capitalization rate begins to increase, the RR exceeds the rate of interest.

[5] Let the interest rate (I), the total return (P), the investment value (V), and the capitalization rate (C) all be considered functions of X, the amount of money borrowed. Then the equation

$$V = \frac{P}{C}$$

expresses the relation between investment value and total return. After a small increase in (P) resulting from additional borrowing

$$V + \Delta V = \frac{P + \Delta P}{C + \Delta C}$$

To determine the RR, it is only necessary to determine the rate of return that will make ΔV vanish. That is

$$\frac{P + \Delta P}{C + \Delta C} = \frac{P}{C}$$

or

$$\frac{P + (\overline{RR} - I)\,\Delta X}{C + \Delta C} = \frac{P}{C}$$

Solving for $\overline{RR}$ gives

$$\overline{RR} = I + \frac{P\Delta C}{(C + \Delta C)\,\Delta X}$$

In the limit this becomes

$$\overline{RR} = I + \frac{P}{C}\,\frac{dC}{dX}$$

and since $\frac{P}{C}$ is equal to (V), the equation given in the text follows immediately.

II THE PROBLEM OF SECURITY APPRAISAL

1 *Two Methods of Capitalizing Earnings*

Any practical application of the principles of the RR necessitates a sound, effective and generally acceptable system of security appraisal. Yet at present no such system exists. Naturally some differences of opinion concerning details may always be expected. But present differences run much deeper than details. On the single question of capitalizing earnings, involved in most appraisal methods, there appear to be two systems in current use that arise from fundamentally different assumptions, lead to substantially different results in calculating the RR, and have radically different implications for financial policy. An analysis of these two systems will therefore prove illuminating and will further highlight the need of providing a sound conceptual groundwork for research on investment problems and the costs of capital.

The accompanying sample balance sheet and income statement contain enough data to illustrate the fundamental difference between the two methods of capitalizing earnings. This hypothetical company is financed partly with bonds, partly with common

TABLE 2

BALANCE SHEET OF THE PDQ MANUFACTURING COMPANY

Assets		
Cash	$ 3,000,000	
Accounts receivable	5,000,000	
Inventory	7,000,000	
Total Current	15,000,000	
Plant and equipment, less depreciation	15,000,000	
TOTAL		$30,000,000
Liabilities		
Accrued items	$ 1,000,000	
Accounts payable	4,000,000	
Total Current	5,000,000	
Bonded debt, 4 percent debentures	5,000,000	
Common stock, 1,500,000 shares at $10 per share	15,000,000	
Earned surplus	5,000,000	
	20,000,000	
TOTAL		$30,000,000

INCOME STATEMENT OF THE PDQ MANUFACTURING COMPANY

Sales	$30,000,000
Cost of goods sold	28,000,000
Net operating income	2,000,000
Interest	200,000

stock; and the problem at hand is to estimate the value of the common stock on the assumption that the bonds, which are well protected, sell in the market at par. Since the purpose of the illustration is to focus attention on the problem of capitalizing earnings, questions of assets and book value will be neglected entirely, and the important matter of the corporate income tax will be deferred for later treatment.

One approach, hereafter called the NOI Method, capitalizes *net operating income* and subtracts the debt as follows:

Net operating income	$2,000,000
Capitalization rate, 10%	× 10
Total value of company	20,000,000
Total bonded debt	5,000,000
Total value of common stock	15,000,000
Value per share, 1,500,000 shares	$10.00

The essence of this approach is that the total value of all bonds and stock must always be the same—$20 million in this example—regardless of the proportion of bonds and stock.[6] Had there been no bonds at all, for example, the total value of the common stock would have been $20 million, and had there been $2.5 million in bonds, the value would have been $17.5 million. Hereafter, the total value of all stocks and bonds will be called the "total investment value" of the company.

The alternative approach, hereafter called the NI Method, capitalizes *net income* instead of net operating income. The calculations are as follows:

Net operating income	$ 2,000,000
Interest	200,000
Net income	1,800,000
Capitalization rate, 10%	× 10
Total value of common stock	18,000,000
Value per share, 1,500,000 shares	$12.00

Under this method the total investment value does not remain constant, but increases with the proportion of bonds in the capital structure. In the table at top of next page, three levels of bond financing are assumed: $5 million, $2.5 million, and no bonds at all. At each level, the value of the stock is obtained, as above, by capitalizing at 10 percent the residual income after bond interest. The implied relation in this table is that an increase of $2.5 million in bonded debt (total capitalization remaining constant) produces a corresponding increase of $1.5 million in total investment value. However, such a relationship cannot continue indefinitely, as the proponents of the NI Method clearly point out. As the debt burden becomes

[6] If the debt burden should be excessive, proponents of the NOI Method might argue that the total value of all bonds and stock would be depressed below $20 million. This argument could be based on the likelihood of insolvency and subsequent forced dissolution of the company.

Assumed amount of bonds	None	$ 2,500,000	$ 5,000,000
Value of common stock	$20,000,000	19,000,000	18,000,000
Total investment value	$20,000,000	$21,500,000	$23,000,000

substantial, the bonds will slip below par, and the stock will cease to be worth ten times earnings.

CHART 3

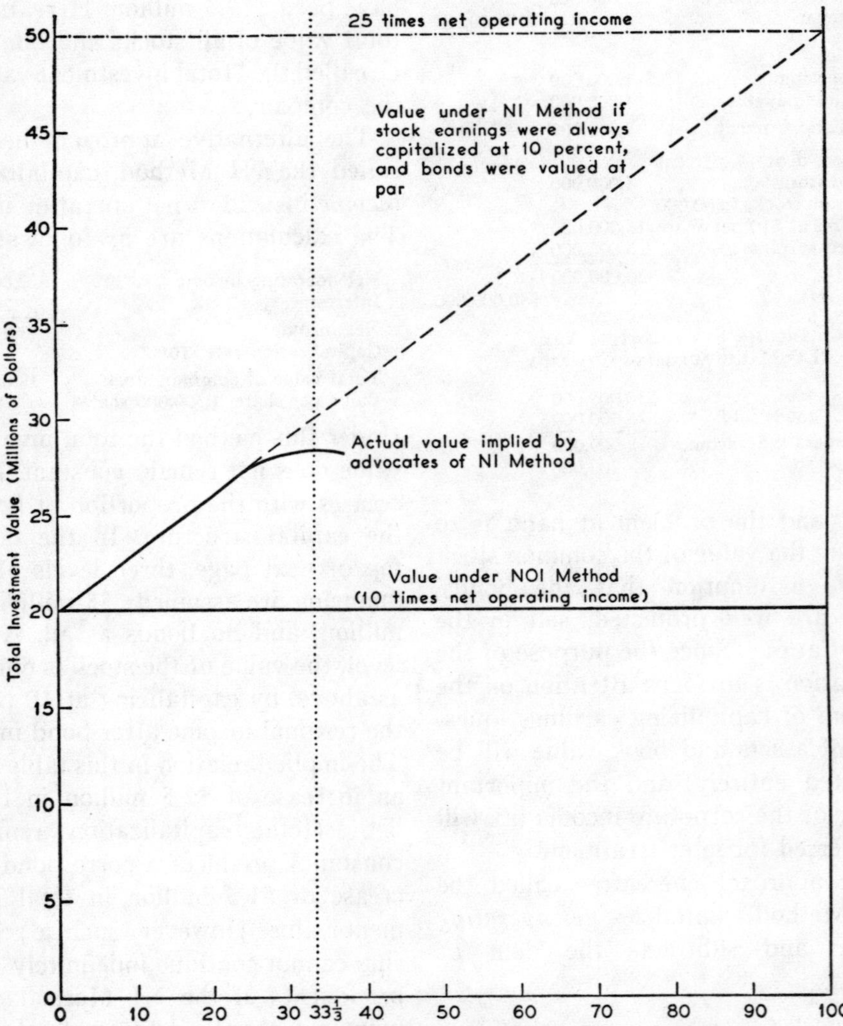

The difference between the two methods is shown graphically in Chart 3. Here the proportion of bonds in the capital structure is indicated by the share of net operating income (always $2 million in this example) that has to be paid to the bondholders. This method has the advantage of showing bond coverage directly; for when 33⅓ percent is paid out in interest (indicated by the dotted line), then the interest coverage is three times. The chart itself contains first a horizontal straight line at $20 million representing the total investment value according to the NOI Method. Second, the chart contains an upward sloping straight line representing the total investment value that would result under the NI Method if the bonds were always valued at par and the stock were always capitalized at 10 percent. Finally, the chart has a curved line showing the total investment value actually implied by the proponents of the NI Method. This curve coincides with the sloping straight line for a considerable distance, but as the proportion of bonds becomes appreciable, the curve falls below the straight line. As drawn here the curve has a definite maximum value, which implies the existence of an optimum capital structure. Naturally, the shape of the total investment value curve and the position of the maximum, near the three-times-interest-coverage point in this chart, are purely conjectural.

The most obvious difference between the two methods is that the NI Method results in a higher total investment value and a higher value for the common stock except for companies capitalized entirely with stock. For such companies the two methods give identical results provided the same capitalization rate is used.[7] This difference alone marks the NI Method as more liberal than the NOI Method, but the distinction between the optimism of the NI Method and the pessimism of the NOI Method will grow sharper as the discussion progresses. The NI Method, it will appear, takes a very sanguine view of the risks incurred in business borrowing; the NOI Method takes a more sober view.

Proponents of the NOI Method argue that the totality of risk incurred by all security holders of a given company cannot be altered by merely changing the capitalization proportions. Such a change could only alter the proportion of the total risk borne by each class of security holder. Thus if the PDQ Company had been capitalized entirely with stock—say 2,000,000 shares instead of 1,500,000 as in Table 1—the stockholders would have borne all the risk. With $5 million in bonds in lieu of the additional 500,000 shares, the bondholders would have incurred a portion of this risk. But because the bonds are so well protected, this portion would be small—say in the order of 5 or 10 percent. Hence the stockholders would still be bearing most of the risk, and with 25 percent fewer shares the risk per share would be substantially greater.[8]

The advocates of the NI Method take a position that is somewhat less

[7] Another exception possibly occurs when a business has an excessive debt burden. If the curve for total investment value under the NI Method (Chart 3) were extended, it would meet the level line for the NOI Method at about the point where bond interest is covered 1¾ times, which is considered an excessive debt burden for an industrial corporation.

[8] This proposition can be stated rigorously in terms of mathematical expectation. In brief, the argument runs along the following lines. The future income of a company has a definite, though perhaps unknown, mathematical expectation. If this income is to be divided up among types of security holder according to some formula, the income of each type will also have a definite mathematical expectation. Finally, the sum of the mathematical expectations for each type will necessarily equal the total for the entire income *no matter how that income is divided up*.

In spite of the logical merits of this proposition, the basic assumption may be objectionable. One of my critics suggests that the totality of risk is increased when a business borrows and that even the NOI Method is optimistic.

straightforward. Those who adhere strictly to this method contend: first, that *conservative* increases in bonded debt do not increase the risk borne by the common stockholders; second, that a package of securities containing a *conservative* proportion of bonds will justifiably command a higher market price than a package of common stock alone. The first contention seems to have little merit; it runs counter to the rigorous analysis offered by the advocates of the NOI Method; and it seems to imply that the security holders of a business can raise themselves by their own bootstraps. Clearly, this contention is a somewhat tempered version of the type of analysis described in Chart 1.[9] The second contention appears to be correct, however, and it certainly merits critical analysis.

Since many investors in the modern world are seriously circumscribed in their actions, there is an opportunity to increase the total investment value of an enterprise by effective bond financing. Economic theorists are fond of saying that in a perfectly fluid world one function of the market is to equalize risks on all investments. If the yield differential between two securities should be greater than the apparent risk differential, arbitragers would rush into the breach and promptly restore the yield differential to its proper value. But in our world, arbitragers may have insufficient funds to do their job because so many investors are deterred from buying stocks or low-grade bonds, either by law, by personal circumstance, by income taxes, or even by pure prejudice. These restricted investors, including all banks and insurance companies, have to bid for high-grade investments almost without regard to yield differentials or the attractiveness of the lower grade investments. And these restricted investors have sufficient funds to maintain yield differentials well above risk differentials. The result is a sort of super premium for safety; and a corporation management can take advantage of this super premium by issuing as many bonds as it can maintain at a high rating grade.

Therefore, a theoretical compromise between the two methods is entirely feasible. One can agree with the advocates of the NOI Method that the totality of risk inherent in the securities of a single company always remains the same, regardless of the capitalization; and one can agree with the advocates of the NI Method that the market will actually and justifiably pay more for the same totality of risk if the company is judicially capitalized with bonds

[9] The argument illustrated in Chart I implies that a business can incur any amount of debt without increasing the proprietors' risk. Recognizing that this is a practical absurdity, the advocates of the NI Method say merely that a business can incur a limited amount of debt without increasing the proprietors' risk.

For example, Benjamin Graham and David L. Dodd, in their book, *Security Analysis* (McGraw-Hill Book Co., second edition, 1940, p. 542), show the effect of indebtedness on earnings by comparing two hypothetical companies. Company A has no bonds at all, and Company B has a conservative bond issue with interest covered more than four times. Because of the leverage imposed by the bond issue, the earnings per common share of Company B fluctuate somewhat more than the earnings per share of Company A. Concerning this, the authors say: "Would it not be fair to assume that the greater sensitivity of Company B to a possible decline in profits is offset by its greater sensitivity to a possible increase?" However, the authors point out that this argument is valid only so long as the indebtedness does not jeopardize the solvency of the company. Should interest be covered only twice (this is an industrial company) the bonds would not be safe and should sell at substantially less than par. The discussion of this point in the third edition of *Security Analysis* (1951, pp. 464 ff.) has been somewhat modified.

and stock, and no inconsistency whatsoever will be introduced.

To illustrate this type of compromise, suppose it could be determined that well protected bonds like those of the PDQ Company should be valued at 5 percent if there were no super premium for safety.[10] That is, a 5 percent differential between bonds at 5 percent and stock at 10 percent would just compensate for the risk differential. Suppose further that the demand for bonds by the restricted investors is sufficient to permit floating the 4 percent bonds of the PDQ Company at par. Hence, 1 percent is the super premium that the restricted investors must pay for safety. But since the stockholders of the PDQ Company have no need to pay this premium, they are justified in writing down the value of their bonds to a 5 percent basis. That is, $5 million of 4 percent bonds would be valued at $4 million in estimating the value of the common stock (because a 4 percent bond is worth 80 at 5 percent). The implied calculations are as follows:

Net operating income	$ 2,000,000
Capitalization rate	× 10
	20,000,000
Stockholders' valuation of bonds (5 percent basis)	4,000,000
Value of common stock	16,000,000
Restricted investors' valuation of bonds (4 percent basis)	5,000,000
Total investment value	$21,000,000

If similar calculations are made for other assumed debt loads—say $2 million, $1 million, and no debt at all—the following values for common stock and total investment value will result:

This implies that whenever $1 million in stock is funded into bonds, the total investment value will be increased $200,000 thereby. Naturally, this relation will not continue indefinitely, because the restricted investors and the market will not pay a super premium for safety if the volume of bonds is too high for adequate coverage.

In all of these calculations the amount of the super premium—1 percent—was arbitrarily assumed, and almost any other amount would have served equally well for illustration. The results, however, would have been different. An increase in the super premium would result in an increase in the value of the stock and the total investment value. This is illustrated graphi-

CHART 4

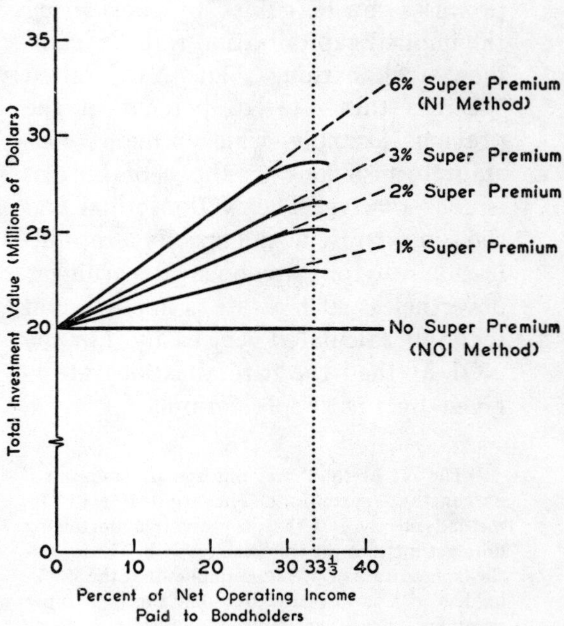

Face value of bonds[11]	None	$ 1,000,000	$ 2,000,000
Value of common stock	$20,000,000	19,200,000	18,400,000
Total investment value	$20,000,000	$20,200,000	$20,400,000

[10] In making this suggestion, I am not ignoring the practical difficulties of actually estimating this super premium.

[11] Assumed equal to the restricted investors' valuation, also the market valuation.

cally in Chart 4, which contains curves showing the relation between total investment value and debt load for five different super premiums. It is interesting to note that a super premium of zero implies the NOI Method, and a super premium of 6 percent is equivalent to the NI Method.[12] Thus it appears that the two methods may be regarded as optimistic and pessimistic extremes between which a more realistic compromise probably lies. However, the difference between the extremes is so great—as will become evident in subsequent discussion of the *RR*—that the choice of a compromise is subject to great leeway.

Further insight into the differences between the NOI Method, the NI Method, and the described set of compromises can be gained by considering the implied capitalization rate for common stock earnings. The NI Method specifies this rate—10 percent in the previous example—which remains constant just so long as the debt burden is conservative. The NOI Method and the compromise do not specify a capitalization rate for common stock earnings; nevertheless such a rate is implied, and it can be calculated very easily. For the NOI Method the capitalization rate is given by the simple formula[13]

$$\frac{1 - P}{10 - 25P}$$

where (P) is the proportion of NOI required for bond interest, the figure 10 is the reciprocal of the 10 percent rate for net operating income, and the figure 25 is the reciprocal of the 4 percent bond rate. For a compromise appraisal assuming a 1 percent super premium, this fraction becomes

$$\frac{1 - P}{10 - 20P}$$

where the figure 20 is the reciprocal of the assumed 5 percent bond rate that would apply if the bonds did not command a super premium. Curves showing the capitalization rates for three appraisal methods at different levels of bond capitalization appear in Chart 5. The point at which the NI curve starts to turn up and the shape of the curve after this point are, of course, conjectural. The other two curves simply represent the mathematical relationships derived above.

2 *Effect of Appraisal Method on Required Return*

If the stockholders (or management) of the PDQ Company should consider raising a moderate amount of new money to finance expansion, they might appropriately ask whether the investment value of their holdings would be enhanced thereby, and they might further ask whether stocks or bonds would

---

[12]The NI Method does not actually imply a 6 percent superpremium. The advocates of the method merely say that conservative borrowing does not increase the stockholders' risk. The idea of the 6 percent super premium implies that the stockholders' risk is increased but that the high super premium—clearly excessive—completely compensates for this risk.

[13]Let (N) be the net operating income and let (B) be the bond interest. Then $10N$ is the total investment value, $25B$ is the value of the bonds, and $10N—25B$ is the value of the stock. The capitalization rate is determined by dividing the net income ($N—B$) by the value of the stock, thus

$$\frac{NB -}{10N - 25B}$$

This fraction can be transformed into the form appearing in the text by letting $P = \frac{B}{N}$, which is the proportion of net operating income required for bond interest.

CHART 5

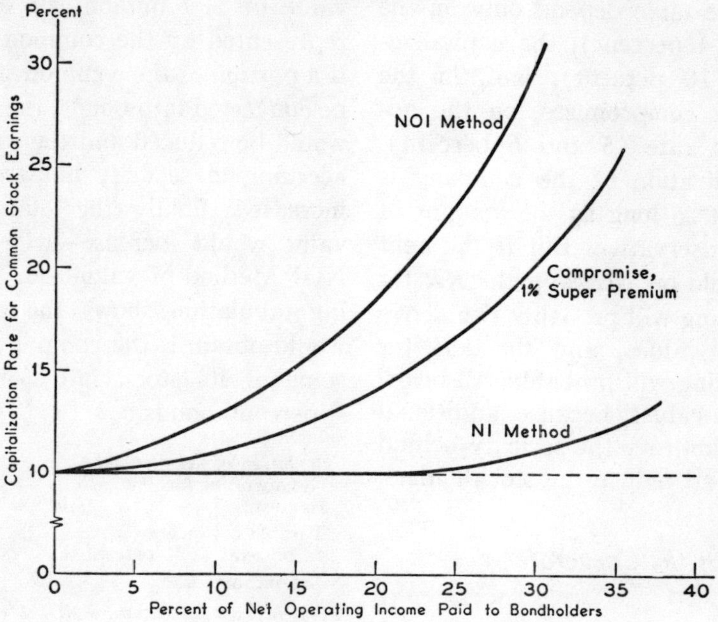

offer the more effective medium. If the stockholders should attempt to use the principle of the *RR* to answer either of these questions, they would discover startling differences in the *RR* for bond financing depending upon the appraisal method used, but they would discover no such differences in the *RR* for stock financing.[14] The following table shows the actual results of calculating *RR*'s on the assumption that 4 percent bonds can be sold at par and that additional common stock can be sold on a 10 percent basis.[15]

	Bonds	*Stock*
NI Method	4%	10%
NOI Method	10	10
Compromise, 1 percent super premium	8	10
Compromise, 2 percent super premium	6⅔	10

[14]I do not wish to imply that all conceivable methods of stock appraisal will result in identical *RR*'s for stock financing. But the NI Method, the NOI Method, and a compromise of the general type described will result in identical *RR*'s.

[15]To illustrate the process, *RR's* for both stock financing and bond financing under the compromise method will be calculated here. Let s be the number of shares of stock, v the investment value per share, N the net operating income, and B the total bond interest. The total investment value is given by the equation

$$sv = 10N - 20B$$

If an additional share of stock is sold at a price equal to v, and if the proceeds are invested, net operating income will increase by an amount ΔN. The *RR* is obtained from solving the equation

$$(s + 1)\ v = 10\ (N + \Delta N) - 20B$$

or

$$v = 10\ \Delta N$$

This means that the additional share must earn 10 percent on its sale price to justify the expansion.

If, on the other hand, an additional 4 percent bond were sold, the interest expense would increase by an amount ΔB, and the equation for determining the *RR* would become

The reader should note that the *RR*'s in the above table depend only on the bond rate (4 percent), the capitalization rate (10 percent), and, in the case of the compromises, on the adjusted bond rate (5 and 6 percent). The capitalization of the company is not relevant so long as the amount of bonds is conservative. But if the debt burden should be excessive, the *RR* for bond financing will probably rise above the quoted values, and the *RR* for stock financing will probably fall below the quoted values because additional equity will improve the security behind the bonds and reduce the stockholders' risk.

3 *Effects of the Corporate Income Tax*

To complete the preceding discussion requires at least brief mention of the corporate income tax. Since bond interest is a deductible expense, the corporation can attain definite tax advantages by bond financing. To illustrate, consider the following abbreviated income statement for an assumed debt-free company.

Sales	$30,000,000
Cost of goods sold	26,666,667
Net operating income (taxable)	3,333,333
Income tax at 40 percent[16]	1,333,333
Net income	$ 2,000,000

If the $2 million net is capitalized at 10 percent, as in the previous examples, the result is a total investment value of $20 million, all of which is represented by the common stock. But if a portion of the common stock should be converted into bonds, the income tax would be reduced and the total amount accruing to security holders would be increased; finally, the total investment value would increase—even under the NOI Method of valuation. The following tabulation shows the results that would obtain if the company converted some of its stock into $5 million of 4 percent bonds.

Calculation of net income:	
Net operating income	$ 3,333,333
Interest	200,000
Taxable net income	3,133,333
Income tax at 40 percent	1,253,333
Net income	$ 1,880,000
Total investment value by NOI Method:	
Net income	$1,880,000
Interest	200,000
Total claims of security holders	2,080,000
Capitalization factor	10
Total investment value	$20,800,000
Total investment value by NI Method:	
Net income	$ 1,880,000
Capitalization factor	10
Value of common stock	18,800,000
Value of bonds	5,000,000
Total investment value	$23,800,000

The advantages of bond financing under the income tax are further illustrated by the *RR*'s shown in the table below. In a tax-free world there might be some doubt about the advantages of bond financing; if the NOI Method should be accepted rigidly, the *RR* for bond financing would exactly equal that for stock financing. But with the corporate income tax the *RR* for bond financing is less than that for stock financing, regardless of the method of evaluation. Furthermore, it is noteworthy that the income tax has the effect of increasing the discrepancy

---

$$sv = 10\,(N + \Delta N) - 20\,(B + \Delta B)$$

or $$0 = 10\,\Delta N - 20\,\Delta B$$

or again $$\Delta N = 2\,\Delta B$$

This means that the new investment must earn twice the rate of interest, or 8 percent.

[16]For the hypothetical examples in this paper, 40 percent is considered a satisfactory approximation to the 38 percent corporation rate — particularly since 40 percent is actually the rate for consolidated returns.

	No Tax[17]	40 Percent Tax[18]
Bond financing, NI Method	4%	4%
Bond financing, NOI Method	10	14
Stock financing, either method	10	16⅔

between the NI Method and the NOI Method. In the real world, therefore, the choice of a proper method of stock appraisal is even more important than in the theoretical world described previously, where income taxes were assumed nonexistent.

4 *Implications for Research*

The foregoing analysis indicates that significant research in problems involving the cost of capital will be seriously handicapped so long as the conflict between the NI Method and the NOI Method remains unresolved. Of course, limited research can probably be done now on the cost of common stock financing because the importance of the valuation problem is much less with common stock financing. A discussion of this problem will appear in the next section. But some of the more significant financial problems of the day involve cost comparisons between bond financing and equity financing—including both stock flotations and retentions—and attempts to make such comparisons without first solving the problem of valuation will probably prove futile and misleading. If a research worker wants to suggest that stock financing is much more costly than bond financing, he can do so very easily by accepting the NI Method, which necessarily implies that the cost of bond financing is roughly equal to the long-term interest rate and that the cost of stock financing is roughly equal to the earnings-price ratio for common stocks. But in doing this, he will probably incur bitter, and on the whole justified, criticism from those who favor the NOI Method—and possibly from some of those who favor a compromise.

As an example, Chart 6 traces the

[17]These are the *RR*'s derived on p. 105.

[18]For bond financing, it is obvious that the *RR* will equal the interest rate under the NI Method. As long as the new investment can earn enough to meet the additional interest burden, the earnings for the common stock will not suffer — taxes or no taxes. It is not quite so obvious that the *RR* for stock financing is equal to 16⅔ percent regardless of appraisal method, but this matter will be amplified further in Section III. Finally, the *RR* for bond financing under the NOI Method will be derived here.

When the hypothetical company is capitalized with $5 million of 4 percent bonds, the total investment value is $20,800,000 as shown, which leaves $15,800,000 for the common stock. If the company sells one more $1,000 bond, the value of the common stock must remain unchanged, and to this end the new investment must earn $140. The following calculations show this.

Value of stock	$15,800,000
Value of bonds after expansion	5,001,000
Total investment value	20,801,000
Required for interest and stock earnings, 10 percent of the above	2,080,100
Bond interest	200,040
Required net income after taxes	1,880,060
Tax	1,253,373
Required taxable income	3,133,433
Interest	200,040
Required net operating income	3,333,473
Net operating income previously available	3,333,333
Additional net operating income required per $1,000	*$140*

CHART 6

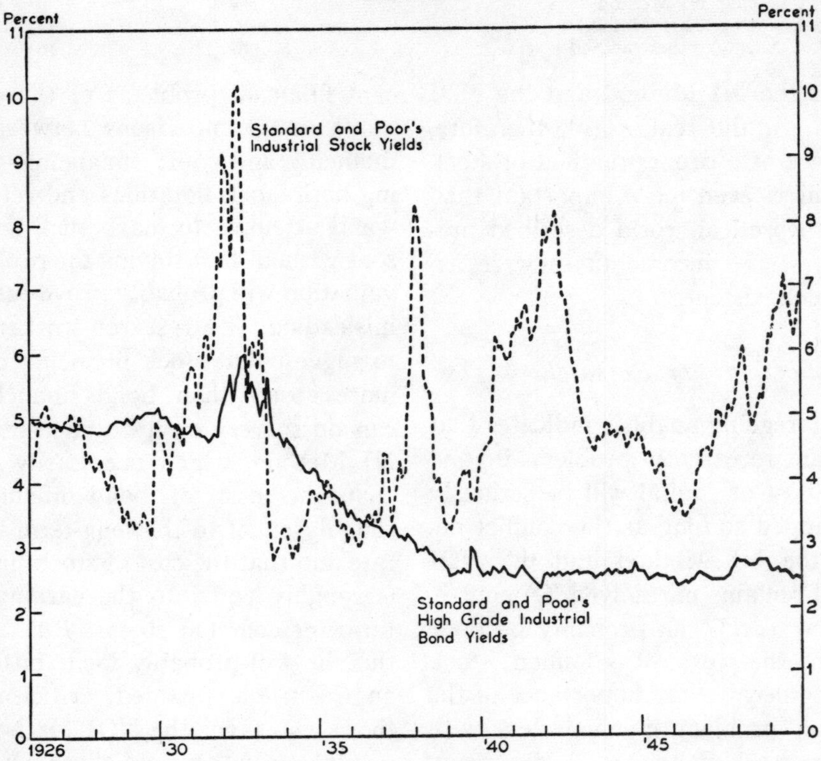

yields of industrial stocks and high-grade industrial bonds from 1926 through 1949.[19] Charts of this type are sometimes used as evidence that the cost of equity capital in relation to debt capital has been substantially higher in the postwar years than in the late twenties. It is true, of course, that this chart is deficient in a number of details: 1) stock yields, which reflect dividends paid, could be adjusted for earnings; 2) stock yields could also be adjusted for the corporate income tax, and 3) both stock and bond yields could be adjusted for flotation expenses. The net effect of all these adjustments would probably increase the apparent cost of equity in the postwar years. But unfortunately, even when these adjustments are made, the chart is still deficient because the basic methodology is not valid unless the NI Method of valuation is wholeheartedly accepted.

5 *Implications for Business Cycle Theory*

According to some writers on business cycle theory the interest rate plays the strategic role of alternately encouraging and discouraging investment. Furthermore, these writers argue, the central monetary authority can exert a substantial stabilizing influence on business by artificially raising the interest

[19]The chart was made up from Standard and Poor's stock and bond yields. The actual figures plotted are averages for the middle month of each quarter — that is, February, May, August, and November.

rate in prosperous periods and lowering it in depressed periods. Clearly, the force of this argument depends upon a tacit assumption that the cost of raising capital is approximately equal to the interest rate. This, in turn, necessitates another assumption accepting the NI Method, for only with this method is the cost of borrowing equal to the interest rate. Hence, the rejection of the NI Method in favor of the NOI Method, or even one of the compromises previously discussed, would cast grave doubts upon the strategic force of the interest rate in economic life. In particular, if the NOI Method should be rigidly accepted, the interest rate would lose virtually all its significance, and in place of it the stock rate (earnings-price ratio) would emerge as the number one determinant of investment on the cost side.

The preceding analysis may throw new light on a statement by John Maynard Keynes concerning easy money policy. It was Keynes' opinion that easy money would provide little stimulus to business in depressions because the marginal efficiency of capital is apt to be extremely low at such times.[20] Keynes was probably right, but perhaps for the wrong reason. He may have misjudged the importance of cost as a determinant of investment. If businessmen accept the NOI Method of valuation, either explicitly or subconsciously, the *RR* for new investment will be extremely high during depressions because of low stock prices, and lowering the interest rate will have almost no effect. Possibly, therefore, the high cost of raising capital may discourage new investment during depressions quite as much as the low marginal efficiency of capital. In everyday language, this merely means that businessmen are loath to incur obligations during a depression, and they will not do so, regardless of the interest rate, unless they can expect a return even higher than the one they would expect in a period of prosperity.[21]

III A BRIEF ANALYSIS OF EQUITY FINANCING

Viewed as a whole, equity financing includes four general types of transactions: common stock flotations, preferred stock flotations, use of earnings retained from operations, and the conversion of rights or other instruments into common stock. This section, however, will deal only with common stock flotations and the retention of earnings. Furthermore, the treatment is extremely sketchy and serves mainly to amplify and fill in the preceding sections.

1 *Variations in Common Stock Financing*

The technique of common stock financing varies considerably from flotation to flotation. This is due partly to state laws, partly to market conditions, and partly to matters of taste and judgment. Sometimes a whole stock issue is sold directly to a syndicate, which has the sole responsibility for distributing

[20]See *The General Theory of Employment, Interest, and Money* (Harcourt, Brace and Co., 1936), p. 316. Here Keynes says: "It is this, indeed, which renders the slump so intractable. Later on, a decline in the rate of interest will be a great aid to recovery and, probably, a necessary condition of it. But for the moment, the collapse in the marginal efficiency of capital may be so complete that no practicable reduction in the rate of interest will be enough."

[21] Using Keynes' language, we might say that businessmen have "a propensity not to borrow" during depressions.

the issue to the public. At the other extreme, an issue is sometimes sold directly to the stockholders through nonmarketable pre-emptive rights with no provision for public sale. More often, however, a combination method is worked out, which may include the issue of marketable pre-emptive rights and the services of an underwriting syndicate to guarantee sale of the entire issue. Since the technique of the flotation may affect costs and *RR*'s, two examples are worked out here: one describing a straight public sale without rights, the other describing a sale to the stockholders through rights, under the assumption that the stockholders exercise their rights.

2 *Stock Flotation by Direct Sale to the Public*

Table 3 contains a hypothetical balance sheet and income statement. Suppose that the stockholders and management of the XYZ Company see an attractive opportunity to buy additional facilities for $5 million. Suppose further that the management opposes depleting the corporate cash reserves and that the stockholders have no available cash themselves; hence it is necessary to sell securities on the open market, and the management elects to sell common stock. Suppose, finally, that the corporation stock is currently selling on the market at 23 and that a syndicate agrees to sell additional stock at 22 (to allow for a bad market), charging a commission of $2.00 a share for the service. The corporation would, therefore, receive $20.00 net for each share sold, and it would have to sell 250,000 new shares to raise the required $5 million. What is the *RR?*

Probably the simplest solution is to calculate a "market capitalization rate"

TABLE 3

BALANCE SHEET OF THE XYZ MANUFACTURING COMPANY

Assets		
Cash	$ 6,000,000	
Accounts receivable	5,000,000	
Inventory	4,000,000	
Total Current	15,000,000	
Plant and equipment, less depreciation	15,000,000	
TOTAL		$30,000,000
Liabilities		
Accrued items	$ 1,000,000	
Accounts payable	4,000,000	
Total Current	5,000,000	
Common stock, 1,000,000 shares at $15 per share	15,000,000	
Surplus	10,000,000	
	25,000,000	
TOTAL		$30,000,000

INCOME STATEMENT OF THE XYZ MANUFACTURING COMPANY

Sales	$11,000,000	
Cost of goods sold	6,000,000	
Net operating income		$5,000,000
Income tax		2,000,000
Net Income		3,000,000
Annual dividends		1,000,000
Transfer to Surplus		$2,000,000

by dividing the market price of 23 into the per share earnings of $3.00. The result is 13.04 percent, or 7.66 times earnings. This provides a suitable multiplier if: 1) the market appraisal is considered correct; 2) the market is expected to continue to appraise the stock at the same rate after expansion (except possibly for a short period during the offering, when the stock may fall to about 22); 3) the dividend rate can be ignored; and 4) individual differences among stockholders, say tax status, can be ignored. By means of this capitalization rate, the following calculations show that the new investment must earn $1,250,000 before taxes—or exactly 25 percent on the additional $5 million—in order to maintain the value of the stock at 23.

ESTIMATED NEW INVESTMENT EARNINGS

Required value per share	$23.00
Capitalization rate	.1304
Required net earnings per share	*$3.00*
Total net earnings, 1,250,000 shares	$3,750,000
Income tax at 40 percent [22]	2,500,000
Total required earnings before tax	6,250,000
Previous earnings before tax	5,000,000
Earnings required on new investments	*$1,250,000*

The above calculations were made in a somewhat roundabout fashion to illustrate an important point: *For debt-free companies selling stock on the open market, the RR will be the same regardless of what capitalization rate is used.* For example, the stockholders might consider that the market undervalued their stock, and they might prefer to capitalize earnings at 10 percent, which would make the stock worth $30.00.[23] The above calculations would have to be changed in two respects only: the required price per share ($30.00) and the capitalization rate (10 percent). These two changes would exactly offset each other, and the required earnings per share would remain $3.00. The subsequent calculations would remain unchanged. All this implies that for debt-free companies selling common stock on the open market, the *RR* is the rate of return required to maintain the original per share earnings—at $3.00 in this example.[24]

This neutral role of the capitalization rate has important practical implications because it considerably simplifies measurement. In actual security appraisal the analyst is ordinarily plagued by two troublesome problems: 1) the estimation of a satisfactory figure for expected earnings, and 2) the choice of a capitalization rate. But if the capitalization rate has no effect on the *RR* for specified types of stock financing, the problem of choosing such a rate can sometimes be sidestepped.

The problem of estimating earnings remains a serious one, however. Actual

[22]For these simple examples 40 percent is a satisfactory approximation to the current 38 percent rate, particularly since 40 percent is actually the rate for consolidated returns.

[23]It is not only possible but quite likely that the stockholders of a company will value their stock at higher than the market price. If they did not put a higher value on their stock, why would they continue to hold it? The reader is apt to ask at this point: "Well, then, why don't they buy more stock in the market and drive the price up to 30"? The answer is simple. The stockholders are limited by the amount of their resources and the need for diversification.

[24]This principle is not strictly true for indebted companies when the NOI Method is used, or for stock flotations with pre-emptive rights. But it appears to be approximately true. I gather this from investigation of two or three examples, which suggest that very large variations in the capitalization rate have a small effect on the calculated *RR* for stock financing in general. This question might bear further investigation.

reported earnings are often not satisfactory because future earnings are more important to stockholders than past earnings. This was brought out dramatically in the early thirties, when many corporations were running deficits and passing dividends; yet their stock was selling substantially above zero on the belief that these corporations had long-run positive earning power. If one should attempt to calculate *RR*'s for the thirties on the basis of the reported deficits, he would obtain perfectly meaningless results. And if he should contemplate estimating the normal, long-run earning power of corporations as it appeared to investors during the thirties—which is the desired figure—he would be facing an almost impossible task.

3 *A Stock Flotation with Pre-emptive Rights*

In the preceding example, the stockholders had inadequate cash reserves, example, however, the stockholders are and the new issue had to be sold on the market by a syndicate. In the following assumed to have sufficient cash to permit buying the issue directly from the company through pre-emptive rights. Suppose that the stockholders are given the right to buy one new share at $21.00 for each four shares held, and that the costs of the flotation are $1.00 a share so that the company again realizes $20.00. This transaction is equivalent to the exchange of $21.00 in cash and four old shares worth $23.00—total $113.00—for five new shares. If the stockholders are not to suffer from the exchange, the five new shares must also be worth $113.00—or $22.60 a share. The necessary calculations for the *RR* are similar to those in the preceding example, except that the required value per share is $22.60 instead of $23.00. The *RR* in this case is $1,141,314 or 22.8 percent. The slightly lower *RR* in this example is due to two factors: 1) the out-of-pocket flotation expenses were assumed to be lower by this method;[25] 2) the opportunity to buy new stock at slightly less than the market price was exercised by the old stockholders, rather than by outsiders, as in the preceding example.

4 *Financing with Cash Earned and Accumulated*

This example serves mainly to show that business retentions should not be regarded as a costless source of capital. Retentions are costless in one sense only: the management incurs no out-of-pocket expenses as it would in floating securities or arranging a loan. But in almost any other sense retentions involve costs like those in other forms of financing. When a management sells stock to the public, it incurs an obligation, through tacit understanding, to invest the proceeds wisely and earn a return for the stockholders. If later the management elects to retain earnings that could be conveniently paid out in dividends, these entail a very clear opportunity cost; for the stockholder loses the opportunity to invest whatever portion of his share of earnings the management chooses to retain. Furthermore, if the management retains earnings and invests them unwisely, the stockholders may incur a very real cost, for the unwise reinvestment of earnings may actually depress the value of the stock.

[25]This is not meant to imply that costs of flotation are typically less for issues floated by means of pre-emptive rights. In fact, a worthwhile project would be to compare actual costs incurred in open market flotations as against pre-emptive rights flotations.

As presented in Table 3, the XYZ Company earned $3 million, or $3.00 a share, and paid out one-third of this in dividends. What is to be done with the remainder? For the purpose of this discussion, it is assumed that the management has only two choices: 1) to pay an extra dividend of $2.00 a share on one million shares of stock, and 2) to divert this money to purchase $2 million worth of new equipment. Which course is more advantageous to the stockholders, provided it is assumed further that the ample cash balance of the XYZ Company can stand the drain of $2 million without impairing liquidity?

The ensuing discussion rests entirely on the assumption of perfect freedom of choice on the part of the management. Yet in practical affairs managements often do not have such freedom. When a corporation has a low current ratio, its management may have to restrict dividends, even though earned, merely to avoid insolvency. A corporation management may also have to restrict dividends, even though earned, because the terms of a loan agreement or bond indenture stipulate that working capital must be maintained at a specified level. Thus a corporation is sometimes virtually forced to retain earnings. In such instances, it is hardly pertinent to ask which course is more advantageous to the stockholders, and it might be misleading to carry through an estimate of the required return in the manner described below. Clearly this entire question of the costs of retentions is a complicated one, requiring a great deal of thoughtful investigation. The present analysis is merely by way of introduction.

But when there is freedom of choice the management may appropriately consider whether the cash would be worth more converted into plant than it would be as cash in the hands of the stockholders. One factor affecting the decision should be the rate of return earnable on the new investment. If the return is low, the stockholders will be better off to receive the dividends and invest the proceeds in other securities; if the rate is high, they will be better off to have the corporation retain the cash.

Another factor that should affect the decision is the incidence of the personal income tax on stockolders. But taking the personal income tax into account is extremely difficult for two reasons: 1) the great variability in rates between the high income brackets and the low income brackets, and 2) the uncertainty of the eventual tax status of possible capital gains that may arise if the corporation invests its retained cash successfully.[26] Therefore, to obain an estimate of the *RR* on the new investment requires one arbitrary assumption concerning the income tax bracket to be represented and another concerning the capital gains tax. To make the calculations as simple as possible, it is assumed that the personal income tax on the cash dividend is 50 percent and that the possibility of an eventual capital gains tax may be ignored.

If the cash dividend is paid, the typical stockholder will have, say, 100 shares of stock worth $23.00 a share[27]

[26]For example, if the typical stockholder holds his stock until death, say twenty years hence, how will his estate be taxed at that time?

[27]Some readers may feel that the previously assumed market price of $23.00 a share should reflect the payment of the $2.00 dividend, and that the stock should be worth less than $23.00 after the

and $100.00 in cash after taxes—a total of $2,400 or $24.00 a share. If the cash is retained, the stockholder will have only his shares, which he hopes will be worth at least $24.00. If the shares are to be worth $24.00, the new investment will have to earn $216,667 or 10.8 percent, as shown below.

Required value per share	$24.00
Capitalization rate	.1304
Required earnings per share	*$ 3.13*
Required earnings, 1,000,000 shares	$3,130,000
Income tax at 40 percent	2,086,667
Required earnings before tax	5,216,667
Income previously available	5,000,000
Additional income required	*$ 216,667*

The *RR* in this example is ever so much lower than in the previous examples, where *RR*'s of over 20 percent resulted. This substantial difference is due mainly to the personal income tax, although the avoidance of out-of-pocket flotation costs is also a factor. If there had been no personal income tax, the stockholders would have enjoyed the entire $2.00 dividend—which, with their stock worth $23.00 a share, would have totaled $25.00. Therefore, the new investment would have to earn $433,333 or 21.6 percent. This is exactly twice as much as the *RR* when the personal income tax is 50 percent. Although it is doubtful whether corporate officials go through these specific calculations in considering use of retained earnings—when choice is possible—they seem to be generally aware that substantial tax savings are possible through the use of retentions.

dividend, say $22.00. This would involve a recalculation of the *RR* to ascertain what rate of return on the new investment would be required to make the stock worth $23.00.

5 *Equity Financing in Conjunction with Debt Financing*

In all the examples discussed heretofore, *RR*'s were calculated on the supposition that the corporation management had to choose one from among such single possibilities as a bond flotation, a stock flotation, or use of retained earnings. Often, however, financing is a combined process involving both debt and equity in various forms and proportions, and as such it presents an intricate problem in joint costs. What would have been the *RR*, or the cost by any other standard, if the XYZ Company had decided to finance its $5 million plant expansion by 1) using $1 million of its own cash, 2) floating $2 million in bonds, 3) by curtailing dividends until the final $2 million could be retained? Could an *RR* or some other measure of cost be determined for the entire transaction? And could the total cost, however determined, be effectively allocated among the three separate sources of funds? This last question is particularly pertinent to the problem of public utility regulation.

This paper does not propose to discuss joint costs beyond merely mentioning them. The problem clearly exists, and it is probably formidable. With joint costs, as with simple costs for a single form of financing, the solution of the problem certainly hinges upon the valuation of business enterprises.

IV CONCLUSION

This paper is limited to a single phase of economic behavior—the financing of assets and the costs incurred therein. By means of a few simple examples I have tried to prove the following proposition: *Given a method of security ap-*

praisal, the costs of raising capital can be both defined and measured. At the same time I have tried to show that there is at present no generally accepted system of appraisal; hence there can be no generally accepted system of measuring costs. It would certainly appear that the first step toward the specific problem of measuring costs is to focus more research on the general problem of appraisal.

"But," the reader is apt to ask at this point, "is there no way to sidestep the appraisal problem and deal with costs directly"? Personally, I think not, though I know of no absolutely conclusive proof. However, any research worker who tries to deal directly with costs is in great danger of falling into one of two rather obvious traps. The first is to define costs in an arbitrary fashion that is amenable to statistical research but irrelevant for economic analysis. An example is the definition of cost currently accepted by many accountants, according to which bond interest is a cost while dividends, even cumulative preferred dividends, are not. If one should accept this definition, he will find a plethora of statistics and a relatively easy problem of measurement, but the "costs" he thus measures will not help him explain the volume of asset expansion or the current preference for debt financing.

The second trap awaiting the unwary research worker is to define costs in a fashion that implies some definite method of appraisal. If, for example, he defines common stock cost as the earnings-price ratio (adjusted for flotation expenses) and bond cost as the interest rate (also adjusted for flotation expenses), he implies the NI Method of valuation; furthermore, he probably implies a belief that borrowing does not entail risk to the borrower. How many of those who support this last definition of cost would also support the view that borrowing entails no extra risk?

Research on the problem of business appraisal does not promise to be easy, by any means. The discussion in this paper has laid chief emphasis on the conflict between the NI Method and the NOI Method of capitalizing earnings. Possibly, this created an impression of oversimplification. Actually, I do not believe that either method, strictly interpreted, is adequate or correct, although I definitely lean in the direction of the NOI Method. But if the NOI Method should be accepted in principle, modifications would almost certainly be required. These might include adjustments for working capital, for book value, and for the super premium for safety, any of which would require careful thought and perhaps considerable statistical analysis.

At the present time, the most fertile field for research on the appraisal problem is probably in the organized security markets. A statistical study of security pricing would probably yield valuable clues for a long-range analysis of capital costs, and it would have the immediate advantage of providing technical information for security analysts and financiers. As conceived here, such a study should be concerned with what might be called "market appraisal," and it would cover such questions as the following: How does an underwriting syndicate arrive at a price to bid for a new security issue? How do investors and traders in the market arrive at prices to bid for traded issues? To what extent do security prices in the market exhibit definite relationships to pertinent factors like earnings prospects and interest coverage? Do the observed relationships imply some specific system of appraisal in use by traders and investors and, if so, is the implied system reasonable? Or, perhaps, is there evidence of many systems? To what extent do traders overlook opportunities for arbitrage between securities?

At the same time a general reformulation of basic economic principles would be highly desirable. What we need is a theory that takes better account of the problem of appraising risks incurred in business expansion. If a project for reformulating basic theory could be incorporated into a statistical analysis of security pricing, two desirable results might be achieved: first, the interpretation of the statistical findings would be less liable to error; second, a truly functional theory of business enterprise would be more likely to emerge.

Discussion:

CLAY J. ANDERSON, *Federal Reserve Bank of Philadelphia*

Mr. Durand's paper represents a fresh approach to the problem of measuring the cost of debt and equity financing, and makes some interesting observations. However, I find myself in disagreement with the basic principles presented by the author.

He states, in his preface to the article, that although his opinions were revised as the paper developed, he expects to stand by two general principles: our basic economic theory needs revision; and security appraisal is the key to measuring the cost of capital. I shall limit my remarks to three main topics—the two general principles just just noted and a few suggestions for research in this area which might be helpful.

Reformulation of Economic Theory

Why does economic theory need revising? If I interpret Mr. Durand's paper correctly, there are two primary reasons. One is that present economic theory proceeds on the assumption that the businessman tries to maximize his income. For example, Mr. Durand states: "Economic theory has used the principle of maximizing income to demonstrate that business expansion will proceed until the marginal return on capital equals the rate of interest." Two major criticisms of this principle are made. In the first place, the principle of maximizing income is "totally meaningless in any world in which income is expected to change." Actually, a businessman planning an investment must compare not only the amount of the additional income expected, but also its time distribution. Since the income from the investment may build up only slowly, the businessman tries "to maximize the discounted value of his future income" instead of maximizing his income.

A second revision is necessary, according to the author, to take account of risk. For example, stockholders considering a bond issue to finance an expansion program must balance the greater return against the greater risk incurred. They can do so by estimating the investment value of their stock. The author then illustrates, by assuming certain per share earnings and the change in the capitalization rate to compensate for the additional risk incurred, how much earnings would have to increase to maintain the investment value of the outstanding stock and therefore to make it worth the stockholders' while to make the additional investment. In short, the illustration really shows how much the per share earnings would have to increase to compensate for the assumed risk incurred by the additional borrowing.

I would like to point out that economic theory, at least in the writings of some well-known authors, has for many years taken these points concerning time distribution and risk into consideration. Irving Fisher, for example, gave a detailed analysis of them in his book *The Rate of Interest*, published in 1907.[1] His theory incorporating the time and risk elements in investment principles was further refined in his book *The Theory of Interest*, published in 1930.[2]

Fisher starts with the general principle that the decision to invest involves comparing optional income streams. In arriving at a decision, the potential investor asks "what difference it makes" which alternative is chosen—difference in terms of disadvantages incurred (costs) for advantages gained (returns). Fisher states that "by cost is meant the comparative loss from one's income stream at first caused by substituting one use of capital for another, and by return is meant the comparative gain which accrues, usually later, by reason of this same substitution. . . . It applies to every possible cost and every possible return."[3] The first approximation of his investment opportunity principle is developed on the assumption that the income stream flowing from any given investment is both fixed and certain. Under these conditions, he says, there is an inducement to invest if the marginal return over cost at present values is equal to or greater than the rate of interest. Recognizing that these assumed conditions do not exist in the real world, he modifies his investment opportunity principle to take account of both the time shape and risk elements.

In his second approximation to the theory of interest, Fisher introduces the fact that optional income streams may differ in size and time shape.[4] In the third approximation, his theory is modified to take into consideration the risk factor or uncertainty.[5] Finally, he arrives at the principle that through investment opportunities one is afforded optional income streams which "differ in size, time shape, composition, and *risk*." The potential investor will select the one which has the maximum present value and will tend to push investment to the point where the "marginal rate of *anticipated* return over cost" tends to equal the rate of interest.[6]

J. M. Keynes is another well-known writer who incorporated these points into his theory.[7] Keynes stated, for example, that Fisher's "rate of return

[1]Irving Fisher, *The Rate of Interest* (Macmillan, 1907), especially Chapters 7, 8, and 11.

[2]Irving Fisher, *The Theory of Interest* (Macmillan, 1930), especially Chapters 7, 8, and 9.

[3]*The Rate of Interest,* Chapter 7; *The Theory of Interest,* pp. 154-58.

[4]*The Rate of Interest,* Chapter 8; *The Theory of Interest,* Chapter 8.

[5]*The Rate of Interest,* Chapter 11; *The Theory of Interest,* Chapter 9.

[6]*The Theory of Interest,* p. 223. Author's italics.

[7]John Maynard Keynes, *The General Theory of Employment, Interest, and Money* (Harcourt, Brace and Co., 1936), pp. 140-41.

over cost" was "identical" with his definition of the "marginal efficiency of capital." He also stressed that the marginal efficiency of capital fluctuates greatly during the business cycle, mainly because of swings in expectations.[8]

These few illustrations are in no sense intended, of course, as a complete coverage of the extent to which economic theory deals with the points raised in Mr. Durand's paper. Well-known authors are cited only as evidence that careful attempts have been made to incorporate into economic theory the discounting of anticipated income, the time shape of an expected income stream, and the risk factors.

SECURITY APPRAISAL

What is the importance of this shift from the maximization of income to that of maximizing investment value, i.e., the discounted value of future income? Mr. Durand states: "This revision is more than mere verbiage. The shift from the maximization of income to the maximization of discounted value has important implications for the measurements of costs and the analysis of investment problems. It emphasizes the basic importance of appraisal and security analysis in molding business decisions. How can the businessman go about maximizing investment value without developing a system of appraisal that is suitable, to him at least?"

With respect to this topic, I want to consider briefly two major points: 1) whether determining investment value, as used by Mr. Durand, is an appropriate method of measuring the costs of debt and equity methods of financing, and 2) whether there is really any basic difference between the two methods of security appraisal analyzed by the author in Section II of his paper.

As to the first question, it seems to me that the answer must be no. Economists have long recognized that capital value does not determine net income, but instead net income (returns over cost) and the rate of interest determine capital value.[9] Furthermore, the truth of this statement has been demonstrated in the market place where the fixed assets of a business are valued mainly on the basis of their earning power. It is essential, therefore, to estimate the net anticipated return over cost, before any reasonable estimate can be made of the effect of a proposed investment on the value of outstanding securites.

Thus, the objective of maximizing the discounted value of future income, instead of maximizing income, does not make security appraisal the key to the problem of measuring cost, as stated by the author. It only introduces time preference — an appraisal of present value as compared to future value.

To derive the investment value of securities by assuming the effect of the new financing on earnings, costs and risk, and then using the investment value to measure costs of the new financing, is circular reasoning. The old theory of regulating public utility rates on the basis of the market value of the securities was discarded for this reason. If the determination of investment value is to be the "key" to measuring financing cost, it must be derived independently. I cannot conceive of any reasonable method of estimating the effects of new financing on the investment value of outstanding securities that does not involve estimating first the additional

[8] *Ibid.*, pp. 313-16

[9] See Fisher, *The Rate of Interest*, p. 15.

income expected in relation to the additional costs incurred, including payments for such factors as risk. Maximizing the present value of anticipated net income is the same as maximizing a prudent investment value of the securities, because net income is the primary determinant of prudent investment value.

Mr. Durand's analysis, however, does not arrive at the effect of proposed new financing on the investment value of the securities independently of income and costs. The effects of the proposed new financing on net income and risk are assumed in estimating the new investment value. For example, in one of the illustrations cited the question is raised as to whether the stockholders of a hypothetical corporation "ABC" could profitably borrow $10 million via 4 percent bonds to finance additional plant expected to earn $800,000 annually. It is stated that the expansion would have the advantage of increasing prospective earnings from $2.50 a share to $2.90 a share, but that it also has the disadvantage of increasing the risk because the proposed bond issue is so large that dividends might be curtailed for several years and if earnings should fall off sharply, the entire financial position of the company might be jeopardized. The author concludes that the assumed increase in per share earnings is not sufficient to compensate for the assumed risk incurred. The illustration is used to make the point that "the risk incurred in borrowing may discourage investment, even though the rate of return on the new investment exceeds the interest cost of borrowed money." The "required return" on a new investment is explained as the amount which must be earned without being actually disadvantageous to the stockholders; in other words, with bond financing it must leave the stock as valuable as before, and with stock financing it must not dilute the per share earnings or the value of the old stock.

The illustration, however, proves only that the increase in earnings must be sufficient to offset or to compensate for the additional risk. The proposed investment to be financed by a 4 percent bond issue would have been ruled out also under Professor Fisher's principles of investment opportunities. Using his investment opportunity principle, the new financing would not be made because the increase in earnings would not be sufficient to provide any excess of returns over costs, including the payment for risk. The illustrations, given to show that investment value must first be determined before the owners of a business can wisely decide as to whether new financing is desirable, are merely a roundabout way of showing that the increase in returns must be sufficient to cover *all costs*.

The second section of Mr. Durand's paper deals with the problem of security appraisal. He states that the practical application of the principle of the required return and the determination of investment value as a means of measuring costs necessitates "a sound, effective, and generally acceptable system of security appraisal. Yet at present no such system exists." Two systems of security appraisal are discussed—the capitalization of net operating income (NOI) and of net income (NI). These two systems, according to the author, arise "from fundamentally different assumptions . . . and have radically different implications for financial policy."

The net-operating-income and the net-income methods represent the same principle or system of security valuation. Both employ the method of capitalizing the net income available to one or more groups of claimants against the assets of the business. The NOI method, in which there is no deduction of interest on bonds, is merely a means of employing the capitalization principle to determine the value of both the stockholders' and bondholders' interest in the assets of the business. The result is the "investment value" of the entire capital structure of the business —bonds and stocks.

The NI method represents exactly the same principle, but it is used for a different purpose. Interest on bonds is deducted and the resulting net income is capitalized, thus giving the value of the stockholders' interest in the business assets. In other words, capitalizing the income available to the stockholders gives the investment value of the stock, not that of the entire business. The difference is not one of method but merely one of the purpose for which it is used. It would be just as logical to deduct preferred stock dividends from the net income and use the residual for determining the capitalized value of the common stock.

MISCELLANEOUS COMMENTS

My remaining comments will be limited to one aspect of Mr. Durand's analysis of the implications of his paper for business cycle theory and to a few suggestions I have for further research on the cost of equity and debt sources of funds.

Mr. Durand points out that for some writers on business cycle theory the interest rate plays a strategic role by encouraging and discouraging investment; therefore the monetary authorities can exert a stabilizing influence by raising and lowering the interest rate. He states, however, that this "depends upon a tacit assumption that the cost of raising capital is approximately equal to the interest rate." With this latter statement—one which frequently appears in writings on this subject—I must take issue. The effectiveness of a flexible interest rate policy by the monetary authorities does not depend upon the influence the interest rate has on the demand for and the supply of capital funds. The real objective of a flexible interest rate is to permit the central bank to exercise effective control over bank reserves and the money supply. If the monetary authorities really exercise effective control, restraint will result in rising interest rates and vice versa. A fixed interest rate policy, however, means that the central bank must supply all of the funds that are demanded at that level of interest rates. The monetary authorities lose control over the volume of bank reserves and deposits. Thus, a flexible interest rate policy is effective not primarily for its direct influence but rather as a necessary corollary of effective control over bank reserves and the money supply.

Finally, I want to suggest a few types of research on the cost of equity and debt funds which might be helpful. Following the usual methods of indicating the relative cost of equity and debt funds—the yield on bonds as compared to the average dividend yield or price-earnings ratio on stocks—we find that the spread has been unusually large during the postwar period. The long-term trends in these measures of cost are given and the deficiencies of this method are discussed in Mr. Durand's paper. Admitting that these measures of the cost of debt and equity financing have serious limitations, I think they do indicate certain lines of research that might be helpful.

The cost of equity as compared to debt funds has been relatively high during the postwar period. This may reflect either the investors' belief that the risk element in stock ownership is increasing or that investors are demanding more compensation for risk-taking. In the sense of the terms on which equity funds are available, there is some evidence of a shortage of equity capital. But there seems to be no evidence that ability to supply equity funds has been deficient. Apparently, it is more a problem of willingness than one of ability.

In view of the limited information available and the importance of a steady flow of equity funds for economic progress, further research is desirable. For example, has there been a redistribution of savings among income classes so that the higher income groups are no longer able to supply as large a quantity of equity funds as formerly? What is the attitude of investors toward stocks as an investment and why? Is an increasing proportion of personal savings going into institutions such as life insurance companies and savings and loan associations, and if so, why? Some research has already been done along these lines, but further studies might be fruitful in providing more information on the important factors influencing the supply of equity capital and the terms on which it will be made available.

MARTIN W. DAVENPORT,
New York University

I would summarize Mr. Durand's argument as follows:

> Businessmen act in what they believe to be their own best interests. Economic theory has presumed that their best interests lie in maximizing income, that the cost of capital is measured by interest rates, and therefore that business expansion requires a marginal rate of return which exceeds the interest rate. This theory must, however, be abandoned for two reasons: 1) the best interests of businessmen consist in maximizing value, not income, and 2) the cost of capital is measured not by the interest rate but by the rate of return on marginal investment necessary to increase the value of the businessman's investment. The key to this approach is a suitable method of appraising investment values of business enterprises and particularly of their common stocks.

I am largely in agreement with Mr. Durand's position, although with certain differences of detail and emphasis. One of these bears upon the use of the words "cost of capital." What really concerns us, I believe, is not the *cost* of raising capital but rather the *effect* of raising capital on investment value. In the accounting sense of the word, at least, there is no cost unless there is some obligation to pay interest; in this sense, retention of net income involves no cost; and yet the effect of retaining earnings on investment value, for better or for worse, may be tremendous.

Mr. Durand has shown that a proposed expansion may promise to raise the income of the owners of an enterprise and yet appear inadvisable because it seems likely to reduce the value of their investment. The standard explanation is that to borrow additional capital increases the "risk" to the junior equity. On purely theoretical grounds, it might seem that the increased danger of loss if things went badly would be counterbalanced by the chances of increased gain if things went well.

However persuasive this argument may appear, it is a fact that the market pays a premium for safety and exacts a discount for risk. Among financial analysts, it is common knowledge that a "leveraged" common stock will sell at a lower multiple of earnings than an "unleveraged" stock of the same company. Nor does this observation apply to these precarious times alone, except in the unusual degree to which it is evident today. I know of no time since 1929 when it has not been generally true that a prior claim to a senior segment of a company's earnings was more valuable than a residual equity to a junior segment of similar amount.

For a very brief period at the top of the 1929 stock market boom, many common stocks sold at a higher ratio to current earnings than did bonds in relation to their claims to interest, but the abnormality was short-lived and was due, I believe, to a degree of optimism as to future increase in earnings so extreme that it could not long face reality. In any case, the relationship that prevailed briefly in 1929 was unusual in the past and may be considered unlikely to prevail in the future.

One of the few portions of this broad field which I have explored involves the relationship between capitalization leverage and the valuation of common stock earnings. For public utility companies, which are peculiarly adaptable to this purpose because of the stability of utility earnings and the availability of a sizable sample of homogeneous companies, my studies showed that even a relatively slight amount of debt or preferred stock would noticeably raise the rate of capitalization of the earnings applicable to the common stock.

If the promise of a return on additional capital sufficient to bring about an increase in common stock *earnings* is unreliable as an indication of the desirability of the transaction for the common stockholders, what test shall we substitute in its place? We need to know the rate of return which will be sufficient to result in an increase in the *market value* of the common stock. Mr. Durand calls it the "required return."

In essence, the required return is that rate of earnings on additional capital which will raise the total market value of the enterprise by an amount at least equal to the market value of the securities issued in order to obtain the new capital. It is a function of the over-all rate of capitalization of the company's total earnings before interest charges, that is, of the relationship between the total market value of the enterprise and the total earnings which are the basis of that value.

Obviously, a theory that depends on a calculation of the effect of a capital addition and its financing on the value of an enterprise requires a method of valuing the enterprise and its securities. Assuming a reasonably reliable estimate of the probable rate of return on additional capital investment—which would be equally necessary under the superseded theory of maximizing income, and which the owners of the enterprise are probably capable of making—all that we need further is the over-all rate of capitalization at which the company's earnings, or the earnings of a similar company, tend to sell in the market place, and a method for determining what portion of this value is assignable to the company's additional securities issued. If we can be content with a reasonably narrow range of rates of capitalization of earnings, and I think we can, then there is no insurmountable obstacle.

In discussing security valuation, Mr. Durand has made much of the alleged conflict between the alternative methods of capitalizing net income or net operating income. In my opinion, he has exaggerated the seriousness of this problem. Because analysts generally understand that the relative amount of leverage senior to a common stock is one of the primary determinants of the rate of capitalization of common stock earnings, I think it would be difficult to find one who in practice uses the pure "net income" method of appraising common stocks.

On the other hand, the "net operating income" method must be made flexible enough to allow for the fact that the type of capital structure has an effect on the total market value of the enterprise. As Mr. Durand has so clearly pointed out, the "institutionalization" of savings in banks, insurance companies and the like, which are wholly or partially restricted in their choice of investments to certain classes of fixed interest-bearing obligations, tends to create a "super premium" for high-grade bonds that provides an opportunity to maximize the total investment value of a company by effective bond financing.

Another important factor is, of course, the corporation income tax. In pure theory, a company financed entirely by interest-bearing debt would be worth 61 percent more than an all-stock company, assuming a 38 percent income tax rate, and the higher the rate, the greater the differential. In practice, of course, all-debt capital structures are financially impracticable and would be disallowed by the Bureau of Internal Revenue. Nevertheless, a considerable amount of debt is entirely feasible for most companies, and its existence raises the total market value of the enterprise, both absolutely and in relation to earnings.

Capital structure probably has other, less obvious, effects on going-concern values. Debt compels, and preferred stock encourages, distributions which might not be made if the capital structure consisted entirely of common stock. From the viewpoint of total investment value, such distribution may be desirable or undesirable, depending on the profitability of available opportunities for reinvestment of earnings in the business. On the other hand, excessive amounts of debt, or even of preferred stock, pose the threat of possible eventual interference with the management or even with operations of the business as a result of transfer of voting control or receivership.

After allowing for these and possibly other factors, there appears to be, for each company, an "optimum" capital structure containing that amount of debt which will maximize the total value of the enterprise. I say "debt" rather than preferred stock because, for reasons relating to income taxes and the "super premium," a reasonable amount of debt tends to maximize the going-concern value of an enterprise, while preferred stock, lacking these advantages, does not. It makes no sense for a strong company like DuPont to sell preferred stock when it could safely and easily sell bonds. I think there is a good chance that statistical research in this area would yield interesting and valuable results.

Assuming, then, that we agree to employ a "net operating income" method of valuation, with appropriate allowance for income taxes, super premium and perhaps other relevant considerations, there are alternative approaches to the problem of determining whether a given method of financing is advantageous to the common stockholders of an enterprise.

By far the simpler alternative, and one designed to show whether the transaction is likely to appear beneficial in the near future, is the method based on current market appraisal of current earnings. If market prices are available for the company's securities, it is fairly simple to determine the approximate over-all rate of capitalization of the current earnings, assuming that the current rate of earnings is known with reasonable accuracy. Underwriters perform such calculations as a matter of routine.

The second method is more complicated and requires a considerably larger element of judgment, since it requires an estimate of what constitutes a "normal" rate of capitalization of earnings for the company. Evidence of what constitutes a normal rate of capitalization can be derived from comparison of past prices and earnings of the company in question, and of other companies similar to it; but since these relationships vary, conclusion from such data will usually take the form of a median or mode or other average with some margin of error implicit.

At first glance it would appear that the two methods are likely to vary widely in their results, since current rates of capitalization of earnings are generally much higher than any "normal" rate that would be derived from the experience of past years prior to 1947. On further study, however, this difficulty tends to vanish.

There has always, except in 1929, been a tendency for earnings to be capitalized at high rates when earnings were historically high, and conversely. Common stocks and entire enterprises are probably selling low in relation to current earnings because the earnings are widely believed to be abnormally high. It seems safe to predict that rates of capitalization will eventually decline toward what we used to consider normal, either because the earnings drop or because the current levels become accepted as normal.

The comments above may become clearer if I illustrate the point in terms of an actual company—Sears, Roebuck. Its capital structure consists solely of common stock. During the past five years, Sears has expanded tremendously by reinvesting about $275 million of undistributed net income. Its major competitor, Montgomery Ward, which is of comparable size and similar as to nature of business, has totally refrained from new capital expenditures. Ward therefore furnishes a convenient standard by which to measure the effects of Sears' expansion on its sales and earnings.

Since 1945, the year before Sears began to expand aggressively, Ward's sales have risen from $654,779,000 to an annual rate of about $1,033,500,000 this year, a gain of about 58 per cent. We may assume that if Sears had not expanded it would also have increased its sales in approximately the same proportion, or from $1,045,259,000 in 1945 to an annual rate of some $1,650,000,000 this year. In actual fact, however, Sears' sales are now running at an annual rate of about $2,330,000,000, and the difference of some $680 million seems a reasonable estimate of the effect on sales of Sears' reinvestment of $275 million of additional capital. I do not know how closely this figure corresponds with the original projections of the Sears management at the time when the expansion program was considered and decided upon. For purposes of illustration, let us assume that their forecasts were closely realized in practice.

During the postwar period, Sears has been able to realize a profit margin of close to 10 per cent of sales, before federal income taxes. After allowing for such taxes at the rate of 38 percent, this profit margin applied to sales of $680 million would indicate an addition to net income of $42,160,000 or 15.3 percent of the $275 million of additional capital. The prewar earnings record suggests, however, that a pretax profit margin of 8 percent would be a much safer guide to the longer term future, and such a margin, with the same $680 million of sales and 38 percent income tax rate, would mean additional net income of $33,728,000 or 12.3 percent of the capital reinvested during the past five years.

What rate of return is required to make this achievement profitable to the company's stockholders in terms of its effect on the market value of their stock? During the postwar years 1946-49, when the stock's earnings were ranging between $4.24 and $5.80 a share and averaging $4.80, the stock sold in the market between a high of 49⅝ and a low of 30⅛, averaging a little less than 40. Earnings of $4.80 on a price of 40 represent a capitalization rate of 12 percent. At the present time, with earnings apparently running at an annual rate of roughly $5.50 a share, the stock is selling around 45 or at a rate of about 12 percent. Comparison of these rates of capitalization with the estimated 15 percent current rate of return on capital reinvested during the past five years indicates that such reinvestment was advantageous to the stockholders.

In the prewar years 1939-40 (omitting the 1938 depression and the stock market collapse accompanying our gradual entry into the war in 1941-42) Sears sold at between 22 and 15, or at an average price of around 18½; in these years it earned $1.65 and $1.58 per share. (All of these figures have been adjusted to reflect the 4-for-1 stock split in 1945.) These earnings were then being capitalized at around 8.7 percent. The 12.3 percent return on invested capital computed on the basis of an 8 percent normal profit margin would clearly justify the company's expansion program. Even a profit margin as low as 6 percent, which would provide a 9.2 percent return on additional capital, would make the reinvestment of earnings appear advantageous, assuming that we can accept 8.7 percent as a "normal" rate of capitalization of earnings for this company.

Sears could, of course, have financed part or all of this expansion by borrowing. Mainly because of the income tax advantage of the interest deduction, this apparently would have been still more favorable in terms of effect on the value of the stock. To provide a 12 percent return on the stock after providing for 38 percent income taxes would have required a return of 19.33 percent before taxes. Assuming that Sears could have raised long-term capital at an interest rate of 2½ percent, a return of 17.83 percent before taxes would have produced a 12 percent return after taxes. The higher the interest rate, the greater the differential between the two required returns before taxes.

The lower rate of return (before income taxes) on additional capital necessary to justify debt financing as compared with equity financing is no doubt an important reason for the relatively minor role of new common stock issues as a source of corporate funds in the postwar period. Out of $23 billion of long-term capital raised by sales of securities during the years 1946-49 inclusive, $18 billion consisted of bonds, mortgages and long-term bank loans, while only $5 billion arose from net new issues of common and preferred stock, and of this only $3 billion was common. Of course, some portion of the $18 billion consisted of convertible bonds, mainly public utility, which may be considered indirect equity financing, in that they are issued with the expectation, or at least the possibility, of eventual conversion into common stock. Even so, the preponderance of debt is striking.

There is only one kind of equity financing that has amounted to much in recent years, and that is retention of earnings, which in 1946-49 amounted to nearly $40 billion, not including some $21 billion of allowances for depreciation. The contrast between the $40 billion of retained earnings and the $3 billion raised from the sale of common stock demands explanation.

Does retention of earnings have any real and substantial advantages over sale of common stock from the standpoint of effect on the value of the stockholders' investment? Obviously it has. To the extent that the corporation would realize less than the current market price—because of selling and underwriting expenses, or because a large issue of common stock might have to be priced appreciably below the market in order to sell—there is a real, though probably in most cases not decisive, advantage to be gained by retaining earnings instead of selling common stock.

There is also, theoretically, a tax advantage, since if instead of reinvesting earnings the corporation first distributed them in dividends and then tried to get them back in payment for stock, the amount that the stockholders could reinvest in the business would be reduced by their personal income taxes on dividends received. But since the company's stockholders would in any case buy only a limited proportion of the new stock, most of the force of this argument evaporates.

These factors no doubt go far to explain the overwhelming preference of corporations for retention of earnings as against sale of common stock. But there is another possible explanation, and it has nothing to do with the best interests of the stockholders. It may be that earnings have been retained and reinvested in the business merely because they were available, without the necessity either of demonstrating the wisdom of their intended use or of facing the verdict that the market would render were additional stock offered for sale.

After all, the interests of management are distinguishable from those of stockholders and may be in conflict with them, in that management has incentives to increase the size of a corporation and to build up its working capital beyond the point to which such actions represent profitable use of stockholders' capital. This line of reasoning, if shown to be valid, would tend to discredit both the old thesis that business expansion will proceed until the marginal return on capital equals the interest rate and Mr. Durand's proposed substitute that expansion will continue until the marginal return on capital equals the "required return."

What is now indicated, in my opinion, is a thorough study to determine to what extent expansion plans of corporations have been based on stockholders' best interests, as measured by probable effect on the value of their stock, and to what extent this expansion and its chosen method of financing have been beneficial or detrimental to their interests. Integral parts of such a survey would be a series of individual studies designed to show what net operating income tends to sell for and what capital tends to earn in various industries, what is the effect of dividend policy on valuation, and what is the optimum capital structure in each industry.

Another approach that might yield interesting conclusions would be a series of interviews with managements of carefully selected enterprises, designed to disclose the reasons behind certain policies and actions which, on the basis of our theory of maximizing value, seem particularly difficult to explain.

There is no doubt in my mind that comprehensive and thorough research in this field would yield data of great value to students of business finance. There is also a good chance that such studies might shed considerable light on the reasons for the fluctuations in business capital expenditures that are so important a determinant of the business cycle.

MEASURING A COMPANY'S COST OF CAPITAL

EZRA SOLOMON*

I. INTRODUCTION

THE aim of this paper is to formulate an explicit and appropriate way of defining and measuring a company's cost of capital. Such a measure is essential to any rational system for making capital-budgeting decisions. Its function is to provide a correct and objective criterion by which management can determine whether it should or should not accept available proposals involving the expenditure of capital. Because of this function, this concept—the cost of capital—has also been called the "minimum required rate of earnings" or the "cutoff" rate for capital expenditures. The determination of a company's capital budget is an intricate process that requires several simultaneous decisions by management: the total extent of capital expenditures; the form these expenditures will take; and the forms of financing to be used in meeting these expenditures. A rational solution to these complex problems involves three steps.

1. Each available expenditure proposal must be measured for the rate of return it promises. When these measured proposals are ranked in descending order of prospective yield, this list provides management with an explicit picture of the company's potential demand for capital funds.

2. Each available source of capital must be measured for its "cost" to stockholders. "Cost" in this context refers to the minimum rate of return that is required to justify the active investment of each succeeding increment of these available funds.[1] When this listing of amounts and expected costs is arrayed in ascending order of cost, it provides management with an explicit picture of the potential supply and cost of funds available to the company.

3. A comparison of these two schedules provides an explicit and correct solution to the capital-budgeting problem. Successive proposals should be accepted from within the descending array as long as the prospective yield from each is higher than the cost of obtaining the increment of funds required for its financing. The first proposal for which capital cost equals or exceeds prospective yield should be rejected, and so should all proposals promising a smaller yield.

RATE OF RETURN

Although there are still wide differences in the methods which are used in practice to evaluate the rate of return promised by a proposal, there is complete agreement at the theoretical level about which measure is the correct one.[2] While

* Associate professor of finance, School of Business, University of Chicago. The author wishes to acknowledge the helpful suggestions of Harry Roberts, Joel Segall, James Lorie, and Eli Shapiro.

[1] Throughout this paper, "cost" will be used to mean "rate of cost." Where another meaning, e.g., dollar cost, is intended, this will be indicated.

[2] The crudest measure of yield is the expected average book earnings (net of tax) divided by the original capital outlay. An alternative version, which amounts to the same thing, is to take the inverse of the pay-out period as a measure of yield. The "scientific method," "investor's method," "compound-discount method," or "discounted cash-flow method," as it is variously called, is to take cash earnings (book earnings, net of tax, plus depreciation allowances attributable to a project) and to find that rate of compound discount which exactly equates these

the actual computation of a project's rate of return in this correct way presents difficult problems of economic forecasting and of accounting, the *concept* itself is a perfectly exact one.

It is also generally agreed that estimating future earnings contributed by a given project requires a comparison between future earnings *without* the project and future earnings *with* the project. This approach is particularly necessary in connection with evaluating so-called "strategic" investments which are designed to prevent a fall in over-all earnings.

COST OF CAPITAL

Although the concept of cost of capital has always played a central part in the theory of capital, the problem of defining and measuring this concept has received almost no attention at all. Quite apart from the practical difficulties of measuring capital costs for a specific company, there is today no explicit and generally acceptable account of what is the correct conceptual approach to its measurement. This gap represents the weakest link in the theory of capital budgeting, and, until it is filled, capital-budgeting theory will remain, at best, only a partial guide to decision-making in this important area of business activity.

With few exceptions, the published literature completely ignores the problem of defining the cost of capital for realistic conditions in which both debt and equity sources are used. The best known exception is the work of Professor Joel Dean, but even his most comprehensive statement regarding the cost of capital is neither explicit nor complete.[3]

Unlike theory, business practice has been unable to avoid the issue. But in the absence of a definitive and acceptable measure of capital cost, business has had to fall back on arbitrary criteria for its capital-budgeting decisions. One common practice is to limit the size of the capital budget in any year to the amount of internally available funds. A second common approach is to postulate an arbitrary "cutoff" rate of the order of 10, 15, or 20 per cent per annum and to use this rate as a minimum requirement for accepting proposals. The use of these methods will, except by accident, involve a breach of the theoretically correct solution—namely, that capital projects should be accepted if the rate of return they promise is higher than the rate of capital cost of the funds needed to implement them.

The problem with which the rest of this paper is concerned is an explicit formulation of a correct and nonarbitrary system of using the concept of capital costs for capital-budgeting decisions. In order to develop such a system, at least

---

earnings with outlays attributable to the project. For detailed accounts of this method see Kenneth E. Boulding, *Economic Analysis* (rev. ed.; New York: Harper & Bros., 1948), pp. 782–830; Joel Dean, *Managerial Economics* (New York: Prentice-Hall, 1951), chap. x; *Capital Budgeting* (New York: Columbia University Press, 1951), chap. ii; "Measuring the Productivity of Capital," *Harvard Business Review*, January–February, 1954, pp. 120–30; and "Better Management of Capital Expenditures through Research," *Journal of Finance*, May, 1953, pp. 119–28; Gordon Shillinglaw, "Measuring the Investment Worth of Capital Proposals," *Modern Management of Capital Expenditures* ("Financial Management Series," No. 105 [New York: American Management Association, 1954]); Horace G. Hill, Jr., *A New Method of Computing Rate-of-Return on Capital Expenditures* (National Society for Business Budgeting, 1953).

[3] *Capital Budgeting*, pp. 36–81. For two other discussions of the problem see David Durand, "Cost of Debt and Equity Funds for Business," *Conference on Research in Business Finance* (New York: National Bureau of Economic Research, 1952), pp. 215–47, and Friedrich and Vera Lutz: *The Theory of Investment of the Firm* (Princeton, Princeton University Press, 1951).

three major difficulties must be faced squarely.

1. The largest part of a company's permanent capital is derived, either internally or externally, from equity funds. These funds do not involve a fixed contractual out-payment. How should the "cost" of such funds be measured? How is this cost likely to vary with the extent of financing envisaged?

2. Most companies derive part of their financing from borrowed funds which have fixed interest and repayment provisions or from preferred stock. But both these forms of financing require that equity capital provide part of the total funds necessary for investment. How should we measure the cost of capital that is derived from more than one source where each component source has not only a different *kind* of cost but a different *rate* of cost?

3. When borrowing is used, the rate of interest charged, the proportion of debt financing available, and the repayment provisions of the loan may all differ as between one type of investment proposal and another. For example, equipment trust certificates can be used for financing certain types of equipment but not for others; bank loans may be available only for particular types of asset expansion; and so on. How should the cost differences arising from access that some investment proposals have to particular kinds of debt financing be treated within the total capital-budgeting framework?

In order to arrive at a solution for these basic problems, this paper proceeds in two stages. In the first stage we will assume that equity funds are the only source of capital. Within this framework the correct measure for each of the sources from which equity funds can be derived will be established. These measures will then be developed into a schedule which shows the incremental cost of deriving successive increments of financing from equity sources alone.

In the second stage of the analysis we will incorporate debt financing and preferred-stock financing into the framework developed in the first stage.

II. THE COST OF EQUITY FUNDS

COMMON STOCK

The cost of capital derived from the issue of new common stock is a difficult concept and one about which little agreement exists in practice. Assuming for the moment that underwriting and flotation costs are zero, there are at least four possible criteria in use for measuring the cost of equity capital. Of these, only one is valid. The four possible criteria are as follows:

a) A project should be accepted if the rate of return which it promises is higher than the rate of return currently being earned on existing corporate capital. The argument made here is that a project is desirable if it raises the average return on the company's investment.

b) A project should be accepted if the rate of return it promises is higher than the present ratio of dividend payments to the market price of existing shares. The argument here is that any rate of return per share that is higher than the dividend rate per share will provide a net return to the corporation's treasury.

c) In order to be acceptable, a project's rate of return has to be higher than present earnings per share relative to present market value per share. By this criterion, the cost of new equity capital is properly measured by the ratio between current earnings per share and current market price per share. We shall refer to this measure as E/P.

d) The fourth, and in the opinion of this writer, the only valid criterion for the cost of new equity capital is a refinement of the simple E/P ratio. Instead of E, the current earnings per share, the numerator should measure management's best estimate of what average future earnings would be if the proposed capital expenditure were not made. We shall refer to this concept as E_A. Assuming that underwriting and flotation costs are zero, the ratio E_A/P is the best conceptual measure of the cost of new equity capital, and the use of this criterion as the cutoff rate for new capital expenditures financed solely by new common stock is the only one that will insure the optimum capital-budgeting decision.

That E_A/P is the correct concept can most easily be defended in terms of an arithmetic example. Let us take a corporation which is considering a specific project involving capital expenditure to be financed by the issue of new equity securities. The following data are given:

1. Total book value of plant and equipment	$30,000,000
2. Total capitalization	One million shares
3. Current earnings, $3.00 per share or	$ 3,000,000
4. Current dividend, $2.00 per share or	$ 2,000,000
5. Current market value, $20.00 per share	
6. Best estimate of future annual earnings without expansion project	$ 3,300,000
7. Best estimate of future annual earnings if expansion project is accepted	$ 4,200,000
8. Salvage value of project*	$ 6,000,000
9. Present outlay required for project	$ 6,000,000
10. Underwriting and flotation expenses	Zero

* The unrealistic salvage value exactly equal to present outlay provides a simple solution for the project's promised rate of return, but in no way affects the validity of the argument.

What we have, then, is a project with a promised return of $900,000 per annum (the difference between items 6 and 7) and a present cost of $6,000,000. The rate of return on this project is therefore 15 per cent per annum.

Our four criteria for the "correct" cost of capital are: (*a*) the present rate of earnings on existing capital (this is 10 per cent, items 1 and 3), (*b*) the present dividend rate as a percentage of present market price (this is also 10 per cent); (*c*) the present earnings rate as a percentage of present market price (this is 15 per cent, items 3 and 5); and (*d*) estimated future average earnings per share without the project (item 6) relative to present market price (this is 16.5 per cent).

By the first two criteria, the project would be clearly acceptable. By the third criterion, it is marginal. By the fourth criterion, it should be rejected. Management, on behalf of its stockholders, needs to find that criterion which will always insure that any accepted project benefits stockholders and that no available project that would benefit stockholders is rejected.

In the long run, the holder of a share of stock is the owner of a stream of earnings from that share, and hence the most pervasive item affecting him in this connection is the impact of policy on future earnings per share. If either of the first two criteria is adopted, the project will be undertaken. It can be shown that this will clearly result in a reduction of per share earnings. The criteria are therefore wrong.

In order to finance the project, $6,000,000 must be raised through new security issues. At current market prices and assuming zero underwriting costs, this will require the sale of 300,000 shares of stock. The new capitalization will be 1,300,000 shares. New earnings *with* the project will be $4,200,000 or $3.23 per share. But *without undertaking the project* and without the new financing, stockholders would have earned $3.30 per share held (items 2 and 6). Assuming that all benefits attributable to the project have been included in the computations, the decision to undertake the project would be a bad one from the point of view of existing stockholders. Continuing the argument, the only condition under which new projects, involving new common-stock financing, should be accepted is if the expected rate of return on these projects exceeds 16.5 per cent (criterion 4). Only then will earnings per share be improved as a result of the venture. Thus, for common-stock financing, the valid concept of capital cost as a criterion for accepting or rejecting proposals is E_A/P. Dividend yields, current rate of earnings on book capital, and other similar concepts affect the cost of new equity capital but are not relevant in *measuring* the cost of new equity capital and should therefore be ignored in this context.[4] The use of E_A/P instead of the simpler concept E/P is important for several reasons.

a) It is conceptually better. The relevant fact with regard to any item of business policy is not the difference between net earnings after the policy item is introduced and present earnings. Rather, it is the difference between net earnings after the policy item is introduced and what earnings *would have been*, had the policy item not been introduced. Admittedly, this refinement adds the need of yet another "estimate" (E_A) to the system in place of an "actual" item (E). But a crude measure of the right concept is far more relevant than the best measure of a wrong concept!

b) In any case, the item E is by no means an unambiguous one, whereas E_A, although it requires an estimate of the future, is at least a perfectly clear concept. Because of cyclical fluctuations in business activity, inventory profits and losses, and the vagaries of accounting practice, current earnings, in the strictest sense of the term, is not a useful number, and some process of averaging and of adjusting past earnings is necessary in order to iron out these fluctuations and exclude the effect of nonrecurring items and conditions.

c) In the case of "growth" companies, the ratio of recent earnings to present market values is especially misleading. Market prices for the stocks of these companies tend to be high relative to recent earnings because earnings are expected to increase in the future. In the case of "growth" companies, it is especially important to use estimated future earnings (assuming the proposed capital expenditure does not take place) as a basis for assaying the desirability of the proposal under consideration.

UNDERWRITING AND FLOTATION EXPENSES

The flotation of new equity securities involves two expenses. In the first place, there are underwriters' commissions, registration expenses, and selling expenses. In the second place, some "underpricing" of the new issue relative to recent market prices is usually necessary to insure success of the issue. These items must be taken into account in computing the cost of new equity capital. Assuming that the net cash receipts per share to the corporation are equal to P_A (as opposed to P, the current market price), the amended concept of capital cost for new equity funds will be E_A/P_A.

[4] Two other criteria commonly referred to in the "practical" literature have not been discussed explicitly in our analysis. One is the effect of a new issue on control over the corporation, and the other is the effect of a new issue on per share book values. The first might be relevant for closely held corporations but hardly applies to widely held going concerns. The book-value criterion will not insure maximum future earnings per share and is therefore a "wrong" standard for evaluating expenditure proposals.

RETAINED EARNINGS

If shareholders were all in the zero income tax bracket and underwriting costs and brokerage fees were also zero, the valid cost of capital funds derived internally from retained earnings would be clearly equal to the cost of externally derived equity funds. Referring to our arithmetic example, it can again be shown that the acceptance of any project and its financing out of retained earnings would hurt stockholders unless the rate of return promised by the project is at least equal to E_A/P_A. If available earnings[5] are paid out rather than retained, shareholders can, for example, reinvest their dividend receipts in shares of the corporation; assuming zero taxes and zero brokerage fees, these investments would yield annual earnings of 16.5 per cent.[6] Management would therefore harm stockholders' interests by retaining earnings for any purpose less lucrative than 16.5 per cent. However, if projects promise to pay more than 16.5 per cent, stockholders benefit if earnings are retained to finance these projects rather than paid out as dividends.

One problem that arises in connection with estimating the cost of retained capital is the problem of alternative outlets open to the stockholder himself. In the foregoing example, 16.5 per cent is the indicated minimum rate for capital-using projects requiring retained earnings. A project yielding 18 per cent would, for example, be clearly acceptable. But what if it is argued that stockholders may have some other alternative use for dividends, e.g., purchase of shares which have an earning rate of 22 per cent in some other company? The only answer to this is that the stock market is sophisticated enough that alternative investment prospects are on a par with one another, taking both earnings rate and risk into account. In other words, in this example the 22 per cent earnings rate on common stock of the outside company is generally considered to be equal to 16.5 per cent on common stock of the company under consideration, and hence a promise of 18 per cent on retained earnings provides a better use of the stockholders' money.

Since shareholders are not in the zero income tax bracket and since neither underwriting expenses nor brokerage fees are zero, several adjustments need to be made in E_A/P_A in order to obtain the correct cost of retained capital. The easiest way to approach these adjustments is to lift one of the restricting assumptions at a time. Taking underwriting expenses and underpricing of new stock into account is simple. The rate E_A/P_A needs to be changed back to E_A/P, where P is the unadjusted market price per share. Brokerage fees are troublesome because the rate differs with the size of purchase. The net effect of taking brokerage fees into account in adapting E_A/P to retained earnings would be to lower the ratio very slightly, because, when a shareholder acquires earnings through retention as opposed to acquisition from reinvestment of dividends, no brokerage fee is involved.[7]

The problem posed by the income tax on dividends presents serious conceptual and practical difficulties. If all shareholders were in the same marginal income tax bracket, e.g, 40 per cent, a simple solution exists. The correct concept of cost of retained capital would be $E_A/P\ (1 - mt)$, where mt is the marginal tax rate.

[5] "Available earnings" refer to book earnings which have not been precommitted in previous budgets or which are not the result of inventory book profits due to price fluctuation and hence automatically tied up within the source from which they are derived.

[6] Assuming no change in the price of the stock.

[7] The minor refinements of making an allowance for brokerage fees is ignored in the rest of the analysis.

In our example, a rate of return of 16.5 × 0.6, or 9.90 per cent, would be the valid cutoff rate if retained earnings alone are used to finance the project.

The fact that stockholders are not all in the same marginal tax bracket creates a difficult problem, and one for which there is no solution at either the conceptual or the operating level. Because stocks are now widely held both by tax-free institutions and by the top income groups in society, the range of tax brackets involved is a very wide one indeed, and this creates latent differences of interest among stockholders with respect to dividend policy. If the company sets the cutoff rate for expansion out of retained earnings at E_A/P, this will make managers and owners of tax-free funds happy. But it may deprive other stockholders of an increment to their earnings which they could not better if they received dividends and reinvested the after-tax proceeds. If the company sets a much lower cutoff rate, e.g., E_A/P (1 − 0.5), it would be depriving stockholders with lower than 50 per cent tax brackets of dividends that they can use more profitably than the company can.

Like any problem involving interpersonal or intergroup comparisons of welfare, no perfect solution is available. Unless management is prepared to assume that it is primarily concerned with stockholders in a specific income bracket, the minimum imputed "cost" of retained earnings should be E_A/P for any company whose stock is held by tax-free funds or by individuals interested in dividend receipts.

DEPRECIATION ALLOWANCES

Depreciation allowances,[8] when earned, represent an important source of reinvestible funds. The problem exists, therefore, of setting a "cost" for such funds. Two relevant situations need consideration: (1) a situation in which these funds are the only source of reinvestible capital and (2) the more usual situation, for a growing company, in which net new funds are invested in addition to the reinvestment of depreciation allowances.

The first situation implies a company with static or shrinking capital assets. In this context the cost of capital is not really relevant for decision-making. The relevant procedure would be for such a company to explore all possible uses of available depreciation funds, including uses for investments outside the company and for the repayment of debts. The problem is simply to allocate the available volume of funds from depreciation to the highest-yielding uses.

In the second situation, the company is a growing one, and this must mean that new equity funds are being invested. In this case the cutoff point for new investment proposals will be determined, on the supply side, by the cost of the other forms of equity capital that are used to finance the expansion of assets.

THE EQUITY SUPPLY SCHEDULE

Our next task is to draw up a cost schedule for equity funds which shows the incremental cost of raising successive amounts of capital from equity sources. Such a schedule (see Fig. 1) would consist of three segments.

A: the total amount of depreciation allowances expected within the budget year. In Figure 1 this is assumed to be $1,000,000.

B: the total amount of available retained earnings. This is equal to expected after-tax book earnings *less* amounts pre-

[8] Depletion allowances and other items of capital consumption allocated as expense in normal financial accounting are also included in the term "depreciation allowances."

committed to working capital, to maintenance of dividends, and to capital projects sanctioned in previous budgets. In Figure 1 this is assumed to be $2,000,000.

The cost of the first dollar of these available retained earnings would be equal to $E_{A'}/P$, where $E_{A'}$ is the expected rate of earnings per share, including earnings expected from the reinvestment of the $1,000,000 of depreciation allowances.

The cost curve will rise for succeeding amounts of retained capital. This is so because, as each succeeding project is accepted, E_A/P rises. However, the contribution of each accepted project to earnings on a per share basis is not likely to be large, and the rise in cost of each succeeding unit of financing will not be steep. The cost of the last unit of available retained earnings is $E_{A''}/P$, where $E_{A''}$ is equal to expected earnings per share, including the earnings expected from projects to be financed from depreciation allowances and retained earnings.

C: after available retained earnings are exhausted, the company can move on to the third segment of equity supply by entering the new-issue market. For this segment, the initial cost is equal to $E_{A''}/P_A$. Since P_A is lower than P, the curve will be discontinuous when the transition is made from internal to external sources.

D: one alternative open to the company is to abstain from the new-equity market and to exploit the retained-earning source by reducing dividend declarations below past levels. Such action is likely to bring about a rapid rise in the cost of these funds because it will generally reduce the market price of stock. When the diversion of dividends has been completely exhausted, the cost of new equity will be much higher because of the lower levels to which the price of stock will have sunk. This alternative is shown in Figure 1 as segment *D*.

III. JOINT FINANCING BY DEBT AND EQUITY

The analysis must now be extended to include the supply of borrowed funds. In order to do this, two problems must be settled: (1) The cash cost of debt funds must be estimated. This is a relatively simple problem. (2) A logical system of rationing must be established which

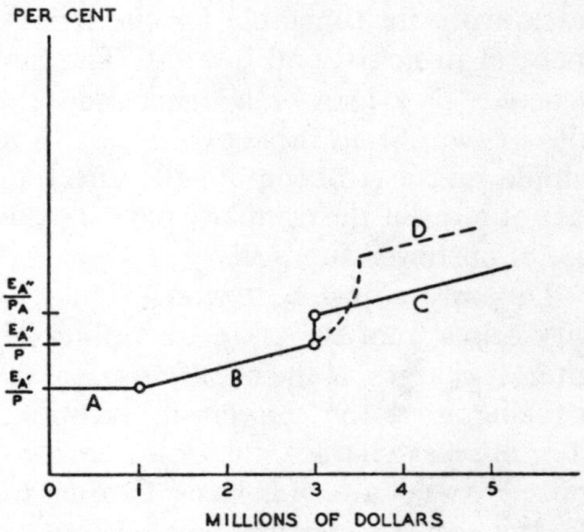

FIG. 1.—The supply schedule of equity funds

treats debt and equity funds within a single unified framework. This is a difficult problem that has not yet been solved in a satisfactory manner. Since borrowed funds must always be accompanied by some proportion of equity funds,[9] a rational system for dealing jointly with these two sources is a fundamental necessity for a complete capital-budgeting framework. The incorporation of debt funds into the analysis introduces a number of difficult issues that must be faced squarely. The use of debt involves latent risks that do not exist when equity

[9] Presumably, some of the recent scandals in connection with FHA loans indicate that exceptions to this general rule do exist.

financing alone is used. The cost and availability of debt funds and the risk to the borrower are different for different kinds of capital expenditure and also vary with the proportion of debt to equity financing. These factors should be taken into account explicitly in order to insure optimum decisions.

CASH COSTS OF BORROWING

Computing the cash costs of borrowed funds is a relatively straightforward problem. The borrowing contract stipulates a precise timetable for the repayment of principal and interest. The net proceeds of a loan or a bond issue are also known. From these two facts, it is a simple matter to compute the effective rate of interest the company pays for the use of borrowed funds.[10]

The only adjustment which is necessary arises from the tax-deductibility of interest charges. If the net after-tax basis is being used for computing earnings, etc., interest charges must also be converted to a net after-tax basis. In order to do this, an assumption must be made with respect to the level of future tax rates. On the basis of such an assumption, gross cash outlays on account of interest and principal can be converted to net cash outlays. From these, the net interest cost of the loan can be measured.

DEBT FUNDS AND EQUITY FUNDS

Conceptually, there are only four ways in which the cost of debt funds can be treated within a capital budget in which both debt and equity are used. Our task is to find and to develop the approach which provides the most suitable guide for the basic problems of capital budgeting, i.e., deciding the extent of the budget and deciding the composition of financing to be used.

APPROACH A

One approach is to take the supply of equity funds as given and to assume that all increments of financing over and above this are derived from borrowing. The relevant cost of new capital is simply the net (after-tax) rate payable on an increment of borrowed funds. Proposals which promise a net rate of return greater than this cost should be accepted.[11]

This approach suffers from a number of serious defects, and it should be rejected. The most important defect is that it fails to recognize that debt funds generally cannot be used without committing some proportion of equity funds, and that these equity funds also involve a "cost" because alternative uses of such funds exist, e.g., dividend payments. Because it ignores the cost of equity funds, approach A provides a wrong criterion for judging the acceptability of investment proposals. Whenever the net cost of equity funds is higher than the net cost of debt funds (and this is the usual case), the use of this approach will lead to the acceptance of proposals that should properly be rejected. This inherent error is easily demonstrated by means of a simple arithmetic example. Let us assume the following facts:

Maximum equity funds available from earnings retention	$300
Rate of return required to justify the use of equity funds*	10%
Borrowing power of company: One dollar of new debt per dollar of earnings reinvested	
Net interest cost of borrowed funds	2%
Projects available this year:	
1. $200 can be invested at 14 per cent	
2. $200 can be invested at 7 per cent	
3. $200 can be invested at 3 per cent	

* This is the rate of earnings that stockholders can buy with each extra dollar of dividends they receive.

[10] The method for deriving the effective rate of interest on a loan is identical to that used for computing the effective rate of return on an investment proposal or for computing the yield to maturity of a bond that is purchased at some price other than par.

[11] This is the approach implied by the familiar textbook diagram, which shows marginal rates of return on capital as a downward sloping line and the

If the criterion of approach A is used, all three projects will be accepted, i.e., $300 will be retained, and $300 will be borrowed. The net increase in earnings that stockholder will enjoy is equal to $42.00 calculated as follows:

$200 @ 14 per cent	$28.00
$200 @ 7 per cent	14.00
$200 @ 3 per cent	6.00
Gross earnings	$48.00
Less net interest on $300	6.00
	$42.00

It can be shown that this is *not* the best result obtainable for the stockholders. For example, if only the first two proposals are accepted, the stockholders will be better off. Only $400 would be invested, $200 from retained earnings (the other $100 would be paid out as dividends) and $200 from borrowing. The net increase in earnings that stockholders will enjoy in this case will be $48.00, calculated as follows:

$200 @ 14 per cent	$28.00
$200 @ 7 per cent	14.00
Gross earnings	$42.00
Less net interest cost on $200	4.00
Net earnings	$38.00
Plus earnings from reinvestment of dividends at 10 per cent	10.00
Total net earnings	$48.00

APPROACH B

An alternative approach is to take the cost of equity funds as the relevant cost for all increments of financing, whether debt or equity sources are used.

The argument on which this approach is based is as follows: The real cost of debt funds to the borrower includes not only the out-of-pocket interest charge incurred but two other factors as well. These are (*a*) constraints placed on the borrower by the terms of the loan, e.g., dividend restriction, amortization payments, etc., and (*b*) the risk of default and the consequences of this contingency. Companies will finance by debt so long as the total real cost of the increment of borrowing is below the cost of financing by new equity funds. But as borrowing increases, the real cost of debt funds rises. This is so because the lender will set higher nominal costs and also because the risk incurred by the borrower will rise as the proportion of debt to equity rises. When borrowing costs have risen to the level of equity costs, the company will turn from debt financing to equity financing. Thus we can assume (*a*) that companies adjust their capitalization structure to the point at which the real cost of new debt and the cost of new equity are equal and (*b*) that the cost of new equity funds is a reasonably good measure of the cost of an increment of financing, regardless of the source from which it is derived.

As a working hypothesis, approach B has much to recommend it. Unlike approach A, it takes borrower's risk into account. The use of the cost of new equity as the minimum acceptable rate for investment proposals provides a safeguard against the kind of error inherent in approach A, namely, the error of accepting proposals that should be rejected. However, approach B suffers from two other limitations:

1. By penalizing all borrowed funds in the budget with the same risk factor, it fails to distinguish between high-risk and low-risk proposals within the budget.[12]

2. By assuming that all firms always maintain a proportion of debt to equity

"rate of interest" as an independent line (usually horizontal but sometimes sloping upward), with the point of intersection being the indicated solution for the capital-budgeting problem.

[12] It is possible, of course, to take these differences into account on the demand side of the analysis by giving risky projects a lower estimated rate of return than they would otherwise warrant.

that makes the marginal cost of borrowing (including risk) equal to the marginal cost of new equity, it ignores the problem of *how* a firm should act in order to achieve this fine balance in its capital structure. In other words, the approach does not provide a guide to one of the problems of capital budgeting, namely, how should the budget be financed?

APPROACH C

The third approach is a variant of approach A. It takes the cost of debt funds as being equal to the net (after-tax) rate of interest. However, it recognizes that debt funds alone cannot be used in financing capital investment and that debt and equity sources must therefore be viewed as a joint supply. In order to find a single combined cost for this joint supply, the approach takes a weighted average of the cost of debt and the cost of equity.[13] Since this method of estimating the cost of capital does not take into account the risk of borrowing, these risks should be adjusted for in estimating the expected rate of return of individual proposals.[14]

The principal deficiency of this method is that there seems to be no clear-cut rule that can be applied in weighting the debt and equity components of the "combined cost" of capital. Presumably, the relevant proportion on which the weights should be based is the ratio of debt to equity in the current year's financing. But this procedure will yield correct results only if the ratio of debt to equity in this year's financing is roughly equal to the ratio of debt to equity in the existing capital structure of the company.

However, for a company which is changing its capital structure, this equality will not exist. For example, it is quite possible that the ratio of debt to equity in current financing could be considerably higher than past ratios. If this should be the case, two important questions arise: (1) How will the change in over-all capitalization affect the market price of the company's stock and hence the cost of equity? and (2) Is it correct to let borrowing power and borrowing rates that are based on existing assets determine the acceptability of new investment proposals? It is possible, for example, to have a situation in which a hitherto debt-free company can borrow all the funds it needs for this year's capital budget without committing a penny of new equity funds for the expansion. In such a case the combined cost of capital would be equal to the net rate of interest (about 2 per cent). Would it be correct to accept this rate as the cutoff point for deciding the acceptability of proposals in this year's budget?

If, in order to avoid these problems, the combined cost is computed using weights based on existing capital structure, such a computation would fail to reflect the correct cost of the funds that are to be rationed. Thus in order to use approach C, a large measure of *ad hoc* judgment may be necessary. Since the basic goal of a rational system of capital budgeting is to minimize *ad hoc* decisions, approach C is not a complete solution.

A SUGGESTED APPROACH

The three approaches discussed and their shortcomings suggest that the problem of determining the optimum ratio of debt to equity and the problem of measuring the cost of capital cannot be treated independently. Both must be solved within the same framework, and

[13] This approach is the one suggested by Joel Dean (see *Capital Budgeting*, p. 50).

[14] See n. 12.

no simple framework is likely to provide such a solution.

The approach suggested in the following pages is more complex than any of the others which have been discussed. However, it requires no basic information that the other approaches do not also need. The essential difference is that the information is used explicitly and systematically. One important concept that is introduced into this suggested approach is the division of a company's borrowing ability into two categories: (*a*) general borrowing power and (*b*) new borrowing power. These two categories can and should be treated separately and differently for capital-budgeting purposes.

GENERAL BORROWING POWER

General borrowing power refers to the latent borrowing power that a company has because of its existing equity in existing assets. It is the power to raise nonequity funds (including preferred-stock sales) without contributing any new equity for the protection of creditors. When a company uses this general borrowing power, the cost of the funds so obtained should *not* enter directly into capital-budgeting calculations. The correct way to view these funds is as follows:

a) What the financing does is to disentangle equity funds previously committed in the company's asset structure. In other words, the supply of usable equity funds can be derived not only from current earnings and new-stock flotations but also from the liquidation of real assets or from borrowing on the strength of these real assets.

b) The equity funds released by general borrowing should be treated, along with other equity funds, in the supply schedule of equity capital available for new investment by the company. If the readjustment of the company's capital structure does not bring about a change in the market price of the stock, the cost of retained earnings and external equity will be unchanged. The basic effect will be a shift of the entire equity supply schedule to the right.

c) All available equity funds, including those released by the exercise of general borrowing power, should be treated as a single pool to be allocated to proposals on the basis of the system outlined below.

NEW BORROWING POWER

In addition to general borrowing power based on existing assets, a company creates new borrowing power when it adds to its working assets. The investment proposals being considered in a capital budget, if implemented, create new borrowing possibilities; these possibilities and the cost of debt funds that can be acquired should enter directly into capital-budgeting decisions. These decisions, in turn, will determine the exact amount of borrowing to be used in financing the capital budget. A suggested framework for dealing with the cost and amount of debt financing is as follows:

a) Each project under considera ion should be allotted a borrowing quota. When there is a definite tie-in between a project and a loan, this borrowing quota is, in effect, determined by the lender. When no such tie-in exists, it must be imputed by management. However, the principles are the same as those used by a prudent lender. Each proposed project has a definable maximum borrowing power. This depends on the *minimum* rate of net operating earnings that a project can reasonably be expected to produce over the uncertain future.[15] The

[15] The rate of return of a project is the most probable rate which it will earn. But since the future is

maximum loan should be set so that the proposal will be able to meet all the debt charges due on a loan of this size, even if it is assumed that it will earn only at its minimum rate. In other words, each project should be viewed as an entity, and its borrowing allotment should be set so that the chance of this entity's "defaulting" is negligible.

b) The total amount of equity financing needed by a proposal is equal to the total financing needed *less* the borrowing allotment granted to it. Likewise, the flow of net earnings promised by the project on this amount of equity is equal to its expected cash earnings *less* the repayment of interest and principal on its borrowing allotment. This flow of net earnings can be expressed as the net rate of return promised by a project on equity funds it uses.

c) What we obtain from this procedure is a schedule that shows, for each proposal, the amount of equity funds it needs and the net rate of yield it promises to return if these funds are granted for it. This schedule should be arranged in descending order of promised yield. Alongside it, we have the schedule showing the "cost" of using succeeding increments of equity capital. The point of intersection of these two schedules is the logical cutoff point for the capital budget.

The suggested framework outlined here bases capital-budgeting decisions on a comparison between a project's net earning rate (net of taxes and debt charges) and the cost of equity funds. Borrowing rates are taken into account on the demand side of the analysis. The system for doing this adjusts explicitly for the risk differences between proposals by allowing the less risky proposals a higher proportion of low-cost debt funds.

The cutoff point indicated by this framework provides a simultaneous solution for both the financing and the investment decisions of capital budgeting: (1) it determines which proposals should be accepted and (2) it determines the amount of debt to be used in financing these proposals. This amount will be equal to the sum of the borrowing allotments on each accepted proposal.

UNSOLVED ISSUES

This paper has been concerned with the problem of determining the extent and financing of a specific capital budget. It has sought a correct way of defining and measuring the cost of capital and a framework for making decisions when more than one source of financing is used. However, it does not take into account a broader problem in capital budgeting. This is the problem of deciding whether a given set of acceptable investment proposals and their financing might not be even more profitable if deferred to a subsequent budget. This broader issue involves a comparison of the present costs of capital goods and financial funds with future costs. If there are strong expectations of net favorable changes in one or both of these basic variables, it might be necessary to postpone decisions indicated by the framework developed previously. However, a consideration of these refinements lies beyond the scope of this paper.

---

uncertain, the actual rate may turn out to be below or above the most probable rate. Risky projects have a wider range of possible earnings than do less risky projects. The minimum rate is that rate below which the actual rate is highly unlikely to fall.

CAPITAL EQUIPMENT ANALYSIS: THE REQUIRED RATE OF PROFIT

MYRON J. GORDON AND ELI SHAPIRO*

THE interest in capital equipment analysis that has been evident in the business literature of the past five years is the product of numerous social, economic, and business developments of the postwar period. No conclusive listing of these developments can be attempted here. However, four should be mentioned which are of particular importance in this search for a more systematic method for discovering, evaluating, and selecting investment opportunities. These are: (1) the high level of capital outlays (in absolute terms); (2) the growth in the size of business firms; (3) the delegation of responsibility for initiating recommendations from top management to the profit center, which has been part of the general movement toward decentralization; and (4) the growing use of "scientific management" in the operations of the business firm.

These developments have motivated the current attempt to develop objective criteria whereby the executive committee in a decentralized firm can arrive at a capital budget. Since each of its profit centers submits capital proposals, the executive committee must screen these and establish an allocation and a level of capital outlays that is consistent with top management's criteria for rationing the firm's funds. Capital budgeting affords the promise that this screening process can be made amenable to some established criteria that are understandable to all the component parts of the firm. Consequently, capital budgeting appeals to top management, for, in the first place, each plant manager can see his proposal in the light of all competing proposals for the funds of the enterprise. This may not completely eliminate irritation among the various parts of the firm, but a rational capital budgeting program can go a long way toward maintaining initiative on the part of a plant manager, even though the executive committee may veto one or all of his proposals. In the second place, the use of a capital budgeting program serves to satisfy top management that each accepted proposal meets adequate predetermined standards and that the budget as a whole is part of a sound, long-run plan for the firm.

What specifically does a capital budgeting program entail? The focal points of capital budgeting are: (1) ascertaining the profit abilities of the array of capital outlay alternatives, and (2) determining the least profitability required to make an investment, i.e., a cut-off point. Capital budgeting also involves administrative procedures and organization designed to discover investment opportunities, process information, and carry out the budget; however, these latter aspects of the subject have been discussed in detail by means of case studies that have appeared in publications of the American Management Association and the National Industrial

† The authors are respectively Associate Professor and Professor in the School of Industrial Management, Massachusetts Institute of Technology.

Conference Board and in periodicals such as the *N.A.C.A. Bulletin.*[1] Hence, we will not concern ourselves with them here.

There are at least four methods for establishing an order-preference array of the capital expenditure suggestions. They are: (1) the still popular "payoff period"; (2) the average investment formula; (3) the present value formula with the rate of interest given; and (4) the present value formula used to find the rate of profit. It is not our intention in this paper to discuss these various methods specifically, since critical analyses of these alternatives are to be found in papers by Dean, by Lorie and Savage, and by Gordon in a recent issue of the *Journal of Business,*[2] which is devoted exclusively to the subject of capital budgeting.

However, it is of interest to note that in each of these methods the future revenue streams generated by the proposed outlays must be amenable to measurement if the method is to be operational. However, improvements in quality, more pleasant working conditions, strategic advantages of integration, and other types of benefits from a capital outlay are still recognized only in qualitative terms, and there is a considerable hiatus in the literature of capital budgeting with respect to the solution of this problem. Hence, in the absence of satisfactory methods for quantifying these types of benefits, the evaluation of alternative proposals is still characterized by intuitive judgments on the part of management, and a general quantitative solution to the capital budgeting problem is not now feasible. It appears to us that this problem affords one of the most promising opportunities for the application of the methods of management science. In fact, we anticipate that techniques for the quantification of the more important factors now treated qualitatively will soon be found.

Given the rate of profit on each capital outlay proposal, the size of the budget and its allocation are automatically determined with the establishment of the rate of profit required for the inclusion of a proposal in the budget. In the balance of this paper, a method for determining this quantity is proposed and its use in capital budgeting is analyzed.

II

We state that the objective of a firm is the maximization of the value of the stockholders' equity. While there may be legitimate differences of opinion as to whether this is the sole motivation of management, we certainly feel that there can be no quarrel with the statement that it is a dominant variable in management's decisions. It has been shown by Lutz and Lutz in their *Theory of the Investment of the Firm*[3] and by

[1] American Management Association, *Tested Approaches to Capital Equipment Replacement,* Special Report No. 1, 1954; American Management Association, *Capital Equipment Replacement; AMA Special Conference,* May 3-4, 1954 (New York, 1954, American Management Association, 105 pp.); J. H. Watson, III, National Industrial Conference Board, *Controlling Capital Expenditures,* Studies in Business Policy, No. 62, April, 1953; C. I. Fellers, "Problems of Capital Expenditure Budgeting", *N.A.C.A. Bulletin,* 26 (May, 1955), 918-24; E. N. Martin, "Equipment Replacement Policy and Application", *N.A.C.A. Bulletin,* 35 (February, 1954), 715-30.

[2] *Journal of Business,* Vol. XXVIII, No. 3 (October, 1955).

[3] Friedrich and Vera Lutz, *The Theory of Investment of the Firm* (Princeton, N. J., 1951, Princeton University Press, 253 pp.) 41-43.

others[4] that this objective is realized in capital budgeting when the budget is set so as to equate the marginal return on investment with the rate of return at which the corporation's stock is selling in the market. The logic and operation of this criterion will be discussed later. Now, we only wish to note the role assigned in capital budgeting to the rate of profit that is required by the market.

At the present time, the dividend yield (the current dividend divided by the price) and the earnings yield (the current income per share divided by the price) are used to measure the rate of profit at which a share is selling. However, both these yields fail to recognize that a share's payments can be expected to grow, and the earnings yield fails to recognize that the corporation's earnings per share are not the payments made to the stockholder.

The practical significance of these failures is evidenced by the qualifications with which these two rate-of-profit measures are used by investment analysts. In the comparative analysis of common stocks for the purpose of arriving at buy or sell recommendation, the conclusions indicated by the dividend and/or the earnings yield are invariably qualified by the presence or absence of the prospect of growth. If it is necessary to qualify a share's yield as a measure of the rate of profit one might expect to earn by buying the share, then it must follow that current yield, whether income or dividend, is inadequate for the purposes of capital budgeting, which is also concerned with the future. In short, it appears to us that the prospective growth in a share's revenue stream should be reflected in a measure of the rate of profit at which the share is selling. Otherwise, its usefulness as the required rate of profit in capital budgeting is questionable.

In his *Theory of Investment Value*,[5] a classic on the subject, J. B. Williams tackled this problem of growth. However, the models he developed were arbitrary and complicated so that the problem of growth remained among the phenomena dealt with qualitatively. It is our belief that the following proposal for a definition of the rate of profit that takes cognizance of prospective growth has merit.

The accepted definition of the rate of profit on an asset is the rate of discount that equates the asset's expected future payments with its price. Let P_0 = a share's price at $t = 0$, let D_t = the dividend expected at time t, and let k = the rate of profit. Then, the rate of profit on a share of stock is the value of k that satisfies

$$(1) \qquad P_0 = \sum_{t=1}^{\infty} \frac{D_t}{(1+k)^t}.$$

It is mathematically convenient to assume that the dividend is paid and discounted continuously at the annual rates D_t and k, in which case

$$(2) \qquad P_0 = \int_0^{\infty} D_t e^{-kt}\, dt.$$

Since P_0 is known, estimating the rate of profit at which a share of stock is selling requires the determination of D_t, $t = 1, 2, \cdots, \infty$.

[4] Joel Dean, *Capital Budgeting: Top Management Policy on Plant, Equipment, and Product Development* (New York, 1951, Columbia University Press, 174 pp.); Roland P. Soule, "Trends in the Cost of Capital", *Harvard Business Review*, 31 (March, April, 1953), 33-47.

[5] J. B. Williams, *The Theory of Investment Value*, (Cambridge, Massachusetts, 1938, Harvard University Press), 87-96.

At the outset it should be made clear that our objective is not to find the rate of profit that *will actually be earned* by buying a share of stock. This requires knowledge of the dividends that will be paid in the future, the price at which the share will be sold, and when it will be sold. Unfortunately, such information is not available to us. The rate of profit of interest here is a relation between the present known price and the *expected future dividends*. The latter will vary among individuals with the information they have on a host of variables and with their personality. Therefore, by expected future dividends we mean an estimate that (1) is derivable from known data in an objective manner, (2) is derived by methods that appear reasonable, i.e., not in conflict with common sense knowledge of corporation financial behavior, and (3) can be used to arrive at a manageable measure of the rate of profit implicit in the expectation.

We arrive at D_t by means of two assumptions. One, a corporation is expected to retain a fraction b of its income after taxes; and two, a corporation is expected to earn a return of r on the book value of its common equity. Let Y_t equal a corporation's income per share of common after taxes at time t. Then the expected dividend at time t is

$$D_t = (1 - b)\, Y_t \tag{3}$$

The income per share at time t is the income at $(t-1)$ plus r percent of the income at $(t-1)$ retained, or

$$Y_t = Y_{t-1} + rbY_{t-1} \tag{4}$$

Equation (4) is simply a compound interest expression so that, if Y_t grows continuously at the rate $g = br$,

$$Y_t = Y_0 e^{gt}. \tag{5}$$

From Equations (3) and (5)

$$D_t = D_0 e^{gt}. \tag{6}$$

Substituting this expression for D_t in Equation (2) and integrating, yields

$$\begin{aligned} P_0 &= \int_0^\infty D_0\, e^{gt}\, e^{-kt}\, dt \\ &= D_0 \int_0^\infty e^{-t(k-g)}\, dt \qquad (7) \\ &= \frac{D_0}{k-g}. \end{aligned}$$

The condition for a solution is $k > g$, a condition that is easily satisfied, for otherwise, P_0 would be infinite or negative.

Solving Equation (7) for k we find that

$$k = \frac{D_0}{P_0} + g. \tag{8}$$

Translated, this means that the rate of profit at which a share of common stock is selling is equal to the current dividend, divided by the current price (the dividend yield), plus the rate at which the dividend is expected to grow. Since there are other possible empirical definitions of the market rate of profit on a share of stock, we will refer to k as the growth rate of profit.

III

Let us now review and evaluate the rationale of the model we have just established. Estimating the rate of profit on a share of stock involves estimating the future dividend stream that it provides, and the fundamental difference between this model and the dividend yield is the assumption of growth. The latter, as can be seen, assumes that the dividend will remain constant. Since growth is generally recognized as a factor in the value of a share and since it is used to explain differences in dividend yield among shares, its explicit recognition appears desirable. Future dividends are uncertain, but the problem cannot be avoided by ignoring it. To assume a constant rate of growth and estimate it to be equal to the current rate appears to be a better alternative.

Under this model the dividend will grow at the rate br, which is the product of the fraction of income retained and the rate of return earned on net worth. It is mathematically true that the dividend will grow at this rate if the corporation retains b and earns r. While we can be most certain that the dividend will not grow uniformly and continuously at some rate, unless we believe that an alternative method for estimating the future dividend stream is superior, the restriction of the model to the assumption that it will grow uniformly at some rate is no handicap. Furthermore, the future is discounted; hence, an error in the estimated dividend for a year in the distant future results in a considerably smaller error in k than an error in estimating the dividend in a near year.

It should be noted that this measure of the rate of profit is suspect, when *both* income and dividend are zero, and it may also be questioned when either falls to very low (or negative) values. In such cases, the model yields a lower rate of profit than one might believe that the market requires on a corporation in such difficulties. It is evident that the dividend and the income yields are even more suspect under these conditions and, hence, are subject to the same limitations.

There are other approaches to the estimation of future dividends than the extrapolation of the current dividend on the basis of the growth rate implicit in b and r. In particular, one can arrive at g directly by taking some average of the past rate of growth in a corporation's dividend. Whether or not this or some other measure of the expected future dividends is superior to the one presented earlier will depend on their relative usefulness in such purposes as the analysis of variation in prices among shares and the preferences of those who want an objective measure of a share's rate of profit.

So far, we have compared the growth rate of profit with the income and dividend yields on theoretical grounds. Let us now consider how they differ in practice, using the same measurement rules for the variables in each case. The numerical difference between the growth rate of profit and the dividend yield is simply the growth rate. However, the income yield, which is the measure of the rate of profit commonly recommended for capital budgeting, differs from the growth rate of profit in a more complex manner, and to establish this difference we first note that

$$(9) \qquad b = \frac{Y - D}{Y} \text{ and } r = \frac{Y}{B}$$

where $B =$ the net worth or book value per share. The growth rate of profit, therefore, may be written as

$$(10) \qquad k = \frac{D}{P} + br = \frac{D}{P} + \frac{Y - D}{B}.$$

Next, the income yield can be decomposed as follows:

$$(11) \qquad y = \frac{Y}{P} = \frac{D}{P} + \frac{Y - D}{P}.$$

We see then that y and k will be equal when book and market values are equal. It can be argued that the income yield overstates a share's payment stream by assuming that each payment is equal to the income per share and understates the payment stream by assuming that it will not grow. Hence, in this special case where book and market values are equal, the two errors exactly compensate each other.

Commonly market and book values differ, and y will be above k when market is below book, and it will be below k when market is above book. Hence, a share of IBM, for example, that is priced far above book had had an earnings yield of two to three percent in 1955. We know that the market requires a higher rate of profit on a common stock, even on IBM, and its growth rate of profit, k, is more in accord with the value suggested by common sense. Conversely, when U. S. Steel was selling at one-half of book value in 1950, the high income yield grossly overstated the rate of profit that the market was, in fact, requiring on the stock.

Furthermore, the growth rate of profit will fluctuate in a narrower range than the earnings yield. For instance, during the last few years, income, dividends, and book value have gone up more or less together, but market price has gone up at a considerably higher rate. Consequently, the growth rate of profit, dependent in part on book value, has fallen less than the earnings yield. Conversely, in a declining market k would rise less rapidly than y.

There is a widespread feeling that many accounting figures, particularly book value per share, are insensitive to the realities of the world, and some may feel that the comparative stability of k is merely a consequence of the limitations of accounting data. This is not true! The behavior of k is not a consequence of the supposed lack of realism in accounting data. Rather, book value appears in the model because it, and not market value, is used to measure the rate of return the corporation earns on investment, which, we have seen, is the rate of return that enters into the determination of the rate at which the dividend will grow. The comparative stability of k follows from the simple fact that, when a revenue stream is expected to grow, a change in the required rate of profit will give rise to a more than proportional change in the asset's price. Conversely, a change in the price reflects a less than proportional change in the rate of profit.

IV

Given the rate of profit expected on each item in the schedule of available investment opportunities and given the rate of profit at which the corporation's stock is selling, what should the capital budget be? As stated earlier, the accepted theory is that the budget should be set so as to equate the marginal return on investment with the rate of profit at which the stock is selling. The reasoning is, if the market requires, let us say, a 10 percent return on investment in the corporation's stock, and if the corporation can earn 15 percent on additional investment, obtaining the funds and making the investment will increase the earnings per share. As the earnings and the dividend per share increase or as the market becomes persuaded that they will increase, the price of the stock will rise. The objective, it will be recalled, is the maximization of the value of the stockholder's equity.

The conclusion drawn implicitly assumes that the corporation can sell additional shares at or above the prevailing market, or if a new issue depresses the market, the fall will be slight, and the price will soon rise above the previous level. However, some other consideration may argue against a new stock issue; for example, the management may be concerned with dilution of control, or the costs of floating a new issue may be very high, or a new issue may be expected to depress the price severely and indefinitely for reasons not recognized in the theory. Hence, it does not automatically follow that a new issue should be floated when a firm's demand for funds exceeds, according to the above criterion, those that are internally available.

In determining whether the required rate of profit is above or below r', the marginal return on investment, one can use y, the earnings yield, or k, the growth rate of profit as the required rate of profit. If y and k differ and if the reasoning in support of k presented earlier is valid, using y to estimate the direction in which a new issue will change the price of the stock may result in a wrong conclusion.

In arriving at the optimum size of a stock issue, the objective is to equate r' and y or k, depending on which is used. Internal data may be used to estimate the marginal efficiency of capital schedule. If the required rate of profit is considered a constant, its definition, $y = Y/P$ or $k = D/P + br$, provides its value. However, the required rate of profit may vary with the size of the stock issue or with the variables that may change as a consequence of the issue. In this event, finding the optimum size of a stock issue requires a model that predicts the variation in the required rate of profit with the relevant variables.

Borrowing is an alternative source of funds for investment. However, an analysis of this alternative requires the measurement of both (1) the variation in risk with debt, and (2) the difference between the rate of profit and the rate of interest needed to cover a given increase in risk. This has not been done as yet, which may explain the widespread practice of arbitrarily establishing a "satisfactory" financial structure and only borrowing to the extent allowed by it.

It has been stated by Dean[6] and Terborgh[7] that the long-term ceiling on a firm's capital outlays is the amount of its internally available funds. However, the share of its income a corporation retains is not beyond the control of its management; and, among the things we want from a capital budgeting model is guidance on whether the share of a corporation's income that is retained for investment should be raised or lowered.

Proceeding along traditional lines, the problem may be posed as follows. A firm estimates its earnings and depreciation allowances for the coming year and deducts the planned dividend to arrive at a preliminary figure for the capital budget. The marginal rate of return on investment in excess of this amount may be above or below the required rate of profit. We infer from theory that the two rates should be equated by (1) raising the budget and

[6]Dean, *op. cit.*, 53-55.

[7]George Willard Terborgh, *Dynamic Equipment Policy* (New York, 1949, McGraw-Hill, 290 pp.), 228-29.

reducing the dividend when the marginal return on investment is above the required rate of return, and (2) raising the dividend and reducing the budget when the reverse holds. The conditions under which this process yields an equilibrium are illustrated in Figure 1. The marginal return on investment, r', should fall as the budget is increased, and the required rate of profit, y or k, should increase or it should fall at a lower rate than r'. The latter case is illustrated by the line y_a or k_a.

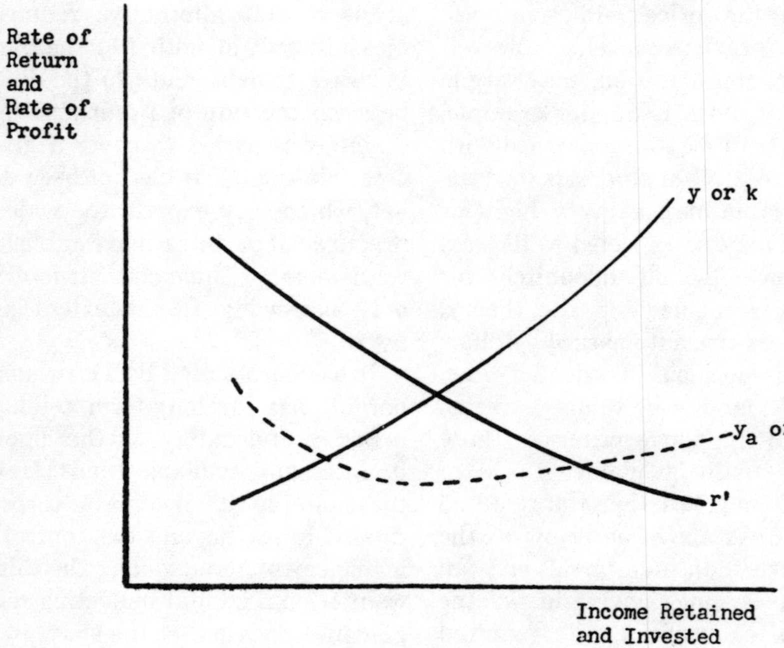

FIG. 1

Changing the dividend so as to equate r' and say y should maximize the price of the stock. For instance, if r' is above y, the company can earn a higher return on investment than stockholders require, and a dollar used this way is worth more to the stockholders than the dollar distributed in dividends. In other words, the price should go up by more than the income retained.

There are, of course, a number of problems connected with the use of this model for arriving at the optimum dividend rate. First, there is the question whether y or k should be used to measure the required rate of profit. Second, there is no question that the required rate of profit varies with the dividend rate. Hence, the current rate of profit given by the definition does not tell what profit rate will be required with a different dividend rate. This requires a model which predicts the variation in y or k with the dividend rate and other variables. Third, there is a very nasty problem of the short and the long run. It is widely believed, though the evidence has limitations, that the price of a share of stock varies with the dividend rate, in which case a corporation should distribute all of its income.

However, it is quite possible that a change in the dividend gives rise to the expectation that earnings and future dividends are changing in the same direction. Further, in the short run, the market is not likely to be informed on a firm's marginal efficiency of capital schedule. For these and other reasons, it is likely that the dividend rate should not be made to vary with short-run changes in the marginal efficiency of capital, and more sophisticated methods than those now in use are needed to establish the variation in price or required rate of profit with the dividend rate.

V

The major points developed in this paper may be summarized as follows. We presented a definition of the rate of profit required by the market on a share of common stock, and we noted some of its advantages. It is theoretically superior to the income and dividend yields because it recognizes that the revenue stream provided by a share can be expected to grow. Furthermore, its empirical characteristics are also superior to those of the income and dividend yields since its value is generally in closer agreement with common sense notions concerning the prevailing rate of profit on a share of stock and since its value fluctuates in a narrower range over time. We next examined some of the problems involved in using this definition of the rate of profit and the earnings yield in capital budgeting models. Finally, we saw that, before capital budgeting theory can be made a reliable guide to action, we must improve our techniques for estimating the future revenue on a capital outlay proposal, and we must learn a good deal more about how the rate of profit the market requires on a share of stock varies with the dividend, the growth rate, and other variables that may influence it.

THE COST OF CAPITAL, CORPORATION FINANCE AND THE THEORY OF INVESTMENT

FRANCO MODIGLIANI AND MERTON H. MILLER†

WHAT IS THE "cost of capital" to a firm in a world in which funds are used to acquire assets whose yields are uncertain; and in which capital can be obtained by many different media, ranging from pure debt instruments, representing money-fixed claims, to pure equity issues, giving holders only the right to a pro-rata share in the uncertain venture? This question has vexed at least three classes of economists: (1) the corporation finance specialist concerned with the techniques of financing firms so as to ensure their survival and growth; (2) the managerial economist concerned with capital budgeting; and (3) the economic theorist concerned with explaining investment behavior at both the micro and macro levels.[1]

In much of his formal analysis, the economic theorist at least has tended to side-step the essence of this cost-of-capital problem by proceeding as though physical assets—like bonds—could be regarded as yielding known, sure streams. Given this assumption, the theorist has concluded that the cost of capital to the owners of a firm is simply the rate of interest on bonds; and has derived the familiar proposition that the firm, acting rationally, will tend to push investment to the point where the marginal yield on physical assets is equal to the market rate of interest.[2] This proposition can be shown to follow from either of two criteria of rational decision-making which are equivalent under certainty, namely (1) the maximization of profits and (2) the maximization of market value.

According to the first criterion, a physical asset is worth acquiring if it will increase the net profit of the owners of the firm. But net profit will increase only if the expected rate of return, or yield, of the asset exceeds the rate of interest. According to the second criterion, an asset is worth acquiring if it increases the value of the owners' equity, *i.e.*, if it adds more to the market value of the firm than the costs of acquisition. But what the asset adds is given by capitalizing the stream it generates at the market rate of interest, and this

† The authors are, respectively, professor and associate professor of economics in the Graduate School of Industrial Administration, Carnegie Institute of Technology. This article is a revised version of a paper delivered at the anual meeting of the Econometric Society, December 1956. The authors express thanks for the comments and suggestions made at that time by the discussants of the paper, Evsey Domar, Robert Eisner and John Lintner, and subsequently by James Duesenberry. They are also greatly indebted to many of their present and former colleagues and students at Carnegie Tech who served so often and with such remarkable patience as a critical forum for the ideas here presented.

1 The literature bearing on the cost-of-capital problem is far too extensive for listing here. Numerous references to it will be found throughout the paper though we make no claim to completeness. One phase of the problem which we do not consider explicitly, but which has a considerable literature of its own is the relation between the cost of capital and public utility rates. For a recent summary of the "cost-of-capital theory" of rate regulation and a brief discussion of some of its implications, the reader may refer to H. M. Somers [20].

2 Or, more accurately, to the marginal cost of borrowed funds since it is customary, at least in advanced analysis, to draw the supply curve of borrowed funds to the firm as a rising one. For an advanced treatment of the certainty case, see F. and V. Lutz [13].

capitalized value will exceed its cost if and only if the yield of the asset exceeds the rate of interest. Note that, under either formulation, the cost of capital is equal to the rate of interest on bonds, regardless of whether the funds are acquired through debt instruments or through new issues of common stock. Indeed, in a world of sure returns, the distinction between debt and equity funds reduces largely to one of terminology.

It must be acknowledged that some attempt is usually made in this type of analysis to allow for the existence of uncertainty. This attempt typically takes the form of superimposing on the results of the certainty analysis the notion of a "risk discount" to be subtracted from the expected yield (or a "risk premium" to be added to the market rate of interest). Investment decisions are then supposed to be based on a comparison of this "risk adjusted" or "certainty equivalent" yield with the market rate of interest.[3] No satisfactory explanation has yet been provided, however, as to what determines the size of the risk discount and how it varies in response to changes in other variables.

Considered as a convenient approximation, the model of the firm constructed via this certainty—or certainty-equivalent — approach has admittedly been useful in dealing with some of the grosser aspects of the processes of capital accumulation and economic fluctuations. Such a model underlies, for example, the familiar Keynesian aggregate investment function in which aggregate investment is written as a function of the rate of interest—the same riskless rate of interest which appears later in the system in the liquidity-preference equation. Yet few would maintain that this approximation is adequate. At the macroeconomic level there are ample grounds for doubting that the rate of interest has as large and as direct an influence on the rate of investment as this analysis would lead us to believe. At the microeconomic level the certainty model has little descriptive value and provides no real guidance to the finance specialist or managerial economist whose main problems cannot be treated in a framework which deals so cavalierly with uncertainty and ignores all forms of financing other than debt issues.[4]

Only recently have economists begun to face up seriously to the problem of the cost of capital *cum* risk. In the process they have found their interests and endeavors merging with those of the finance specialist and the managerial economist who have lived with the problem longer and more intimately. In this joint search to establish the principles which govern rational investment and financial policy in a world of uncertainty two main lines of attack can be discerned. These lines represent, in effect, attempts to extrapolate to the world of uncertainty each of the two criteria—profit maximization and market value maximization—which were seen to have equivalent implications in the special case of certainty. With the recognition of uncertainty this equivalence vanishes. In fact, the profit maxi-

[3] The classic examples of the certainty-equivalent approach are found in J. R. Hicks [8] and O. Lange [11].

[4] Those who have taken a "case-method" course in finance in recent years will recall in this connection the famous Liquigas case of Hunt and Williams, [9, pp. 193-96] a case which is often used to introduce the student to the cost-of-capital problem and to poke a bit of fun at the economist's certainty-model.

mization criterion is no longer even well defined. Under uncertainty there corresponds to each decision of the firm not a unique profit outcome, but a plurality of mutally exclusive outcomes which can at best be described by a subjective probability distribution. The profit outcome, in short, has become a random variable and as such its maximization no longer has an operational meaning. Nor can this difficulty generally be disposed of by using the mathematical expectation of profits as the variable to be maximized. For decisions which affect the expected value will also tend to affect the dispersion and other characteristics of the distribution of outcomes. In particular, the use of debt rather than equity funds to finance a given venture may well increase the expected return to the owners, but only at the cost of increased dispersion of the outcomes.

Under these conditions the profit outcomes of alternative investment and financing decisions can be compared and ranked only in terms of a *subjective* "utility function" of the owners which weighs the expected yield against other characteristics of the distribution. Accordingly, the extrapolation of the profit maximization criterion of the certainty model has tended to evolve into utility maximization, sometimes explicitly, more frequently in a qualitative and heuristic form.[5]

The utility approach undoubtedly represents an advance over the certainty or certainty-equivalent approach. It does at least permit us to explore (within limits) some of the implications of different financing arrangements, and it does give some meaning to the "cost" of different types of funds. However, because the cost of capital has become an essentially subjective concept, the utility approach has serious drawbacks for normative as well as analytical purposes. How, for example, is management to ascertain the risk preferences of its stockholders and to compromise among their tastes? And how can the economist build a meaningful investment function in the face of the fact that any given investment opportunity might or might not be worth exploiting depending on precisely who happen to be the owners of the firm at the moment?

Fortunately, these questions do not have to be answered; for the alternative approach, based on market value maximization, can provide the basis for an operational definition of the cost of capital and a workable theory of investment. Under this approach any investment project and its concomitant financing plan must pass only the following test: Will the project, as financed, raise the market value of the firm's shares? If so, it is worth undertaking; if not, its return is less than the marginal cost of capital to the firm. Note that such a test is entirely independent of the tastes of the current owners, since market prices will reflect not only their preferences but those of all potential owners as well. If any current stockholder disagrees with management and the market over the valuation of the project, he is free to sell out and reinvest elsewhere, but will still benefit from the capital appreciation resulting from management's decision.

The potential advantages of the market-value approach have long been appreciated; yet analytical results have been meager. What appears to be keep-

[5] For an attempt at a rigorous explicit development of this line of attack, see F. Modigliani and M. Zeman [14].

ing this line of development from achieving its promise is largely the lack of an adequate theory of the effect of financial structure on market valuations, and of how these effects can be inferred from objective market data. It is with the development of such a theory and of its implications for the cost-of-capital problem that we shall be concerned in this paper.

Our procedure will be to develop in Section I the basic theory itself and to give some brief account of its empirical relevance. In Section II, we show how the theory can be used to answer the cost-of-capital question and how it permits us to develop a theory of investment of the firm under conditions of uncertainty. Throughout these sections the approach is essentially a partial-equilibrium one focusing on the firm and "industry." Accordingly, the "prices" of certain income streams will be treated as constant and given from outside the model, just as in the standard Marshallian analysis of the firm and industry the prices of all inputs and of all other products are taken as given. We have chosen to focus at this level rather than on the economy as a whole because it is at the level of the firm and the industry that the interests of the various specialists concerned with the cost-of-capital problem come most closely together. Although the emphasis has thus been placed on partial-equilibrium analysis, the results obtained also provide the essential building blocks for a general equilibrium model which shows how those prices which are here taken as given, are themselves determined. For reasons of space, however, and because the material is of interest in its own right, the presentation of the general equilibrium model which rounds out the analysis must be deferred to a subsequent paper.

I. THE VALUATION OF SECURITIES, LEVERAGE, AND THE COST OF CAPITAL

A. *The Capitalization Rate for Uncertain Streams*

As a starting point, consider an economy in which all physical assets are owned by corporations. For the moment, assume that these corporations can finance their assets by issuing common stock only; the introduction of bond issues, or their equivalent, as a source of corporate funds is postponed until the next part of this section.

The physical assets held by each firm will yield to the owners of the firm—its stockholders—a stream of "profits" over time; but the elements of this series need not be constant and in any event are uncertain. This stream of income, and hence the stream accruing to any share of common stock, will be regarded as extending indefinitely into the future. We assume, however, that the mean value of the stream over time, or average profit per unit of time, is finite and represents a random variable subject to a (subjective) probability distribution. We shall refer to the average value over time of the stream accruing to a given share as the return of that share; and to the mathematical expectation of this average as the expected return of the share.[6] Although

[6] These propositions can be restated analytically as follows: The assets of the *i*th firm generate a stream:

$$X_i(1), X_i(2) \cdots X_i(T)$$

whose elements are random variables subject to the joint probability distribution:

$$\chi_i[X_i(1), X_i(2) \cdots X_i(t)].$$

The return to the *i*th firm is defined as:

individual investors may have different views as to the shape of the probability distribution of the return of any share, we shall assume for simplicity that they are at least in agreement as to the expected return.[7]

This way of characterizing uncertain streams merits brief comment. Notice first that the stream is a stream of profits, not dividends. As will become clear later, as long as management is presumed to be acting in the best interests of the stockholders, retained earnings can be regarded as equivalent to a fully subscribed, pre-emptive issue of common stock. Hence, for present purposes, the division of the stream between cash dividends and retained earnings in any period is a mere detail. Notice also that the uncertainty attaches to the mean value over time of the stream of profits and should not be confused with variability over time of the successive elements of the stream. That variability and uncertainty are two totally different concepts should be clear from the fact that the elements of a stream can be variable even though known with certainty. It can be shown, furthermore, that whether the elements of a stream are sure or uncertain, the effect of variability per se on the valuation of the stream is at best a second-order one which can safely be neglected for our purposes (and indeed most others too).[8]

The next assumption plays a strategic role in the rest of the analysis. We shall assume that firms can be divided into "equivalent return" classes such that the return on the shares issued by any firm in any given class is proportional to (and hence perfectly correlated with) the return on the shares issued by any other firm in the same class. This assumption implies that the various shares within the same class differ, at most, by a "scale factor." Accordingly, if we adjust for the difference in scale, by taking the *ratio* of the return to the expected return, the probability distribution of that ratio is identical for all shares in the class. It follows that all relevant properties of a share are uniquely characterized by specifying (1) the class to which it belongs and (2) its expected return.

The significance of this assumption is that it permits us to classify firms into groups within which the shares of different firms are "homogeneous," that is, perfect substitutes for one another. We have, thus, an analogue to the familiar concept of the industry in which it is the commodity produced by the firms that is taken as homogeneous. To complete this analogy with Marshallian price theory, we shall assume in the analysis to follow that the shares concerned are traded in perfect markets

---

$$X_i = \lim_{T \to \infty} \frac{1}{T} \sum_{t=1}^{T} X_i(t).$$

X_i is itself a random variable with a probability distribution $\Phi_i(X_i)$ whose form is determined uniquely by χ_i. The expected return $\overline{X}_i$ is defined as $\overline{X}_i = E(X_i) = \int x_i X_i \Phi_i(X_i) dX_i$. If N_i is the number of shares outstanding, the return of the ith share is $x_i = (1/N)X_i$ with probability distribution $\phi_i(x_i)dx_i = \Phi_i(Nx_i)d(Nx_i)$ and expected value $= \overline{x}_i\ (1/N)\ \overline{X}_i$.

[7]To deal adequately with refinements such as differences among investors in estimates of expected returns would require extensive discussion of the theory of portfolio selection. Brief references to these and related topics will be made in the succeeding article on the general equilibrium model.

[8]The reader may convince himself of this by asking how much he would be willing to rebate to his employer for the privilege of receiving his annual salary in equal monthly installments rather than in irregular amounts over the year. See also J. M. Keynes [10, esp. pp. 53-54].

under conditions of atomistic competition.[9]

From our definition of homogeneous classes of stock it follows that in equilibrium in a perfect capital market the price per dollar's worth of expected return must be the same for all shares of any given class. Or, equivalently, in any given class the price of every share must be proportional to its expected return. Let us denote this factor of proportionality for any class, say the kth class, by $1/\rho_k$. Then if p_j denotes the price and $\bar{x}_j$ is the expected return per share of the jth firm in class k, we must have:

$$(1) \qquad p_j = \frac{1}{\rho_k} \bar{x}_j;$$

or, equivalently,

$$(2) \qquad \frac{\bar{x}_j}{p_j} = \rho_k$$

a constant for all firms j in class k.

The constants ρ_k (one for each of the k classes) can be given several economic interpretations: (a) From (2) we see that each ρ_k is the expected rate of return of any share in class k. (b) From (1) $1/\rho_k$ is the price which an investor has to pay for a dollar's worth of expected return in the class k. (c) Again from (1), by analogy with the terminology for perpetual bonds, ρ_k can be regarded as the market rate of capitalization for the expected value of the uncertain streams of the kind generated by the kth class of firms.[10]

B. *Debt Financing and Its Effects on Security Prices*

Having developed an apparatus for dealing with uncertain streams we can now approach the heart of the cost-of-capital problem by dropping the assumption that firms cannot issue bonds. The introduction of debt-financing changes the market for shares in a very fundamental way. Because firms may have different proportions of debt in their capital structure, shares of different companies, even in the same class, can give rise to different probability distributions of returns. In the language of finance, the shares will be subject to different degrees of financial risk or "leverage" and hence they will no longer be perfect substitutes for one another.

To exhibit the mechanism determining the relative prices of shares under these conditions, we make the following two assumptions about the nature of bonds and the bond market, though they are actually stronger than is necessary and will be relaxed later: (1) All bonds (including any debts issued by households for the purpose of carrying shares) are assumed to yield a constant income per unit of time, and this income is regarded as certain by all traders

[9] Just what our classes of stocks contain and how the different classes can be identified by outside observers are empirical questions to which we shall return later. For the present, it is sufficient to observe: (1) Our concept of a class, while not identical to that of the industry is at least closely related to it. Certainly the basic characteristics of the probability distributions of the returns on assets will depend to a significant extent on the product sold and the technology used. (2) What are the appropriate class boundaries will depend on the particular problem being studied. An economist concerned with general tendencies in the market, for example, might well be prepared to work with far wider classes than would be appropriate for an investor planning his portfolio, or a firm planning its financial strategy.

[10] We cannot, on the basis of the assumptions so far, make any statements about the relationship or spread between the various ρ's or capitalization rates. Before we could do so we would have to make further specific assumptions about the way investors believe the probability distributions vary from class to class, as well as assumptions about investors' preferences as between the characteristics of different distributions.

regardless of the issuer. (2) Bonds, like stocks, are traded in a perfect market, where the term perfect is to be taken in its usual sense as implying that any two commodities which are perfect substitutes for each other must sell, in equilibrium, at the same price. It follows from assumption (1) that all bonds are in fact perfect substitutes up to a scale factor. It follows from assumption (2) that they must all sell at the same price per dollar's worth or return, or what amounts to the same thing must yield the same rate of return. This rate of return will be denoted by r and referred to as the rate of interest or, equivalently, as the capitalization rate for sure streams. We now can derive the following two basic propositions with respect to the valuation of securities in companies with different capital structures:

Proposition I. Consider any company j and let $\overline{X}_j$ stand as before for the expected return on the assets owned by the company (that is, its expected profit before deduction of interest). Denote by D_j the market value of the debts of the company; by S_j the market value of its common shares; and by $V_j \equiv S_j + D_j$ the market value of all its securities or, as we shall say, the market value of the firm. Then, our Proposition I asserts that we must have in equilibrium:

$$(3) \qquad V_j \equiv (S_j + D_j) = \overline{X}_j/\rho_k,$$

for any firm j in class k.

That is, the *market value of any firm is independent of its capital structure and is given by capitalizing its expected return at the rate* ρ_k *appropriate to its class.*

This proposition can be stated in an equivalent way in terms of the firm's "average cost of capital," $\overline{X}_j/V_j$, which is the ratio of its expected return to the market value of all its securities. Our proposition then is:

$$(4) \qquad \frac{\overline{X}_j}{(S_j + D_j)} \equiv \frac{\overline{X}_j}{V_j} = \rho_k,$$

for any firm j, in class k.

That is, *the average cost of capital to any firm is completely independent of its capital structure and is equal to the capitalization rate of a pure equity stream of its class.*

To establish Proposition I we will show that as long as the relations (3) or (4) do not hold between any pair of firms in a class, arbitrage will take place and restore the stated equalities. We use the term arbitrage advisedly. For if Proposition I did not hold, an investor could buy and sell stocks and bonds in such a way as to exchange one income stream for another stream, identical in all relevant respects but selling at a lower price. The exchange would therefore be advantageous to the investor quite independently of his attitudes toward risk.[11] As investors exploit these arbitrage opportunities, the value of the overpriced shares will fall and that of the underpriced shares will rise, thereby tending to eliminate the discrepancy between the market values of the firms.

[11] In the language of the theory of choice, the exchanges are movements from inefficient points in the interior to efficient points on the boundary of the investor's opportunity set; and not movements between efficient points along the boundary. Hence for this part of the analysis nothing is involved in the way of specific assumptions about investor attitudes or behavior other than that investors behave consistently and prefer more income to less income, *ceteris paribus*.

By way of proof, consider two firms in the same class and assume for simplicity only, that the expected return, $\overline{X}$, is the same for both firms. Let company 1 be financed entirely with common stock while company 2 has some debt in its capital structure. Suppose first the value of the levered firm, V_2, to be larger than that of the unlevered one, V_1. Consider an investor holding s_2 dollars' worth of the shares of company 2, representing a fraction α of the total outstanding stock, S_2. The return from this portfolio, denoted by Y_2, will be a fraction α of the income available for the stockholders of company 2, which is equal to the total return X_2 less the interest charge, rD_2. Since under our assumption of homogeneity, the anticipated total return of company 2, X_2, is, under all circumstances, the same as the anticipated total return to company 1, X_1, we can hereafter replace X_2 and X_1 by a common symbol X. Hence, the return from the initial portfolio can be written as:

$$(5) \qquad Y_2 = \alpha(X - rD_2).$$

Now suppose the investor sold his αS_2 worth of company 2 shares and acquired instead an amount $s_1 = \alpha(S_2 + D_2)$ of the shares of company 1. He could do so by utilizing the amount αS_2 realized from the sale of his initial holding and borrowing an additional amount αD_2 on his own credit, pledging his new holdings in company 1 as a collateral. He would thus secure for himself a fraction $s_1/S_1 = \alpha(S_2 + D_2)/S_1$ of the shares and earnings of company 1. Making proper allowance for the interest payments on his personal debt αD_2, the return from the new portfolio, Y_1, is given by:

$$(6) \qquad Y_1 = \frac{\alpha(S_2 + D_2)}{S_1} X - r\alpha D_2$$

$$= \alpha \frac{V_2}{V_1} X - r\alpha D_2.$$

Comparing (5) with (6) we see that as long as $V_2 > V_1$ we must have $Y_1 > Y_2$, so that it pays owners of company 2's shares to sell their holdings, thereby depressing S_2 and hence V_2; and to acquire shares of company 1, thereby raising S_1 and thus V_1. We conclude therefore that levered companies cannot command a premium over unlevered companies because investors have the opportunity of putting the equivalent leverage into their portfolio directly by borrowing on personal account.

Consider now the other possibility, namely that the market value of the levered company V_2 is less than V_1. Suppose an investor holds initially an amount s_1 of shares of company 1, representing a fraction α of the total outstanding stock, S_1. His return from this holding is:

$$Y_1 = \frac{s_1}{S_1} X = \alpha X.$$

Suppose he were to exchange this initial holding for another portfolio, also worth s_1, but consisting of s_2 dollars of stock of company 2 and of d dollars of bonds, where s_2 and d are given by:

$$(7) \qquad s_2 = \frac{S_2}{V_2} s_1, \qquad d = \frac{D_2}{V_2} s_1.$$

In other words the new portfolio is to consist of stock of company 2 and of bonds in the proportions S_2/V_2 and D_2/V_2, respectively. The return from the stock in the new portfolio will be a fraction s_2/S_2 of the total return of stockholders of company 2, which is

$(X - rD_2)$, and the return from the bonds will be rd. Making use of (7), the total return from the portfolio, Y_2, can be expressed as follows:

$$\begin{aligned} Y_2 &= \frac{s_2}{S_2}(X - rD_2) + rd \\ &= \frac{s_1}{V_2}(X - rD_2) + r\frac{D_2}{V_2}s_1 \\ &= \frac{s_1}{V_2}X = \alpha\frac{S_1}{V_2}X \end{aligned}$$

(since $s_1 = \alpha S_1$). Comparing Y_2 with Y_1 we see that, if $V_2 < S_1 \equiv V_1$, then Y_2 will exceed Y_1. Hence it pays the holders of company 1's shares to sell these holdings and replace them with a mixed portfolio containing an appropriate fraction of the shares of company 2.

The acquisition of a mixed portfolio of stock of a levered company j and of bonds in the proportion S_j/V_j and D_j/V_j respectively, may be regarded as an operation which "undoes" the leverage, giving access to an appropriate fraction of the unlevered return X_j. It is this possibility of undoing leverage which prevents the value of levered firms from being consistently less than those of unlevered firms, or more generally prevents the average cost of capital $\bar{X}_j/V_j$ from being systematically higher for levered than for nonlevered companies in the same class. Since we have already shown that arbitrage will also prevent V_2 from being larger than V_1, we can conclude that in equilibrium we must have $V_2 = V_1$, as stated in Proposition I.

Proposition II. From Proposition I we can derive the following proposition concerning the rate of return on common stock in companies whose capital structure includes some debt: the expected rate of return or yield, i, on the stock of any company j belonging to the kth class is a linear function of leverage as follows:

$$(8) \quad i_j = \rho_k + (\rho_k - r)\, D_j/S_j.$$

That is, *the expected yield of a share of stock is equal to the appropriate capitalization rate ρ_k for a pure equity stream in the class, plus a premium related to financial risk equal to the debt-to-equity ratio times the spread between ρ_k and r*. Or equivalently, the market price of any share of stock is given by capitalizing its expected return at the continuously variable rate i_j of (8).[12]

A number of writers have stated close equivalents of our Proposition I although by appealing to intuition rather than by attempting a proof and only to insist immediately that the results were not applicable to the actual capital markets.[13] Proposition II, how-

[12]To illustrate, suppose $\bar{X}=1000$, $D=4000$, $r=5$ per cent and $\rho_k=10$ per cent. These values imply that $V=10{,}000$ and $S=6000$ by virtue of Proposition I. The expected yield or rate of return per share is then:

$$\begin{aligned} i &= \frac{1000 - 200}{6000} \\ &= .1 + (.1 - .05)\frac{4000}{6000} = 13\tfrac{1}{3} \text{ per cent.} \end{aligned}$$

[13]See, for example, J. B. Williams [21, esp. pp. 72-73]; David Durand [3]; and W. A. Morton [15]. None of these writers describe in any detail the mechanism which is supposed to keep the average cost of capital constant under changes in capital structure. They seem, however, to be visualizing the equilibrating mechanism in terms of switches by investors between stocks and bonds as the yields of each get out of line with their "riskiness." This is an argument quite different from the pure arbitrage mechanism underlying our proof, and the difference is crucial. Regarding Proposition I as resting on investors' attitudes toward risk leads inevitably to a misunderstanding of many factors influencing relative yields such as, for example, limitations on the portfolio composition of financial institutions. See below, esp. Section I.D.

ever, so far as we have been able to discover is new.[14] To establish it we first note that, by definition, the expected rate of return, *i*, is given by:

$$(9) \qquad i_j \equiv \frac{\bar{X}_j - rD_j}{S_j}.$$

From Proposition I, equation (3), we know that:

$$\bar{X}_j = \rho_k(S_j + D_j).$$

Substituting in (9) and simplifying, we obtain equation (8).

C. *Some Qualifications and Extensions of the Basic Propositions*

The methods and results developed so far can be extended in a number of useful directions, of which we shall consider here only three: (1) allowing for a corporate profits tax under which interest payments are deductible; (2) recognizing the existence of a multiplicity of bonds and interest rates; and (3) acknowledging the presence of market imperfections which might interfere with the process of arbitrage. The first two will be examined briefly in this section with some further attention given to the tax problem in Section II. Market imperfections will be discussed in Part D of this section in the course of a comparison of our results with those of received doctrines in the field of finance.

Effects of the Present Method of Taxing Corporations. The deduction of interest in computing taxable corporate profits will prevent the arbitrage process from making the value of all firms in a given class proportional to the expected returns generated by their physical assets. Instead, it can be shown (by the same type of proof used for the original version of Proposition I) that the market values of firms in each class must be proportional in equilibrium to their expected return net of taxes (that is, to the sum of the interest paid and expected net stockholder income). This means we must replace each $\bar{X}_j$ in the original versions of Propositions I and II with a new variable $\bar{X}_j^{\tau}$ representing the total income net of taxes generated by the firm:

(10)

$$\bar{X}_j^{\tau} \equiv (\bar{X}_j - rD_j)(1 - \tau) + rD_j \equiv \bar{\pi}_j^{\tau} + rD_j,$$

where $\bar{\pi}_j^{\tau}$ represents the expected net income accruing to the common stockholders and τ stands for the average rate of corporate income tax.[15]

After making these substitutions, the propositions, when adjusted for taxes, continue to have the same form as their originals. That is, Proposition I becomes:

$$(11) \quad \frac{\bar{X}_j^{\tau}}{V_j} = \rho_k^{\tau}, \text{ for any firm in class } k,$$

and Proposition II becomes

(12)

$$i_j \equiv \frac{\bar{\pi}_j^{\tau}}{S_j} = \rho_j^{\tau} + (\rho_k^{\tau} - r)D_j/S_j$$

where ρ_k^{τ} is the capitalization rate for income net of taxes in class *k*.

Although the form of the propositions is unaffected, certain interpretations must be changed. In particular, the after-tax capitalization rate ρ_k^{τ} can

[14] Morton does make reference to a linear yield function but only "... for the sake of simplicity and because the particular function used makes no essential difference in my conclusions" [15, p. 443, note 2].

[15] For simplicity, we shall ignore throughout the tiny element of progression in our present corporate tax and treat τ as a constant independent of $(\bar{X} - rD_j)$.

no longer be identified with the "average cost of capital" which is $\rho_k = \overline{X}_j / V_j$. The difference between ρ_k^{τ} and the "true" average cost of capital, as we shall see, is a matter of some relevance in connection with investment planning within the firm (Section II). For the description of market behavior, however, which is our immediate concern here, the distinction is not essential. To simplify presentation, therefore, and to preserve continuity with the terminology in the standard literature we shall continue in this section to refer to ρ_k^{τ} as the average cost of capital, though strictly speaking this identification is correct only in the absence of taxes.

Effects of a Plurality of Bonds and Interest Rates. In existing capital markets we find not one, but a whole family of interest rates varying with maturity, with the technical provisions of the loan and, what is most relevant for present purposes, with the financial condition of the borrower.[16] Economic theory and market experience both suggest that the yields demanded by lenders tend to increase with the debt-equity ratio of the borrowing firm (or individual). If so, and if we can assume as a first approximation that this yield curve, $r = r(D/S)$, whatever its precise form, is the same for all borrowers, then we can readily extend our propositions to the case of a rising supply curve for borrowed funds.[17]

Proposition I is actually unaffected in form and interpretation by the fact that the rate of interest may rise with leverage; while the average cost of *borrowed* funds will tend to increase as debt rises, the average cost of funds from *all* sources will still be independent of leverage (apart from the tax effect). This conclusion follows directly from the ability of those who engage in arbitrage to undo the leverage in any financial structure by acquiring an appropriately mixed portfolio of bonds and stocks. Because of this ability, the ratio of earnings (*before* interest charges) to market value—*i.e.*, the average cost of capital from all sources—must be the same for all firms in a given class.[18] In other words, the in-

[16] We shall not consider here the extension of the analysis to encompass the time structure of interest rates. Although some of the problems posed by the time structure can be handled within our comparative statics framework, an adequate discussion would require a separate paper.

[17] We can also develop a theory of bond valuation along lines essentially parallel to those followed for the case of shares. We conjecture that the curve of bond yields as a function of leverage will turn out to be a nonlinear one in contrast to the linear function of leverage developed for common shares. However, we would also expect that the rate of increase in the yield on new issues would not be substantial in practice. This relatively slow rise would reflect the fact that interest rate increases by themselves can never be completely satisfactory to creditors as compensation for their increased risk. Such increases may simply serve to raise r so high relative to ρ that they become self-defeating by giving rise to a situation in which even normal fluctuations in earnings may force the company into bankruptcy. The difficulty of borrowing more, therefore, tends to show up in the usual case not so much in higher rates as in the form of increasingly stringent restrictions imposed on the company's management and finances by the creditors; and ultimately in a complete inability to obtain new borrowed funds, at least from the institutional investors who normally set the standards in the market for bonds.

[18] One normally minor qualification might be noted. Once we relax the assumption that all bonds have certain yields, our arbitrage operator faces the danger of something comparable to "gambler's ruin." That is, there is always the possibility that an otherwise sound concern—one whose long-run expected income is greater than its interest liability—might be forced into liquidation as a result of a run of temporary losses. Since reorganization generally involves costs, and because the operation of the firm may be hampered during the period of

creased cost of borrowed funds as leverage increases will tend to be offset by a corresponding reduction in the yield of common stock. This seemingly paradoxical result will be examined more closely below in connection with Proposition II.

A significant modification of Proposition I would be required only if the yield curve $r = r\ (D/S)$ were different for different borrowers, as might happen if creditors had marked preferences for the securities of a particular class of debtors. If, for example, corporations as a class were able to borrow at lower rates than individuals having equivalent personal leverage, then the average cost of capital to corporations might fall slightly, as leverage increased over some range, in reflection of this differential. In evaluating this possibility, however, remember that the relevant interest rate for our arbitrage operators is the rate of brokers' loans and, historically, that rate has not been noticeably higher than representative corporate rates.[19] The operations of holding companies and investment trusts which can borrow on terms comparable to operating companies represent still another force which could be expected to wipe out any marked or prolonged advantages from holding levered stocks.[20]

Although Proposition I remains unaffected as long as the yield curve is the same for all borrowers, the relation between common stock yields and leverage will no longer be the strictly linear one given by the original Proposition II. If r increases with leverage, the yield i will still tend to rise as D/S increases, but at a decreasing rather than a constant rate. Beyond some high level of leverage, depending on the exact form of the interest function, the yield may even start to fall.[21] The relation between i and D/S could conceivably take the form indicated by the curve MD in Figure 2, although in practice the curvature would be much less pronounced. By contrast, with a constant rate of interest, the relation would be linear throughout as shown by line MM', Figure 2.

The downward sloping part of the curve MD perhaps requires some comment since it may be hard to imagine why investors, other than those who

reorganization with lasting unfavorable effects on earnings prospects, we might perhaps expect heavily levered companies to sell at a slight discount relative to less heavily indebted companies of the same class.

19Under normal conditions, moreover, a substantial part of the arbitrage process could be expected to take the form, not of having the arbitrage operators go into debt on personal account to put the required leverage into their portfolios, but simply of having them reduce the amount of corporate bonds they already hold when they acquire underpriced unlevered stock. Margin requirements are also somewhat less of an obstacle to maintaining any desired degree of leverage in a portfolio than might be thought at first glance. Leverage could be largely restored in the face of higher margin requirements by switching to stocks having more leverage at the corporate level.

20An extreme form of inequality between borrowing and lending rates occurs, of course, in the case of preferred stocks, which can not be directly issued by individuals on personal account. Here again, however, we would expect that the operations of investment corporations plus the ability of arbitrage operators to sell off their holdings of preferred stocks would act to prevent the emergence of any substantial premiums (for this reason) on capital structures containing preferred stocks. Nor are preferred stocks so far removed from bonds as to make it impossible for arbitrage operators to approximate closely the risk and leverage of a corporate preferred stock by incurring a somewhat smaller debt on personal account.

21Since new lenders are unlikely to permit this much leverage (*cf.* note 17), this range of the curve is likely to be occupied by companies whose earnings prospects have fallen substantially since the time when their debts were issued.

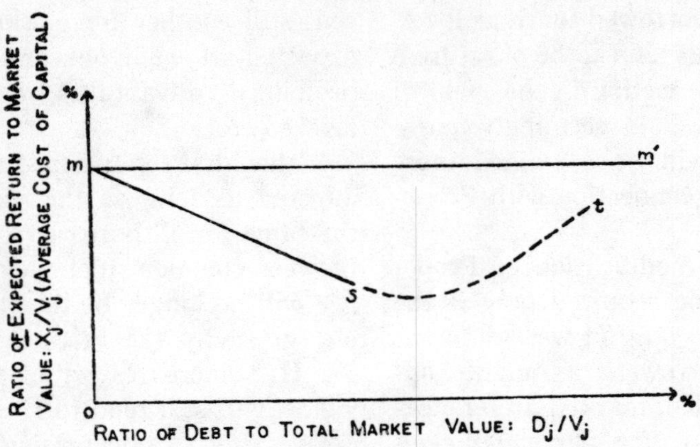

FIGURE 1

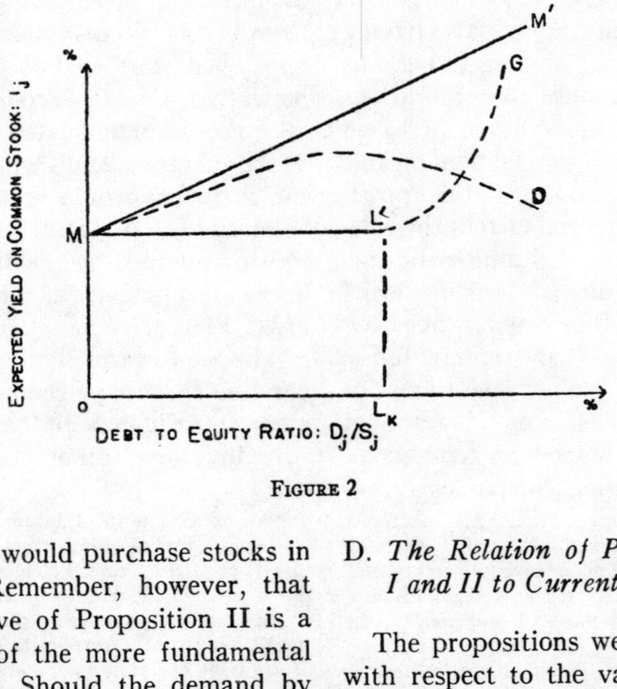

FIGURE 2

like lotteries, would purchase stocks in this range. Remember, however, that the yield curve of Proposition II is a consequence of the more fundamental Proposition I. Should the demand by the risk-lovers prove insufficient to keep the market to the peculiar yield-curve *MD*, this demand would be reinforced by the action of arbitrage operators. The latter would find it profitable to own a pro-rata share of the firm as a whole by holding its stock *and* bonds, the lower yield of the shares being thus offset by the higher return on bonds.

D. *The Relation of Propositions I and II to Current Doctrines*

The propositions we have developed with respect to the valuation of firms and shares appear to be substantially at variance with current doctrines in the field of finance. The main differences between our view and the current view are summarized graphically in Figures 1 and 2. Our Proposition I [equation (4)] asserts that the average cost of capital, $\overline{X}_j^{\tau}/V_j$, is a constant for all firms j in class k, independently of their financial structure. This implies that, if we were to take a sample of firms in a given class, and if for each firm we were to plot the ratio of expected return to market value against some measure of leverage or financial structure, the points would tend to fall on a horizontal straight line with intercept ρ_k^{τ}, like the solid line mm' in Figure 1.[22] From Proposition I we derived Proposition II [equation (8)] which, taking the simplest version with r constant, asserts that, for all firms in a class, the relation between the yield on common stock and financial structure, measured by D_j/S_j, will approximate a straight line with slope $(\rho_k^{\tau} - r)$ and intercept ρ_k^{τ}. This relationship is shown as the solid line MM' in Figure 2, to which reference has been made earlier.[23]

By contrast, the conventional view among finance specialists appears to start from the proposition that, other things equal, the earnings-price ratio (or its reciprocal, the times-earnings multiplier) of a firm's common stock will normally be only slightly affected by "moderate" amounts of debt in the firm's capital structure.[24] Translated into our notation, it asserts that for any firm j in the class k,

(13)

$$\frac{\bar{X}_j^{\tau} - rD_j}{S_j} \equiv \frac{\bar{\pi}_j^{\tau}}{S_j} = i_k^*, \text{ a constant for } \frac{D_j}{S_j} \leq L_k$$

or, equivalently,

$$(14) \qquad S_j = \bar{\pi}_j^{\tau}/i_k^*.$$

Here i_k^* represents the capitalization rate of earnings-price ratio on the common stock and L_k denotes some amount of leverage regarded as the maximum "reasonable" amount for firms of the class k. This assumed relationship between yield and leverage is the horizontal solid line ML' of Figure 2. Beyond L', the yield will presumably rise sharply as the market discounts "excessive" trading on the equity. This possibility of a rising range for high leverages is indicated by the broken-line segment $L'G$ in the figure.[25]

If the value of shares were really given by (14) then the over-all market value of the firm must be:

(16)

$$V_j \equiv S_j + D_j = \frac{\bar{X}_j^{\tau} - rD_j}{i_k^*} + D_j = \frac{\bar{X}_j^{\tau}}{i_k^*} + \frac{(i_k^* - r)\,D_j}{i_k^*}.$$

[22] In Figure 1 the measure of leverage used is D_j/V_j (the ratio of debt to market value) rather than D_j/S_j (the ratio of debt to equity), the concept used in the analytical development. The D_j/V_j measure is introduced at this point because it simplifies comparison and contrast of our view with the traditional position.

[23] The line MM' in Figure 2 has been drawn with a positive slope on the assumption that $\rho_k^{\tau} > r$, a condition which will normally obtain. Our Proposition II as given in equation (8) would continue to be valid, of course, even in the unlikely event that $\rho_k^{\tau} < r$, but the slope of MM' would be negative.

[24] See, *e.g.*, Graham and Dodd [6, pp. 464-66]. Without doing violence to this position, we can bring out its implications more sharply by ignoring the qualification and treating the yield as a virtual constant over the relevant range. See in this connection the discussion in Durand [3, esp. pp. 225-37] of what he calls the "net income method" of valuation.

[25] To make it easier to see some of the implications of this hypothesis as well as to prepare the ground for later statistical testing, it will be helpful to assume that the notion of a critical limit on leverage beyond which yields rise rapidly, can be epitomized by a quadratic relation of the form:

(15)

$$\pi_j^{\tau}/S_j = i_k^* + \beta(D_j/S_j) + \alpha(D_j/S_j)^2, \quad \alpha > 0.$$

That is, for any given level of expected total returns after taxes ($\overline{X}_j^\tau$) and assuming, as seems natural, that $i_k^* > r$, the value of the firm must tend to ***rise*** with debt;[26] whereas our Proposition I asserts that the value of the firm is completely independent of the capital structure. Another way of contrasting our position with the traditional one is in terms of the cost of capital. Solving (16) for $\overline{X}_j^\tau / V_j$ yields:

(17)

$$\overline{X}_j^\tau / V_j = i_k^* - (i_k^* - r)\, D_j / V_j.$$

According to this equation, the average cost of capital is not independent of capital structure as we have argued, but should tend to *fall* with increasing leverage, at least within the relevant range of moderate debt ratios, as shown by the line *ms* in Figure 1. Or to put it in more familiar terms, debt-financing should be "cheaper" than equity-financing if not carried too far.

When we also allow for the possibility of a rising range of stock yields for large values of leverage, we obtain a U-shaped curve like *mst* in Figure 1.[27] That a yield-curve for stocks of the form *ML′G* in Figure 2 implies a U-shaped cost-of-capital curve has, of course, been recognized by many writers. A natural further step has been to suggest that the capital structure corresponding to the trough of the U is an "optimal capital structure" towards which management ought to strive in the best interests of the stockholders.[28] According to our model, by contrast, no such optimal structure exists—all structures being equivalent from the point of view of the cost of capital.

Although the falling, or at least U-shaped, cost-of-capital function is in one form or another the dominant view in the literature, the ultimate rationale of that view is by no means clear. The crucial element in the position—that the expected earnings-price ratio of the stock is largely unaffected by leverage up to some conventional limit—is rarely even regarded as something which requires explanation. It is usually simply taken for granted or it is merely asserted that this is the way the market behaves.[29] To the extent that the constant earnings-price ratio has a rationale at all we suspect that it reflects in most cases the feeling that moderate amounts of debt in "sound" corporations do not really add very much to the "riskiness" of the stock. Since the extra risk is slight, it seems natural to suppose that firms will not have to pay noticeably higher yields in order to in-

[26] For a typical discussion of how a promoter can, supposedly, increase the market value of a firm by recourse to debt issues, see W. J. Eiteman [4, esp. pp. 11-13].

[27] The U-shaped nature of the cost-of-capital curve can be exhibited explicitly if the yield curve for shares as a function of leverage can be approximated by equation (15) of footnote 25. From that equation, multiplying both sides by S_j we obtain: $\overline{\pi}_j^\tau = \overline{X}_j^\tau - rD_j = i_k^* S_j + \beta D_j + \alpha D_j^2 / S_j$ or, adding and subtracting $i_k^* D_k$ from the right-hand side and collecting terms,

(18)

$$\overline{X}_j^\tau = i_k^*(S_j + D_j) + (\beta + r - i_k^*)D_j + \alpha D^2{}_j / S_j.$$

Dividing (18) by V_j gives an expression for the cost of capital:

(19) $$\overline{X}_j^\tau / V_j = i_k^* - (i_k^* - r - \beta)D_j/V_j + \alpha D_j^2 / S_j V_j = i_k^* - (i_k^* - r - \beta)D_j/V_j + \alpha(D_j/V_j)^2/(1 - D_j/V_j)$$

which is clearly U-shaped since α is supposed to be positive.

[28] For a typical statement see S. M. Robbins [16, p. 307]. See also Graham and Dodd [6, pp. 468-74].

[29] See *e.g.*, Graham and Dodd [6, p. 466].

duce investors to hold the stock.[30]

A more sophisticated line of argument has been advanced by David Durand [3, pp. 231-33]. He suggests that because insurance companies and certain other important institutional investors are restricted to debt securities, nonfinancial corporations are able to borrow from them at interest rates which are lower than would be required to compensate creditors in a free market. Thus, while he would presumably agree with our conclusions that stockholders could not gain from leverage in an unconstrained market, he concludes that they can gain under present institutional arrangements. This gain would arise by virtue of the "safety superpremium" which lenders are willing to pay corporations for the privilege of lending.[31]

The defective link in both the traditional and the Durand version of the argument lies in the confusion between investors' subjective risk preferences and their objective market opportunities. Our Propositions I and II, as noted earlier, do not depend for their validity on any assumption about individual risk preferences. Nor do they involve any assertion as to what is an adequate compensation to investors for assuming a given degree of risk. They rely merely on the fact that a given commodity cannot consistently sell at more than one price in the market; or more precisely that the price of a commodity representing a "bundle" of two other commodities cannot be consistently different from the weighted average of the prices of the two components (the weights being equal to the proportion of the two commodities in the bundle).

An analogy may be helpful at this point. The relations between $1/\rho_k$, the price per dollar of an unlevered stream in class k; $1/r$, the price per dollar of a sure stream, and $1/i_j$, the price per dollar of a levered stream j, in the kth class, are essentially the same as those between, respectively, the price of whole milk, the price of butter fat, and the price of milk which has been thinned out by skimming off some of the butter fat. Our Proposition I states that a firm cannot reduce the cost of capital—*i.e.*, increase the market value of the stream it generates—by securing part of its capital through the sale of bonds, even though debt money appears to be cheaper. This assertion is equivalent to the proposition that, under perfect markets, a dairy farmer cannot in general earn more for the milk he produces by skimming some of the butter fat and selling it separately, even though butter fat per unit weight, sells for more than whole milk. The advantage from skimming the milk

30 A typical statement is the following by Guthmann and Dougall [7, p. 245]: "Theoretically it might be argued that the increased hazard from using bonds and preferred stocks would counterbalance this additional income and so prevent the common stock from being more attractive than when it had a lower return but fewer prior obligations. In practice, the extra earnings from 'trading on the equity' are often regarded by investors as more than sufficient to serve as a 'premium for risk' when the proportions of the several securities are judiciously mixed."

31 Like Durand, Morton [15] contends "that the actual market deviates from [Proposition I] by giving a changing over-all cost of money at different points of the [leverage] scale" (p. 443, note 2, inserts ours), but the basis for this contention is nowhere clearly stated. Judging by the great emphasis given to the lack of mobility of investment funds between stocks and bonds and to the psychological and institutional pressures toward debt portfolios (see pp. 444-51 and especially his discussion of the optimal capital structure on p. 453) he would seem to be taking a position very similar to that of Durand above

rather than selling whole milk would be purely illusory; for what would be gained from selling the high-priced butter fat would be lost in selling the low-priced residue of thinned milk. Similarly our Proposition II—that the price per dollar of a levered stream falls as leverage increases—is an exact analogue of the statement that the price per gallon of thinned milk falls continuously as more butter fat is skimmed off.[32]

It is clear that this last assertion is true as long as butter fat is worth more per unit weight than whole milk, and it holds even if, for many consumers, taking a little cream out of the milk (adding a little leverage to the stock) does not detract noticeably from the taste (does not add noticeably to the risk). Furthermore the argument remains valid even in the face of institutional limitations of the type envisaged by Durand. For suppose that a large fraction of the population habitually dines in restaurants which are required by law to serve only cream in lieu of milk (entrust their savings to institutional investors who can only buy bonds). To be sure the price of butter fat will then tend to be higher in relation to that of skimmed milk than in the absence such restrictions (the rate of interest will tend to be lower), and this will benefit people who eat at home and who like skim milk (who manage their own portfolio and are able and willing to take risk). But it will still be the case that a farmer cannot gain by skimming some of the butter fat and selling it separately (firm cannot reduce the cost of capital by recourse to borrowed funds).[33]

Our propositions can be regarded as the extension of the classical theory of markets to the particular case of the capital markets. Those who hold the current view—whether they realize it or not—must assume not merely that there are lags and frictions in the equilibrating process—a feeling we certainly share,[34] claiming for our propositions

[32] Let M denote the quantity of whole milk, B/M the proportion of butter fat in the whole milk, and let p_M, p_B and p_α denote, respectively, the price per unit weight of whole milk, butter fat and thinned milk from which a fraction α of the butter fat has been skimmed off. We then have the fundamental perfect market relation:

$$\text{(a)} \quad p_\alpha(M - \alpha B) + p_B \alpha B = p_M M, \quad 0 \leq \alpha \leq 1,$$

stating that total receipts will be the same amount $p_M M$, independently of the amount αB of butter fat that may have been sold separately. Since p_M corresponds to $1/\rho$, p_B to $1/r$, p_α to $1/i$, M to $\bar{X}$ and αB to rD, (a) is equivalent to Proposition I, $S+D = \bar{X}/\rho$. From (a) we derive:

$$\text{(b)} \qquad p_\alpha = p_M \frac{M}{M - \alpha B} - p_B \frac{\alpha B}{M - \alpha B}$$

which gives the price of thinned milk as an explicit function of the proportion of butter fat skimmed off; the function decreasing as long as $p_B > p_M$. From (a) also follows:

(c)

$$1/p_\alpha = 1/p_M + (1/p_M - 1/p_B)\frac{p_B \alpha B}{p_\alpha(M - \alpha B)}$$

which is the exact analogue of Proposition II, as given by (8).

[33] The reader who likes parables will find that the analogy with interrelated commodity markets can be pushed a good deal farther than we have done in the text. For instance, the effect of changes in the market rate of interest on the over-all cost of capital is the same as the effect of a change in the price of butter on the price of whole milk. Similarly, just as the relation between the prices of skim milk and butter fat influences the kind of cows that will be reared, so the relation between i and r influences the kind of ventures that will be undertaken. If people like butter we shall have Guernseys; if they are willing to pay a high price for safety, this will encourage ventures which promise smaller but less uncertain streams per dollar of physical assets.

[34] Several specific examples of the failure of the arbitrage mechanism can be found in Graham and Dodd [6, *e.g.*, pp. 646-48]. The price discrepancy described on pp. 646-47 is particularly curious since it persists even today despite the fact that

only that they describe the central tendency around which observations will scatter—but also that there are large and *systematic* imperfections in the market which permanently bias the outcome. This is an assumption that economists, at any rate, will instinctively eye with some skepticism.

In any event, whether such prolonged, systematic departures from equilibrium really exist or whether our propositions are better descriptions of long-run market behavior can be settled only by empirical research. Before going on to the theory of investment it may be helpful, therefore, to look at the evidence.

E. *Some Preliminary Evidence on the Basic Propositions*

Unfortunately the evidence which has been assembled so far is amazingly skimpy. Indeed, we have been able to locate only two recent studies—and these of rather limited scope—which were designed to throw light on the issue. Pending the results of more comprehensive tests which we hope will soon be available, we shall review briefly such evidence as is provided by the two studies in question: (1) an analysis of the relation between security yields and financial structure for some 43 large electric utilities by F. B. Allen [1], and (2) a parallel (unpublished) study by Robert Smith [19], for 42 oil companies designed to test whether Allen's rather striking results would be found in an industry with very different characteristics.[35] The Allen study is based on average figures for the years 1947 and 1948, while the Smith study relates to the single year 1953.

The Effect of Leverage on the Cost of Capital. According to the received view, as shown in equation (17) the average cost of capital, $\bar{X}^\tau/V$ should decline linearly with leverage as measured by the ratio D/V, at least through most of the relevant range.[36] According to Proposition I, the average cost of capital within a given class k should tend to have the same value $\rho_k{}^\tau$ independently of the degree of leverage. A simple test of the merits of the two alternative hypotheses can thus be carried out by correlating $\bar{X}^\tau/V$ with D/V. If the traditional view is correct, the correlation should be significantly negative; if our view represents a better approximation to reality, then the correlation should not be significantly different from zero.

Both studies provide information about the average value of D—the market value of bonds and preferred stock—and of V—the market value of all securities.[37] From these data we can

---

a whole generation of security analysts has been brought up on this book!

[35]We wish to express our thanks to both writers for making available to us some of their original worksheets. In addition to these recent studies there is a frequently cited (but apparently seldom read) study by the Federal Communications Commission in 1938 [22] which purports to show the existence of an optimal capital structure or range of structures (in the sense defined above) for public utilities in the 1930's. By current standards for statistical investigations, however, this study cannot be regarded as having any real evidential value for the problem at hand.

[36]We shall simplify our notation in this section by dropping the subscript j used to denote a particular firm wherever this will not lead to confusion.

[37]Note that for purposes of this test preferred stocks, since they represent an *expected* fixed obligation, are properly classified with bonds even though the tax status of preferred dividends is different from that of interest payments and even though preferred dividends are really fixed only as to their maximum in any year. Some difficulty of classification does arise in the case of convertible

readily compute the ratio D/V and this ratio (expressed as a percentage) is represented by the symbol d in the regression equations below. The measurement of the variable $\bar{X}^\tau/V$, however, presents serious difficulties. Strictly speaking, the numerator should measure the expected returns net of taxes, but this is a variable on which no direct information is available. As an approximation, we have followed both authors and used (1) the average value of actual net returns in 1947 and 1948 for Allen's utilities; and (2) actual net returns in 1953 for Smith's oil companies. Net return is defined in both cases as the sum of interest, preferred dividends and stockholders' income net of corporate income taxes. Although this approximation to expected returns is undoubtedly very crude, there is no reason to believe that it will systematically bias the test in so far as the sign of the regression coefficient is concerned. The roughness of the approximation, however, will tend to make for a wide scatter. Also contributing to the scatter is the crudeness of the industrial classification, since especially within the sample of oil companies, the assumption that all the firms belong to the same class in our sense, is at best only approximately valid.

Denoting by x our approximation to X^τ/V (expressed, like d, as a percentage), the results of the tests are as follows:

Electric Utilities $x = 5.3 + .006d$
$(\pm .008)$
$r = .12$

Oil Companies $x = 8.5 + .006d$
$(\pm .024)$
$r = .04.$

The data underlying these equations are also shown in scatter diagram form in Figures 3 and 4.

The results of these tests are clearly favorable to our hypothesis. Both correlation coefficients are very close to zero and not statistically significant. Furthermore, the implications of the traditional view fail to be supported even with respect to the sign of the correlation. The data in short provide no evidence of any tendency for the cost of capital to fall as the debt ratio increases.[38]

preferred stocks (and convertible bonds) selling at a substantial premium, but fortunately very few such issues were involved for the companies included in the two studies. Smith included bank loans and certain other short-term obligations (at book values) in his data on oil company debts and this treatment is perhaps open to some question. However, the amounts involved were relatively small and check computations showed that their elimination would lead to only minor differences in the test results.

[38] It may be argued that a test of the kind used is biased against the traditional view. The fact that both sides of the regression equation are divided by the variable V which may be subject to random variation might tend to impart a positive bias to the correlation. As a check on the results presented in the text, we have, therefore, carried out a supplementary test based on equation (16). This equation shows that, if the traditional view is correct, the market value of a company should, for given $\bar{X}^\tau$, increase with debt through most of the relevant range; according to our model the market value should be uncorrelated with D, given $\bar{X}^\tau$. Because of wide variations in the size of the firms included in our samples, all variables must be divided by a suitable scale factor in order to avoid spurious results in carrying out a test of equation (16). The factor we have used is the book value of the firm denoted by A. The hypothesis tested thus takes the specific form:

$$V/A = a + b(\bar{X}^\tau/A) + c(D/A)$$

and the numerator of the ratio X^τ/A is again approximated by actual net returns. The partial correlation between V/A and D/A should now be positive according to the traditional view and zero according to our model. Although division by A should, if anything, bias the results in favor of the traditional hypothesis, the partial correlation turns out to be only .03 for the oil companies and —.28 for the electric utilities. Neither of these coefficients is significantly different from zero and the larger one even has the wrong sign.

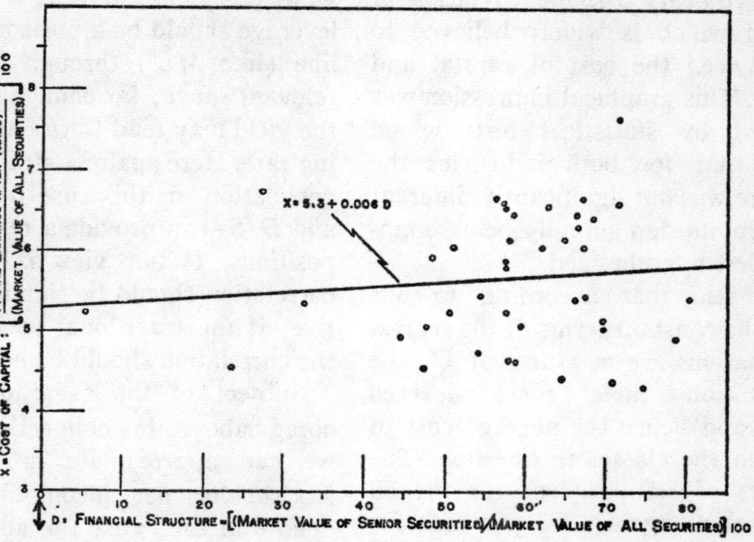

FIGURE 3. COST OF CAPITAL IN RELATION TO FINANCIAL STRUCTURE FOR 43 ELECTRIC UTILITIES, 1947–48

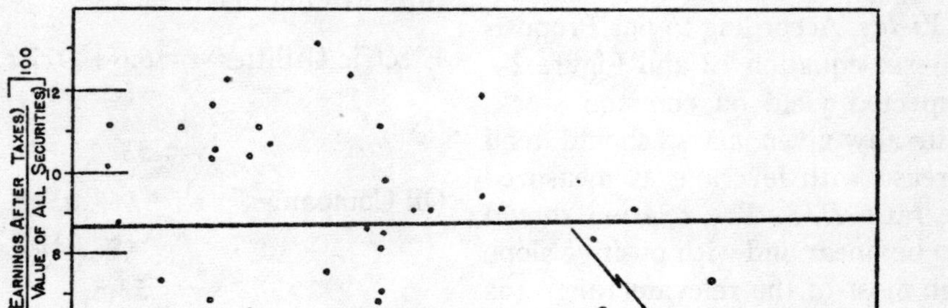

FIGURE 4. COST OF CAPITAL IN RELATION TO FINANCIAL STRUCTURE FOR 42 OIL COMPANIES, 1953

It should also be apparent from the scatter diagrams that there is no hint of a curvilinear, U-shaped, relation of the kind which is widely believed to hold between the cost of capital and leverage. This graphical impression was confirmed by statistical tests which showed that for both industries the curvature was not significantly different from zero, its sign actually being opposite to that hypothesized.[39]

Note also that according to our model, the constant terms of the regression equations are measures of $\rho_k{}^\tau$, the capitalization rates for unlevered streams and hence the average cost of capital in the classes in question. The estimates of 8.5 per cent for the oil companies as against 5.3 per cent for electric utilities appear to accord well with a priori expectations, both in absolute value and relative spread.

The Effect of Leverage on Common Stock Yields. According to our Proposition II—see equation 12 and Figure 2—the expected yield on common stock, $\bar{\pi}^\tau/S$, in any given class, should tend to increase with leverage as measured by the ratio D/S. The relation should tend to be linear and with positive slope through most of the relevant range (as in the curve MM' of Figure 2), though it might tend to flatten out if we move far enough to the right (as in the curve MD'), to the extent that high leverage tends to drive up the cost of senior capital. According to the conventional view, the yield curve as a function of leverage should be a horizontal straight line (like ML') through most of the relevant range; far enough to the right, the yield may tend to rise at an increasing rate. Here again, a straight-forward correlation—in this case between $\bar{\pi}^\tau/S$ and D/S—can provide a test of the two positions. If our view is correct, the correlation should be significantly positive; if the traditional view is correct, the correlation should be negligible.

Subject to the same qualifications noted above in connection with $\bar{X}^\tau$, we can approximate $\bar{\pi}^\tau$ by actual stockholder net income.[40] Letting z denote in each case the approximation to $\bar{\pi}^\tau/S$ (expressed as a percentage) and letting h denote the ratio D/S (also in percentage terms) the following results are obtained:

Electric Utilities $z = 6.6 + .017h$
$(\pm .004)$

$r = .53$

Oil Companies $z = 8.9 + .051h$
$(\pm .012)$

$r = .53.$

These results are shown in scatter diagram form in Figures 5 and 6.

[39] The tests consisted of fitting to the data the equation (19) of footnote 27. As shown there, it follows from the U-shaped hypothesis that the coefficient α of the variable $(D/V)^2/(1-D/V)$, denoted hereafter by d^*, should be significant and positive. The following regression equations and partials were obtained:

Electric Utilities $x = 5.0 + .017d - .003d^*$;
$r_{xd^*\cdot d} = -.15$

Oil Companies $x = 8.0 + .05d - .03d^*$;
$r_{xd^*\cdot d} = -.14.$

[40] As indicated earlier, Smith's data were for the single year 1953. Since the use of a single year's profits as a measure of expected profits might be open to objection we collected profit data for 1952 for the same companies and based the computation of $\bar{\pi}^\tau/S$ on the average of the two years. The value of $\bar{\pi}^\tau/S$ was obtained from the formula:

$$\left(\text{net earnings in 1952} \cdot \frac{\text{assets in '53}}{\text{assets in '52}} + \text{net earnings in 1953}\right) \tfrac{1}{2}$$

$$\div \text{(average market value of common stock in '53).}$$

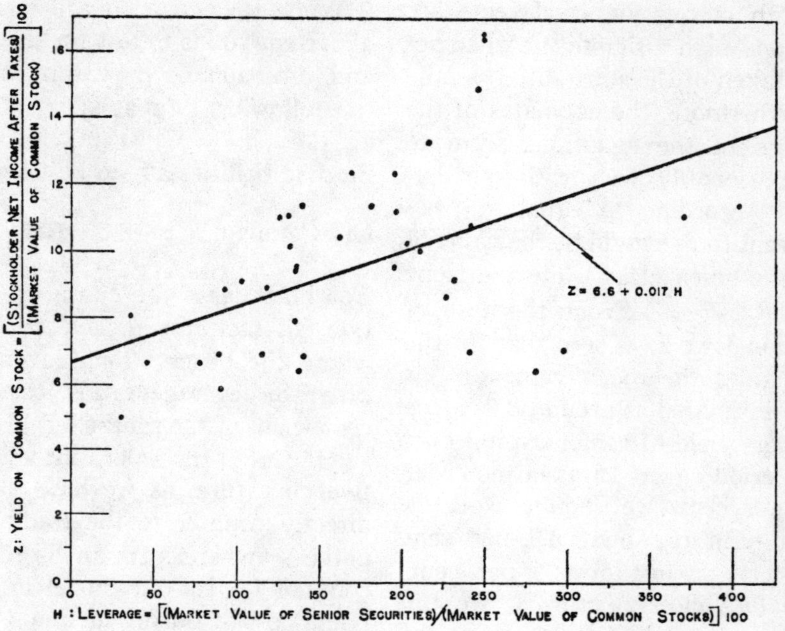

Figure 5. Yield on Common Stock in Relation to Leverage for 43 Electric Utilities, 1947–48

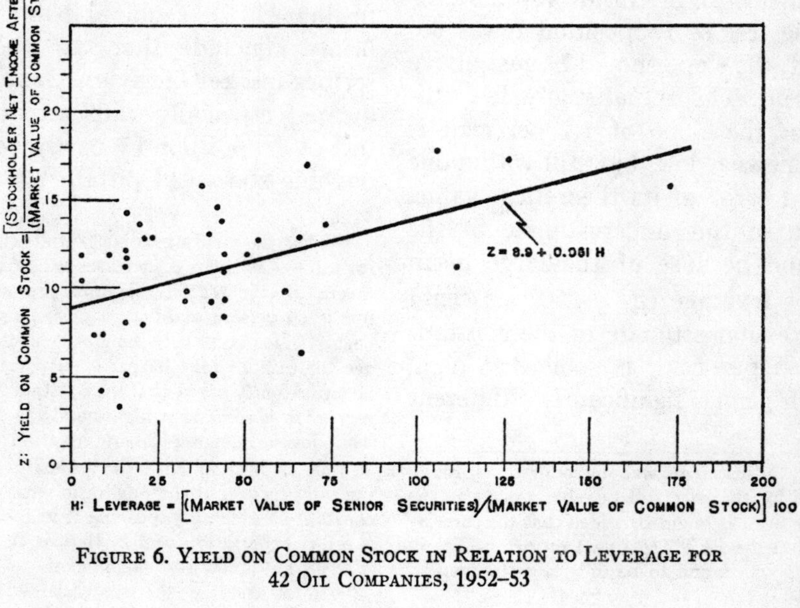

Figure 6. Yield on Common Stock in Relation to Leverage for 42 Oil Companies, 1952–53

Here again the implications of our analysis seem to be borne out by the data. Both correlation coefficients are positive and highly significant when account is taken of the substantial sample size. Furthermore, the estimates of the coefficients of the equations seem to accord reasonably well with our hypothesis. According to equation (12) the constant term should be the value of ρ_k^τ for the given class while the slope should be $(\rho_k^\tau - r)$. From the test of Proposition I we have seen that for the oil companies the mean value of ρ_k^τ could be estimated at around 8.7. Since the average yield of senior capital during the period covered was in the order of 3½ per cent, we should expect a constant term of about 8.7 per cent and a slope of just over 5 per cent. These values closely approximate the regression estimates of 8.9 per cent and 5.1 per cent respectively. For the electric utilities, the yield of senior capital was also on the order of 3½ per cent during the test years, but since the estimate of the mean value of ρ_k^τ from the test of Proposition I was 5.6 per cent, the slope should be just above 2 per cent. The actual regression estimate for the slope of 1.7 per cent is thus somewhat low, but still within one standard error of its theoretical value. Because of this underestimate of the slope and because of the large mean value of leverage ($\bar{h}$ = 160 per cent) the regression estimate of the constant term, 6.6 per cent, is somewhat high, although not significantly different from the value of 5.6 per cent obtained in the test of Proposition I.

When we add a square term to the above equations to test for the presence and direction of curvature we obtain the following estimates:

Electric Utilities $z = 4.6 + .004h - .007h^2$

Oil Companies $z = 8.5 + .072h - .016h^2$.

For both cases the curvature is negative. In fact, for the electric utilities, where the observations cover a wider range of leverage ratios, the negative coefficient of the square term is actually significant at the 5 per cent level. Negative curvature, as we have seen, runs directly counter to the traditional hypothesis, whereas it can be readily accounted for by our model in terms of rising cost of borrowed funds.[41]

In summary, the empirical evidence we have reviewed seems to be broadly consistent with our model and largely inconsistent with traditional views. Needless to say much more extensive testing will be required before we can firmly conclude that our theory describes market behavior. Caution is indicated especially with regard to our test of Proposition II, partly because of possible statistical pitfalls[42] and partly

The asset adjustment was introduced as rough allowance for the effects of possible growth in the size of the firm. It might be added that the correlation computed with $\bar{\pi}^\tau / S$ based on net profits in 1953 alone was found to be only slightly smaller, namely .50.

[41] That the yield of senior capital tended to rise for utilities as leverage increased is clearly shown in several of the scatter diagrams presented in the published version of Allen's study. This significant negative curvature between stock yields and leverage for utilities may be partly responsible for the fact, previously noted, that the constant in the linear regression is somewhat higher and the slope somewhat lower than implied by equation (12). Note also in connection with the estimate of ρ_k^τ that the introduction of the quadratic term reduces the constant considerably, pushing it in fact below the a priori expectation of 5.6, though the difference is again not statistically significant.

[42] In our test, *e.g.*, the two variables z and h are

because not all the factors that might have a systematic effect on stock yields have been considered. In particular, no attempt was made to test the possible influence of the dividend pay-out ratio whose role has tended to receive a great deal of attention in current research and thinking. There are two reasons for this omission. First, our main objective has been to assess the prima facie tenability of *our* model, and in this model, based as it is on rational behavior by investors, dividends per se play no role. Second, in a world in which the policy of dividend stabilization is widespread, there is no simple way of disentangling the true effect of dividend payments on stock prices from their apparent effect, the latter reflecting only the role of dividends as a proxy measure of long-term earning anticipations.[43] The difficulties just mentioned are further compounded by possible interrelations between dividend policy and leverage.[44]

both ratios with S appearing in the denominator, which may tend to impart a positive bias to the correlation (*cf.* note 38). Attempts were made to develop alternative tests, but although various possibilities were explored, we have so far been unable to find satisfactory alternatives.

[43] We suggest that failure to appreciate this difficulty is responsible for many fallacious, or at least unwarranted, conclusions about the role of dividends.

[44] In the sample of electric utilities, there is a substantial negative correlation between yields and pay-out ratios, but also between pay-out ratios and leverage, suggesting that either the association of yields and leverage or of yields and pay-out ratios may be (at least partly) spurious. These difficulties however do not arise in the case of the oil industry sample. A preliminary analysis indicates that there is here no significant relation between leverage and pay-out ratios and also no significant correlation (either gross or partial) between yields and pay-out ratios.

II. IMPLICATIONS OF THE ANALYSIS FOR THE THEORY OF INVESTMENT

A. *Capital Structure and Investment Policy*

On the basis of our propositions with respect to cost of capital and financial structure (and for the moment neglecting taxes), we can derive the following simple rule for optimal investment policy by the firm:

Proposition III. If a firm in class k is acting in the best interest of the stockholders at the time of the decision, it will exploit an investment opportunity if and only if the rate of return on the investment, say ρ^*, is as large as or larger than ρ_k. That is, *the cut-off point for investment in the firm will in all cases be* ρ_k *and will be completely unaffected by the type of security used to finance the investment.* Equivalently, we may say that regardless of the financing used, the marginal cost of capital to a firm is equal to the average cost of capital, which is in turn equal to the capitalization rate for an unlevered stream in the class to which the firm belongs.[45]

To establish this result we will consider the three major financing alternatives open to the firm—bonds, retained earnings, and common stock issues—and show that in each case an investment is worth undertaking if, and only if, $\rho^* \geqq \rho_k$.[46]

[45] The analysis developed in this paper is essentially a comparative-statics, not a dynamic analysis. This note of caution applies with special force to Proposition III. Such problems as those posed by expected changes in r and ρ_k over time will not be treated here. Although they are in principle amenable to analysis within the general framework we have laid out, such an undertaking is sufficiently complex to deserve separate treatment. *Cf.* note 17.

[46] The extension of the proof to other types of

Consider first the case of an investment financed by the sale of bonds. We know from Proposition I that the market value of the firm before the investment was undertaken was:[47]

$$(20) \qquad V_0 = \bar{X}_0/\rho_k$$

and that the value of the common stock was:

$$(21) \qquad S_0 = V_0 - D_0.$$

If now the firm borrows I dollars to finance an investment yielding ρ^* its market value will become:

$$(22) \qquad V_1 = \frac{\bar{X}_0 + \rho^* I}{\rho_k} = V_0 + \frac{\rho^* I}{\rho_k}$$

and the value of its common stock will be:

$$(23) \qquad S_1 = V_1 - (D_0 + I) = V_0 + \frac{\rho^* I}{\rho_k} - D_0 - I$$

or using equation 21,

$$(24) \qquad S_1 = S_0 + \frac{\rho^* I}{\rho_k} - I.$$

Hence $S_1 \gtreqless S_0$ as $\rho^* \gtreqless \rho_k$.[48]

To illustrate, suppose the capitalization rate for uncertain streams in the kth class is 10 per cent and the rate of interest is 4 per cent. Then if a given company had an expected income of 1,000 and if it were financed entirely by common stock we know from Proposition I that the market value of its stock would be 10,000. Assume now that the managers of the firm discover an investment opportunity which will require an outlay of 100 and which is expected to yield 8 per cent. At first sight this might appear to be a profitable opportunity since the expected return is double the interest cost. If, however, the management borrows the necessary 100 at 4 per cent, the total expected income of the company rises to 1,008 and the market value of the firm to 10,080. But the firm now will have 100 of bonds in its capital structure so that, paradoxically, the market value of the stock must actually be reduced from 10,000 to 9,980 as a consequence of this apparently profitable investment. Or, to put it another way, the gains from being able to tap cheap, borrowed funds are more than offset for the stockholders by the market's discounting of the stock for the added leverage assumed.

Consider next the case of retained earnings. Suppose that in the course of its operations the firm acquired I dollars of cash (without impairing the earning power of its assets). If the cash is distributed as a dividend to the stockholders their wealth W_0, after the

financing, such as the sale of preferred stock or the issuance of stock rights is straightforward.

[47] Since no confusion is likely to arise, we have again, for simplicity, eliminated the subscripts identifying the firm in the equations to follow. Except for ρ_k, the subscripts now refer to time periods.

[48] In the case of bond-financing the rate of interest on bonds does not enter explicitly into the decision (assuming the firm borrows at the market rate of interest). This is true, moreover, given the conditions outlined in Section I.C, even though interest rates may be an increasing function of debt outstanding. To the extent that the firm borrowed at a rate other than the market rate the two I's in equation (24) would no longer be identical and an additional gain or loss, as the case might be, would accrue to the shareholders. It might also be noted in passing that permitting the two I's in (24) to take on different values provides a simple method for introducing underwriting expenses into the analysis.

distribution will be:

$$W_0 = S_0 + I = \frac{\bar{X}_0}{\rho_k} - D_0 + I \tag{25}$$

where $\bar{X}_0$ represents the expected return from the assets exclusive of the amount I in question. If however the funds are retained by the company and used to finance new assets whose expected rate of return is ρ^*, then the stockholders' wealth would become:

$$W_1 = S_1 = \frac{\bar{X}_0 + \rho^* I}{\rho_k} - D_0 = S_0 + \frac{\rho^* I}{\rho_k}. \tag{26}$$

Clearly $W_1 \gtreqless W_0$ as $\rho^* \gtreqless \rho_k$ so that an investment financed by retained earnings raises the net worth of the owners if and only if $\rho^* > \rho_k$.[49]

Consider finally, the case of common-stock financing. Let P_0 denote the current market price per share of stock and assume, for simplicity, that this price reflects currently expected earnings only, that is, it does not reflect any future increase in earnings as a result of the investment under consideration.[50] Then if N is the original number of shares, the price per share is:

$$P_0 = S_0/N \tag{27}$$

and the number of new shares, M, needed to finance an investment of I dollars is given by:

$$M = \frac{I}{P_0}. \tag{28}$$

As a result of the investment the market value of the stock becomes:

$$S_1 = \frac{\bar{X}_0 + \rho^* I}{\rho_k} - D_0 = S_0 + \frac{\rho^* I}{\rho_k} = NP_0 + \frac{\rho^* I}{\rho_k}$$

and the price per share:

$$P_1 = \frac{S_1}{N + M} = \frac{1}{N + M}\left[NP_0 + \frac{\rho^* I}{\rho_k}\right]. \tag{29}$$

Since by equation (28), $I = MP_0$, we can add MP_0 and subtract I from the quantity in bracket, obtaining:

$$P_1 = \frac{1}{N + M}\left[(N + M)P_0 + \frac{\rho^* - \rho_k}{\rho_k} I\right] = P_0 + \frac{1}{N + M}\,\frac{\rho^* - \rho_k}{\rho_k} I > P_0 \text{ if,} \tag{30}$$

and only if, $\rho^* > \rho_k$.

Thus an investment financed by common stock is advantageous to the current stockholders if and only if its yield exceeds the capitalization rate ρ_k.

Once again a numerical example may help to illustrate the result and make it clear why the relevant cut-off rate is ρ_k and not the current yield on common stock, i. Suppose that ρ_k is 10 per cent, r is 4 per cent, that the original expected income of our company is 1,000 and that management has the oppor-

49 The conclusion that ρ_k is the cut-off point for investments financed from internal funds applies not only to undistributed net profits, but to depreciation allowances (and even to the funds represented by the current sale value of any asset or collection of assets). Since the owners can earn ρ_k by investing funds elsewhere in the class, partial or total liquidating distributions should be made whenever the firm cannot achieve a marginal internal rate of return equal to ρ_k.

50 If we assumed that the market price of the stock did reflect the expected higher future earnings (as would be the case if our original set of assumptions above were strictly followed) the analysis would differ slightly in detail, but not in essentials. The cut-off point for new investment would still be ρ_k, but where $\rho^* > \rho_k$ the gain to the original owners would be larger than if the stock price were based on the pre-investment expectations only.

tunity of investing 100 having an expected yield of 12 per cent. If the original capital structure is 50 per cent debt and 50 per cent equity, and 1,000 shares of stock are initially outstanding, then, by Proposition I, the market value of the common stock must be 5,000 or 5 per share. Furthermore, since the interest bill is $.04 \times 5{,}000 = 200$, the yield on common stock is $800/5{,}000 = 16$ per cent. It may then appear that financing the additional investment of 100 by issuing 20 shares to outsiders at 5 per share would dilute the equity of the original owners since the 100 promises to yield 12 per cent whereas the common stock is currently yielding 16 per cent. Actually, however, the income of the company would rise to 1,012; the value of the firm to 10,120; and the value of the common stock to 5,120. Since there are now 1,020 shares, each would be worth 5.02 and the wealth of the original stockholders would thus have been increased. What has happened is that the dilution in expected earnings per share (from .80 to .796) has been more than offset, in its effect upon the market price of the shares, by the decrease in leverage.

Our conclusion is, once again, at variance with conventional views,[51] so much so as to be easily misinterpreted. Read hastily, Proposition III seems to imply that the capital structure of a firm is a matter of indifference; and that, consequently, one of the core problems of corporate finance—the problem of the optimal capital structure for a firm—is no problem at all. It may be helpful, therefore, to clear up such possible misunderstandings.

B. *Proposition III and Financial Planning by Firms*

Misinterpretation of the scope of Proposition III can be avoided by remembering that this Proposition tells us only that the type of instrument used to finance an investment is irrelevant to the question of whether or not the investment is worth while. This does not mean that the owners (or the managers) have no grounds whatever for preferring one financing plan to another; or that there are no other policy or technical issues in finance at the level of the firm.

That grounds for preferring one type of financial structure to another will still exist within the framework of our model can readily be seen for the case of common-stock financing. In general, except for something like a widely publicized oil-strike, we would expect the market to place very heavy weight on current and recent past earnings in forming expectations as to future returns. Hence, if the owners of a firm discovered a major investment opportunity which they felt would yield much more than ρ_k, they might well prefer not to finance it via common stock at the then ruling price, because this price may fail to capitalize the new venture. A better course would be a pre-emptive issue of stock (and in this connection it should be remembered that stockholders are free to borrow and buy). Another possibility would be to finance the project initially with debt. Once the project had reflected itself in increased actual earnings, the debt could be retired either with an equity issue at much better prices or

[51] In the matter of investment policy under uncertainty there is no single position which represents "accepted" doctrine. For a sample of current formulations, all very different from ours, see Joel Dean [2, esp. Ch. 3], M. Gordon and E. Shapiro [5], and Harry Roberts [17].

through retained earnings. Still another possibility along the same lines might be to combine the two steps by means of a convertible debenture or preferred stock, perhaps with a progressively declining conversion rate. Even such a double-stage financing plan may possibly be regarded as yielding too large a share to outsiders since the new stockholders are, in effect, being given an interest in any similar opportunities the firm may discover in the future. If there is a reasonable prospect that even larger opportunities may arise in the near future and if there is some danger that borrowing now would preclude more borrowing later, the owners might find their interests best protected by splitting off the current opportunity into a separate subsidiary with independent financing. Clearly the problems involved in making the crucial estimates and in planning the optimal financial strategy are by no means trivial, even though they should have no bearing on the basic decision to invest (as long as $\rho^* \geqq \rho_k$).[52]

Another reason why the alternatives in financial plans may not be a matter of indifference arises from the fact that managers are concerned with more than simply furthering the interest of the owners. Such other objectives of the management—which need not be necessarily in conflict with those of the owners—are much more likely to be served by some types of financing arrangements than others. In many forms of borrowing agreements, for example, creditors are able to stipulate terms which the current management may regard as infringing on its prerogatives or restricting its freedom to maneuver. The creditors might even be able to insist on having a direct voice in the formation of policy.[53] To the extent, therefore, that financial policies have these implications for the management of the firm, something like the utility approach described in the introductory section becomes relevant to financial (as opposed to investment) decision-making. It is, however, the utility functions of the managers per se and not of the owners that are now involved.[54]

In summary, many of the specific considerations which bulk so large in traditional discussions of corporate finance can readily be superimposed on our simple framework without forcing any drastic (and certainly no systematic) alteration of the conclusion which is our principal concern, namely that for investment decisions, the mar-

52 Nor can we rule out the possibility that the existing owners, if unable to use a financing plan which protects their interest, may actually prefer to pass up an otherwise profitable venture rather than give outsiders an "excessive" share of the business. It is presumably in situations of this kind that we could justifiably speak of a shortage of "equity capital," though this kind of market imperfection is likely to be of significance only for small or new firms.

53 Similar considerations are involved in the matter of dividend policy. Even though the stockholders may be indifferent as to payout policy as long as investment policy is optimal, the management need not be so. Retained earnings involve far fewer threats to control than any of the alternative sources of funds and, of course, involve no underwriting expense or risk. But against these advantages management must balance the fact that sharp changes in dividend rates, which heavy reliance on retained earnings might imply, may give the impression that a firm's finances are being poorly managed, with consequent threats to the control and professional standing of the management.

54 In principle, at least, this introduction of management's risk preferences with respect to financing methods would do much to reconcile the apparent conflict between Proposition III and such empirical findings as those of Modigliani and Zeman [14] on the close relation between interest rates and the ratio of new debt to new equity issues; or of John Lintner [12] on the considerable stability in target and actual dividend-payout ratios.

ginal cost of capital is ρ_k.

C. *The Effect of the Corporate Income Tax on Investment Decisions*

In Section I it was shown that when an unintegrated corporate income tax is introduced, the original version of our Proposition I,

$$\bar{X}/V = \rho_k = \text{a constant.}$$

must be rewritten as:

(11)

$$\frac{(\bar{X} - rD)(1 - \tau) + rD}{V} \equiv \frac{\bar{X}^\tau}{V} = \rho_k^\tau = \text{a constant.}$$

Throughout Section I we found it convenient to refer to $\bar{X}^\tau/V$ as the cost of capital. The appropriate measure of the cost of capital relevant to investment decisions, however, is the ratio of the expected return *before* taxes to the market value, *i.e.*, $\bar{X}/V$. From (11) above we find:

$$(31) \qquad \frac{\bar{X}}{V} = \frac{\rho_k^\tau - \tau r(D/V)}{1 - \tau} = \frac{\rho_k^\tau}{1 - \tau}\left[1 - \frac{\tau r D}{\rho_k^\tau V}\right],$$

which shows that the cost of capital now depends on the debt ratio, decreasing, as D/V rises, at the constant rate $\tau r/(1-\tau)$.[55] Thus, with a corporate income tax under which interest is a deductible expense, gains can accrue to stockholders from having debt in the capital structure, even when capital markets are perfect. The gains however are small, as can be seen from (31), and as will be shown more explicitly below.

From (31) we can develop the tax-adjusted counterpart of Proposition III by interpreting the term D/V in that equation as the proportion of debt used in any additional financing of V dollars. For example, in the case where the financing is entirely by new common stock, $D = 0$ and the required rate of return $\rho_k{}^S$ on a venture so financed becomes:

$$(32) \qquad \rho_k{}^S = \frac{\rho_k{}^\tau}{1 - \tau}.$$

For the other extreme of pure debt financing $D = V$ and the required rate of return, $\rho_k{}^D$, becomes:

(33)

$$\rho_k{}^D = \frac{\rho_k^\tau}{1 - \tau}\left[1 - \tau\frac{r}{\rho_k^\tau}\right] = \rho_k{}^S\left[1 - \tau\frac{r}{\rho_k^\tau}\right] = \rho_k{}^S - \frac{\tau}{1 - \tau}r.$$[56]

---

[55] Equation (31) is amenable, in principle, to statistical tests similar to those described in Section I.E. However we have not made any systematic attempt to carry out such tests so far, because neither the Allen nor the Smith study provides the required information. Actually, Smith's data included a very crude estimate of tax liability, and, using this estimate, we did in fact obtain a negative relation between $\bar{X}/V$ and D/V. However, the correlation (—.28) turned out to be significant only at about the 10 per cent level. While this result is not conclusive, it should be remembered that, according to our theory, the slope of the regression equation should be in any event quite small. In fact, with a value of τ in the order of .5, and values of $\rho_k{}^\tau$ and r in the order of 8.5 and 3.5 per cent respectively (*cf.* Section I.E.) an increase in D/V from 0 to 60 per cent (which is, approximately, the range of variation of this variable in the sample) should tend to reduce the average cost of capital only from about 17 to about 15 per cent.

[56] This conclusion does not extend to preferred stocks even though they have been classed with debt issues previously. Since preferred dividends except for a portion of those of public utilities are not in general deductible from the corporate tax, the cut-off point for new financing via preferred stock is exactly the same as that for common stock.

For investments financed out of retained earnings, the problem of defining the required rate of return is more difficult since it involves a comparison of the tax consequences to the individual stockholder of receiving a dividend versus having a capital gain. Depending on the time of realization, a capital gain produced by retained earnings may be taxed either at ordinary income tax rates, 50 per cent of these rates, 25 per cent, or zero, if held till death. The rate on any dividends received in the event of a distribution will also be a variable depending on the amount of other income received by the stockholder, and with the added complications introduced by the current dividend-credit provisions. If we assume that the managers proceed on the basis of reasonable estimates as to the average values of the relevant tax rates for the owners, then the required return for retained earnings $\rho_k{}^R$ can be shown to be:

(34)

$$\rho_k{}^R = \rho_k{}^\tau \frac{1}{1-\tau}\frac{1-\tau_d}{1-\tau_g} = \frac{1-\tau_d}{1-\tau_g}\rho_k{}^S$$

where τ_d is the assumed rate of personal income tax on dividends and τ_g is the assumed rate of tax on capital gains.

A numerical illustration may perhaps be helpful in clarifying the relationship between these required rates of return. If we take the following round numbers as representative order-of-magnitude values under present conditions: an after-tax capitalization rate $\rho_k{}^\tau$ of 10 per cent, a rate of interest on bonds of 4 per cent, a corporate tax rate of 50 per cent, a marginal personal income tax rate on dividends of 40 per cent (corresponding to an income of about $25,000 on a joint return), and a capital gains rate of 20 per cent (one-half the marginal rate on dividends), then the required rates of return would be: (1) 20 per cent for investments financed entirely by issuance of new common shares; (2) 16 per cent for investments financed entirely by new debt; and (3) 15 per cent for investments financed wholly from internal funds.

These results would seem to have considerable significance for current discussions of the effect of the corporate income tax on financial policy and on investment. Although we cannot explore the implications of the results in any detail here, we should at least like to call attention to the remarkably small difference between the "cost" of equity funds and debt funds. With the numerical values assumed, equity money turned out to be only 25 per cent more expensive than debt money, rather than something on the order of 5 times as expensive as is commonly supposed to be the case.[57] The reason

[57] See *e.g.*, D. T. Smith [18]. It should also be pointed out that our tax system acts in other ways to reduce the gains from debt financing. Heavy reliance on debt in the capital structure, for example, commits a company to paying out a substantial proportion of its income in the form of interest payments taxable to the owners under the personal income tax. A debt-free company, by contrast, can reinvest in the business all of its (smaller) net income and to this extent subject the owners only to the low capital gains rate (or possibly no tax at all by virtue of the loophole at death). Thus, we should expect a high degree of leverage to be of value to the owners, even in the case of closely held corporations, primarily in cases where their firm was not expected to have much need for additional funds to expand assets and earnings in the future. To the extent that opportunities for growth were available, as they presumably would be for most successful corporations, the interest of the stockholders would tend to be better served by a structure which permitted maximum use of retained earnings.

for the wide difference is that the traditional view starts from the position that debt funds are several times cheaper than equity funds even in the absence of taxes, with taxes serving simply to magnify the cost ratio in proportion to the corporate rate. By contrast, in our model in which the repercussions of debt financing on the value of shares are taken into account, the *only* difference in cost is that due to the tax effect, and its magnitude is simply the tax on the "grossed up" interest payment. Not only is this magnitude likely to be small but our analysis yields the further paradoxical implication that the stockholders' gain from, and hence incentive to use, debt financing is actually smaller the lower the rate of interest. In the extreme case where the firm could borrow for practically nothing, the advantage of debt financing would also be practically nothing.

III. CONCLUSION

With the development of Proposition III the main objectives we outlined in our introductory discussion have been reached. We have in our Propositions I and II at least the foundations of a theory of the valuation of firms and shares in a world of uncertainty. We have shown, moreover, how this theory can lead to an operational definition of the cost of capital and how that concept can be used in turn as a basis for rational investment decision-making within the firm. Needless to say, however, much remains to be done before the cost of capital can be put away on the shelf among the solved problems. Our approach has been that of static, partial equilibrium analysis. It has assumed among other things a state of atomistic competition in the capital markets and an ease of access to those markets which only a relatively small (though important) group of firms even come close to possessing. These and other drastic simplifications have been necessary in order to come to grips with the problem at all. Having served their purpose they can now be relaxed in the direction of greater realism and relevance, a task in which we hope others interested in this area will wish to share.

REFERENCES

1. F. B. ALLEN, "Does Going into Debt Lower the 'Cost of Capital'?" *Analysts Jour.*, Aug. 1954, *10*, 57–61.
2. J. DEAN, *Capital Budgeting*. New York 1951.
3. D. DURAND, "Costs of Debt and Equity Funds for Business: Trends and Problems of Measurement" in Nat. Bur. Econ. Research, *Conference on Research in Business Finance*. New York 1952, pp. 215–47.
4. W. J. EITEMAN, "Financial Aspects of Promotion," in *Essays on Business Finance* by M. W. Waterford and W. J. Eiteman. Ann Arbor, Mich. 1952, pp. 1–17.
5. M. J. GORDON and E. SHAPIRO, "Capital Equipment Analysis: The Required Rate of Profit," *Manag. Sci.*, Oct. 1956, *3*, 102–10.
6. B. GRAHAM and L. DODD, *Security Analysis*, 3rd ed New York 1951.
7. G. GUTHMANN and H. E. DOUGALL, *Corporate Financial Policy*, 3rd ed. New York 1955.
8. J. R. HICKS, *Value and Capital*, 2nd ed. Oxford 1946.
9. P. HUNT and M. WILLIAMS, *Case Problems in Finance*, rev. ed. Homewood, Ill. 1954.
10. J. M. KEYNES, *The General Theory of Employment, Interest and Money*. New York 1936.
11. O. LANGE, *Price Flexibility and Employment*. Bloomington, Ind. 1944.
12. J. LINTNER, "Distribution of Incomes of Corporations among Dividends, Retained Earnings and Taxes," *Am. Econ. Rev.*, May 1956, *46*, 97–113.
13. F. LUTZ and V. LUTZ, *The Theory of Investment of the Firm*. Princeton 1951.
14. F. MODIGLIANI and M. ZEMAN, "The Effect of the Availability of Funds, and the Terms Thereof, on Business Investment" in Nat. Bur. Econ. Research, *Conference on Research in Business Finance*. New York 1952, pp. 263–309.
15. W. A. MORTON, "The Structure of the Capital Market and the Price of Money," *Am. Econ. Rev.*, May 1954, *44*, 440–54.

16. S. M. Robbins, *Managing Securities.* Boston 1954.
17. H. V. Roberts, "Current Problems in the Economics of Capital Budgeting," *Jour. Bus.*, 1957, *30* (1), 12–16.
18. D. T. Smith, *Effects of Taxation on Corporate Financial Policy*. Boston 1952.
19. R. Smith, "Cost of Capital in the Oil Industry," (hectograph). Pittsburgh: Carnegie Inst. Tech. 1955.
20. H. M. Somers, " 'Cost of Money' as the Determinant of Public Utility Rates," *Buffalo Law Rev.*, Spring 1955, *4*, 1–28.
21. J. B. Williams, *The Theory of Investment Value*. Cambridge, Mass. 1938.
22. U. S. Federal Communications Commission, *The Problem of the "Rate of Return" in Public Utility Regulation*. Washington 1938.

THE COST OF CAPITAL IN AN IMPERFECT MARKET: A REPLY TO MODIGLIANI AND MILLER

DAVID DURAND†

In a recent contribution on security valuation and the cost of capital Messrs. Modigliani and Miller [13] (hereafter MM) have enunciated three propositions that contradict widely accepted beliefs and some conclusions stated earlier by myself [3]. In itself, the contradiction is hardly surprising, since MM's propositions rest on rather special assumptions not ordinarily entertained. What is surprising is that MM propose to erect [13, p. 264] "an operational definition of the cost of capital and a workable theory of investment" upon these assumptions, which are somewhat subtle and, on analysis, turn out to be extremely restrictive. This paper will not attempt to deny MM's propositions in their own properly limited theoretical context; instead, it will consider the nature of MM's underlying assumptions and the difficulties of applying them operationally.

Of MM's propositions the first will provide adequate material for discussion; it underlies the second and third, and the assumptions upon which it rests are those of primary interest. Proposition I states that, in a perfect market, the total value of all the outstanding securities of a firm is independent of the capital structure. More specifically, if the firm j has outstanding stock and debt instruments valued at S_j and D_j, and if its expected average earnings are $\overline{X}_j$ before interest, then the total value of its securities [13, p. 268, equation(3)] is

$$V_j \equiv S_j + D_j = \overline{X}_j/\rho_k,$$

where ρ_k is a constant capitalization factor applicable to all firms within "equivalent return class" k (to be defined later).

There seem to be three obvious devices that will aid in building a foundation under Proposition I. One is to assume that arbitrage is possible between securities in an "equivalent return class." Another is to assume that a "firm" falls into none of the three standard categories — proprietorship, partnership, or corporation — but is a sort of hybrid, having marketable securities like a corporation, proration of income like a partnership, and allocation of financial responsibility like neither. A third device is to assume a long-run equilibrium in which stocks sell at book value. But none of these devices is realistic, and MM have not accepted any of them wholeheartedly. Thus, while they speak of arbitrage, the process they actually describe is not arbitrage at all, but a switch. Or again, they include all firms in one category—calling them corporations, but failing to bring out the essential differences between corporations and partnerships. And finally, although they do not discuss the question of stocks selling at book value, some but not all of their treatment of dividend policy seems to assume just this. This paper will expose the difficulties of justifying Proposition I for real, live corporations in a world

† The author is professor of industrial management at the Massachusetts Institute of Technology.

where arbitrage is usually impossible, and where stocks do not sell at book value.

I. *Proposition I and Arbitrage: An Illustrative Example*

True arbitrage, when possible in the corporate security markets, is a powerful equalizer; but it is not ordinarily possible, and its overall influence is therefore limited. To clarify the issue, this section will present an artificial example of an "equivalent return class" of corporations in which the possibility of arbitrage will practically guarantee Proposition I; the subsequent sections will then show how this example fails to account for the real problems of corporation finance.

Petrolease is a fictitious corporation whose business consists in leasing oil properties; it earns $10 per share on the average, all of which it pays out in dividends. Leverage Fund is a fictitious open-end investment trust, whose assets consist solely of Petrolease shares. It operates under the following conditions, some of which are unusual: (1) for every share of Petrolease that it holds, it must have outstanding one share of its own stock and one $100 bond paying interest at 5 percent; (2) it incurs no expenses and pays out all earnings; (3) as an open-end fund, it will issue on demand one share and one bond while simultaneously acquiring, by purchase or exchange, a Petrolease share, or it will redeem on demand one share and one bond while divesting itself of a Petrolease share; (4) it makes no loading charge so that the buyer (or seller) of a bond and share pays (or receives) the same combined price that Leverage Fund pays (or receives) for a share of Petrolease; (5) in the open market, securities of both Petrolease and Leverage Fund trade without commissions. As a result of conditions (1) and (2), Leverage Fund is a transmission line for the uncertainties and vicissitudes of Petrolease. The investor who buys a bond and share of Leverage Fund will receive exactly the same income over the years ($5 per year from the bond plus an average of $5 from the share) as another investor who buys a share of Petrolease. Thus these two corporations constitute an "equivalent return class" in the sense of MM.

The peculiarities of Leverage Fund and Petrolease virtually guarantee that Proposition I will hold between them; together a bond and share of the one must sell for the same price as a share of the other. Suppose, for example, the following prices to obtain in the open market:

Petrolease		Leverage Fund	
stock	160	bonds	100
		stock	68
			168

Then, the $8 discrepancy between the two corporations will provide investors and speculators with opportunities for profit, the exploitation of which will tend to reduce and eventually eliminate the discrepancy.

One such opportunity is through arbitrage. A speculator who owns none of the securities in question can, nevertheless, realize a quick profit of $800 by buying 100 shares of Petrolease and simultaneously selling short 100 bonds and shares of Leverage Fund. Then, at his leisure, he exchanges his long Petrolease shares for Leverage Fund securities and delivers the latter against his short commitment. A single aggressive arbitrager can thus exert terrific equalizing pressure, for he can continue his operations just as long as any discrepancy remains. Indeed, if a discrepancy should persist—owing to sluggishness of other operators—the arbitrager might eventually buy up and exchange all outstanding shares of Petrolease; then, the discrepancy would necessarily disappear, there being no more Petrolease shares to trade.

But, it is important to note, the effectiveness of this arbitrage depends upon the possibility of exchange between Petrolease and Leverage Fund, not upon the income equivalence of the two corporations. If, for example, personal income from bond interest should be taxed at a lower rate than dividends, any astute investor would prefer a bond and share of Leverage Fund to a share of Petrolease and would regard a price discrepancy as normal. The arbitragers, however, would still profit by buying Petrolease and selling Leverage Fund.

Another opportunity for profit is through what might be called a straddle position,[1] designed to provide income without investment. An operator who sells short 100 bonds and shares of Leverage Fund and immediately invests the proceeds in 105 shares of Petrolease will derive from the transaction a net income equal to the dividends on 5 shares of Petrolease. In this hypothetical transaction, the straddle operator avoids the normal risks of maintaining a short position—since he can always convert 100 shares of Petrolease into Leverage Fund securities and use these to discharge his short commitment. He can, therefore, expand his position almost indefinitely and exert terrific equalizing pressure, much like the arbitrager.

A third opportunity for profit is through the switching of investment accounts from Leverage Fund into Petrolease. MM refer to this type of transaction as arbitrage—a rather common error among market outsiders. But there is more at stake here than the mere careless use of technical terms by laymen. Having learned that genuine arbitrage, when possible, can be tremendously effective as an equalizing force, one may improperly impute some of this effectiveness to other operations by ill-advisedly referring to them as arbitrage. But this is like an attempt to increase the offensive power of a Brown Bess rechristening it Big Bertha.

The essential ingredient of arbitrage, in this context, is some provision for exchange or conversion.[2] Although Petrolease shares carry no intrinsic right of exchange, the operation of Leverage Fund has the effect of rendering them exchangeable. MM repeatedly speak of one security as a "perfect substitute" for another, merely on the

[1] The term 'straddle' is used here, perhaps a little loosely, by analogy to a straddle in the commodity markets, which consists in buying one future, say May, and going short of another, say July. There is no relation between this kind of straddle and the stock option of the same name.

[2] Arbitrage between Petrolease and Leverage Fund belongs to a category known as 'kind' arbitrage. According to Weinstein [18, p. 2], a transaction of this type may be defined as "the simultaneous purchase and sale of equivalent articles or securities in the same or different markets." But the meaning of equivalence here is rather special, implying that the articles or securities are essentially different but, "through the terms of their issuance or through special circumstance, may become equal or equivalent to each other." Later [18, p. 66], Weinstein specifies: "By equivalent securities is meant a convertible bond or stock, a right or option warrant, or a stock of one company which may be exchanged for the stock of the same or another company." By this view, a share of Petrolease is equivalent to a bond and share of Leverage Fund because of the exchange opportunity —and not because of the income equivalence.

Before Switching				
300 Closed Corp.	at $68	value $20,400	yielding	$1500
After Switching				
340 Petrolease	at 160	54,400	yielding	3400
Margin loan at 5% interest[3]		34,000	costing	1700
Net		$20,400		$1700

grounds that it has a claim to an equal amount of income. Now, in point of fact, a share of Petrolease is a perfect substitute for any other share—in legal terms Petrolease shares are fungible—but it is not a perfect substitute for a bond and share of Leverage Fund; the Petrolease stockholder has no vote for Leverage Fund directors. A share of Petrolease is, however, a good enough substitute for a bond and share of Leverage Fund, and vice versa, to permit the arbitrage operations that will assure the validity of Proposition I. The importance of these details becomes apparent if Leverage Fund is simply transformed into a closed-end trust—bearing, say, the name Closed Corp. Then, even though one share of Petrolease still stands solidly behind a bond and share of Closed Corp.—maintaining income equivalence, just as with Leverage Fund—no exchange is possible between the securities of the two companies. This precludes arbitrage and places the burden of equalizing the market on the straddle operators and the investors who switch long-term holdings.

A straddle position between Petrolease and Closed Corp. is technically possible. But it may be difficult to arrange, owing to the institutional restrictions on short selling; and it is highly hazardous because the straddle operator no longer has the option of exchanging Petrolease to liquidate his short position in the event of emergency, such as a corner. (See Macaulay [12, pp. vii-viii, 19-20]). Although corners are not so common as formerly, the recent episode of Bruce Corporation on the American Stock Exchange indicates that the danger is still present.

A switch of investment funds into Petrolease from Closed Corp. is about as easy as a switch from Leverage Fund. According to MM, a leverage-loving investor who holds Closed Corp. stock outright should sell it, and then buy just enough Petrolease on margin to reproduce the leverage of Closed Corp. in his own private account. If, to be specific, he should start with 300 shares of Closed Corp., he would change his position as in table at top of page. Thus he achieves an increase of $200 in net income with no loss of income stability; for, by arranging to pay out in interest exactly $5 of his dividend receipts from each share of Petrolease, which is what Closed Corp. pays, he assures himself that his net income will exhibit exactly the same percentage fluctuations as Closed Corp. dividends. From such considerations MM [13, p. 270] "conclude therefore that levered companies cannot command a premium over unlevered companies because investors have the opportunity of putting the equivalent leverage into their portfolio [sic] directly by borrowing on personal account." But outside the world of pure fantasy or science fiction, this is only a limited opportunity for

[3] MM [13, p. 268] assume that the investor pays the same rate on his margin loan that Leverage Fund pays on its bonds.

most investors, who are deterred from aggressive margin buying by its intrinsic risks (see Section II) or by the legal and institutional restrictions placed upon it (see Section III).

Because of these deterrents, Proposition I can be no more than an inequality for Petrolease and Closed Corp. In simplest terms, Closed Corp. securities enjoy a wider market than does Petrolease stock. Almost any investor who would buy a share of Petrolease would find a satisfactory—though not perfect—substitute in a bond and share of Closed Corp., and he should willingly switch if the substitute fell to a discount.[4] Thus, as long as investors are fairly alert, Closed Corp. cannot sell much below Petrolease. But the reverse does not hold; for Closed Corp. stock has a special appeal to risk takers, and the bonds have a special appeal both to those who want to play safe and to those who are barred from buying stock. For Closed Corp. to command a premium, it is necessary only that this specialized demand should exceed the available supply. After all, the essential difference between Closed Corp. and Leverage Fund is the limitation on the amount of securities that the former can conveniently issue. When Leverage Fund commands a premium, the arbitragers can buy up and exchange Petrolease shares, thus increasing the supply of Leverage Fund securities; but they cannot do this for Closed Corp. Consequently, income equivalence alone does not suffice to assure value equivalence for corporations having different capital structures.

[4] There will be a few exceptions—that is, institutions that are required to invest only in common stock. The College Retirement Equities Fund is an example.

II. *Limited Liability vs. The Risk of Margin Buying*

One reason for the growth of the modern business corporation over the past hundred years has been the protection afforded stockholders by the principle of limited liability. According to Ballantine [1, p. 1]:

> "Much of the industrial and commercial development of the nineteenth and twentieth centuries has been made possible by the corporate mechanism. By its use investors may combine their capital and participate in the profits of large or small scale business enterprises under a centralized management, with a risk limited to the capital contributed and without peril to their other resources and business. The amount of capital needed for modern business could hardly have been assembled and combined in any other way."

Indeed, the principle of limited liability offers the aggressive enterpriser a sort of heads-I-win-tails-you-lose opportunity. Not long after the passage of the Limited Liability Act of 1855 and the Companies Act of 1862,[5] which established limited liability in Britain, a member of the bar, and famous social critic, commented as follows:

> "Some seven men form an Association (if possible, all Peers and Baronets), they start off with a public declaration to what extent they mean to pay their debts. That's called their Capital: if they are wary they will not quote it at a sum immense. The figure's immaterial —it may vary from eighteen million down to eighteenpence. *I* should put it rather low; the good sense of doing so will be evident at once to any debtor. . . . They then proceed to trade with all who'll trust 'em, quite irrespective of their capital (it's shady, but it's sanctified by custom); Bank, Railway, Loan, or Panama Canal. You can't embark on trading too tremendous—it's strictly fair, and based on common sense—if you succeed, your profits are stupendous—and if you fail, pop goes your eighteenpence. . . . If you come to

[5] See Ballantine [1, pp. 34-35].

grief, and creditors are craving (for nothing that is planned by mortal head is certain in this Vale of Sorrow—saving that one's Liability is Limited),—do you suppose that signifies perdition? If so you're but a monetary dunce—you merely file a Winding-Up Petition, and start another Company at once! Though a Rothschild you may be in your own capacity, as a Company you've come to utter sorrow—but the Liquidators say, 'Never mind —you needn't pay,' so you start another Company tomorrow!" (Gilbert [7, pp. 490-491]).

The aggressive investor who wishes to enjoy some of the benefits of leverage can do so without throwing all discretion to the winds; he borrows through a corporate intermediary. The leverage-loving investor of the last example, who holds 300 shares of Closed Corp. outright at 68, has, in effect, a levered position in Petrolease; and on this he faces a maximum loss of $20,400, since he has no liability to Closed Corp. bondholders. If he switches into 340 shares of Petrolease on margin, as MM recommend, he incurs a liability of $34,000 for his margin loan, and his maximum loss increases to $54,400. In practice, of course, he runs very little risk of losing the entire $54,400 because his broker-lender, in self-defense, will attempt to sell him out before Petrolease becomes worthless. But this protection against maximum loss greatly increases the risk of lesser loss. Many a margin trader has been liquidated as the result of a strictly temporary decline in the price of the stock margined. The essential point is that the margin loan is a demand loan; and in spite of MM's assertion [13, p. 268] "that all bonds are in fact perfect substitutes up to a scale factor," a demand loan cannot possibly be regarded as a perfect substitute for Closed Corp. bonds, which have a definite term, say 20 years.

MM ask us to believe that the protection afforded by limited liability is not worth a premium, even though individuals or partnerships may often incorporate and incur appreciable double taxation just to enjoy this protection. In fact, MM [13, p. 269] argue that the investor requires no protection in switching from Closed Corp. outright to Petrolease on margin, since he merely exchanges "one income stream for another stream, identical in all relevant respects but selling at a lower price." But this view is correct only if corporate earnings are quite stable. If Petrolease earnings should drop below $5 per share, net income would drop into the red for the margined investor, but it could not go below zero for the outright investor in Closed Corp. Possibly MM intended to eliminate the possibility of negative income on margin accounts when they wrote [13, p. 268]: "All bonds (including any debts issued by households for the purpose of carrying shares) are assumed to yield a constant income per unit of time, and this income is regarded as certain by all traders regardless of the issuer." But this is a strange statement for anyone committed to "an operational definition of the cost of capital" in a world where nothing is certain—except, perhaps, that one's liability is limited! Although later [13, p. 274, ftn. 18] MM offer a "minor qualification" to the effect that income may temporarily fall below interest requirements "as a result of a run of temporary losses," they fail to grapple with the essential problems of business and financial risk: that Petrolease wells may unexpectedly run dry, that Closed Corp. bonds may default and become worthless, that mortgages may be foreclosed, or that margin traders may be whipsawed by temporary fluctuations in the price—not necessarily the income—of the stock margined. These are the real risks of market life; and no one who excludes them can expect to qualify among the economists who have [13, p. 263] "begun to face up seriously to the problem of the cost of capital *cum* risk."

III. *Market Restrictions: A Clarification and a Rebuttal*

Since indiscriminate margin buying may jeopardize not only the buyer but also the lender, and possibly even the public at large, a host of protective restrictions have grown up—taking such varied forms as institutional traditions, investment taboos, and actual legal prohibitions. Very important among these are the institutional arrangements that prevent some of our largest investors from doing any margin trading whatsoever. Virtually all of the mutual funds and a good share of the closed-end trusts are thus prohibited by their charters. All together, these companies control some $10,000,000,000 of assets, most of them in common stocks. It is against such windmills of entrenched wealth that MM expect the remaining rugged, but quixotic, individuals to do battle, buying a few hundred shares of this or that on margin.

The individuals, moreover, and such institutions as are not flatly prohibited, do not enjoy unbridled license in their margin trading. Even before the days of Regulation X, stock brokers curtailed margin commitments. Today, the 90 percent limit would prohibit an investor from borrowing $34,000 to buy $54,400 of Petrolease stock on margin, as part of the switching operation described in Section I. Thus, the kind of margin switching described by MM as a basis for supporting Proposition I is illegal in extreme forms, as well as hazardous in all.

In discussing a previous analysis of market restrictions and the cost of capital, MM [13, pp. 278-279] write:

> "A more sophisticated line of argument has been advanced by David Durand [3, pp. 231-33]. He suggests that because insurance companies and certain other important institutional investors are restricted to debt securities, nonfinancial corporations are able to borrow from them at interest rates which are lower than would be required to compensate creditors in a free market. Thus, while he would presumably agree with our conclusions that stockholders could not gain from leverage in an unconstrained market, he concludes that they can gain under present institutional arrangements. . . . The defective link in both the traditional and the Durand version of the argument lies in the confusion between investors' subjective risk preferences and their objective market opportunities."

Now who is confusing subjective preferences with objective opportunities? The statement [3, p. 231] that "these restricted investors, including all banks and insurance companies, have to bid for high-grade investments almost without regard to yield differentials or the attractiveness of the lower grade investments" implies not so much that life insurance companies buy bonds out of choice, although some of them do, as that they shun stocks under duress. Possibly [3], written when several life companies were campaigning to broaden their objective market opportunities to buy stocks, may have slighted margin restrictions; but it did not preclude them! Most institutions prohibited from buying stocks outright will be automatically prevented from buying them on margin.

MM illustrate their position on market restrictions with an amazing, but informative, analogy to the price of milk, arguing that a corporation cannot profit by selling both debt and equity any more than a farmer can profit by separating his milk into cream and skimmed milk. They say [13, p. 280]:

"Furthermore the argument remains valid even in the face of institutional [sic] limitations of the type envisaged by Durand. For suppose that a large fraction of the population habitually dines in restaurants which are required by law to serve only cream in lieu of milk (entrust their savings to institutional investors who can only buy bonds). To be sure the price of butter fat will then tend to be higher in relation to that of skimmed milk than in the absence [sic] such restrictions (the rate of interest will tend to be lower), and this will benefit people who eat at home and who like skim milk (who manage their own portfolio [sic] and are able and willing to take risk). But it will still be the case that a farmer cannot gain by skimming some of the butter fat and selling it separately (firm cannot reduce the cost of capital by recourse to borrowed funds).

MM are probably correct in thinking that their legal restriction on restaurants does not suffice, all by itself, to raise the price of separated milk to a premium over whole milk. But if they are willing to admit one legal restriction in order to achieve a little realism, they can hardly exclude others. A restriction on milk separators, especially in conjunction with that on restaurants, might well force the price of separated milk to a premium. At any rate, the facts indicate that a premium of around 40 percent actually exists in the retail markets.[6]

A restriction on milk separators in the milk market would be analogous to the existing restrictions on arbitrage and margin trading in the financial markets. In the example of Petrolease and Leverage Fund Proposition I was bound to hold because the arbitragers stood ready to separate Petrolease whole milk into Leverage Fund skimmed milk and cream if these components rose to a premium, and equally ready to recombine the components if they fell to a discount. But the transformation of Leverage Fund into Closed Corp eliminated the arbitragers, thus depriving the market of its most potent leveling mechanism and Proposition I of its most forceful justification. Of course, when Closed Corp. skimmed milk and cream command a premium, a few sharp operators will still attempt to separate Petrolease whole milk by selling Closed Corp. bonds short or by borrowing (selling their own bonds in MM's terminology) to buy Petrolease on margin. But these operators may lack the financial strength necessary to equalize the market value of Petrolease and Closed Corp.; they have only limited resources —there being virtually no mutual funds or other large institutional investors among them—and only limited freedom to employ these resources under present legal and institutional restrictions on short selling and margin buying.

IV. *The Problem of Retention and Growth*

Discussion of all preceding examples, except for arbitrage in Leverage Fund and Petrolease, has assumed 100 percent dividend payout. This assumption would be completely realistic for part-

[6] On a recent visit to the Cambridge Stop-and-Shop, I found fat-free milk selling at two quarts for 51¢, whole milk (unhomogenized) at the same price, and heavy cream at 35¢ per half pint. By mixing four fifths of a half pint of the cream (about 40 percent butterfat) with two quarts of fat-free milk, one would obtain a product comparable to whole milk (about 4 percent butterfat). The cost of this mixture, 79¢ for 2.2 quarts, represents a premium of about 40 percent over the two quart price of 51¢ for whole milk.

nerships, since the law considers that a partner receives his pro-rata share of the firm's income, whether paid out or not; and it is almost realistic for certain types of corporations, such as regulated investment trusts. But it will not do for corporations at large. MM do not actually assume 100 percent payout; instead they say [13, p. 266]: "As will become clear later, as long as management is presumed to be acting in the best interests of the stockholders, retained earnings can be regarded as equivalent to a fully subscribed, preemptive issue of common stock. Hence, for present purposes, the division of the stream between cash dividends and retained earnings in any period is a mere detail." But what do "present purposes" include? Obviously not the execution of Form 1040 or presentation in a court of law! And a little thought will indicate that they do not even include the delineation of an "equivalent return class," which "plays a strategic role" [p. 266] in MM's argument. Suppose, for example, that two equity-financed corporations earn regularly a definite rate ρ^* on assets of A, and that they retain no earnings. Then the assets of each will remain constant at A, and the earnings will remain at $A\rho^*$ per year. Earnings per share will then differ at most by a scale factor, and the two corporations must, according to MM's definition [13, pp. 265-66, esp. ftn. 6], belong to the same "equivalent return class." But now suppose that one corporation should start to retain earnings and to invest them profitably; then its assets and earnings would both begin to increase, and its earnings per share would differ from those of the other corporation by more than a scale factor. This would suffice to transfer the retaining corporation into a new class.

MM's proposal to regard retentions as a fully subscribed, pre-emptive stock issue may get them out of this difficulty in the special case of a long-run equilibrium with stocks selling at book value, but will not help them if stocks sell appreciably above or below book value. Before the corporation of the preceding paragraph started to expand, it earned $A\rho^*$ — or $A\rho^*/N$ per share on N shares having book value $B_0 = A/N$. With a market capitalization rate of ρ_k, the stock sold at a price of $P_0 = A\rho^*/\rho_k N$, with a ratio to book value $P_0/B_0 = \rho^*/\rho_k$. Now, in the first year of its expansion, the corporation retains an amount $I = A\rho^* X$, which it reinvests to yield the same rate ρ^*; and this enables it to earn $A\rho^*(1 + \rho^* X)$. MM wish us to regard I, the amount retained, as the proceeds of a stock sale, but they neglect to inform us of the price P_f at which their hypothetical transaction is to take place—a detail, perhaps, but an important one! No single price P_f for the hypothetical stock issue will meet both of two requirements: first, to maintain earnings per share unchanged and thus keep the corporation in the same class; and second, to provide a genuine equation between the amount retained and the stock issue.

A price of $P_f = B_0$ for example, will meet only the first requirement. At this price the corporation must issue

$$\frac{I}{B_0} = \frac{A\rho^* X}{A/N} = \rho^* N X$$

new shares, and these together with N old shares will earn per share

$$\frac{A\rho^* (1 + \rho^* X)}{N (1 + \rho^* X)} = A\rho^*/N,$$

exactly the same as before expansion. But this price $P_f = B_0$ will not meet the second condition, because the subscriber to the hypothetical stock issue is, in effect, forced to acquire additional shares at B_0 when the market price is P_0; and he must, consequently, either enjoy a profit $P_0 - B_0$ or sustain a loss $B_0 - P_0$.

Finding a price P_f that will meet the second requirement and actually equate a dollar's worth of retentions to a dollar's worth of issued stock is difficult. Such a price will depend, when $\rho^* \neq \rho_k$ and $P_0 \neq B_0$, on the entire future growth of the corporation; and to obtain a solution, one must stipulate an arbitrary future growth pattern. From the standpoint of algebra, one of the more tractable growth patterns is a uniform growth rate of $\rho^* X$, resulting from the retention and reinvestment each year of a fraction X of earnings to yield precisely ρ^*. Then the required price is given by

$$\frac{A\rho^*(1 - X)}{(\rho_k - \rho^* X)N},$$

which is a standard actuarial formula for the present value of an income stream starting at $A\rho^*(1 - X)/N$, growing at a rate $\rho^* X$, and discounted at ρ_k (cf. Todhunter [16, pp. 48-49]). When $\rho^* = \rho_k$, the above gives $P_f = B_0 = A/N$ for $1 > X \geqslant 0$; but when $\rho^* > \rho_k$ and $X > 0$, it gives $P_f > B_0$, with P_f approaching infinity as $\rho^* X$ approaches ρ_k. Thus, in addition to resting on highly artificial assumptions, the above formula sometimes leads to absurdities (cf. Durand [6]). Williams [8, pp. 87-89, 129-34] suggests some growth formulae that are also artificial but at least avoid the absurdities.

Whether the corporation succeeds in finding, for its hypothetical stock issue, the exact price P_f that meets the second requirement, its choice of any price $P_f \neq B_0$ will affect earnings per share and transfer it into a new "equivalent return class."[7] In particular, when $\rho^* > \rho_k$, each hypothetical issue above book value will raise earnings per share, thus offering investors a potential element of long-term appreciation in excess of the nominal earnings-price ratio ρ_k. Moreover, although this result has been derived for a special corporation, it is remarkably general. It applies to real stock issues and bond issues as well as to hypothetical stock issues, and it applies to corporations growing at irregular rates.[8]

If MM wish to include in their "equivalent return classes" a reasonable variety of companies expanding at various rates, and if they wish to make sure that retained earnings are equivalent to a fully-subscribed, pre-emptive stock issue, then they must assume some sort of long-run equilibrium condition in which $\rho^* = \rho_k$ and price equals book value. Indeed, they have explicitly [13, pp. 288-91] assumed $\rho^* \geqslant \rho_k$, on the grounds that investments yielding ρ^*

[7] Possibly this argument contains a subtlety that requires explanation. A corporation can, of course, start in a given "equivalent return class," go through a period of expansion, and return to the same class at the close of its expansion—even if it earns $\rho^* > \rho_k$ on its investments. But this is not the point. It is the prospect of expansion, not the act itself, that causes the difficulty. Oddly enough, MM recognize [13, p. 290, ftn. 50] that a proposed expansion may, because of its potential affect on earnings per share, influence stock prices; but they seem to have overlooked the havoc that this kind of anticipation plays with their concept of an "equivalent return class."

[8] There is a good deal of literature describing the mechanism by which this additional element of appreciation is realized. See, for example, Durand [5, Chapt. 4], Gordon and Shapiro [9], Modigliani and Miller [13, pp. 288-91], Tatham [15].

$< \rho_k$ are unprofitable and detrimental to the stockholders. They could equally well have ruled out $\rho^* > \rho_k$ on grounds of competition; if an area of investment opportunity offers rates of return $\rho^* > \rho_k$, it will attract additional capital until the discrepancy disappears. Such an argument can be no great hurdle for those who believe the presence of [13, p. 281] "large and *systematic* imperfections in the market which permanently bias the outcome . . . is an assumption that economists, at any rate, will instinctively eye with some skepticism."

Paradoxically enough, although an outright assumption that $\rho^* = \rho_k$ and that price equals book value would have done much to shore up MM's theoretical argument, it would have done nothing to establish this argument as realistic or operational. In the operating world stocks do not sell at book value—not even approximately. A list recently released by the New York Stock Exchange [14, pp. 10-11] shows great variation in popular stocks—ranging from New York Central, selling at about one tenth book value, to International Business Machines, at about seven times book value. Moreover, there is some question whether an exact equality between price and book value will induce investors to contribute the large amounts of capital required by a vigorously growing economy. Writing on the utility industry, where this problem is well recognized, Tatham [15] points out that utility stocks have, in recent years, generally commanded a premium over book value, thus assuring investors of a "potential increase in value and earnings during a period of expansion," which "provides one of the basic attractions of utility common stocks for investment purposes." By this "potential increase" Tatham [15, p. 36] refers specifically to the growth in earnings per share that results from successive issues of stock above book value; but the same sort of growth also results from expansion financed through borrowing or retentions, provided $\rho^* > \rho_k$ and stocks sell above book value.

Since so many considerations indicate that investors should not regard dividend policy as a mere detail, some empirical evidence of their actual behavior is needed; and by now a good deal is available (cf. Durand [4] and [5], Gordon [8], Graham and Dodd [10, Chapt. 34], Johnson, Shapiro, and O'Meara [11]). Table 1 summarizes a regression analysis of price P on book value B, earnings E, and dividends D, for a group of 25 bank stocks—one of six groups analyzed recently.[9] The special arrangement in the table is designed to show the successive reductions in the sum of residual squares due first to earnings, E, and then to the ratio of dividends to earnings, D/E. In particular, the reduction due to D/E (.094283 − .036081 = .058202) is far too great to attribute to chance (since the F-ratio .058202 × 21/.036081 = 33.88 far exceeds even the .001 point for one and 21 degrees of freedom) and indicates that the payout ratio exerts a significant influence on price—even after the combined influence of book value and earnings have been taken into account. Table 2 summarizes regression analyses of four groups of public utility stocks.[10]

[9] For further analysis, see Durand [5]. The original data for this example appear in [5, p. 29, Table 5].

[10] These analyses come from a larger study on public utility stock prices and the cost of capital, financed by a grant from the Sloan Research Fund of the School of Industrial Management at Massachusetts Institute of Technology. The main results

TABLE 1
REGRESSION ANALYSIS OF THE STOCKS OF 25 LARGE BANKS OUTSIDE NEW YORK CITY, EARLY 1953

Regression Equations	*Sum of Residual Squares*
$\log_{10}P = .07 + .97\log_{10}B$	.151298
$\log_{10}P = .54 + .49\log_{10}B + .54\log_{10}E$	.094283
$\log_{10}P = .96 + .22\log_{10}B + .91\log_{10}E + .70\log_{10}D/E$	.036081

TABLE 2
REGRESSION ANALYSIS OF FOUR GROUPS OF PUBLIC UTILITY STOCKS (20 STOCKS PER GROUP), EARLY 1955

Group	*Regression Equations*	*Sum of Residual Squares*
I (Northeast)		
	$\log_{10}P/B = 1.18 + .96\log_{10}E/B$	.031033
	$\log_{10}P/B = 1.32 + 1.04\log_{10}E/B + .60\log_{10}D/E$	.017997
	$F = 17x.013036/.017997 = 12.314$	.013036
II (Midwest)		
	$\log_{10}P/B = .90 + .70\log_{10}E/B$	.019481
	$\log_{10}P/B = 1.16 + .90\log_{10}E/B + .46\log_{10}D/E$	.011770
	$F = 17x.007711/.011770 = 11.137$	.007711
III (West)		
	$\log_{10}P/B = .97 + .77\log_{10}E/B$	.042596
	$\log_{10}P/B = 1.11 + .87\log_{10}E/B + .28\log_{10}D/E$	.040625
	$F = 17x.001971/.040625 = .825$	.001971
IV (South)		
	$\log_{10}P/B = 1.13 + .90\log_{10}E/B$	.049213
	$\log_{10}P/B = 1.27 + 1.00\log_{10}E/B + .30\log_{10}D/E$	.041994
	$F = 17x.007219/.041994 = 2.922$	.007219

Here the ratio of price to book value, P/B, is related to earnings over book value, E/B, and dividends over earnings, D/E. The reduction in the sum of squares is highly significant in the first two groups, but not at all significant in the last two. The combined experience of all groups taken together is significant.

MM are inclined to scoff at evidence like the above, arguing that [13, pp. 287-88] "in a world in which the policy of dividend stabilization is widespread, there is no simple way of disentangling the true effect of dividend payments on stock prices from their apparent effect, the latter reflecting only the role of dividends as a proxy measure of long-term earning anticipations." Are not MM trying to extinguish the fire by pouring on more fuel? In addition to the true effect, they introduce an apparent effect, which may also affect stock prices and the cost of capital.

Unfortunately MM do not explain what they mean by the "true effect of dividend payments." Possibly they refer to the practical inability of some investors, notably institutions, to regard retentions as a pre-emptive stock issue; after all, there is a distinction between capital gains and income—and especially between unrealized capital gains and realized income. Or again, MM may refer to the influence, discussed earlier in this section, of dividend policy on the earnings prospects of a company

have yet to be published. The computations were performed on the I.B.M. 704 computer at the newly established M.I.T. Computation Center.

when $\rho^* \neq \rho_k$. In this light, MM's statement on the apparent effect seems to imply that dividend policy may exert, in addition to its genuine influence, a psychological influence on the public's appraisal of earnings prospects—presumably by creating or correcting wrong impressions. In the earlier and less responsible days of Wall Street, an unscrupulous insider—like General Daniel E. Sickles of the Erie (cf. Dewing [2, p. 744, ftn. 6])—might often attempt to mislead the public by manipulating dividends and issuing false earnings statements. And even today, when blatant manipulation is far less common, psychological influences remain. If a conscientious corporation manager believes the public is underestimating the earning power of his company and that a dividend change might improve the public's estimate, should he not make the change? To put it briefly there are many ways, some devious, by which dividend policy can influence stock prices and the cost of capital; and the available evidence indicates conclusively that at least some of them are effective.

Even though the available evidence does not suffice to disentangle all these influences, it offers some interesting hints. The bank stocks covered by Table 1 had an average price about 5 percent above book value—with a range from 22 percent below for The National Shawmut to 83 percent above for The Bank of America. The utility stocks covered by Table 2 all sold above book value—with a range from 11 percent for Consolidated Edison and Pennsylvania Water and Power to 222 percent for Scranton Electric. Under such circumstances, investors seeking long-term appreciation should prefer stocks paying low dividends—at least, according to the argument advanced earlier in this section; and if such investors dominate the market, negative regression coefficients for D/E are the natural result. The positive coefficients in Tables 1 and 2 imply dominance by another type of investor—possibly one who looks at dividend data instead of analyzing the earnings account, but more probably one with a genuine need for regular dividend income (cf. Durand [5, p. 47]). In effect, our evidence on dividend policy is just good enough to be frustrating: it leaves us no doubt whatsoever that dividend policy exerts an influence on stock prices and the cost of capital, while leaving us tremendous doubts about the nature and significance of this influence.

V. *Problems of Empirical Analysis*

The empiricist who would investigate the cost of capital for corporations will encounter a host of obstacles, and among the first will be the gathering of data that are reliable and pertinent. He will find price quotations sometimes hard to acquire and often erratic—particularly quotations for corporate bonds, most of which are rather inactively traded nowadays, and some of which, the so-called private placements, are not even traded at all. He will find dividend rates, although easy enough to ascertain for regular payers like American Telephone and Telegraph, very troublesome when irregular payments, stock dividends, and extras are the rule. And he will find earnings even harder to ascertain precisely than dividends, for they are subject to the vagaries of accounting practice as well as the vicissitudes of business conditions.

Another obstacle, which is crucial for

MM's approach, is the difficulty of assembling a sample of corporations capable of supporting a comparative, or cross-section, type of analysis. The empirical analyst will be unable to assemble any sample meeting the rigid requirements of MM's "equivalent return class;" but this in itself is hardly disastrous, since samples showing no variation in dividend policy and growth rate will not yield much information. The real difficulty is to find samples that are reasonably homogeneous in most respects, and yet show enough variation in growth rate, capital structure, and the like, to bring out the influences of these factors. One can often find two or three, and sometimes several, corporations with characteristics sufficiently uniform to justify significant comparisons—a device long known and used by security analysts. But if an analyst restricts his samples in order to keep them homogeneous, he must perforce keep them small; and as he attempts to expand them to the point where they are numerically satisfactory, he must pay a price in lost homogeneity. This problem arose recently in a study of 117 bank stocks (Durand [4] and [5]). A sample of 117 would be large enough to support a fairly respectable cross-section analysis—provided it were homogeneous. But a division of this sample into six subsamples, coupled with some tests for homogeneity, revealed striking differences. Within the subsamples, moreover, there was further evidence of heterogeneity; in fact, a surprisingly large number of banks exhibited characteristics that rendered them virtually unique (Durand [5, pp. 19-20 and 60-62]).

Taken all together these obstacles of sparse market prices, uncertain dividends, ambiguous earnings, and heterogeneous stock groups rather narrowly limit the ability of the empirical analyst to detect, let alone measure, the various factors affecting the cost of capital. Indeed, only the strongest factors can be expected to exert a discernible influence through the haze of extraneous perturbations; and the subtler ones may easily remain unnoticed. To date, in fact, one of the few relations that have been strong enough to observe repeatedly is that between price and dividend payout; and even this has proved neither clear cut nor easy to interpret. Although the evidence suffices to establish the existence of such a relation, it does not demonstrate universality or uniformity; it does not indicate whether stockholders are using dividend data to forecast company prospects or are merely expressing an honest preference for cash income; and finally, it does not remove the element of guess and conjecture from decisions on dividend policy by the operating corporation manager who may wish to provide low-cost capital for his company, or to meet the needs of a wide variety of stockholders in vastly different personal circumstances and income tax brackets.

The influence, if any, of leverage on cost of capital has so far escaped detection—either in the two groups of securities (oils and utilities) mentioned by MM, or in the sample of 117 bank stocks. But in view of the difficulties of detection, this is not very convincing evidence; it does not preclude the possibility of some influence any more than the inability to hear coherent speech over a noisy telephone line during a thunderstorm precludes the possibility that someone is trying to say something in a low voice at the other end. On MM's scatter diagram [13, p. 283, Fig. 3], relating cost of capital to financial structure for 43 utilities, the ratio of "total earnings after taxes" to "market value of all securities" (i.e., cost by their definition) ranges from about 4¼% to about 7½%, with well over a third of the observations falling outside the range from 5% to 6½%. In the face of so much scatter, could anyone be assured of detecting a consistent variation of, say, ¼% in the depicted ratio over the range of observed financial structures? And a possible variation of this magnitude is not to be regarded as financially insignificant by a corporation manager or by a public utilities commission. On assets of $1,000,000,000 savings of ¼% would amount to the tidy sum of $2,500,000 per year. I submit that the real significance of MM's negative evidence, even supported by similar evidence already available, is only to warn us that many important questions in corporation finance, the cost of capital, and the theory of investment are not to be easily answered by such financial data as are ordinarily available.

VI. *Conclusion*

MM have cut out for themselves the extremely difficult, if not impossible, task of being both pure and practical at the same time. Starting with a perfect market in a perfect world, they have introduced small modifications in the direction of realism; but they have not made significant progress in this direction, considering their avowed aim of achieving an "operational definition of the cost of capital." Their treatment of risk affords, perhaps, the clearest example. In allowing corporate earnings to fluctuate somewhat — presumably around a fairly definite central value—MM have postulated a world that is not 100 percent riskless; but it is a remarkably safe world—being free from the risk of bond default, margin calls, foreclosures, or major disasters of any sort. In a world so safe, a proprietor would have little inducement to incorporate so as to avoid some of the risks of borrowing on private account.

Or again, MM have made little progress in coming to grips with market restrictions. To the practical man, a perfect market, if not perfect nonsense, is one in which traders make the best possible use of such objective opportunities as are actually available. Thus, margin trading is an opportunity open to a limited class of traders and investors whose individual commitments are circumscribed by Regulation X and other institutional constraints; and the task of the practical analyst is to estimate how much of a leveling effect such a circumscribed class can actually exert. MM do not propose to eliminate all "lags and frictions in the equilibrating process," claiming [13, p. 281] for their "propositions only that they describe the central tendency around which observations will scatter." But even under this interpretation the market will, in its deviations from equilibrium, often offer extraordinary opportunities to the alert. In particular, when bonds command a premium, a fast-acting corporation may be able actually to reduce its cost of capital by issuing bonds; and in doing so it will naturally tend to eliminate the premium and deprive other corporations of the same opportunity. Oddly enough, in assuring corporate management that it cannot reduce the cost of capital by borrowing, MM have put themselves in the paradoxical position of promoting an institutional friction that will impede the restoration of their cherished equilibrium.

Finally, and most important of all, MM have underestimated the difficulty of setting up an equivalent return class," which is the cornerstone of their theory. To the practically minded, it is unthinkable to postulate the existence of two or more distinct corporations with income streams that can fluctuate at random and yet be perfectly correlated from now until doomsday; and the artificial example of Petrolease and Closed Corp. provides no exception because these two corporations are not completely distinct. But the difficulty goes much deeper. MM face the unpleasant dilemma either of assuming a long-run equilibrium with stocks at book value or of limiting each equivalent return class to corporations growing at the same rate. Either choice is unrealistic, and neither gives MM any claim to "an operational definition of the cost of capital and a workable theory of investment."

It is no easy task to formulate an operational definition of the cost of capital for a world where markets are imperfect, where separated milk commands a 40-percent premium over whole milk, where the ratio of stock prices to book value varies from one tenth to seven, where growth is the order of the day, and where investors and their advisory services insist on a distinction between income and long term appreciation. Indeed, it may turn out to be an impossible task. But we shall make more progress in the long run by frankly recognizing the obstacles to achievement than we shall by accepting such false goals as are attainable by wishing these obstacles out of the way.

1. H. W. BALLANTINE, *Ballantine on Corporations,* rev. ed. Chicago 1946.
2. A. S. DEWING, *The Financial Policy of Corporations,* 5th ed. New York 1953, Vol. 1.
3. D. DURAND, "Costs of Debt and Equity Funds for Business: Trends and Problems of Measurement" in Nat. Bur. Econ. Research, *Conference on Research in Business Finance.* New York 1952, pp. 215—47.
4. D. DURAND, "Bank Stocks and the Analysis of Covariance, *Econometrica,* Jan. 1955, *23,* 30—45.
5. D. DURAND, *Bank Stock Prices and the Bank Capital Problem,* (Occasional Paper 54, Nat. Bur. Econ. Research), New York 1957.
6. D. DURAND, "Growth Stocks and the Petersburg Paradox," *Jour. Finance,* Sept. 1957, *12,* 348—63.
7. SIR W. S. GILBERT, "Limited Liability," The Bab Ballads, 6th ed. London 1953, pp. 490—91.
8. M. J. GORDON, "Dividends, Earnings, and Stock Prices," *Rev. Econ. Stat.* Feb. 1959, *41.*
9. M. J. GORDON and E. SHAPIRO, "Capital Equipment Analysis: The Required Rate of Profit," *Manag. Sci.,* Oct. 1956, *3,* 102—10.
10. B. J. GRAHAM and D. L. DODD in collaboration with C. TATHAM, JR., *Security Analysis,* 3rd ed. New York 1951.
11. L. R. JOHNSON, E. SHAPIRO, and J. O'MEARA, JR., "Valuation of Closely Held Stock for Federal Tax Purposes: Approach to an Objective Method," *Univ. Pennsylvania Law Rev.* Nov. 1951, *100,* 166—195.
12. F. R. MACAULAY in collaboration with D. DURAND, *Short Selling on the New York Stock Exchange* (Twentieth Century Fund, mimeo.). New York 1951.
13. F. MODIGLIANI and M. H. MILLER, "The Cost of Capital, Corporation Finance and the Theory of Investment," *Am. Econ. Rev.,* June 1958, *48,* 261—97.
14. New York Stock Exchange, "Book Value and Market Value," *The Exchange,* June 1958, *19,* 9—11.
15. C. TATHAM, JR., "Book Value and Market Prices of Electric Utility Common Stocks," *Analysts Jour.,* Nov. 1953, *9,* 33—36.
16. R. TODHUNTER, *The Institute of Actuaries' Text-Book on Compound Interest and Annuities Certain,* 4th ed., revised by R. C. Simmonds and T. P. Thompson. Cambridge 1937.
17. M. H. WEINSTEIN, *Arbitrage in Securities.* New York and London, 1931.
18. J. B. WILLIAMS, *The Theory of Investment Value.* Cambridge, Mass. 1938.

CURRENT PROBLEMS IN THE ECONOMICS OF CAPITAL BUDGETING

HARRY V. ROBERTS*

INTRODUCTION

Two books of great potential significance for business practice were published in 1951: *Capital Budgeting*, by Joel Dean, and *Theory of Investment of the Firm*, by Friedrich and Vera Lutz.[1] Both were applications of formal economic theory to business decisions about internal investments and the financing of these investments. Dean's orientation was mainly conditioned by concrete problems that he had faced; the Lutzes', by a long stream of economic thought usually described under the name "capital theory." Dean's book and his subsequent writing and research have had great influence on the development of what is now generally called "capital budgeting." Dean and the others who have cultivated this field have done much to make both businessmen and academic specialists aware of the limitations of intuitive decisions about capital expenditures and especially of the rules of thumb (e.g., pay-out period) that are often alleged to guide these decisions. The Lutzes' book, by contrast, appears to have received little attention by those interested in capital budgeting, though it contains much of relevance to almost every phase of business finance.

This paper is aimed at stating and extending certain points in the Lutzes' argument that are germane to problems in capital budgeting. It is intended neither to present a systematic exposition of their book nor to propose solutions to all outstanding problems in capital budgeting. Rather it is hoped to dispel more confusion than it creates—a not trivial objective in this difficult field—and to stimulate others to draw more from the Lutzes' rich though technical analysis.

The specific problems here discussed are these: (1) definition of "cost of capital"; (2) treatment of borrowing costs; (3) selection of optimal financial arrangements; and (4) treatment of income streams of differing lengths.

DEFINITION OF "COST OF CAPITAL"

The most deep-seated conceptual problem in capital budgeting today centers around the unfortunate term "cost of capital," a phrase that has caused as much confusion as the expression "rate of interest" in the literature of theoretical economics. The confusion stems from the simple fact that one term, "cost of capital," has been used for two distinct ideas: (1) the rate at which funds can be borrowed or new equity capital obtained and (2) the rate at which a stream of future cash flows should be discounted to measure its present value. The Lutzes' book calls these rates, respectively, the "borrowing rate" and the "lending rate," and these terms will be used henceforth in this paper.[2] For many purposes of economic analysis, including much of the

* Associate professor of statistics, School of Business, University of Chicago.

[1] Joel Dean, *Capital Budgeting* (New York: Columbia University Press, 1951); Friedrich and Vera Lutz, *The Theory of Investment of the Firm* (Princeton, N.J.: Princeton University Press, 1951).

[2] Friedrich and Vera Lutz, *op. cit.*, pp. 22–24, 35–37, 38, 39, 60, 131, 195–97.

Lutzes' book, these two rates can be and are assumed identical. For almost any purpose of business decision-making, they should not be assumed to be equal.

The borrowing rate is the rate of interest the firm must pay for funds. Under the simplest assumption this rate is a constant; in most practical situations it is a function of other variables, such as the total amount of debt already existing.

The lending rate is the rate that can be obtained outside the firm "in the loan market or in some other enterprise."[3] The key idea is this: "We assume that the entrepreneur discounts his own profits at an outside *lending rate* which is constant and is [not] identical with the borrowing rate."[4] This rate is assumed constant because of the (realistic) assumption that "there is perfect competition in the market for funds," that is, that actions of the firm will have no perceptible influence on market rates. By contrast, "the rate at which [the entrepreneur] borrows is an increasing function of the amount he borrows solely on account of the increasing credit risk assumed by the lender."[5]

The basic idea of discounting profits at the outside lending rate is a straightforward application of the principle of opportunity costs, and the Lutzes apparently feel that it is self-evident. Indeed, the idea is self-evident; it simply states that, at the margin, no entrepreneur should undertake an investment within his company when he can do better elsewhere.[6]

Dean's basic book, like practically all the capital-budgeting literature, conceives of cost of capital in the sense of a borrowing rate. Dean, however, has made at least one brief but clear statement of the idea of lending rate, though not by that name: "In theory, the cost of capital plays another role. It shows the return that could be made by diverting cash out of the firm's business into alternative market investments."[7] He then almost immediately discarded this concept, however: "This opportunity-cost principle has a tone of unreality, however, since it implies that the stockholder is king and that financial policy is aimed solely at maximizing the value of his capital."[8]

It is conceivable, of course, that financial policy might indeed be aimed at something other than maximizing the value of the stockholders' capital. It is hard, however, to see what the other something would be. Even a corporate management completely removed from ownership and concerned only with maximizing their personal net worth (e.g., by increasing salaries) would appear to be in the best position to do this if they made *investment and financing decisions* in a way designed to maximize the present value of future cash streams. Of course, the outside lending rate would then be that rate perceived by "management" rather than "the entrepreneur" or "the stockholders," but this would be true in any fiduciary relationship in which one person or group must represent the interests of others.

The idea that future cash streams should be discounted at some outside

[3] *Ibid.*, pp. 22 and 194.

[4] *Ibid.*, p. 22.

[5] *Ibid.*

[6] It should be mentioned that important legal and tax considerations will affect the entrepreneur's opportunities for outside investments and the precise mechanisms by which these investments will be made. We will not explore these important problems here.

[7] Dean, *op. cit.*, pp. 43–44.

[8] *Ibid.*, p. 44.

lending rate seems to be the only way of bringing clarity to the theory of capital budgeting. It does not tell how the lending rate should be determined. The borrowing rate, on the other hand, poses measurement difficulties that are much simpler in principle; forecasts can be and are made, for example, of the cost of a specific bank loan or a bond issue. Ease of measurement appears to have won out over logical clarity, and practical attempts to measure the *rate of discounting the future* have been, in fact, attempts at measuring the cost of borrowed funds[9] or of some average of costs of different forms of borrowing arrangements. These measurements are of value because borrowing costs are relevant to capital-budgeting decisions; but to use a borrowing rate for the purpose that should be served by the lending rate is to substitute arbitrary rule of thumb for logic.

For the most part the Lutzes assume that "the alternative to investing [the entrepreneur's] funds in his own business [is] to invest them in securities with no 'credit risk' (e.g., in government bonds)." In this case, the lending rate will be smaller than the borrowing rate when the two diverge. But they also note that "investment in any of the maturities in the loan market may not be the entrepreneur's only alternative to using funds in his own business. Usually another possibility exists, i.e. investment in other firms in other lines of business which also yield uncertain returns."[10] The Lutzes give two explanations for this: first, at some point further investment in the entrepreneur's own firm adds little to its estimated present value and may also substantially increase the degree of riskiness; second, there are advantages to be obtained by spreading risks by diversification.

While the Lutzes do not seem to come specifically to the following suggestion, my proposal is that the lending rate should be measured by the expected rate of return on equity investments outside the firm that appear to the entrepreneur[11] to involve a degree of riskiness similar to those contemplated within the firm.

This statement is somewhat vague and implies a criterion that must be in part subjective. It is subjective because, as in much of economic theory, the decision-maker's knowledge and anticipations of the future are taken as givens. An economist or statistician may, of course, furnish relevant information to the decision-maker and advise him of technical ways in which such information can be used to maximize present value. Only the decision-maker, however, can ultimately decide what he conceives to be the outside alternatives to investments within his firm and make the predictions necessary to establish their rate of return. Hence the lending rate is not a number that can be measured objectively and authoritatively by economists or statisticians, except in so far as they can determine what the decision-maker has in mind.

The statement is vague because of the introduction of the factor of uncertainty, for which there is so far no very satisfactory treatment.[12] Until more precise formulations are evolved, vagueness is inevitable, and the proposal here seems to

[9] For capital-budgeting and financial decisions, new equity financing should be regarded in the same light as debt financing (see, e.g., Friedrich and Vera Lutz, *op. cit.*, pp. 43 and 200–204).

[10] *Ibid.*, pp. 195–96.

[11] More generally, to the person or group by whom capital-budgeting decisions are made.

[12] To my knowledge, the best attempts are Friedrich and Vera Lutz, *op. cit.*, chap. xv, and Harry Markowitz, "Portfolio Selection," *Journal of Finance*, VII (1952), 77–91.

be a defensible guide to practical action and a good starting point for further development of the theory.[13]

TREATMENT OF BORROWING COSTS

Given the lending rate proposed in the preceding section for discounting future income streams, we can now quote the fundamental criterion for capital-budgeting decisions when there are no arbitrary constraints: "Proposals should be selected that have positive present values when discounted at the firm's cost of capital.[14] The things to discount are the net cash flows resulting from the investments, and these cash flows should take taxes into account."[15] The only thing that needs to be made explicit in this statement is that the net cash flows in question should reflect the incremental effects of any debt-repayment schedule that would be incurred as a consequence of accepting the proposal.[16] If incremental debt costs cannot be associated with a single proposal, the relevant decision unit is the group of proposals for which it is possible to associate such costs, unless, of course, no debt is to be incurred.[17] The measure of incremental debt costs does, of course, raise the usual problems of assessing indirect as well as direct effects. In principle, these problems are similar to those involved in estimating long-run costs and revenues in pricing decisions.

SELECTION OF OPTIMAL FINANCIAL ARRANGEMENTS

One of the most appealing properties of the method of the two preceding sections is that the method contains within itself instructions as to optimal financing. It is easy to see why this is so. For any investment proposal and financing arrangement a present value of future cash flows can be measured. Given any financing arrangement, investment proposals can be selected to maximize present value; conversely, given any investment proposal, the financing arrangement can be chosen so as to maximize present value. Though this brief statement of principle begs a host of detailed problems of application that will not be taken up here, it serves as a point of departure for decisions about financing.[18]

[13] The lending rate may for some purposes not be constant: (1) it will depend on the riskiness of the internal investments under consideration, since the outside investments are to be of "a comparable degree of riskiness," and (2) it may be expected to vary in future time periods. As to the second point, future income streams can be discounted according to the lending rates anticipated at each point of the stream.

[14] In our terminology, "cost of capital" should be replaced by "lending rate."

[15] James H. Lorie and Leonard J. Savage, "Three Problems in Rationing Capital," *Journal of Business*, XXVIII (1955), 229. The criterion for mutually exclusive projects is, except for possible discontinuities, to choose that project for which the ratio of present value to initial cost is highest, assuming present value exceeds cost. Here we mean "present value" to exclude initial cost; in the Lorie-Savage quotation above, "present value" includes initial cost as a negative entry in the calculation.

[16] In Durand's terminology, this is the net income (NI) as opposed to net operating income (NOI) approach (see David Durand, "Costs of Debt and Equity Funds for Business: Trends and Problems of Measurement," in *Conference on Research in Business Finance* [New York: National Bureau of Economic Research, Inc., 1952], pp. 215–47). The reader is also reminded that outside equity financing should be regarded as debt financing for the present purpose (see n. 9 above). We pass the problems of retention of earnings versus payment of dividends.

[17] A project to be financed entirely out of earnings provides a clear illustration of the logic of using the lending rate instead of the borrowing rate for discounting future cash streams; an even clearer one is a decision that involves no investment at all but requires discounting future revenues and costs, e.g., a pricing decision.

[18] See, e.g., Friedrich and Vera Lutz, *op. cit.*, chaps. xiii, xiv, xvi, and xvii.

TREATMENT OF INCOME STREAMS OF DIFFERING LENGTHS

Capital-budgeting decisions should be made against the background of "the entrepreneur's 'horizon' . . . a . . . future date beyond which the entrepreneur does not envisage operations of any kind."[19] We shall not here take up the various assumptions about the "horizon" explored by the Lutzes.[20] The assumption that seems to us to be typically relevant in capital budgeting is this: The entrepreneur contemplates keeping his capital invested, either within or outside the firm, for a period at least as long as the longest future income stream for any contemplated internal investment. At any time, of course, that there are not enough internal investments, he will invest the balance of his capital at the lending rate. To determine the lending rate itself, the entrepreneur must in principle forecast his potential outside investment opportunities up to the horizon for such investments, selecting for each period of time the best investment for that period; this process may, of course, lead to a schedule of future lending rates instead of a single rate (see n. 13).

Given this formulation, the present-value method always correctly evaluates income streams of different lengths.

[19] *Ibid.*, p. 25.

[20] *Ibid.*, pp. 25–27.

COMMENTS

This paper has been concerned with some of the logical criteria for capital-budgeting decisions when the aim is to maximize the firm's present value.[21] There is a long step from the formulation of logical criteria to the practical world in which decisions are actually made, and awareness of the logic of any situation is not always helpful to those who have acquired the intuitive skill that sometimes comes from experience. Yet, to the extent that decisions are to be subjected to analytical scrutiny, the clear formulation of logic is an indispensable step. I do not underestimate the difficulty of getting the data needed to implement the general logical criteria or the need to work out the criteria in detail to meet the many perplexing special problems that arise in practice. These requirements, however, are easier to the extent that the basic criteria are well formulated.

The most serious deficiency in the present state of knowledge about capital budgeting is the absence of a satisfactory framework for incorporating uncertainty into the analysis. Much of the ultimate success or failure of analytical methods in aiding or superseding intuitive methods of capital budgeting will hinge on future developments in the treatment of uncertainty.

[21] And therefore its net worth at all points in time (see Lorie and Savage, *op. cit.*, p. 231).

IV

General Solutions to Optimal Investment Decisions

ON THE THEORY OF OPTIMAL INVESTMENT DECISION[1]

J. HIRSHLEIFER
University of Chicago

THIS article is an attempt to solve (in the theoretical sense), through the use of isoquant analysis, the problem of optimal investment decisions (in business parlance, the problem of capital budgeting). The initial section reviews the principles laid down in Irving Fisher's justly famous works on interest[2] to see what light they shed on two competing rules of behavior currently proposed by economists to guide business investment decisions—the present-value rule and the internal-rate-of-return rule. The next concern of the paper is to show how Fisher's principles must be adapted when the perfect capital market assumed in his analysis does not exist—in particular, when borrowing and lending rates diverge, when capital can be secured only at an increasing marginal borrowing rate, and when capital is "rationed." In connection with this last situation, certain non-Fisherian views (in particular, those of Scitovsky and of the Lutzes) about the correct ultimate goal or criterion for investment decisions are examined. Section III, which presents the solution for multiperiod investments, corrects an error by Fisher which has been the source of much difficulty. The main burden of the analysis justifies the contentions of those who reject the internal rate of return as an investment criterion, and the paper attempts to show where the error in that concept (as ordinarily defined) lies and how the internal rate must be redefined if it is to be used as a reliable guide. On the positive side, the analysis provides some support for the use of the present-value rule but shows that even that rule is at best only a partial indicator of optimal investments and, in fact, under some conditions, gives an incorrect result.

More recent works on investment decisions, I shall argue, suffer from the neglect of Fisher's great contributions—the attainment of an optimum through balancing consumption alternatives over time and the clear distinction between production opportunities and exchange opportunities. It is an implication of this analysis, though it cannot be pursued here in detail, that solutions to the problem of investment decision recently proposed by Boulding, Samuelson, Scitovsky, and the Lutzes are at least in part erroneous. Their common error lay in searching for a rule or formula which would indicate optimal investment decisions *independently of consumption decisions*. No such search can succeed, if Fisher's analysis is sound which regards investment as not an end in itself but rather a process for distributing consumption over time.

The present paper deals throughout with a highly simplified situation in which the costs and returns of alternative individual investments are known *with certainty*, the problem being to select the scale and the mix of invest-

[1] I should like to express indebtedness to many of my colleagues, and especially to James H. Lorie and Martin J. Bailey, for valuable suggestions and criticisms.

[2] Irving Fisher, *The Theory of Interest* (New York: Macmillan Co., 1930), is most widely known. His earlier work, *The Rate of Interest* (New York: Macmillan Co., 1907), contains most of the essential ideas.

ments to be undertaken. To begin with, the analysis will be limited to investment decisions relating to two time periods only. We shall see in later sections that the two-period analysis can be translated immediately to the analysis of investments in perpetuities. For more general fluctuating income streams, however, additional difficulties arise whose resolution involves important new questions of principle. The restriction of the solution to perfect-information situations is, of course, unfortunate, since ignorance and uncertainty are of the essence of certain important observable characteristics of investment decision behavior. The analysis of optimal decisions under conditions of certainty can be justified, however, as a first step toward a more complete theory. No further apology will be offered for considering this oversimplified problem beyond the statement that theoretical economists are in such substantial disagreement about it that a successful attempt to bring the solution within the standard body of economic doctrine would represent a real contribution.

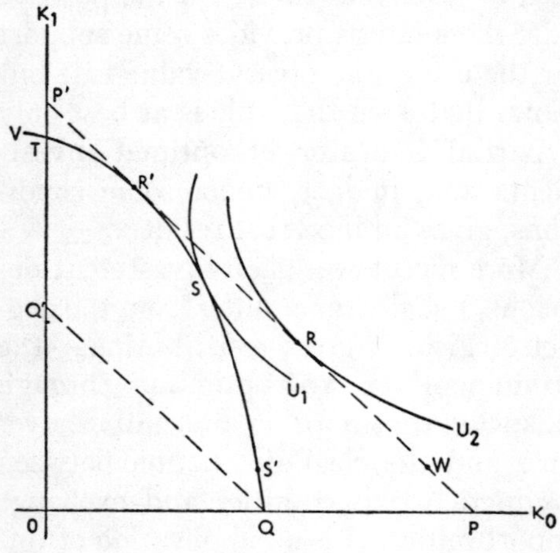

FIG. 1.—Fisher's solution

I. TWO-PERIOD ANALYSIS

A. BORROWING RATE EQUALS LENDING RATE (FISHER'S SOLUTION)

In order to establish the background for the difficult problems to be considered later, let us first review Fisher's solution to the problem of investment decision.[3] Consider the case in which there is a given rate at which the individual (or firm)[4] may borrow that is unaffected by the amount of his borrowings; a given rate at which he can lend that is unaffected by the amount of his loans; and in which these two rates are equal. These are the conditions used by Fisher; they represent a perfect capital market.

In Figure 1 the horizontal axis labeled K_0 represents the amount of actual or potential income (the amount consumed or available for consumption) in period 0; the vertical axis K_1 represents the amount of income in the same sense in period 1. The individual's decision problem is to choose, within the opportunities available to him, an optimum point on the graph—that is, an optimal time pattern of consumption. His starting point may conceivably be a point on either axis (initial income falling all in period 0 or all in period 1), such as points T or P, or else it may be a point in the positive quadrant (initial income falling partly in period 0 and partly in period 1), such as points W or S'. It may even lie in the second or fourth quadrants—where his initial situation involves negative income either in period 0 or in period 1.

[3] Fisher's contributions to the theory of capital go beyond his solution of the problem discussed in this paper—optimal investment decision. He also considers the question of the equilibrium of the capital market, which balances the supplies and demands of all the decision-making agencies.

[4] This analysis does not distinguish between individuals and firms. Firms are regarded solely as agencies or instruments of individuals.

The individual is assumed to have a preference function relating income in periods 0 and 1. This preference function would be mapped in quite the ordinary way, and the curves U_1 and U_2 are ordinary utility-indifference curves from this map.

Finally, there are the investment opportunities open to the individual. Fisher distinguishes between "investment opportunities" and "market opportunities." The former are real productive transfers between income in one time period and in another (what we usually think of as "physical" investment, like planting a seed); the latter are transfers through borrowing or lending (which naturally are on balance offsetting in the loan market). I shall depart from Fisher's language to distinguish somewhat more clearly between "production opportunities" and "market opportunities"; the word "investment" will be used in the more general and inclusive sense to refer to both types of opportunities taken together. Thus we may invest by building a house (a sacrifice of present for future income through a production opportunity) or by lending on the money market (a sacrifice of present for future income through a market or exchange opportunity). We could, equivalently, speak of purchase and sale of capital assets instead of lending or borrowing in describing the market opportunities.

In Figure 1 an investor with a starting point at Q faces a market opportunity illustrated by the dashed line QQ'. That is, starting with all his income in time 0, he can lend at some given lending rate, sacrificing present for future income, any amount until his K_0 is exhausted—receiving in exchange K_1 or income in period 1. Equivalently, we could say that he can buy capital assets—titles to future income K_1—with current income K_0. Following Fisher, I shall call QQ' a "market line."[5] The line PP', parallel to QQ', is the market line available to an individual whose starting point is P on the K_0 axis. By our assumption that the borrowing rate is also constant and equal to the lending rate, the market line PP' is also the market opportunity to an individual whose starting point is W, within the positive quadrant.

Finally, the curve $QSTV$ shows the range of productive opportunities available to an individual with starting point Q. It is the locus of points attainable to such an individual as he sacrifices more and more of K_0 by productive investments yielding K_1 in return. This attainability locus Fisher somewhat ambiguously calls the "opportunity line"; it will be called here the "productive opportunity curve" or "productive transformation curve." Note that in its concavity to the origin the curve reveals a kind of diminishing returns to investment. More specifically, productive investment projects may be considered to be ranked by the expression $(\Delta K_1)/(-\Delta K_0) - 1$, which might be called the "productive rate of return."[6] Here ΔK_0 and ΔK_1 represent the changes in income of periods 0 and 1 associated with the project in question.

We may conceive of whole projects being so ranked, in which case we get the average productive rate of return for each such project. Or we may rank infinitesimal increments to projects, in which case we can deal with a marginal productive rate of return. The curve $QSTV$ will be continuous and have a

[5] The slope of the market line is, of course, $-(1 + i)$, where i is the lending-borrowing rate. That is, when one gives up a dollar in period 0, he receives in exchange $1 + i$ dollars in period 1.

[6] For the present it is best to avoid the term "internal rate of return." Fisher uses the expressions "rate of return on sacrifice" or "rate of return over cost."

continuous first derivative under certain conditions relating to absence of "lumpiness" of individual projects (or increments to projects), which we need not go into. In any case, $QSTV$ would represent a sequence of projects so arranged as to start with the one yielding the highest productive rate of return at the lower right and ending with the lowest rate of return encountered when the last dollar of period 0 is sacrificed at the upper left.[7] It is possible to attach meaning to the portion of $QSTV$ in the second quadrant, where K_0 becomes negative. Such points could not be optimal with indifference curves as portrayed in Figure 1, of course, but they may enter into the determination of an optimum. (This analysis assumes that projects are independent. Where they are not, complications ensue which will be discussed in Sections E and F below.)

As to the solution itself, the investor's objective is to climb onto as high an indifference curve as possible. Moving along the productive opportunity line $QSTV$, he sees that the highest indifference curve it touches is U_1 at the point S. But this is not the best point attainable, for he can move along $QSTV$ somewhat farther to the point R', which is on the market line PP'. He can now move in the reverse direction (borrowing) along PP', and the point R on the indifference curve U_2 is seen to be the best attainable.

The investor has, therefore, a solution in two steps. The "productive" solution—the point at which the individual should stop making additional productive investments—is at R'. He may then move along his market line to a point better satisfying his time preferences, at R. That is to say, he makes the best investment from the productive point of view and then "finances" it in the loan market. A very practical example is building a house and then borrowing on it through a mortgage so as to replenish current consumption income.

We may now consider, in the light of this solution, the current debate between two competing "rules" for optimal investment behavior.[8] The first of these, the present-value rule, would have the individual or firm adopt all projects whose present value is positive at the market rate of interest. This would have the effect of maximizing the present value of the firm's position in terms of income in periods 0 and 1. Present value, under the present conditions, may be defined as $K_0 + (K_1)/(1 + i)$, income in period 1 being discounted by the factor $1 + i$, where i is the lending-borrowing rate. Since the market lines are defined by the condition that a sacrifice of one dollar in K_0 yields $1 + i$ dollars in K_1, these market lines are nothing but lines of constant present value. The equation

[7] An individual starting at S' would also have a "disinvestment opportunity."

[8] The present-value rule is the more or less standard guide supported by a great many theorists. The internal-rate-of-return rule, in the sense used here, has also been frequently proposed (see, e.g., Joel Dean, *Capital Budgeting* [New York: Columbia University Press, 1951], pp. 17–19). Citations on the use of alternative investment criteria may be found in Friedrich and Vera Lutz, *The Theory of Investment of the Firm* (Princeton, N.J.: Princeton University Press, 1951), p. 16. The internal-rate-of-return rule which we will consider in detail (i.e., adopt all projects and increments to projects for which the internal rate of return exceeds the market rate of interest) is *not* the same as that emphasized by the Lutzes (i.e., adopt that pattern of investments maximizing the internal rate of return). The rule considered here compares the incremental or marginal rate of return with a market rate; the other would maximize the average internal rate of return, without regard to the market rate. The latter rule will be shown to be fundamentally erroneous, even in the form the Lutzes accept as their ultimate criterion (maximize the internal rate of return on the investor's owned capital). This point will be discussed in connection with capital rationing in Sec. D, below.

for these lines is $K_0 + (K_1)/(1 + i) = C$, C being a parameter. The present-value rule tells us to invest until the highest such line is attained, which clearly takes place at the point R'. So far so good, but note that the rule says nothing about the "financing" (borrowing or lending) also necessary to attain the final optimum at R.

The internal-rate-of-return rule, in the form here considered, would have the firm adopt any project whose internal rate is greater than the market rate of interest. The internal rate for a project in the general case is defined as that discounting rate ρ which reduces the stream of net returns associated with the project to a present value of zero (or, equivalently, which makes the discounted value of the associated cost stream equal to the discounted value of the receipts stream). We may write

$$0 = \Delta K_0 + \frac{\Delta K_1}{1+\rho} + \frac{\Delta K_2}{(1+\rho)^2} + \dots + \frac{\Delta K_n}{(1+\rho)^n}.$$

In the two-period case ρ is identical with the productive rate of return, $(\Delta K_1)/(-\Delta K_0) - 1$. As in the discussion above, if infinitesimal changes are permitted, we may interpret this statement in the marginal sense. The marginal (two-period) internal rate of return is measured by the slope of the productive opportunity curve minus unity. In Figure 1 at each step we would compare the steepness of $QSTV$ with that of the market lines. We would move along $QSTV$ as long as, and just so long as, it is the steeper. Evidently, this rule would have us move along $QSTV$ until it becomes tangent to a market line at R'. Again, so far so good, but nothing is said about the borrowing or lending then necessary to attain the optimum.

At least for the two-period case, then, the present-value rule and the internal-rate-of-return rule lead to identical answers[9] which are the same as that reached by our isoquant analysis, so far as *productive* investment decisions are concerned. The rules are both silent, however, about the market exchange between K_0 and K_1, which remains necessary if an optimum is to be achieved. This second step is obviously part of the solution. Had there been no actual opportunity to borrow or lend, the point S would have been the best attainable, and the process of productive investment should not have been carried as far as R'. We cannot say that the rules are definitely wrong, however, since with no such market opportunities there would have been no market rate of interest i for calculating present values or for comparison with the marginal internal rate of return. It remains to be seen whether these rules can be restated or generalized to apply to cases where a simple market rate of interest is not available for unlimited borrowing and lending. But it should be observed that, in comparison with isoquant analysis, each of the rules leads to only a partial answer.

B. WHEN BORROWING AND LENDING RATES DIFFER

We may now depart from Fisher's analysis, or rather extend it, to a case he did not consider. The borrowing and lending rates are still assumed to be constant, independent of the amounts taken or supplied by the individual or firm under consideration. However, it is now assumed that these rates are not equal, the borrowing rate being higher than the

[9] In fact, for the two-period case the rules are identical: it is possible to show that any project (or increment to a project) of positive present value must have an internal rate of return greater than the rate of interest.

lending rate.[10] In Figure 2 there is the same preference map, of which only the isoquant U_1 is shown. There are now, however, two sets of market lines over the graph; the steeper (*dashed*) lines represent borrowing opportunities (note the direction of the arrows), and the flatter (*solid*) lines represent lending opportunities. The heavy solid lines show two possible sets of productive opportunities, both of which lead to solutions along U_1. Starting with amount *OW* of K_0, an in-

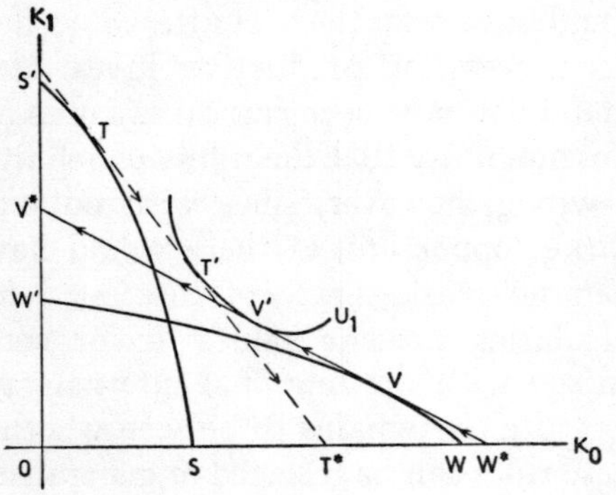

FIG. 2.—Extension of Fisher's solution for differing borrowing and lending rates.

vestor with a production opportunity *WVW'* would move along *WVW'* to *V*, at which point he would *lend* to get to his time-preference optimum—the tangency with U_1 at *V'*. The curve *STS'* represents a much more productive possibility; starting with only *OS* of K_0, the investor would move along *STS'* to *T* and then *borrow* backward along the dashed line to get to *T'*, the tangency point with U_1. Note that the total opportunity set (the points attainable through any combination of the market and productive opportunities) is *WVV** for the first opportunity, and *S'TT** for the second.

More detailed analysis, however, shows that we do not yet have the full solution—there is a third possibility. An investor with a productive opportunity locus starting on the K_0 axis will never stop moving along this locus in the direction of greater K_1 as long as the marginal productive rate of return is still above the borrowing rate—nor will he ever push along the locus beyond the point where the marginal productive rate of return falls below the lending rate. Assuming that some initial investments are available which have a higher productive rate of return than the borrowing rate, the investor should push along the locus until the borrowing rate is reached. If, at this point, it is possible to move up the utility hill by borrowing, productive investment should cease, and the borrowing should take place; the investor is at some point like *T* in Figure 2. If borrowing decreases utility, however, more productive investment is called for. Suppose investment is then carried on until diminishing returns bring the marginal productive rate of return down to the lending rate. If lending then increases utility, productive investment should halt there, and the lending take place; the investor is at some point like *V* in Figure 2. But suppose that now it is found that lending also decreases utility! This can only mean that a tangency of the productive opportunity locus and an indifference curve took place when the marginal productive rate of return was somewhere *between* the lending and the borrowing rates. In this case neither lending nor borrowing is called for, the optimum being reached directly in the productive investment decision by equating the marginal productive rate of re-

[10] If the borrowing rate were lower than the lending rate, it would be possible to accumulate infinite wealth by borrowing and relending, so I shall not consider this possibility. Of course, financial institutions typically borrow at a lower average rate than that at which they lend, but they cannot expand their scale of operations indefinitely without changing this relationship.

turn with the marginal rate of substitution (in the sense of time preference) along the utility isoquant.

These solutions are illustrated by the division of Figure 3 into three zones. In Zone I the borrowing rate is relevant. Tangency solutions with the market line at the borrowing rate like that at T are carried back by borrowing to tangency with a utility isoquant at a point like T'. All such final solutions lie along the curve OB, which connects all points on the utility isoquants whose slope equals that of the *borrowing* market line. Correspondingly, Zone III is that zone where the productive solution involves tangency with a lending market line (like V), which is then carried forward by lending to a final tangency optimum with a utility isoquant along the line OL at a point like V'. This line connects all points on the utility isoquants with slope equal to that of the *lending* market line. Finally, Zone II solutions occur when a productive opportunity locus like QRQ' is steeper than the lending rate throughout Zone III but flatter than the borrowing rate throughout Zone I. Therefore, such a locus must be tangent to one of the indifference curves somewhere in Zone II.

By analogy with the discussion in the previous section, we may conclude that the *borrowing* rate will lead to correct answers (to the productive investment decision, neglecting the related financing question) under the present-value rule or the internal-rate-of-return rule—when the situation involves a Zone I solution. Correspondingly, the *lending* rate will be appropriate and lead to correct investment decisions for Zone III solutions. For Zone II solutions, however, neither will be correct. There will, in fact, be some rate between the lending and the borrowing rates which would lead to the correct results. Formally speaking, we could describe this correct discount rate as the marginal productive opportunity rate,[11] which will at equilibrium equal the marginal subjective time-preference rate. In such a case neither rule is satisfactory in the sense of providing the productive solution without reference to the utility isoquants; knowledge of the comparative slopes of the utility isoquant and the productive opportunity frontier is all that is necessary, however. Of course, even when the rules in question are considered "satisfactory," they are misleading in implying that productive investment decisions can be correctly made independently of the "financing" decision.

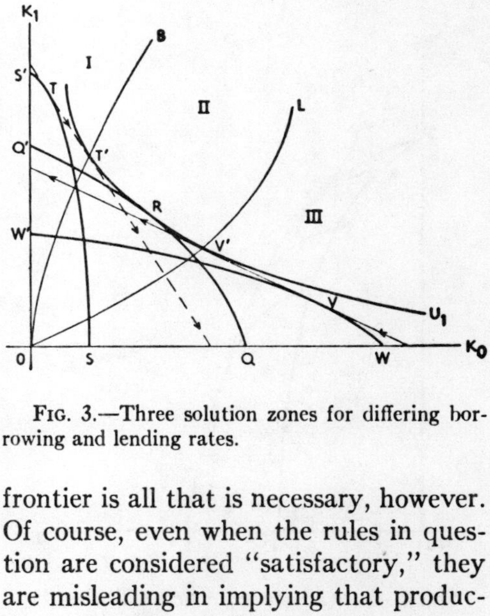

FIG. 3.—Three solution zones for differing borrowing and lending rates.

This solution, in retrospect, may perhaps seem obvious. Where the productive opportunity, time-preference, and

[11] The marginal productive opportunity rate, or marginal internal rate of return, measures the rate of return on the best alternative project. Assuming continuity, it is defined by the slope of QRQ' at R in Fig. 3. Evidently, a present-value line tangent to U_1 and QRQ' at R would, in a formal sense, make the present-value rule correct. And comparing this rate with the marginal internal rate of return as it varies along QRQ' would make the internal-rate-of-return rule also correct in the same formal sense.

market (or financing) opportunities stand in such relations to one another as to require borrowing to reach the optimum, the borrowing rate is the correct rate to use in the productive investment decision. The lending rate is irrelevant because the decision on the margin involves a balancing of the cost of borrowing and the return from further productive investment, both being higher than the lending rate. The lending opportunity is indeed still available, but,

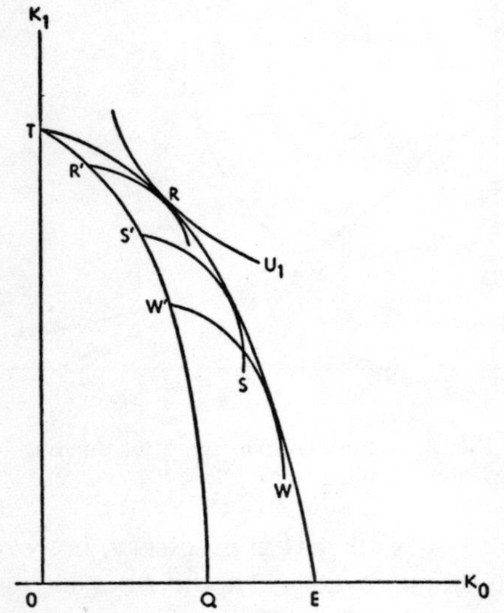

FIG. 4.—Increasing marginal cost of borrowing

the rate of return on lending being lower than the lowest marginal productive rate of return we would wish to consider in the light of the borrowing rate we must pay, lending is not a relevant alternative. Rather the relevant alternative to productive investment is a reduction in borrowing, which in terms of saving interest is more remunerative than lending. Similarly, when the balance of considerations dictates lending part of the firm's current capital funds, borrowing is not the relevant cost incurred in financing productive investment. The relevant alternative to increased productive investment is the amount of lending which must be foregone. While these considerations may be obvious, there is some disagreement in the literature as to whether the lending or the borrowing rate is *the* correct one.[12]

C. INCREASING MARGINAL COST OF BORROWING

While it is generally considered satisfactory to assume a constant lending rate (the investor does not drive down the loan rate as a consequence of his lendings), for practical reasons it is important to take account of the case in which increased borrowing can only take place at increasing cost. As it happens, however, this complication does not require any essential modification of principle.

Figure 4 shows, as before, a productive opportunity locus $QR'T$ and an indifference curve U_1. For simplicity, assume that marginal borrowing costs rise at the same rate whether the investor begins to borrow at the point R', S', or W' or at any other point along $QR'T$ (he cannot, of course, start borrowing at Q, having no K_1 to offer in exchange for more K_0). Under this assumption we can then draw market curves, now concave to the origin, like $R'R$, $S'S$, and $W'W$. The curve TE represents the total opportunity set as the *envelope* of these market curves, that is, TE connects all the points on the market curves representing the maximum K_0 attainable for any given K_1. By the nature of an envelope curve, TE will be tangent to a market

[12] The borrowing rate (the "cost of capital") has been recommended by Dean and by Lorie and Savage (see Joel Dean, *Capital Budgeting* [New York: Columbia University Press, 1951], esp. pp. 43–44; James H. Lorie and Leonard J. Savage, "Three Problems in Rationing Capital," *Journal of Business*, XXVIII [October, 1955], 229–39, esp. p. 229). Roberts and the Lutzes favor the use of the lending rate (see Friedrich and Vera Lutz, *op. cit.*, esp. p. 22; Harry V. Roberts, "Current Problems in the Economics of Capital Budgeting," *Journal of Business*, XXX [January, 1957], 12–16).

curve at each such point. The optimum is then simply found where TE is tangent to the highest indifference curve attainable—here the curve U_1 at R. To reach R, the investor must exploit his productive opportunity to the point R' and then borrow back along his market curve to R.

The preceding discussion applies solely to what was called a Zone I (borrowing) solution in the previous section. Depending upon the nature of the productive opportunity, a Zone II or Zone III solution would also be possible under the assumptions of this section. With regard to the present-value and the internal-rate-of-return rules, the conclusions are unchanged for Zone II and III solutions, however. Only for Zone I solutions is there any modification.

The crucial question, as always, for these rules is what rate of discount to use. Intuition tells us that the rate representing *marginal* borrowing cost should be used as the discount rate for Zone I solutions, since productive investment will then be carried just to the point justified by the cost of the associated increment of borrowing.[13] That is, the slope of the envelope for any point on the envelope curve (for example, R), is the same as the slope of the productive opportunity curve at the corresponding point (R') connected by the market curve.[14] If this is the case, the discount rate determined by the slope at a tangency with U_1 at a point like R will also lead to productive investment being carried to R' by the rules under consideration. Of course, this again is a purely formal statement. Operationally speaking, the rules may not be of much value, since the discount rate to be used is not known in advance independently of the utility (time-preference) function.

D. RATIONING OF "CAPITAL"—A CURRENT CONTROVERSY

The previous discussion provides the key for resolving certain current disputes over what constitutes optimal invest-

[13] I should like to thank Joel Segall for insisting on this point in discussions of the problem. Note that the rate representing marginal borrowing cost is not necessarily the borrowing rate on marginal funds—an increment of borrowing may increase the rate on infra-marginal units.

[14] While this point can be verified geometrically, it follows directly from the analytic properties of an envelope curve.

To simplify notation, in this note I shall denote K_1 of Figure 4 as y and K_0 as x. The equation of the productive opportunity locus may be written

$$y_0 = f(x_0)\,. \tag{a}$$

The family of market curves can be expressed by $y - y_0 = g(x - x_0)$, or

$$F(x, x_0) = f(x_0) + g(x - x_0)\,. \tag{b}$$

An envelope, $y = h(x)$, is defined by the condition that any point on it must be a point of tangency with some member of the family (b). Thus we have

$$h(x) = F(x, x_0)\,, \tag{c}$$

$$\frac{dh}{dx} = \frac{\partial F(x, x_0)}{\partial x}\,. \tag{d}$$

The second condition for an envelope is that the partial derivative of the function (b) with respect to the parameter must equal zero:

$$\frac{\partial F(x, x_0)}{\partial x_0} = 0\,. \tag{e}$$

But

$$\frac{\partial F(x, x_0)}{\partial x_0} = \frac{d f(x_0)}{d x_0} + (-1)\frac{d g(x - x_0)}{d(x - x_0)}$$

Hence

$$\frac{d f(x_0)}{d x_0} = \frac{d g(x - x_0)}{d(x - x_0)}\,.$$

Also

$$\frac{\partial F(x, x_0)}{\partial x} = \frac{d g(x - x_0)}{d(x - x_0)}\,.$$

So, finally,

$$\frac{d f(x_0)}{d x_0} = \frac{d g(x - x_0)}{d(x - x_0)} = \frac{\partial F(x, x_0)}{\partial x} = \frac{dh}{dx}\,.$$

Thus the slope of the productive opportunity locus is the same as the slope of the envelope at points on the two curves connected by being on the same market curve.

ment decision under a condition of "capital rationing" or "fixed capital budget." This condition is said to exist when the firm, or individual, or perhaps department of government under consideration cannot borrow additional "capital" but is limited instead to making the best use of the "capital" already in its possession or allocated to it.[15] In theoretical literature a closely related idea is expressed by Scitovsky, who, regarding the availability of capital (in the sense of "current capital funds") as the fixed factor limiting the size of the firm, proposes as the investment criterion the maximization of "profit per unit capital invested."[16] Lutz and Lutz, in contrast, assert as their ultimate investment criterion the maximization of the rate of return on the entrepreneur's *owned* capital, which they regard as fixed.[17]

It is of some interest to analyze these concepts in greater detail in terms of our Fisherian model. Scitovsky defines "capital" as current capital funds (our K_0) required to bridge the time lapse between factor input and product output.[18] Under this definition, however, "capital" would be fixed to the firm only under rather peculiar conditions; specifically, if there is a discontinuity in the capital funds market such that the marginal borrowing rate suddenly becomes infinite at the firm's level of borrowings.[19] Without discontinuity, an infinitely high marginal borrowing rate could never represent an equilibrium position for the borrower, unless indeed his preference for present income over future income was absolute. And, of course, if the marginal borrowing rate is not infinite, current capital funds could not be said to be fixed. Nevertheless, while this case may be considered peculiar and unlikely to arise in any strict sense, it may be acceptable as a reasonable approximation of certain situations which occur in practice—especially in the short run, perhaps as a result of previous miscalculations. A division of a firm or a department of government may at times be said to face an infinite marginal borrowing rate once a budget constraint is reached—until the next meeting of the board of directors or the Congress provides more funds.

On the other hand, it is difficult to decipher the Lutzes' meaning when they speak of the firm's *owned* capital as fixed. In the Fisherian analysis, "ownership" of current or future assets is a legal form without analytical significance—to buy an asset yielding future income, with current funds, is simply to lend, while selling income is the same as borrowing. In a more fundamental sense, however, we could think of the firm as "owning"

[15] The expression "capital rationing" was used some time ago by Hart to refer to a non-price limitation on the acquisition of debt or equity financing (see A. G. Hart, "Anticipations, Business Planning, and the Cycle," *Quarterly Journal of Economics*, LI [1937], 273–97). His use of the term does not seem to imply a definitely fixed quantity available and can, in fact, be interpreted simply as indicating a rising marginal cost of capital funds. See also Joel Dean, *Managerial Economics* (Englewood Cliffs, N.J.: Prentice-Hall, Inc., 1951), pp. 586–600. In the sense of a definitely fixed quantity of funds, the term has been used by various authors discussing business or government problems. See J. Margolis, "The Discount Rate and the Benefits-Cost Justification of Federal Irrigation Investment," (Department of Economics, Stanford University, Technical Report No. 23 [Stanford, Calif., 1955]); Lorie and Savage, *op. cit.*, and R. McKean, *Efficiency in Government through Systems Analysis* (New York: John Wiley & Sons, 1958).

[16] T. Scitovsky, *Welfare and Competition* (Chicago: Richard D. Irwin, Inc., 1951), pp. 208–9.

[17] *Op. cit.*, pp. 16–48, esp. pp. 17, 20, 42.

[18] *Op. cit.*, p. 194

[19] Scitovsky appears to leap from the acceptable argument in the earlier part of his discussion that willingness to lend and to borrow are not *unlimited* to the unacceptable position in his later discussion that current capital funds are *fixed* (*ibid.*, pp. 193–200, 208–9).

the opportunity set or at least the physical productive opportunities available to it, and this perhaps is what the Lutzes have in mind. Thus, Robinson Crusoe's house might be considered as his "owned capital"—a resource yielding consumption income in both present and future. The trouble is that the Lutzes seem to be thinking of "owned capital" as the *value* of the productive resources (in the form of capital goods) owned by the firm,[20] but owned physical capital goods cannot be converted to a capital *value* without bringing in a rate of discount for the receipts stream. But since, as we have seen, the relevant rate of discount for a firm's decisions is not (except where a perfect capital market exists) an independent entity but is itself determined by the analysis, the *capital value* cannot in general be considered to be fixed independently of the investment decision.[21]

While space does not permit a full critique of the Lutzes' important work, it is worth mentioning that—from a Fisherian point of view—it starts off on the wrong foot. They search first for an ultimate criterion or formula with which to gauge investment decision rules and settle upon "maximization of the rate of return on the investor's owned capital" on what seem to be purely intuitive grounds. The Fisherian approach, in contrast, integrates investment decision with the general theory of choice—the goal being to maximize utility subject to certain opportunities and constraints. In these terms, certain formulas can be validated as useful proximate rules for some classes of problems, as I am attempting to show here. However, the ultimate Fisherian criterion of choice—the optimal balancing of consumption alternatives over time—cannot be reduced to any of the usual formulas.

Instead of engaging in further discussion of the various senses in which "capital" may be said to be fixed to the firm, it will be more instructive to see how the Fisherian approach solves the problem of "capital rationing." I shall use as an illustration what may be called a "Scitovsky situation," in which the investor has run against a discontinuity making the marginal borrowing rate infinite. I regard this case (which I consider empirically significant only in the short run) as the model situation underlying the "capital rationing" discussion.

An infinite borrowing rate makes the dashed borrowing lines of Figures 2 and 3 essentially vertical. In consequence, the curve OB in Figure 3 shifts so far to the left as to make Zone I disappear for all practical purposes. There are then only Zone II and Zone III solutions. An investment-opportunity locus like WVW' in Figure 3 becomes less steep than the lending slope in Zone III, in which case the investor will carry investment up to the point V where this occurs and then lend until a tangency solution is reached at V', which would be somewhere along the curve OL of Figure 3. If an invest-

[20] Lutz and Lutz, *op. cit.*, pp. 3–13.

[21] It is possible, however, that the Lutzes had in mind only the case in which an investor starts off with current funds but no other assets. In this case no discounting problems would arise in defining owned capital, so their ultimate criterion could not be criticized on that score. The objection raised below to the Scitovsky criterion, however—that it fails to consider the *consumption* alternative, which is really the heart of the question of investment decision—would then apply to the Lutzes' rule. In addition, a rule for an investor owning solely current funds is hardly of general enough applicability to be an ultimate criterion. The Lutzes themselves recognize the case of an investor owning no "capital" but using only borrowed funds, and for this case they themselves abandon their ultimate criterion (*ibid.*, p. 42, n. 32). The most general case, of course, is that of an investor with a productive opportunity set capable of yielding him alternative combinations of present and future income.

ment-opportunity locus like *QRQ'* in Figure 3 is still steeper than the lending rate after it crosses *OL*, investment should be carried until tangency with an indifference curve like U_1 is attained somewhere to the left of *OL*, with no lending or borrowing taking place.

In terms of the present-value or internal-rate-of-return rules, under these conditions the decisions should be based on the *lending* rate (as the discounting rate or the standard of comparison) if the solution is a Zone III one. Here lending actually takes place, since movement upward and to the left still remains desirable when the last investment with a rate of return greater than the lending rate is made. If the solution is a Zone II one, the lending rate must not be used. Investments showing positive present value at the lending rate (or, equivalently, with an internal rate of return higher than the lending rate) will be nevertheless undesirable after a tangency point equating the investment-opportunity slope and the time-preference slope is reached. The correct rate, formally speaking, is the marginal opportunity rate.

The solution changes only slightly when we consider an isolated individual like Robinson Crusoe or a self-contained community like a nation under autarchy (or like the world economy as a whole). In this situation neither borrowing nor lending is possible in our sense, only productive opportunities existing. Only Zone II solutions are then possible. This case is the most extreme remove from the assumption of perfect capital markets.[22]

As in the case of the Zone II solutions arising without capital rationing, the present-value or internal-rate-of-return rules can be formally modified to apply to the Zone II solutions which are typical under capital rationing. The discount rate to be used for calculating present values or as a standard of comparison against the internal rate of project increments is the rate given by the slope of the Zone II tangency (the marginal productive rate of return); with this rate, the rules give the correct answer. But this rate cannot be discovered until the solution is attained and so is of no assistance in reaching the solution. The exception is the Zone III solution involving lending which can arise in a "Scitovsky situation." Here the lending rate should of course be used. The undetermined discount rate that gives correct results when the rules are used for Zone II solutions can, in some problems, be regarded as a kind of shadow price reflecting the productive rate of return on the best alternative opportunity not being exploited.

The reader may be curious as to why, in the Scitovsky situation, the outcome of the analysis was not Scitovsky's result—that the optimal investment decision is such as to maximize the (average) internal rate of return on the firm's present capital funds (K_0). Thus, in Figure 3, for a firm starting with *OQ* of K_0 and faced with the productive opportunity locus *QRQ'*, the average rate of return (K_1 received per unit of K_0 sacrificed) is a maximum for an infinitesimal movement along *QRQ'*, since, the farther it moves, the more the marginal and average productive rates of return fall. Such a rule implies staying at *Q*—which is obviously the wrong decision.

[22] We could, following the principles already laid down, work out without great difficulty the solution for the case in which borrowing is permitted but only up to a certain fixed limit. The effect of such a provision is to provide a kind of "attainability envelope" as in Fig. 4, but of a somewhat different shape.

How does this square with Scitovsky's intuitively plausible argument that the firm always seeks to maximize its returns on the fixed factor, present capital funds being assumed here to be fixed?[23] The answer is that this argument is applicable only for a factor "fixed" in the sense of no alternative uses. Here present capital funds K_0 are assumed to be fixed, but not in the sense Scitovsky must have had in mind. The concept here is that no additional borrowing can take place, but the possibility of *consuming* the present funds as an alternative to investing them is recognized. For Scitovsky, however, the funds *must* be invested. If in fact current income K_0 had no uses other than conversion into future income K_1 (this amounts to absolute preference for future over current income), Scitovsky's rule would correctly tell us to pick that point on the K_1 axis which is the highest.[24] Actually, our time preferences are more balanced; there *is* an alternative use (consumption) for K_0. Therefore, even in Scitovsky situations, we will balance K_0 and K_1 on the margin—and not simply accept the maximum K_1 we can get in exchange for all our "fixed" K_0.[25] The analyses of Scitovsky, the Lutzes, and many other recent writers frequently lead to incorrect solutions because of their failure to take into account the alternative consumption opportunities which Fisher integrated into his theory of investment decision.

E. NON-INDEPENDENT INVESTMENT OPPORTUNITIES

Up to this point, following Fisher, investment opportunities have been assumed to be independent so that it is possible to rank them in any desired way. In particular, they were ordered in Figures 1 through 4 in terms of decreasing productive rate of return; the resultant concavity produced unique tangency solutions with the utility or market curves. But suppose, now, that there are two mutually exclusive sets of such investment opportunities. Thus we may consider building a factory in the East or the West, but not both—contemplating the alternatives, the eastern opportunities may look like the locus $QV'V$, and the western opportunities like $QT'T$ in Figure 5.[26]

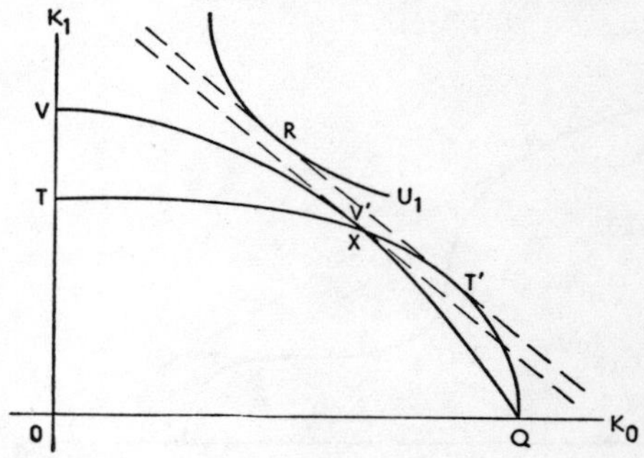

FIG. 5.—Non-independent investment opportunities—two alternative productive investment loci.

Which is better? Actually, the solutions continue to follow directly from Fisher's principles, though too much non-independence makes for troublesome calculations in practice, and in some classes

[23] *Op. cit.*, p. 209.

[24] That is, the point Q' in Fig. 3. This result is of course trivial. Scitovsky may possibly have in mind choice among non-independent sets of investments (discussed in the next section), where each set may have a different intersection with the K_1 axis. Here a non-trivial choice could be made with the criterion of maximizing the average rate of return.

[25] Scitovsky may have in mind a situation in which a certain fraction of current funds K_0 are set apart from consumption (on some unknown basis) to become the "fixed" current capital funds. In this case the Scitovsky rule would lead to the correct result if it happened that just so much "fixed" capital funds were allocated to get the investor to the point R' on his productive transformation locus of Fig. 3.

[26] It would, of course, reduce matters to their former simplicity if one of the loci lay completely within the other, in which case it would be obviously inferior and could be dropped from consideration.

of cases the heretofore inerrant present-value rule fails. In the simplest case, in which there is a constant borrowing-lending rate (a perfect capital market), the curve $QV'V$ is tangent to its highest attainable present-value line at V'—while the best point on $QT'T$ is T'. It is only necessary to consider these, and the one attaining the higher present-value line ($QT'T$ at T' in this case) will permit the investor to reach the highest possible indifference curve U_1 at R. In contrast, the internal-rate-of-return rule would locate the points T' and V' but could not discriminate between them. Where borrowing and lending rates differ, as in Figure 2 (now interpreting the productive opportunity loci of that figure as mutually exclusive alternatives), it may be necessary to compare, say, a lending solution at V with a borrowing solution at T. To find the *optimum optimorum*, the indifference curves must be known (in Fig. 2 the two solutions attain the same indifference curve). Note that present value is *not* a reliable guide here; in fact, the present value of the solution V ($=W^*$) at the relevant discount rate for it (the lending rate) far exceeds that of the solution T ($=T^*$) at its discount rate (the borrowing rate), when the two are actually indifferent. Assuming an increasing borrowing rate creates no new essential difficulty.

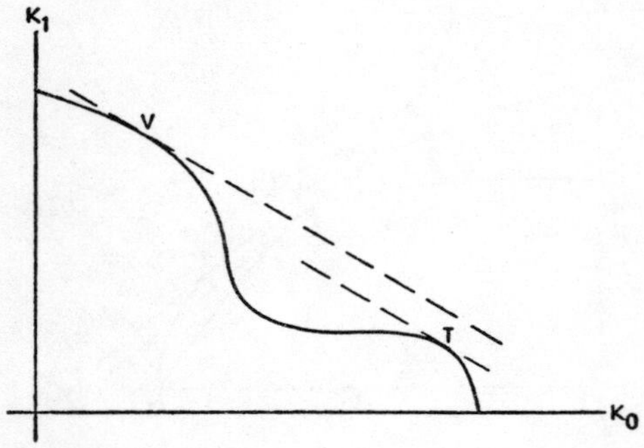

FIG. 6.—Non-independent investment opportunities—poorer projects prerequisite to better ones.

Another form of non-independence, illustrated in Figure 6, is also troublesome without modifying principle. Here the projects along the productive investment locus QQ' are not entirely independent, for we are constrained to adopt some low-return ones before certain high-return ones. Again, there is a possibility of several local optima like V and T, which can be compared along the same lines as used in the previous illustration.

F. CONCLUSION FOR TWO-PERIOD ANALYSIS

The solutions for optimal investment decisions vary according to a two-way classification of cases. The first classification refers to the way market opportunities exist for the decision-making agency; the second classification refers to the absence or presence of the complication of non-independent productive opportunities. The simplest, extreme cases for the first classification are: (*a*) a perfect capital market (market opportunities such that lending or borrowing in any amounts can take place at the same, fixed rate) and (*b*) no market opportunities whatsoever, as was true for Robinson Crusoe. Where there is a perfect capital market, the total attainable set is a triangle (considering only the first quadrant) like OPP' in Figure 1, just tangent to the productive opportunity locus. Where there is no capital market at all, the total attainable set is simply the productive opportunity locus itself. It is not difficult to see how the varying forms of imperfection of the capital market fit in between these extremes.

When independence of physical (productive) opportunities holds, the opportunities may be ranked in order of descending productive rate of return.

Geometrically, if the convenient (but inessential) assumption of continuity is adopted, independence means that the productive opportunity locus is everywhere concave to the origin, like $QS'TV$ in Figure 1. Non-independence may take several forms (see Figs. 5 and 6), but in each case that is not trivial non-independence means that the effective productive opportunity locus is not simply concave. This is obvious in Figure 6. In Figure 5 each of the two alternative loci considered separately is concave, but the effective locus is the scalloped outer edge of the overlapping sets of points attainable by either—that is, the effective productive opportunity locus runs along $QT'T$ up to X and then crosses over to $QV'V$.

With this classification a detailed tabulation of the differing solutions could be presented; the following brief summary of the general principles involved should serve almost as well, however.

1. The internal-rate-of-return rule fails wherever there are multiple tangencies—the normal outcome for non-independent productive opportunities.

2. The present-value rule works whenever the other does and, in addition, correctly discriminates among multiple tangencies whenever a perfect capital market exists (or, by extension, whenever a unique discount rate can be determined for the comparison—for example when all the alternative tangencies occur in Zone I or else all in Zone III).

3. Both rules work only in a formal sense when the solution involves direct tangency between a productive opportunity locus and a utility isoquant, since the discount rate necessary for use of both rules is the marginal opportunity rate—a product of the analysis.

4. The cases when even the present-value rule fails (may actually give wrong answers) all involve the comparison of multiple tangencies arising from non-independent investments when, in addition, a perfect capital market does not exist. One important example is the comparison of a tangency involving borrowing in Zone I with another involving lending in Zone III. Only reference to the utility map can give correct answers for such cases.

5. Even when one or both rules are correct in a not merely formal sense, the answer given is the "productive solution"—only part of the way toward attainment of the utility optimum. Furthermore, this productive decision is optimal only when it can be assumed that the associated financing decision will in fact be made.

II. A BRIEF NOTE ON PERPETUITIES

A traditional way of handling the multiperiod case in capital theory has been to consider investment decisions as choices between current funds and perpetual future income flows. For many purposes this is a valuable simplifying idea. It cannot be adopted here, however, because the essence of the practical difficulties which have arisen in multiperiod investment decisions is the *reinvestment* problem—the necessity of making productive or market exchanges between incomes in future time periods. In fact, the consideration of the perpetuity case is, in a sense, only a variant of the two-period analysis, in which there is a single present and a single future. In the case of perpetuity analysis, the future is stretched out, but we cannot consider transfer between different periods of the future.

All the two-period results in Section I can easily be modified to apply to the choice between current funds and perpetuities. In the figures, instead of income K_1 in period 1 one may speak of an annual rate of income k. Productive opportunity loci and time-preference curves will retain their familiar shapes. The lines of constant present value (borrow-lend lines) are expressed by the equation $C = K_0 + (k/i)$ instead of $C = K_0 + (K_1)/(1 + i)$. The "internal rate of return" will equal $(k)/(-\Delta K_0)$. The rest of the analysis follows directly, but, rather than trace it out, I shall turn to the consideration of the multiperiod case in a more general way.

III. MULTIPERIOD ANALYSIS

Considerable doubt prevails on how to generalize the principles of the two-period analysis to the multiperiod case. The problems which have troubled the analysis of the multiperiod case are actually the result of inappropriate generalizations of methods of solution that do lead to correct results in the simplified two-period analysis.

A. INTERNAL-RATE-OF-RETURN RULE VERSUS PRESENT-VALUE RULE

In the multiperiod analysis there is no formal difficulty in generalizing the indifference curves of Figure 1 to indifference shells in any number of dimensions. Also the lines of constant present value or market lines become hyperplanes with the equation (in the most general form)

$$K_0 + \frac{K_1}{1+i_1} + \frac{K_2}{(1+i_1)(1+i_2)} + \dots + \frac{K_n}{(1+i_1)(1+i_2)\dots(1+i_n)} = C,$$

C being a parameter, i_1 the discount rate between income in period 0 and 1, i_2 the discount rate between periods 1 and 2, and so forth.[27] Where $i_1 = i_2 = \dots i_n = i$, the expression takes on the simpler and more familiar form

$$K_0 + \frac{K_1}{1+i} + \frac{K_2}{(1+i)^2} + \dots + \frac{K_n}{(1+i)^n} = C.$$

The major difficulty with the multiperiod case turns upon the third element of the solution—the description of the productive opportunities, which may be denoted by the equation $f(K_0, K_1, \dots, K_n) = 0$. The purely theoretical specification is not too difficult, however, if the assumption is made that all investment options are independent. The problem of non-independence is not essentially different in the multiperiod case and in the two-period case, and it would enormously complicate the presentation to consider it here. Under this condition, then, and with appropriate continuity assumptions, the productive opportunity locus may be envisaged as a shell[28] concave to the origin in all directions. With these assumptions, between income in any two periods K_r and K_s

[27] I shall not, in this section, consider further the possible divergences between the lending and borrowing rates studied in detail in Sec. I but shall speak simply of "the discount rate" or "the market rate." The principles involved are not essentially changed in the multiperiod case; I shall concentrate attention on certain other difficulties that appear only when more than two periods are considered. We may note that in the most general case the assumption of full information becomes rather unrealistic—e.g., that the pattern of interest rates i_1 through i_n is known today.

[28] As in the two-period case, the locus represents not all the production opportunities but only the *boundary* of the region represented by the production opportunities. The boundary consists of those opportunities not dominated by any other; any opportunity represented by an interior point is dominated by at least one boundary point.

(holding K_t for all other periods constant) there will be a two-dimensional productive opportunity locus essentially like that in Figure 1.[29]

Now suppose that lending or borrowing can take place between any two successive periods r and s at the rate i_s. The theoretical solution involves finding the multidimensional analogue of the point R' (in Fig. 1)—that is, the point on the highest present-value hyperplane reached by the productive opportunity locus. With simple curvature and continuity assumptions, R' will be a tangency point, thus having the additional property that, between the members of any such pair of time periods, the marginal productive rate of return between K_r and K_s (holding all other K_t's constant) will be equal to the discount rate between these periods. Furthermore, if the condition is met between all pairs of successive periods, it will also be satisfied between any pairs of time periods as well.[30] Again, as in the two-period case, the final solution will involve market lending or borrowing ("financing") to move along the highest present-value hyperplane at-

[29] The assumption of n-dimensional continuity is harder to swallow than two-dimensional continuity as an approximation to the nature of the real world. Nevertheless, the restriction is not essential, though it is an enormous convenience in developing the argument. One possible misinterpretation of the continuity assumption should be mentioned: it does not necessarily mean that the only investment opportunities considered are two-period options between pairs of periods in the present or future. Genuine multiperiod options are allowable—for example, the option described by cash-flows of -1, $+4$, $+2$, and $+6$ for periods 0, 1, 2, and 3, respectively. The continuity assumption means, rather, that if we choose to move from an option like this one in the direction of having more income in period 1 and less, say, in period 3, we can find other options available like -1, $+4+e_1$, $+2$, $+6-e_3$, where e_1 and e_3 represent infinitesimals. In other words, from any point on the locus it is possible to trade continuously between incomes in any pair of periods.

[30] Maximizing the Lagrangian expression $C-\lambda f(K_0, \ldots, K_n)$, we derive the first-order conditions

$$\begin{cases} \dfrac{\partial C}{\partial K_0} = 1 & -\lambda \dfrac{\partial f}{\partial K_0} = 0 \\ \dfrac{\partial C}{\partial K_1} = \dfrac{1}{1+i_1} & -\lambda \dfrac{\partial f}{\partial K_1} = 0 \\ \cdots\cdots & \cdots\cdots \\ \dfrac{\partial C}{\partial K_n} = \dfrac{1}{(1+i_1)(1+i_2)\ldots(1+i_n)} & -\lambda \dfrac{\partial f}{\partial K_n} = 0\,. \end{cases}$$

Eliminating λ between any pair of successive periods:

$$\frac{\partial f/\partial K_r}{\partial f/\partial K_s} = \frac{(1+i_1)(1+i_2)\ldots(1+i_r)(1+i_s)}{(1+i_1)(1+i_2)\ldots(1+i_r)}$$

$$\left.\frac{\partial K_s}{\partial K_r}\right|_{\substack{K_j \\ (j\neq r,s)}} = 1+i_s\,.$$

Between non-successive periods:

$$\left.\frac{\partial K_t}{\partial K_r}\right|_{\substack{K_j \\ (j\neq r,t)}} = (1+i_{r+1})(1+i_{r+2})\ldots(1+i_{t-1})(1+i_t)\,.$$

tained from the intermediate productive solution R' to the true preference optimum at R. Note that, as compared with the present value or direct solution, the principle of equating the marginal productive rate of return with the discount rate requires certain continuity assumptions.

Now it is here that Fisher, who evidently understood the true nature of the solution himself, appears to have led others astray. In his *Rate of Interest* he provides a mathematical proof that the optimal investment decision involves setting what is here called the marginal productive rate of return equal to the market rate of interest *between any two periods.*[31] By obvious generalization of the result of the two-period problem, this condition is identical with that of finding the line of highest present value (the two-dimensional projection of the hyperplane of highest present value) between these time periods. Unfortunately, Fisher fails to state the qualification "between any two time-periods" consistently and at various places makes flat statements to the effect that investments will be made wherever the "rate of return on sacrifice" or "rate of return on cost" between any two options exceeds the rate of interest.[32]

Now the rate of return on sacrifice is, for two-period comparisons, equivalent to the productive rate of return. More generally, however, Fisher defines the rate of return on sacrifice in a *multiperiod* sense; that is, as that rate which reduces to a present value of zero the entire sequence of positive and negative periodic differences between the returns of any two investment options.[33] This definition is, for our purposes, equivalent to the so-called "internal rate of return."[34] This latter rate (which will be denoted ρ) will, however, be shown to lead to results which are, in general, not correct if the procedure is followed of adopting or rejecting investment options on the basis of a comparison of ρ and the market rate.[35]

B. FAILURE OF THE GENERALIZED "INTERNAL RATE OF RETURN"

Recent thinking emphasizing the internal rate of return seems to be based upon the idea of finding a purely "internal" measure of the time productivity of an investment—that is, the rate of growth of capital funds invested in a project—for comparison with the market

[31] *Rate of Interest*, pp. 398–400. Actually, the proof refers only to successive periods, but this is an inessential restriction.

[32] *Ibid.*, p. 155; *Theory of Interest*, pp. 168–69.

[33] *Rate of Interest*, p. 153; *Theory of Interest*, pp. 168–69.

[34] For some purposes it is important to distinguish between the rate which sets the present value of a series of receipts from an investment equal to zero and that rate which does the same for the series of *differences* between the receipts of two alternative investment options (see A. A. Alchian, "The Rate of Interest, Fisher's Rate of Return over Cost, and Keynes' Internal Rate of Return," *American Economic Review*, XLV [December, 1955], 938–43). For present purposes there is no need to make the distinction because individual investment options are regarded as independent increments—so that the receipts of the option in question are in fact a sequence of differences over the alternative of not adopting that option.

[35] As another complication, Fisher's mathematical analysis compares the two-period marginal rates of return on sacrifice with the interest rates between those two periods, the latter not being assumed constant throughout. In the multiperiod case Fisher nowhere states how to combine the differing period-to-period interest rates into an over-all market rate for comparison with ρ. It is possible that just at this point Fisher was thinking only of a rate of interest which remained constant over time, in which case the question would not arise. The difficulty in the use of the "internal rate" when variations in the market rate over time exist will be discussed below.

rate.[36] But the idea of rate of growth involves a ratio and cannot be uniquely defined unless one can uniquely value initial and terminal positions. Thus the investment option characterized by the annual cash-flow sequence $-1, 0, 0, 8$ clearly involves a growth rate of 100 per cent (compounding annually), because it really reduces to a two-period option with intermediate compounding. Similarly, a savings deposit at 10 per cent compounded annually for n years may seem to be a multiperiod option, but it is properly regarded as a series of two-period options (the "growth" will take place only if at the beginning of each period the decision is taken to reinvest the capital plus interest yielded by the investment of the previous period). A savings-account option without reinvestment would be: $-1, .10, .10, .10, \ldots, 1.10$ (the last element being a terminating payment); with reinvestment, the option becomes $-1, 0, 0, 0, \ldots, (1.10)^n$, n being the number of compounding periods after the initial deposit.

Consider, however, a more general investment option characterized by the sequence $-1, 2, 1$. (In general, all investment options considered here will be normalized in terms of an assumed $1.00 of initial outlay or initial receipt.) How can a rate of growth for the initial capital outlay be determined? Unlike the savings-account opportunity, no information is provided as to the rate at which the intermediate receipt or "cash throw-off" of $2.00 can be reinvested. If, of course, we use some external discounting rate (for example, the cost of capital or the rate of an outside lending opportunity), we will be departing from the idea of a purely *internal* growth rate. In fact, the use of an external rate will simply reduce us to a present-value evaluation of the investment option.

In an attempt to resolve this difficulty, one mathematical feature of the two-period marginal productive rate of return was selected for generalization by both Fisher and his successors. This feature is the fact that, when ρ (in the two-period case equal to the marginal productive rate of return $[\Delta K_1]/[-\Delta K_0] - 1$) is used for discounting the values in the receipt-outlay stream, the discounted value becomes zero. This concept lends itself to easy generalization: for any multiperiod stream there will be a similar discounting rate ρ which will make the discounted value equal to zero (or so it was thought). This rate seems to be purely internal, not infected by any market considerations. And, in certain simple cases, it does lead to correct answers in choosing investment projects according to the rule: Adopt the project if ρ is greater than the market rate r.

For the investment option $-1, 2, 1$ considered above, ρ is equal to $\sqrt{2}$, or 141.4 per cent. And, in fact, if the borrowing rate or the rate on the best alternative opportunity (whichever is the appropriate comparison) is less than $\sqrt{2}$, the investment is desirable. Figure 7 plots the present value C of the option as a function of the discounting interest rate, i, assumed to be constant over the two discounting periods. Note that the present value of the option diminishes as i increases throughout the entire relevant range of i, from $i = -1$ to $i = \infty$.[37] The internal rate of return ρ is that i for which the present value curve cuts the horizontal axis. Evidently, for any $i < \rho$, present value is positive; for

[36] See K. E. Boulding, *Economic Analysis* (rev. ed.; New York: Harper & Bros., 1948), p. 819.

[37] Economic meaning may be attached to negative interest rates; these are rates of shrinkage of capital. I rule out the possibility of shrinkage rates greater than 100 per cent, however.

$i > \rho$, it is negative.

However, the fact that the use of ρ leads to the correct decision in a particular case or a particular class of cases does not mean that it is correct in prin-

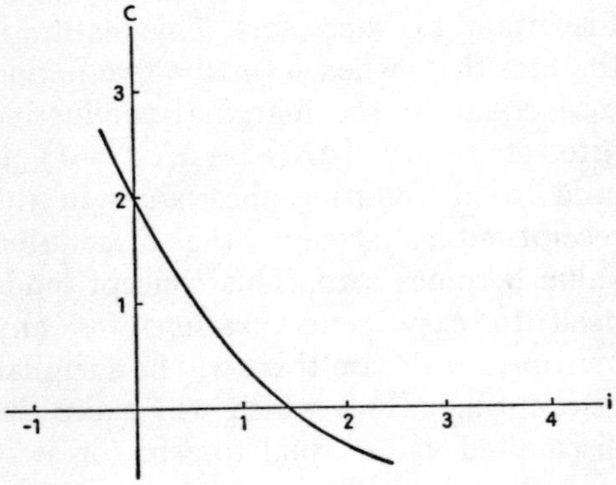

FIG. 7.—Sketch of present value of the option −1, 2, 1.

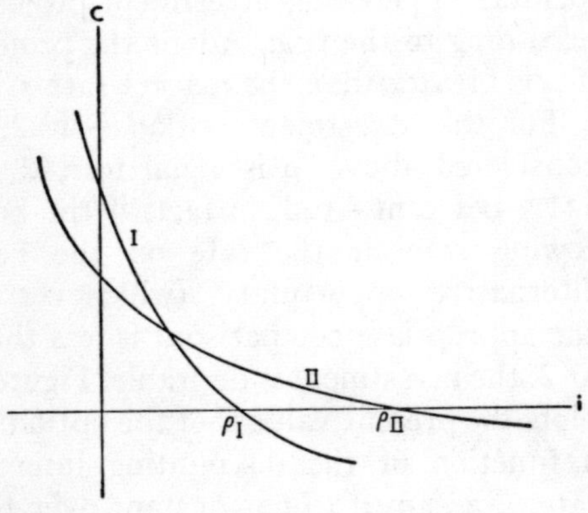

FIG. 8.—Two alternative options

ciple. And, in fact, cases have been adduced where its use leads to incorrect answers. Alchian has shown that, in the comparison of two investment options which are alternatives, the choice of the one with a higher ρ is not in general correct—in fact, the decision cannot be made without knowledge of the appropriate external discounting rate.[38] Figure 8 illustrates two such options, I being preferable for low rates of interest and II for high rates. The i at which the cross-over takes place is Fisher's rate of return on sacrifice between these two options. But II has the higher internal rate of return (that is, its present value falls to zero at a higher discounting rate) regardless of the actual rate of interest. How can we say that I is preferable at low rates of interest? Because its present value is higher, it permits the investor to move along a higher hyperplane to find the utility optimum attained somewhere on that hyperplane. If II were adopted, the investor would also be enabled to move along such a hyperplane, but a lower one. Put another way, with the specified low rate of interest, the investor adopting I could, if he chose, put himself in the position of adopting II by appropriate borrowings and lendings together with throwing away some of his wealth.[39]

Even more fundamentally, Lorie and Savage have shown that ρ may not be unique.[40] Consider, for example, the in-

[38] Alchian, *op. cit.*, p. 939.

[39] Some people find this so hard to believe that I shall provide a numerical example. For investment I, we may use the annual cash-flow stream −1, 0, 4—then the internal rate of return is 1, or 100 per cent. For investment option II, we may use the option illustrated in Figure 7: −1, 2, 1. For this investment ρ is equal to $\sqrt{2}$, or 141.4 per cent. So the internal rate of return is greater for II. However, the present value for option I is greater at an interest rate of 0 per cent, and in fact it remains greater until the cross-over rate, which happens to be at 50 per cent for these two options. Now it is simple to show how, adopting I, we can get to the result II at any interest rate lower than 50 per cent—10 per cent, for example. Borrowing from the final time period for the benefit of the intermediate one, we can convert −1, 0, 4 to −1, 2.73, 1 (I have subtracted 3 from the final period, crediting the intermediate period with $3/1.1 = 2.73$). We can now get to option II by throwing away the 0.73, leaving us with −1, 2, 1. The fact that we can get to option II by throwing away some wealth demonstrates the superiority of I even though $\rho_{II} > \rho_I$, provided that borrowing and lending can take place at an interest rate less than the cross-over discounting rate of 50 per cent.

[40] *Op. cit.*, pp. 236–39.

vestment option −1, 5, −6. Calculation reveals that this option has a present value of zero at discounting rates of both 100 per cent and 200 per cent. For this investment option present value as a function of the discounting rate is sketched in Figure 9. While Lorie and Savage speak only of "dual" internal rates of return, any number of zero values of the present-value function are possible in principle. The option −1, 6, −11, 6, illustrated in Figure 10, has

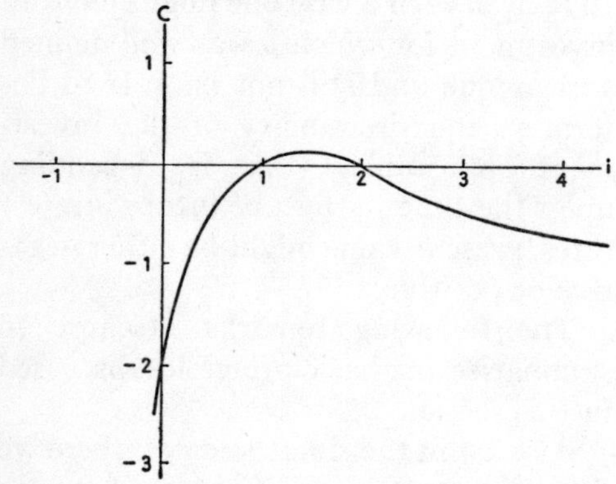

Fig. 9.—Sketch of present value of the investment option −1, 5, −6.

zero present value at the discounting rates 0 per cent, 100 per cent, and 200 per cent, for example.[41]

[41] The instances discussed above suggest that the alternation of signs in the receipt stream has something to do with the possibility of multiple ρ's. In fact, Descartes's rule of signs tells us that the number of solutions in the allowable range (the number of points where present value equals zero for $i > -1$) is at most equal to the number of reversals of sign in the terms of the receipts sequence. Therefore, a two-period investment option has at most a single ρ, a three-period option at most a dual ρ, and so forth. There is an interesting footnote in Fisher which suggests that he was not entirely unaware of this difficulty. Where more than a single-sign alternation takes place, he suggests the use of the present-value method rather than attempting to compute "the rate of return on sacrifice" (*Rate of Interest*, p. 155). That any number of zeros of the present value function can occur was pointed out by Paul A. Samuelson in "Some Aspects of the Pure Theory of Capital," *Quarterly Journal of Economics*, LI (1936–37), 469–96 (at p. 475).

In fact, perfectly respectable investment options may have *no* real internal rates (the present value equation has only imaginary roots). The option −1, 3, $-2\frac{1}{2}$ is an example; a plot would show that its present value is negative throughout the relevant range.[42] It is definitely not the case, however, that all options

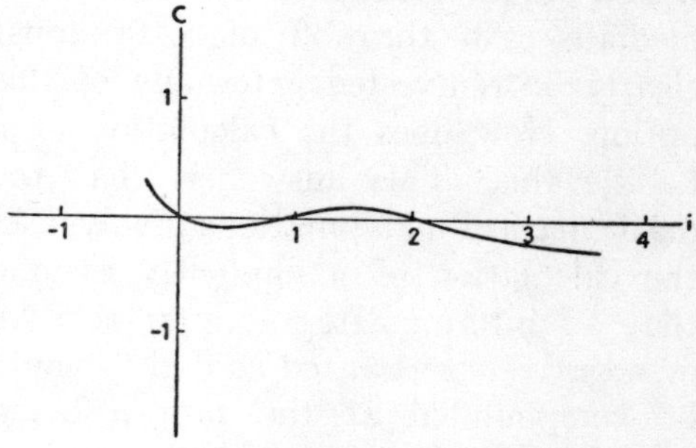

Fig. 10.—Sketch of present value of the investment option −1, 6, −11, 6.

for which the internal rate cannot be calculated are bad ones. If we merely reverse the signs on the option above to get 1, −3, $2\frac{1}{2}$, we have an option with positive present value at all rates of discount.

These instances of failure of the multiperiod internal-rate-of-return rule (note that in each case the present-value rule continues to indicate the correct answer unambiguously, setting aside the question of the appropriate discounting rate which was discussed in Sec. I) are, of course, merely the symptom of an underlying erroneous conception. It is clear

[42] Mathematically, the formula for the roots of a three-period option n_0, n_1, n_2 where $n_0 = -1$ is:

$$i = \frac{(n_1 - 2) \pm \sqrt{n_1^2 + 4n_2}}{2}.$$

If $-4n_2$ exceeds n_1^2, the roots will be imaginary, and an internal rate of return cannot be calculated. A necessary condition for this result is that the sum of the undiscounted cash flows be negative, but this condition should not rule out consideration of an option (note the option −1, 5, −6 in Fig. 9).

that the idea that ρ represents a growth rate in any simple sense cannot be true; a capital investment of \$1.00 cannot grow at a rate both of 100 per cent and of 200 per cent. Even more fundamentally, the idea that ρ is a purely *internal* rate is not true either. Consider the option -1, 2, 1 discussed earlier, with a unique p equal to $\sqrt{2}$. The intermediate cash throwoff of \$2.00 must clearly be reinvested externally of this option. How does the calculation of ρ handle this? This answer is that the mathematical manipulations involved in the calculation of ρ implicitly assume that all intermediate receipts, positive or negative, are treated as if they could be compounded at the rate ρ being solved for.[43] The rate ρ has been characterized rather appropriately as the "solving rate" of interest. But note that this mathematical manipulation, even where it does lead to a unique answer (and, in general, it will not), is unreasonable in its economic implications. There will not normally be other investment opportunities arising for investment of intermediate cash proceeds at the rate ρ, nor is it generally true that intermediate cash inflows (if required) must be obtained by borrowing at the rate ρ. The rate ρ, arising from a mathematical manipulation, will only by rare coincidence represent relevant economic alternatives.

The preceding arguments against the use of the usual concept of the "internal rate of return" do not take any account of the possibility of non-constant interest rates over time. Martin J. Bailey has emphasized to me that it is precisely when this occurs (when there exists a known pattern of future variation of i) that the internal-rate-of-return rule fails most fundamentally. For in the use of that rule all time periods are treated on a par; the only discounting is via the solving rate defined only in terms of the sequence of cash flows. But with (a known pattern of) varying future i, shifts in the relative desirability of income in different periods are brought about. In the usual formulation the internal rate of return concept can take no account of this. In fact, in such a case one might have an investment for which ρ was well defined and unique and still not be able to determine the desirability of the investment opportunity (that is, depending upon the time pattern of future interest rates, present value might be either negative or positive).

The following remarks attempt to summarize the basic principles discussed in this section.

At least in the simplest case, where we do not worry about differences between borrowing and lending rates but assume these to be equal and also constant (constant with respect to the amount borrowed or lent—not constant over time), the multidimensional solution using the present-value rule is a straightforward generalization of the two-period solution. The principle is to push productive investment to the point where the highest attainable level of present value is reached and then to "finance" this investment by borrowing or lending between time periods to achieve a time-preference optimum.

The main burden of these remarks has been to the effect that the internal-rate-of-return rule, unlike the present-value rule, does not generalize to the multi-period case if the usual definition of the internal rate ρ is adopted—that is, as that rate which sets the present value of

[43] The true significance of the reinvestment assumption was brought out in Ezra Solomon, "The Arithmetic of Capital-budgeting Decisions," *Journal of Business*, XXIX (April, 1956), 124–29, esp. pp. 126–27.

the discounted income stream equal to zero. I have tried to show the multiperiod generalization which *would* make the internal-rate-of-return rule still correct: between *every pair* of time periods, the marginal internal rate of return in the sense of the marginal productive rate of return between those two periods, holding income in other periods constant, should be set equal to the market discount rate between those periods. That the usual interpretation of the internal-rate-of-return rule is not in general correct has been illustrated by its failure in particular cases and has been explained by exposing the implicit assumption made in the mathematical manipulation which finds ρ—that all intermediate cash flows are reinvested (or borrowed, if cash flows are negative) at the rate ρ itself. In addition, ρ does not allow for varying interperiod preference rates (or interest rates) over time. This generalized multiperiod internal rate of return is, therefore, not really internal, nor is the assumption implied about the external opportunities generally correct or even generally reasonable.

IV. CONCLUDING COMMENTS

The preceding analysis has slighted a great many questions. In addition, lack of time has precluded comparative discussion of the works of other authors, however helpful this might have been.[44]

I have not attempted to generalize the results to the multiperiod case with non-independent investments or with differing or non-constant borrowing and lending rates. On the latter points intuition suggests that whether the borrowing or lending rate in calculating present value is to be used for any time period does not depend upon any characteristics of the investment option under consideration in isolation; it depends rather upon the over-all cash position after adoption of that option as an increment. If, after such adoption, time preference dictates shifting to less income in period r and more in period t, any income associated with the option in question falling in period r should be discounted back to the next earlier period at the lending rate (and that for period t at the borrowing rate). Income in any period s may then have been successively discounted at borrowing rates for a number of periods and lending rates for a number of others before being reduced to a present value.

The main positive conclusion of the paper is that the present-value rule for investment decisions is correct in a wide variety of cases (though not universally) and in a limited sense. The rule tells us to attain the highest possible level of present value, but the point at which this condition is satisfied (that is, the distribution of incomes in various time periods) is not the final solution. It is, rather, an intermediate "productive" solution which must then be modified by borrowing or lending ("financing") to find the over-all optimum. This becomes particularly clear when we consider the case where lending and borrowing rates differ and thus enter the subcontroversy

[44] I should comment, though, on the important article by Samuelson, *op. cit.* The results here are in part consistent with his, with the following main differences: (1) He limits himself to the analysis of a single investment, whereas I consider the entire investment-consumption pattern over time. (2) He concludes in favor of the present-value rule, discounting at *the* market rate of interest. I have attempted to consider explicitly the problem of what to do when the borrowing and lending rates diverge, or vary as a function of the amount borrowed, and I do not find the present-value rule to be universally valid. Of these differences, the first is really crucial. It is the heart of Fisher's message that investments *cannot* be considered in isolation but only in the context of the other investment and consumption alternatives available. Nevertheless, Samuelson's article suffices to refute a number of fallacies still current in this field of economic theory.

between those who favor the use of present-value discounting at the cost of capital and those who would discount at the alternative lending rate. Which is correct depends upon the financing necessary to approach the time-preference optimum. Furthermore, if a tangency takes place between the productive opportunity locus and the time-preference utility isoquant at a rate between the lending and the borrowing rates, the "productive" solution requires no financing and the present-value principle is only correct in a formal sense. The present-value rule fails to give correct answers only for certain cases which combine the difficulties of non-independent investments and absence of a perfect capital market. When a perfect capital market exists, the present-value rule is universally correct in the limited sense referred to above. With independent investments but an imperfect capital market, the present-value rule will give answers which are correct but possibly only in a formal sense (the discounting rate used is not an external opportunity but an internal shadow price which comes out of the analysis).

The main negative conclusion is that the internal-rate-of-return rule for the multiperiod case is not generally correct, if the usual definition of the internal rate is adopted as that discount rate which makes the present value of the income stream associated with an investment option equal to zero. The so-called internal rate will only give correct answers in general if restricted to two-period comparisons; I have called this two-period internal rate the productive rate of return. For multiperiod investments the usual internal-rate-of-return rule (compare ρ with the market rate r) is not generally correct; however, given certain continuity assumptions, the correct answer will be arrived at by setting the marginal productive rate of return between each *pair* of time periods equal to the discount or market rate between those periods.

More important than the specific detailed conclusions is the demonstration that the Fisherian approach—the analysis of investment decisions as a means of balancing consumption incomes over time, together with the distinction between productive and market investment opportunities—is capable of solving (in the theoretical sense) all the problems posed. This solution is, furthermore, not an excrescence upon the general economic theory of choice but entirely integrated with it, constituting another dimension, so to speak. Since Fisher, economists working in the theory of investment decision have tended to adopt a mechanical approach—some plumping for the use of this formula, some for that. From a Fisherian point of view, we can see that none of the formulas so far propounded is universally valid. Furthermore, even where the present-value rule, for example, is correct, few realize that its validity is conditional upon making certain associated financing decisions as the Fisherian analysis demonstrates. In short, the Fisherian approach permits us to define the range of applicability and the shortcomings of all the proposed formulas—thus standing over against them as the general theoretical solution to the problem of investment decision under conditions of certainty.

APPLICATION OF LINEAR PROGRAMMING TO FINANCIAL BUDGETING AND THE COSTING OF FUNDS*

A. CHARNES,† W. W. COOPER,‡ AND M. H. MILLER§

I. INTRODUCTION

The purpose of this paper is to explore ways in which the theorems and computational apparatus of linear programming might be brought to bear on the allocation of funds within an enterprise. The rational deployment of a firm's resources requires (simultaneous) consideration of at least the following closely related questions.

1. Given the structure of the firm's assets, what operating program—in the sense of plans for production, purchases, and sales over the relevant planning interval—will yield the firm the greatest prospective net returns in the light of its profit and other objectives? That linear programming can contribute to a solution here has been amply demonstrated by its many successful applications to such planning problems (some quite large) in a variety of contexts.[1] For a number of reasons reported applications have so far been concentrated heavily in the production area; but, as we shall try to show, there is no reason why the same techniques cannot be used for financial planning or, more to the point, joint operating and financial planning.

2. What is the "yield" to the firm of each of the various possible changes in its asset structure, assuming that these assets are employed to maximum advantage? Here linear programming offers a way of bypassing some of the technical difficulties which have been encountered in connection with attempts to evaluate projects (as prosposed, e.g., in [16] or [21]) on the basis of their "rates of return."[2] In addition, with a programming formulation, some of the harder parts of the task of tracing through the interactions of proposed investments with each other and with existing facilities can be left to the mathematics.

3. What is the opportunity cost of funds in the firm, in the sense of the prospective rate of yield on an increment of funds committed to the enterprise

* This paper is a revised version of an ONR research report which was first presented at the Symposium on Operational Models, jointly sponsored by the Chemical Corps Engineering Command and New York University held at Army Chemical Center, Maryland, January 17, 1957. Part of the research underlying this paper was undertaken for the project "Planning and Control of Industrial Operations" at Carnegie Institute of Technology and part for the project Methodological Aspects of Management Research" at Purdue University. Both projects are under contract with the United States Office of Naval Research. Reproduction of this paper in whole or in part is permitted for any purpose of the United States government, Contract Nonr-760-(01), Project NR047-011, and Contract Nonr-1100-(05), Project NR047-016.

† Research professor of applied mathematics and economics, Northwestern University.

‡ Ford Distinguished Research Professor, Graduate School of Industrial Administration, Carnegie Institute of Technology.

§ Associate professor of economics and industrial administration, Carnegie Institute of Technology.

[1] See, e.g., [6] (in the Bibliography) and the references therein.

[2] Rate of return is defined for this purpose as that rate of interest which makes the present value of the project equal to its cost. For discussions of the technical deficiencies of this method of ranking projects (which include possible non-uniqueness and possible inability to rank mutually exclusive projects) see [26], [29], and [22].

and optimally employed during the planning interval? Knowledge of this opportunity cost is required for determining, among other things, whether the "yield" of a proposed investment is sufficient to justify its undertaking. Under some conditions this opportunity cost of funds can be determined in advance and independently of the actual operating and investment decisions. Such is the case when the firm has the power to borrow or lend unlimited quantities of funds in the capital markets at a constant rate. When, on the other hand, the firm is subject to "capital rationing"[3] or when its planning must be undertaken subject to liquidity constraints, the use of some predetermined external yield rate for purposes of internal allocations is not, in general, appropriate or feasible.[4] Here, again, however, a linear programming approach may represent one way to bypass some of the difficulties. It is possible, as we shall show, to modify standard linear programming formulations by incorporating the funds components of the profit objective directly among the constraining relations on programs. This procedure provides a measure of the marginal internal yield of funds and one which takes account of the feedback between operations and finance when funds are limited. It can also be made to yield evaluations of some of the "qualitative" restrictions which are features of many actual financing arrangements.

Since linear programming is still a relatively new tool of management, it may perhaps be well to begin with some preliminary remarks about its nature.

II. LINEAR PROGRAMMING: DIRECT AND DUAL RELATIONS

Consider, for example, the following ingredients of a very simple buying, selling, and storage problem for a warehouse manager contemplating possible purchase, sale, and storage patterns over the $j = 1, 2, \ldots, n$ periods which constitute his "planning horizon." Let

B = the fixed warehouse capacity;

A = the initial stock of inventory in the warehouse;

x_j = the amount to be purchased in period j;

y_j = the amount to be sold in period j; (1)

p_j = sales price per unit prevailing in period j; and

c_j = purchase price per unit prevailing in period j.

Given the p_j and c_j, how should this firm program its activities—that is, determine values x_j and y_j—in order to maximize its profits?

All programs must honor the constraints. As an example, let it be assumed that the firm sells under conditions of "perfect competition" so that potential sales at a given price p_j may be of any size. Sales must, however, be executed from inventory on hand at the start of any period so that at, say, period i the cumulative sales of the firm must conform to

$$\sum_{j=1}^{i} y_j \leq A + \sum_{j=1}^{i-1} x_j .$$

[3] For the analysis presented here "capital rationing" will be taken in its familiar sense of implying a situation in which a firm has access to only a maximal amount of funds. Higher offer prices either will not call forth additional funds or will call them only on terms which are unacceptable—as when creditors or new investors stipulate significant changes in the control of the firm (see [14], [15], and [20]).

[4] In particular, it is not feasible to use an external rate for, say, computing "present values" of proposed projects or to serve as a "cut-off" rate for screening projects. For a demonstration of the inadequacy of these standard approaches when capital markets are imperfect see [22].

Also, while the firm can buy any quantity of goods, it cannot store more than its net available capacity allows; that is,

$$\sum_{j=1}^{i} x_j \leq B - A + \sum_{j=1}^{i} y_j .$$

The problem as described can be represented by the following mathematical model:[5]

$$\text{maximize } \pi = \sum_{j=1}^{n} p_j y_j - \sum_{j=1}^{n} c_j x_j \quad (2a)$$

subject to the $i = 1, 2, \ldots, n$ buying constraints,

$$-\sum_{j=1}^{i} x_j - \sum_{j=1}^{i} y_j \leq B - A , \quad (2b)$$

and to the n selling constraints,

$$-\sum_{j=1}^{i-1} x_j + \sum_{j=1}^{i} y_j \leq A . \quad (2c)$$

Also the variables

$$x_j, y_j \geq 0, \; j = 1, 2, \ldots, n \quad (2d)$$

for all purchases and sales are constrained to assume non-negative values.

If each of the mathematical expressions (2*b*)–(2*c*) are written explicitly for $i = 1, 2, \ldots, n$, the kinds of expressions obtained are shown in (3*a*) and (3*b*).

When the coefficients which appear alongside the variables in these expressions are detached and arrayed, as in Figure 1, a rather striking pattern, called the "structure" of the model, emerges. The non-zero coefficients[6] are either $+1$ or -1. They can be arrayed as a series of triangles (with one smaller than the others) positioned as shown. To check that this is so, simply drop the variables shown at the top of the table (corresponding to the stub labeled "λ") along-

[5] Notice that what is being maximized is *undiscounted* cumulative profits. This assumption can be interpreted as implying that an "adequate" allotment of funds has been granted to the manager and that no further decisions about withdrawals of funds or new commitment of funds are to be made until the horizon period is reached. Later examples will cover cases in which the funds allotted may not be "adequate" to permit the manager to undertake every profitable transaction as well as cases in which external market opportunities for borrowing and lending are considered explicitly. The relation of these and other cases to the standard discounting approach in dynamic models will be discussed further below.

[6] I.e., the first expression in (3*a*) may be considered to be the same as $+1x_1 + 0x_2 + \ldots + 0x_n - 1y_1 - 0y_2 - \ldots - 0y_n \leq B - A$, and the same kinds of expressions may be written for the other constraints. All coefficients are then seen to be $+1$, -1, or 0.

$$\begin{array}{lll}
x_1 & -y_1 & \leq B - A \\
x_1 + x_2 & -y_1 - y_2 & \leq B - A \\
\cdots\cdots & \cdots\cdots & \cdots\cdots \\
x_1 + x_2 + \ldots + x_n & -y_1 - y_2 - \ldots - y_n & \leq B - A
\end{array} \quad (3a)$$

and

$$\begin{array}{lll}
 & y_1 & \leq A \\
-x_1 & +y_1 + y_2 & \leq A \\
-x_1 - x_2 & +y_1 + y_2 + y_3 & \leq A \\
\cdots\cdots & \cdots\cdots & \cdots\cdots \\
-x_1 - x_2 - \ldots - x_{n-1} & +y_1 + y_2 + y_3 + \ldots + y_n & \leq A .
\end{array} \quad (3b)$$

side the 1's, 0's, and −1's as schematically indicated by the triangles in the body of the table. Form the resulting expressions, one for each row of the diagram. The triangles opposite the t's (in the stub) will then give the expressions (3*a*). Those alongside the u's will give the expressions (3*b*). Finally, if the process is continued into the last row (labeled "p"), the functional (2*a*), for which a maximum is sought, can be secured.

The algebraic expressions thus secured may be called the "direct" problem. To each such direct linear programming problem there is always another (linear programming) problem which can be formed from exactly the same data. It is called the "dual" problem.

The dual to (2) is

$$\text{minimize } E = \sum_{k=1}^{n} (B-A)\,t_k + \sum_{k=1}^{n} A\,u_k \quad (4\,b)$$

subject to

$$\sum_{i=k}^{n} t_i - \sum_{i=k+1}^{n} u_i \geq -c_k,\ k = 1, 2, \ldots, n \quad (4\,c)$$

and to

$$-\sum_{i=r}^{n} t_i + \sum_{i=r}^{n} u_i \geq p_r,\ r = 1, 2, \ldots, n\,. \quad (4\,c)$$

That is, values are sought for the variables u and t which make E a minimum while honoring the $2n$ expressions, (4*b*) and (4*c*), along with the non-negativity requirements

$$t_i,\ u_i \geq 0,\ i = 1, 2, \ldots, n\,. \quad (4d)$$

The schema of Figure 1 assists in forming the dual as well as the direct problem. Whereas the direct problem was formed from the *rows*, its dual is formed from the *columns* of this same table. Thus, at $k = 1$, the first dual inequality is secured by positioning the variables t and u alongside the +1's, the −1's (and the single zero) on the left margins of the two left-hand triangles to give $t_1 + t_2 + \ldots + t_k + \ldots + t_n - u_2 - u_3 - \ldots - u_r - \ldots - u_n \geq -c_1$. Continuing in this same manner until the right-hand vertices of these two triangles on the left are reached, the final dual constraint for (4*b*) is found to give $t_n \geq -c_n$, since u_n has a zero coefficient in this column. Continuing to the margin of the next two triangles, the first of the n expressions in (4*c*) is found to be $-t_1 - t_2 - \ldots - t_k - \ldots - t_n + u_1 + u_2 + \ldots +$

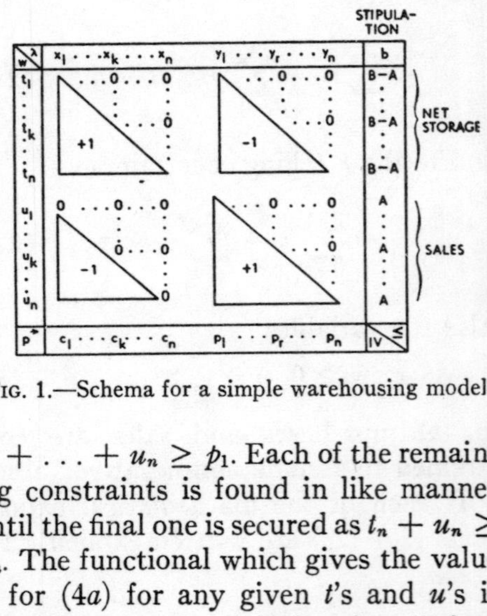

FIG. 1.—Schema for a simple warehousing model

$u_r + \ldots + u_n \geq p_1$. Each of the remaining constraints is found in like manner until the final one is secured as $t_n + u_n \geq p_n$. The functional which gives the value E for (4*a*) for any given t's and u's is obtained from the right-hand or "stipulations" *column* as

$$(B-A)\,t_1 + (B-A)\,t_2 + \ldots$$
$$+ (B-A)\,t_n + A\,u_1 + A\,u_2 \ldots + A\,u_n\,.$$

There is a theorem, known as the "dual theorem of linear programming,"[7] which asserts that the optimum values, min. $E = E^*$ and max. $\pi = \pi^*$,[8] are

[7] See [24(2)], where it was first given.

[8] Certain additional refinements which are primarily directed to questions of mathematical consistency and the existence of solutions are also

equal, so that $E^* = \pi^*$.[9] In the present case this gives

$$\sum_{j=1}^{n} p_j y_j^* - \sum_{j=1}^{n} c_j x_j^* = \sum_{k=1}^{n} (B - A)\, t_k^* - \sum_{k=1}^{n} A u_k^* . \tag{5a}$$

To make sense as an equation, both sides of these expressions must give the same units of measure. The p_j's and c_j's are in terms of dollars per unit and the y_j's and x_j's are in terms of the units—say, tons—in which purchases and sales can be effected in period j. Thus, π^* represents the total dollars (of profit) which can be (optimally) obtained over the entire horizon $j = 1, 2, \ldots, n$. The right-hand side, which gives E^*, must therefore equal the same number of dollars. Now $(B - A)$ is, say, tons of net warehouse capacity available, while A represents tons of starting inventory. Therefore, t_k^* must be stated in terms of dollars per ton of net warehouse capacity available in period k, and u_k^* must, similarly, be in dollars per unit of initial (opening) inventory considered at period k.

The t^*'s and u^*'s can therefore be used to "evaluate" these assets. To see what is involved, suppose the firm acquires (or wishes to consider acquiring) in, say, period 1 an extra ton of warehouse capacity. Then these same dual evaluators may apply[10] to give[11]

$$\sum_{k=1}^{n} (B+1)\, t_k^* - \sum_{k=1}^{n} A\, (t_k^* - u_k^*) = (B+1) \sum_{k=1}^{n} t_k^* - A \sum_{k=1}^{n} (t_k^* - u_k^*) , \tag{5b}$$

with a new total dollar value E^{**} which is larger than E^* by

$$\sum_{k=1}^{n} t_k^* .$$

Since the dual theorem also applies to this new problem, it asserts (without requiring advance knowledge of the actual direct program composition) that optimal use of this new resource makes possible new program values which will give a new total profit

$$\pi^{**} = \pi^* + \sum_{k=1}^{n} t_k^* \geq \pi^* .^{12}$$

In this sense the values of the dual variables serve as "evaluators." They provide, beforehand, a means of determining the consequent increments (or decrements) in profits, costs—and like values—which can be secured if optimal use is made of proposed asset changes.[13]

contained in this theorem but will not be dealt with here (see [24(2)]). For a more elementary exposition (and related management interpretations) see [10]. The relation of this theorem to general economic questions is studied in [17].

[9] Starred values will be used to indicate optimum values.

[10] These remarks will be qualified later to indicate how ranges within which the t^*'s and u^*'s remain unchanged can be ascertained.

[11] Note that $\Sigma(t_k^* - u_k^*)$ gives the net inventory value, the terms t_k^* representing costs (i.e., opportunity costs) resulting from the utilization of otherwise available warehouse space and the u_k^* representing gains resulting from either (or both) purchase economies or selling possibilities. Cf. [5] for further discussion.

[12] The inequality allows the case $\pi^{**} = \pi^*$ but never $\pi^{**} < \pi^*$, because, by virtue of the nonnegativity constraints, every $t_k^* \geq 0$, so that

$$\sum_{k=1}^{n} t_k^* \geq 0 .$$

[13] More generally, these are called changes in the "stipulations" to allow for the fact that they are not confined to physical assets but may also apply to constraints arising from prescribed policies of the business, legal requirements, etc. For example,

The enhanced power that linear programming receives from the relations of duality that have been established will be illustrated in the sections to follow. This will be done by tracing through, *mutatis mutandis*, the simultaneous interactions of asset changes and optimal program compositions which can be generated from one type of demonstration model. It will then be apparent how the dual theorem makes it possible to consider one linear problem in place of what might otherwise appear as a series of complicated non-linear problems.

This last statement is predicated on the choice of a suitable rule of computation. That is, the rule must be selected so that, in solving one problem (direct or dual), a solution to the other one is also secured without extra calculations. Since such rules of computation are available (e.g., the simplex method of Dantzig [24(1)]), this choice can always be made, and there need be no trouble on this point.

III. FINANCIAL CONSTRAINTS AND THEIR EVALUATION

To see how the methods of linear programming (including duality) can help to disentangle some of the interactions between financial and operating policies, consider what happens when the dual theorem is applied to financial (liquidity) constraints such as

$$\sum_{j=1}^{i} c_{j-\epsilon} x_{j-\epsilon} - \sum_{j=1}^{i} p_{j-\tau} y_{j-\tau} \leq M_0 - \underline{M} \equiv \overline{M}, \; i = 1, \ldots, n\,. \tag{6}$$

In these expressions the subscripts indicate lags,[14] $j - \epsilon$ and $j - \tau$, in, respectively, payments and receipts; M_0 represents initial cash[15] available; and $\underline{M}$, a balance which it is (for whatever reasons)[16] desired to maintain at all times.

Each of these financial stipulations in equation (6)—whose force is to limit purchases by the manager to the original allotment of funds plus the cash in excess of required minimal holdings generated by operations—can be associated with a dual variable. Let these variables be called v_k. The dimensional analysis given in connection with equations (5*a*) and (5*b*) can be immediately extended to these new constraining relations. It is then seen that the v's must be stated in terms of dollars per dollar invested—assuming optimal use of the additional investment—or, more precisely, dollars per unit time per dollar invested (or withdrawn). These are the dimensions of compound interest.

IV. LINEAR PROGRAMMING AND MODEL TYPES

At this point it may be helpful to outline the strategy which will be followed in the remaining sections of this paper. Attention will be centered on questions of interpretation rather than on issues, such as computational efficiency or mathematical theory. Numerical examples and schematic illustrations (such as Fig. 1) will therefore be used to carry the

a policy which requires "relatively stable" employment may become a constraining relation with a stipulation. A constraining relation is to be distinguished from the "objective" (e.g., profit maximization), which is incorporated in the functional. See [10] for further discussion.

[14] Leads may also be inserted, and even more complicated expressions may be used. For this exposition, however, only the simplest cases (which retain some degree of interest) will be examined.

[15] Other measures of liquidity may, of course, be used if desired, and constraints may be entered for each relevant component of liquidity at any or all time periods for which they may be pertinent.

[16] E.g., because of an allotment schedule, transaction or precautionary motivation, etc. If desired, the stipulations may be altered to M_i, different for each time period.

burden of the analysis. These examples (and resulting interpretations) will be oriented mainly toward standard constructs in economics and finance, and only the simplest kinds of cases will be used. For example, even though it may seem to lend an air of artificiality to the "financial constraints," risk and related considerations will be left aside in order to avoid introducing still further complications into this exposition.[17]

The prototype from which these examples will be synthesized has already been given in the expressions (2). In that form it is known as the "warehousing model" of linear programming. Originally formulated by Cahn [2],[18] this model has been generalized from its original formulation as a single-commodity, one-warehouse, fixed-price example to include multiple warehouses and products, prices which vary with quantities bought and sold, etc.[19]

The warehousing model to be used here will cover only the single-product, one-warehouse case. Suitably adjusted, it contains all essentials which are required for the proposed yield analyses in extremely simple form. These include fixed facilities, inventory carrying charges (to be imputed), and transactions across time which involve payables and receivables (and, therefore, a distinction between cash flows and accruals).

Attention should be drawn toward one other aspect of these models. Most linear programming applications to management planning have revealed families of rather striking structural similarities in a wide variety of situations. These structural elements have made it possible to devise analytical and computational techniques which, when compared with more general techniques, are highly efficient for models with these structural properties. This has made it possible to deal with problems whose size would otherwise be forbidding.

The transportation model of linear programming is an example which can be used to illustrate one such "model type." Originally formulated for optimal movement of goods from origins to destinations,[20] it has since been generalized[21] in ways which also make it applicable to such seemingly alien problems as the assignment of personnel to jobs, the analysis of electrical networks,[22] etc. Moreover, when "model approximations"[23] are allowed, still wider classes of problems are encompassed within this one type. Thus, as exhibited in [6],[24] machine- and shop-loading models of certain kinds can also be included in this category.

As a different example, consider the problem of blending gasolines in a refinery.[25] If the elements for a "blending model" are diagrammed, a rather striking pattern of rectangles and echelons

[17] Cf. [11] for further discussion. Later papers will include such probabilistic (risk) considerations.

[18] The formulation given here, however, rests on the one first used in [3] and [5].

[19] See [5] for further discussion and suggested methods of computation for these models. See also [1] for a formulation of one case into functional equations—a formulation which is equivalent in that it yields the same (optimum) solutions as its algebraic counterpart.

[20] See, e.g., [24(3)].

[21] These generalizations have become known as "distribution models," which are intended to be comprehended here as models of "transportation type."

[22] Including non-linear networks of both electrical and hydraulic varieties. See, e.g., [7].

[23] I.e., models which have (or can be made to have) approximately the structure of a known (exact) model type.

[24] See this reference for further discussion, including a discussion of methods for securing and controlling the approximations.

[25] Cf. [9]; see also [19] for a report of further extensions and applications.

is obtained for the non-zero coefficients. These same elements are found in many processes of chemical manufacture, in mixing formula feeds for animals, and even in models that have been used for studying the traffic flows in a network of city streets.[26]

Still other examples could be cited. The potential importance of these model types as a guide for applications is probably sufficiently clear. In any event, these ideas have been discussed elsewhere and therefore need not be repeated here in full detail.[27] The essential notion is that many (if not most) problems of management planning can be synthesized from various combinations of a few model types (or approximations) which serve as basic ingredients.

Operations research, or related activities, will provide the tests required to establish the exact scope of potential applications of the model-type constructs. In the meantime there is a sufficient accumulation of evidence to make a study of any member of one of these classes a worthwhile scientific pursuit.[28]

There is little question that the warehouse model, suitably generalized, is an important member of one such class: "The warehousing problem is of interest in its own right. It is also worthy of study for other reasons. On the one hand it represents a generalization of simpler transportation models;[29] on the other hand it is the simplest example of a large and important class of dynamic models."[30] Indeed, in the latter connection, it may serve as a model approximation for much more complicated problems.[31]

V. WAREHOUSE MODEL WITH A FINANCIAL CONSTRAINT

Instead, therefore, of considering a large and complicated example of the kind that might occur in practice, a smaller one can be used to study essential properties of the larger ones in ways which can be usefully applied to them as well. For this purpose a small "warehouse model" involving only ten variables and fifteen constraints[32] can be used to initiate the desired explorations. Further possible extensions (e.g., from a one-commodity to multiple-commodity cases) will become evident as the discussion proceeds.

To simplify the presentation (and analysis), it is desirable to transform the problem, commencing with Figure 1, into a simpler equivalent. Therefore, by reference to equation (4), define the new cumulative variables

$$T_k = \sum_{i=k}^{n} t_i \qquad U_k = \sum_{i=k}^{n} u_i \tag{7}$$

so that $T_n \equiv t_n$ and $U_n \equiv u_n$. Then the entire problem in (4) may be stated in the following simpler form:

$$\min. E = (B - A)T_1 + A\,U_1$$

[26] See [4].

[27] See [5] and [6].

[28] E.g., for purposes of devising special methods of analysis, study of its properties in relation to other members of the class, etc.

[29] Cf. [28] for an explicit formulation given after these remarks were published.

[30] Quoted from [5]. See also [12] for a formulation with financial constraints in the context of "dyadic" linear programming models.

[31] See the model discussed in [6] for scheduling (over time) the flows of oil from a series of wells, while allowing for non-linearities arising from pressure drops due to the oil flows.

[32] There are actually twenty-five constraints when non-negativity (of each variable) is also counted. (Undue worry about questions of consistency or uniqueness may be avoided by noting that the basic orientation is toward *inequalities* rather than *equations*.)

subject to

$$T_k \geq U_{k+1} - c_k, T_{k-1} \geq T_k, T_n \geq -c_n ,$$
$$U_r \geq T_r + p_r, U_{r-1} \geq U_r , \quad (8)$$
$$T_r, U_r \geq 0 ,$$

where $U_0 \equiv U_1$, $T_0 \equiv T_1$, by reference to these cumulative variables.[33]

The relevance of the dual relation between (2) and (4) has already been noted. This same relation evidently holds between (2) and (8), since the latter, in essence, simply cumulates the variables (and hence their values) in (4). In other words, the proper cumulants for any solution of (4) give the results required in (8); conversely, by a suitable arrangement for decumulation, any results secured for (8) can be used to give the corresponding values of (4).

An optimal solution of a direct problem such as (2) automatically provides the values w_i^* for the corresponding dual variables. They may be read immediately from the optimum "tableau"[34] of the direct problem. The possibility of altering any stipulation in the direct problem without necessarily altering the (optimal) values for any dual variable has already been noted. Indeed, it is possible (in general) to vary more than one stipulation at a time without altering any of the dual evaluators, but such variations cannot be arbitrarily undertaken. Because of existing methods of computation, however, no great trouble need arise in practical applications. It is possible quickly to ascertain whether any proposed set of variations will affect the values w_i^*.[35] If such alterations are encountered, it is then possible to ascertain new optimum values w_i^* (and the new direct programs) without having to initiate calculations from scratch.[36]

Although the required adjustments to the program and dual variables can readily be generated in actual computation, for simplicity of presentation, it will be assumed, unless otherwise noted, that only variations in stipulations which permit maintenance of the "previous pattern" of direct activities are of interest.[37]

[33] Henceforth all values c_j, p_j will be assumed to be non-negative so that constraints such as $T_n \geq -c_n$ may be regarded as redundant and eliminated from further consideration.

[34] A tableau refers to the tabular arrangement used to effect the calculations. See [10] for further details on this or other technical terms used in this paper.

[35] A sufficient condition for the values of the dual variables w_i^* to remain unchanged when stipulations change is that no change in the optimum set of "basis vectors" occurs. Call this collection of basis vectors G and its inverse G^{-1}. Let $G^{-1}b = Y_0 \geq 0$ represent the optimum program achieved from the set b of initial stipulations. If b is replaced by a new set $\hat{b}$, the new program $G^{-1}\hat{b} = \hat{Y}_0$ may be readily generated. If $\hat{Y}_0 \geq 0$, then the new program is also optimal, and a fortiori the values w_i^*, achieved with b, will remain unaffected by the change from b to $\hat{b}$. See [10].

[36] E.g., by the modified simplex method of Charnes and Lemke [13] and the dual method of Lemke [25]. The dual method starts with a solution $\hat{Y}$, not necessarily non-negative but does arrange to have $w^* \geq 0$. With this start, the dual method continues to an optimum at

$$\hat{\hat{Y}}^* \geq 0, \hat{\hat{w}}^* \geq 0 .$$

This is precisely what is required when alterations in the initial $w_i^* \geq 0$ are to be considered. Machine codes (due to R. Graves, of Standard Oil Co., Indiana) are available, it may be noted, which combine the dual and modified simplex methods for use on electronic calculators.

[37] In the specific context of the warehousing problem under discussion, a pattern may be described as follows. Under the initial set of stipulations, purchases and sales will be undertaken at positive levels in some periods and at zero levels in others. This will form a "pattern" of non-zero values—these values occurring in the periods when transactions actually occur. This pattern will be regarded as constant under any variation in the stipulations only so long as none of the previously zero levels becomes positive. This characterization is, rigorously speaking, too strong (see n. 35). All that is really required (as a sufficient condition) is that no change in "basis" shall occur. This constant-pattern assumption may be regarded as an

To the basic warehousing model, (2), a financial constraint of the following simple form of (6) is now added:

$$\sum_{j=1}^{i} c_j x_j - \sum_{j=1}^{i-1} p_j y_j \leq \bar{M} \qquad (6a)$$

$$i = 1, 2, \ldots, n .$$

In this case all purchases are made in cash, and sales are made on an accrual basis with realization in cash one period later.

Figure 2 extends the schema of Figure 1 to incorporate these n additional "financial constraints." The two new triangles at the bottom contain the c_k and $-p_k$, respectively, drawn from (6a). Also new dual variables, v_k, $k = 1, 2, \ldots, n$ are inserted in the w column to facilitate formation of the dual constraints.

Defining new cumulative variables

$$V_k = \sum_{i=k}^{n} v_i \qquad (9)$$

$$W_k = 1 + V_k$$

in a fashion analogous to equation (7), the dual of this problem may be stated as

$$\min. E = (B - A) T_1 + A U_1 + \bar{M} V_1$$

subject to

$$T_k \geq U_{k+1} - c_k; W_k, T_{k-1} \geq T_k \geq 0 ,$$

$$U_r \geq T_r + p_r; W_{r+1}, U_{r-1} \geq U_r \geq 0 , \qquad (10)$$

$$W_{r-1} \geq W_r \geq 1 .$$

The values T_1^*, U_1^*, and W_1^* which these variables assume at an optimum then provide the desired (incremental) evaluators: T_1^* applies to $(B - A)$; U_1^*, to A; and V_1^*, to $\bar{M}$. In particular, V_1^* is the incremental (opportunity cost) cumulative, or compound, internal yield rate. It shows the net amount to which an additional dollar invested in the firm will accumulate if left to mature to the end of the planning horizon.

This relation of duality may be stated in economic as well as mathematical terms. Management can proceed by either of the following routes: either it can proceed directly to maximize profits subject to its capital (and physical) limitations or, alternatively, it can proceed to allocate its resources, including liquid resources, by a minimizing principle.

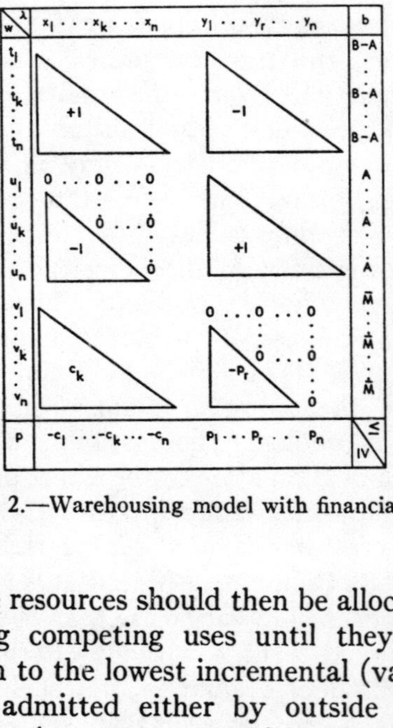

FIG. 2.—Warehousing model with financial constraint.

These resources should then be allocated among competing uses until they are driven to the lowest incremental (value) level admitted either by outside conditions (e.g., the market) or by nonnegativity—whichever holds first.

VI. A NUMERICAL ILLUSTRATION

The data of Table 1 can be used for a readily calculated example. The results are shown in Figure 3. Here the direct program variables are written in the body and their (numerical) optimizing values at the top. The purchase prices, c, and the selling prices, p, are shown at the bottom. By inserting the

extension or adaptation of the usual type of *ceteris paribus* assumptions.

numbers at the top for each x and y and the numbers at the bottom for each c and p, it is found that all constraints are satisfied either as equations or as the inequalities shown in the column which is second from the right-hand end. Also, the program profits, \$6,825, may be calculated as the difference between cash receipts and expenditures where the former are extended to include the collections at the end of period 5.[38] This "profit" includes the sale of the initial inventory but not the "cost" thereof, since this cost was presumably incurred prior to the planning interval and hence does not enter into optimizing decisions during the interval.[39]

TABLE 1

DATA FOR WAREHOUSING MODEL WITH SIMPLE FINANCIAL CONSTRAINT: ONE-PERIOD LAG

A = 100 = opening inventory } "Tons" or equivalent units
B = 125 = warehouse capacity }
M_0 = 1,000 = initial cash balance
$\underline{M}$ = 500 = minimum cash balance
n = 5 = number of "periods"

Period (j)	Unit Cost (c_j)	Unit Sales Price (p_j)
1.	25	20
2.	25	35
3.	25	30
4.	35	25
5.	45	50

It will be observed that the solution of the direct problem involves the purchase of 20 units in the first period—the maximum quantity permitted by the available funds ($M_0 - \underline{M}$) of \$500—and the sale in period 2 of these units plus the initial 100 units of opening inventory. The proceeds of this sale are realized in cash by period 3, and the funds generated are reinvested in 125 units of inventory in the period—the maximum permitted by the warehouse capacity. The inventory acquired in period 3 is then liquidated in period 5.

The values for the dual variables appear in the stub of Figure 3. The profit figure (and also optimality) may therefore be readily checked by reference to the dual theorem. Substitution in equation (10) yields

$$\begin{aligned} \min. E = E^* = (B - A)T_1^* + A\,U_1^* \\ + \bar{M}\,V^* = 25 \times 25 + 100 \times 60 \quad (11) \\ + 500 \times 2/5 = \$6{,}825\,, \end{aligned}$$

the same as $\pi^* = \max.\ \pi$ as required by the dual theorem.

The values $T_1^* = \$25$ and $U_1^* = \$60$ used above are, of course, simply the cumulants of the t^*'s and u^*'s shown in the stub of Figure 3. The value $T_1^* =$ \$25 asserts that a one-unit increment in net warehouse capacity $(B - A)$ will, if used optimally (i.e., by permitting the purchase of an additional unit of inventory in period 3), increase the total profit by \$25. An additional unit of initial inventory will provide an increment of $U_1^* - T_1^* = \$35$. That is, if a new direct problem is constructed with $\hat{A} =$ 101 in place of $A = 100$, the profit level will increase by \$35 to a new level of \$6,860, as may be readily verified.

These valuations hold, of course, only within prescribed limits. Thus, if the firm acquires more than 168 "tons" of warehouse capacity, a new value $T_1^* = 0$ will obtain. At this capacity level—or greater—the warehouse restriction would never be binding.[40] Moreover, a mini-

[38] Or beginning of period 6. The awkwardness arising from a fixed finite horizon will be dealt with in subsequent papers which are being prepared in collaboration with J. Dreze.

[39] Except when taxes (and like matters) are considered. It is then necessary to include specific rules—LIFO, FIFO, etc.—on inventory valuation.

[40] Excess capacity has, of course, a zero opportunity cost over the alternatives considered. If leasing out, or leasing in, were also included in the model, however, this value would change.

mum capacity of 120 "tons" is necessary to validate the result $T_1^* = \$25$, since reductions below this level would render the net storage capacity rather than the cash constraint binding in period 1.[41] In short, the evaluations $T_1^* = \$25$ and $U_1^* - T_1^* = \$35$ are valid only so long as the status of a previously critical constraint is not altered.[42]

Dual \ Direct	x: 20 0 125 0 0	y: 0 120 0 0 125	In-equality	Stipu-lation
$0 = t_1$	x_1	$-y_1$	< 25	
$0 = t_2$	$x_1 + x_2$	$-y_1 - y_2$	< 25	
$10 = t_3$	$x_1 + x_2 + x_3$	$-y_1 - y_2 - y_3$	$= 25$	$B - A$
$15 = t_4$	$x_1 + x_2 + x_3 + x_4$	$-y_1 - y_2 - y_3 - y_4$	$= 25$	
$0 = t_5$	$x_1 + x_2 + x_3 + x_4 + x_5$	$-y_1 - y_2 - y_3 - y_4 - y_5$	< 25	
$0 = u_1$		y_1	< 100	
$0 = u_2$	$-x_1$	$y_1 + y_2$	$= 100$	
$10 = u_3$	$-x_1 - x_2$	$y_1 + y_2 + y_3$	$= 100$	A
$0 = u_4$	$-x_1 - x_2 - x_3$	$y_1 + y_2 + y_3 + y_4$	< 100	
$50 = u_5$	$-x_1 - x_2 - x_3 - x_4$	$y_1 + y_2 + y_3 + y_4 + y_5$	$= 100$	
$0 = v_1$	c_1x_1		$= 500$	
$2/5 = v_2$	$c_1x_1 + c_2x_2$	$-p_1y_1$	$= 500$	
$0 = v_3$	$c_1x_1 + c_2x_2 + c_3x_3$	$-p_1y_1 - p_2y_2$	< 500	$\bar{M}$
$0 = v_4$	$c_1x_1 + c_2x_2 + c_3x_3 + c_4x_4$	$-p_1y_1 - p_2y_2 - p_3y_3$	< 500	
$0 = v_5$	$c_1x_1 + c_2x_2 + c_3x_3 + c_4x_4 + c_5x_5$	$-p_1y_1 - p_2y_2 - p_3y_3 - p_4y_4$	< 500	
Dual Values \ Direct Prices	−25 −25 −25 −35 −45 $-c$	20 35 30 25 50 p		

FIG. 3.—Variables and values for the illustration of Table 1

For the financial constraint, Figure 3 shows values of $V_1^* = 2/5$ or $W_1^* = 1 + V_1^* = 7/5$. The financial constraint is binding only in period 1. An extra dollar committed in period 1 would permit additional purchases in period 1 and hence additional sales in period 2. Thus each extra dollar would accrue to $\$35/\$25 = 7/5 = W_1^* = 1 + V_1^*$ by period 2.[43] Thereafter no further accumulation takes place, since physical capacity rather than cash is the effective constraint on purchases. If the financial constraint were binding in other periods as well as the first, then, by equation (9), new values v_j^* and $j \geq 3$ would be added to V_1^* which would reflect the possibility of further accruals realized not only from the initial cash but also from the profits realized from their (optimal) employment. In the present example, since all values subsequent to v_2^* are zero, $W_3^* = W_4^* = W_5^* = 1$, and no further accretion occurs.

VII. JOINT ANALYSIS OF FINANCIAL AND OTHER CONSTRAINTS

The internal yield rates V_j^* acquire added interest insofar as they can be used to assess alternative applications of funds—for example, as they can be used to evaluate alterations of other stip-

[41] Information of this character, rendered in schedular form, would present a "demand curve" for warehouse capacity, given the level of the other constraints (see [10]).

[42] See n. 35 above for a more exact statement.

[43] Just as the value $T_1^* = \$25$ remained valid for variations $120 \leq B \leq 168$ so the value $V_1^* = 2/5$ remains valid for variations $\underline{M} \leq M_0 \leq \$1,125$, or $0 \leq \bar{M} \leq \$625$.

ulations such as warehouse capacity. Consider, therefore, the desirability of altering $B = 125$ to $\hat{B} = 126$, with $\bar{M} =$ \$500. As previously noted, this would yield an increment to total profit of $T_1^* =$ \$25 by permitting a one-unit increase in the following transaction: Buy in period 3 at \$25 and sell in period 5 at \$50.

Of course, the cost of securing this additional unit of capacity must also be considered. Suppose this cost to be \$20 and suppose, furthermore, that the additional facility will be worth nothing at the end of the fifth period. The net return on the investment, $5/20 = 25$ per cent, is clearly not sufficient to justify a diversion of funds from the original allotment, since the cost of the cash diversion as measured by V_1^* is 2/5, or 40 per cent. Moreover, the investment in this added facility would not be warranted even if an extra \$20 could be secured at zero cost from external sources. Any increment $\Delta M_0 <$ \$125, in liquid funds, can be more profitably employed in effecting purchases at period 1 prices and selling them in period 2.

On the other hand, under the liquidity constraints assumed for the firm, the extra warehouse space might be worth acquiring provided "suitable" financing terms were offered by the builder. If, for example, the builder were willing to give terms of 50 per cent down and 50 per cent in period 3, then the cost of the diversion of funds would be only \$10 V_1^* + \$10 V_3^* = \$4, which is less than the \$5 net increment to profit which can be generated from the extra space. Thus, even at the same "interest rate" (here zero), the form of the financing arrangement enters significantly into the resource-allocating decisions when liquidity is to be considered as an appropriate part of the profit-maximizing machinery.

Other such "financial effects" (which can enter to modify standard propositions about rational patterns of profit maximization behavior) might be considered at this point. Suppose, for example, that a tax payment of \$1,100 is due in period 2 and that, in anticipation of this payment, the firm eliminates all other considerations of liquidity in this period. In particular, the requirement $\bar{M} =$ \$500 is replaced by $\bar{M} = -$\$100, the entire available cash resources being held in readiness for the payment. Under these conditions the constant pattern assumption cannot be maintained.[44] In particular, the firm is required to undertake "distress sales." At an optimum it must discontinue its "profitable" period 1 purchases and replace $x_1^* = 20$ by $\hat{x}_1^* = 0$. Also it will replace $y_1 = 0$ by $\hat{y}_1^* = 5$ and reduce $y_2 = 120$ to $\hat{y}_2^* = 95$, and leave the remaining transactions at their previous levels.[45]

The pattern variation encountered in this (tax) example also alters the dual evaluators. In particular, the value $v_2^* =$

[44] If this same tax were imposed and collected in period 1, a contradiction would appear. Under the stated conditions there is no way to generate the funds required. This can be interpreted as causing the firm "to go out of business." (The dual would then show either an infinite value or no solution. Because this aspect of the dual theorem is not really being examined in this paper, no further attention will be paid to it here.) Note, however, that, if the model were altered so that the firm might allow discounts for immediate (cash) payment by customers, it would then be able to continue operations. They way to incorporate such features in the model will be evident from subsequent discussion.

[45] That these alterations must occur is apparent from an examination of the second-period financial constraint: $c_1x_1 + c_2x_2 - p_1y_1 \leq -100$ or $y_1 = (100 + c_1x_1 + c_2x_2)/p_1$, which shows that any values $x_1, x_2 \geq 0$ force larger period 1 sales under any regime of positive prices. The minimum of such "loss sales" (in this example all reproduction costs are higher) occurs with $\hat{x}_1^* = \hat{x}_2^* = 0$ and $\hat{y}_1^* = 5$.

2/5 in changed to $\hat{v}_2^* = 3/4$. This alteration provides a measure of what may be called the "money cost" (incremental and compounded) of this tax. The same tax collected in other periods would have no such money cost. Thus the period 2 collection of $1,100 reduces the level of total profit from $6,825 to $5,550, so that the profit reduction exceeds the $1,100 tax by $175. Alternatively, a later collection period would allow this firm to reap an extra $175 of profit.[46]

Not only can the dual variables be used in this way to evaluate investment and financing opportunities but they can be made to yield most of the standard constructs of the theory of investment.

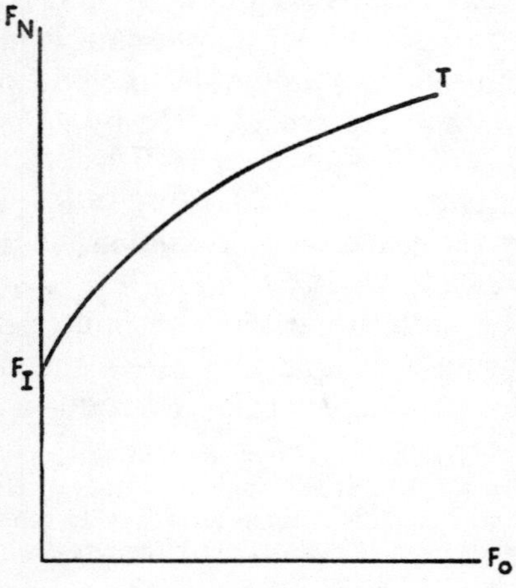

FIG. 4A

Consider, for example, the question: "What is the maximum cost at which another unit of warehouse capacity would be just worth acquiring out of opening funds?" This may be rephrased analytically as find the value β which satisfies

$$(1 + V_1^*)\,\beta \equiv W_1^*\beta = T_1^*. \qquad (12)$$

With $T_1^* = \$25$ and $W_1^* = 7/5$, the solution is $\beta = \$17\frac{6}{7}$ per unit. An analogous procedure may be used, of course, to find the maximum amount to pay for an additional unit of opening inventory. This value, $\hat{\beta}$, can readily be shown to be $25, since the values of W_1^*, U_1^*, and T_1^* in the expression $W_1^*\,\hat{\beta} = U_1^* - T_1^*$ are 7/5, $60, and $25, respectively. The values obtained for β and $\hat{\beta}$ can be interpreted as the "present value" of each kind of additions to the firm's physical assets, assuming their optimal employment over the planning interval. Alternatively, W_1^* can be interpreted as an (internal) "discount factor"—one

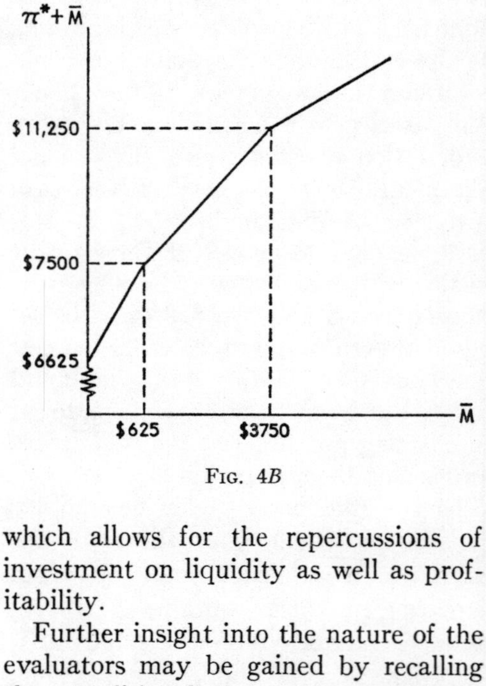

FIG. 4B

which allows for the repercussions of investment on liquidity as well as profitability.

Further insight into the nature of the evaluators may be gained by recalling that traditional theory represents the productive opportunities for funds by a function such as the one shown in Figure 4A. Here F_0 represents initial funds and F_n final funds, when opportunities are utilized to maximum advan-

[46] See n. 45, where a still earlier collection period would cause a contradiction in the problem as stated. Notice, also, that this raises a question of optimum collection periods, as well as amounts, as part of the problem of the tax-revenue policy. Questions can also evidently be raised about standard versions of shifting and incidence theory.

tage over the horizon.[47] For ease of comparison with the present case, this diagram has been modified to allow for the presence of initial inventory. This has a conversion value such that, even when $F_0 = \$0$ is invested, an accumulation ot $F_n = F_I$ will nevertheless occur via sale of inventory[48] on the most advantageous terms. Such a sale, of course, converts inventory first to receivables and then to cash which is thereafter available for reinvestment.

The range $0 - F_I$ in Figure 4*A* is perhaps best regarded as a discontinuity, or "jump," at $F_0 = \$0$, and the slope of T thereafter can be interpreted (in the usual fashion) as 1 plus the marginal rate of return on invested funds for $F_0 > \$0$. More precisely, it should be called the "marginal productive rate of return" (see [22]) in order to avoid possible confusion with what has come to be known as the "internal rate of return" in the literature of capital budgeting.[49]

The productive opportunity locus does not appear explicitly in the programming formulation. It is, however, implicit in the formulation and can be derived by parametric variations of the cash stipulation. Such a locus for the example of Figure 3 is given in Figure 4*B*. For this example, $F_0 = M_0 - \underline{M}$ and $F_N = \pi^* + \bar{M}$. The function consists of three linear segments. The first segment reflects the return when $F_0 = \$0$, so that the inventory conversion ultimately gives $\pi^* = \$6{,}625$. As positive allotments of liquid funds are made, the profits of the firm rise at a constant rate to the point B, where $M_0 - \underline{M} = \$625$. The slope of the curve in this section—i.e., one plus the marginal productive rate of return—is, of course, $W_1^* = 1 + V_1^* = 7/5$, which maintains over the range $0 < M_0 - \underline{M} < \$625$. From \$625 to \$3750, W_1^* has a value of 6/5. Beyond this range, liquid funds cease to be a binding constraint on production, and the marginal productive rate of return becomes zero.

VIII. EVALUATION OF THE INDIVIDUAL PERIOD CONSTRAINTS

There are additional analogues between the standard constructs of marginal productivity analysis and the lower-case variables t_k^*, u_k^*, and v_k^*. They are, however, of a rather looser sort—in part because of the lack of a standard dynamic version of the firm in economic theory and in part because of semantic problems. Logically, there is no trouble with the status of the dual variables in this or any other programming problem. The trouble, if any, arises only when an attempt is made to make these symbols correspond with real-world counterparts in existing economic institutions.

Consider, for example, the value $u_3^* = \$10$ in Figure 3. This is associated with variations of A, the "initial" inventory,

[47] For simplicity of exposition investment is here shown as increasing from left to right. This reverses the usual portrayal of the opportunity function. See, e.g., [22].

[48] Other assets may also be liquidated and the diagram adjusted further for these possibilities if desired.

[49] See, e.g., Dean [16] or Hill [21]. As noted earlier (n. 5 above), this concept has serious deficiencies as a means for making capital budgeting decisions. In particular, these internal rates do not always give correct rankings of investment opportunities even when liquidity considerations can be ignored. When liquidity considerations are present, ever more severe difficulties are encountered. The use of "present values" as a basis for ranking projects has been suggested as an alternative to "internal rates of return," at least when liquidity considerations are absent. But, as noted in [22], ambiguous results are possible even in this case—e.g., when borrowing and lending rates differ. Then the proper discount rate is not a given (independent of decisions) but, as is the case for W_1^*, is a variable whose value is to be ascertained as part of the problem. These remarks apply a fortiori when rationing or liquidity considerations are present.

in period 3. It is desired to study the consequences of varying only the value $A = 100$ in period 3 and only in the selling constraint. In particular, no comparable variation in the stipulation $(B - A)$ which applies to the third-period buying constraint will be admitted.

To interpret such a variation, it is necessary once more to consider the nature of this selling constraint. It states, essentially, that all sales must be made from inventory. Thus, if $A = 100$ is replaced by $\hat{A} = 99$ in the third period, the following adjustments occur to achieve a new optimum: $y_2^* = 120$ is replaced by $\hat{y}_2^* = 119$, and $x_3^* = 125$ is replaced by $\hat{x}_3^* = 124$. All other program values are unaffected. Tracing through the effect of the indicated adjustment, it is found that total profit is reduced by the indicated amount, $u_3^* = \$10$.

It might seem that the reduced purchases in period 3 would cause a reduction in the highly profitable period 5 sales. It must be remembered, however, that only a period 3 variation in "initial" inventory is being considered. All other values of A are held constant. In fact, the one-unit reduction in period 2 sales is effected precisely to avoid this contingency and to allow the more profitable period 5 sales to be executed at their previous (maximal) level.

The effect of varying A in a selling and not in the corresponding buying constraint is to "free" the associated purchases from the necessity of clearing through the warehouse. In subsequent periods, however, adjustments must be made, since the values of A in the selling constraint have their counterparts in the buying constraints as well. A study of the structure of Figure 3 will reveal that in certain circumstances this can cause the firm to sell "forward" by increasing some preceding value of y in order to "make room" for the subsequent purchases. That is, the sale is made, even though goods are not on hand, on condition that a subsequent purchase will also be made "to cover" the transaction.

The present example does not permit an easy illustration when A is varied upward; that is, any upward variation of A in the inventory constraint requires the computation of a new optimum program and thereby violates the constant-pattern assumption. For example, if $A = 100$ is replaced by $\hat{A} = 101$, the value $y_3^* = 0$ is replaced by $\hat{y}_3^* = 1$, and $x_3^* = 125$ is replaced by $\hat{x}_3^* = 126$.[50] Essentially, then, the firm is selling a unit purchased in the same period under these circumstances.

As an alternative method of illustrating the nature of the selling constraint and its evaluators, consider the possibility of altering A in two periods. Let $A = 100$ be changed to $\hat{A} = 101$ in periods 2 and 3. The firm will then utilize this across-period possibility by selling an additional unit at \$35 in period 2 and buying an additional unit in period 3 at \$25, for a total incremental gain of $u_3^* = \$10$.

A similar across-period approach helps to clarify the interpretation of the variables t^* as they apply to net warehouse capacity. Here the variation is on B while A is held constant. An additional unit of warehouse space in period 4, which is available until sales are effected in period 5, is worth $t_4^* = \$15$, since it would make possible a purchase in period

[50] Also $u^* = 10$ and $u_2^* = 0$ are replaced, respectively, by $\hat{u}_3 = 5$ and $\hat{u}_2 = 5$, while $v_2^* = 2/5$ and all other $v^* = 0$ is replaced by $v_2^* = 1/5$ and $v_1^* = 1/5$. The cumulants $U_1^* = 60$ and $V_1^* = 2/5$ are not affected, but their constituent elements (the items now being examined) are. This variation also illustrates why the constant-pattern assumption is too strong with respect to the upper-case dual evaluators.

4 at \$35 for sale in period 5 at \$50. If available one period earlier, the space gains an additional value $t_3 = \$10$, since the extra purchase can be made at period 3 prices, which are \$10 less than those of period 4.[51]

In this interpretation the values t_j^* measure the added profit which can be secured by having extra capacity available one period earlier than $j + 1$. These values are, so to speak, the "time derivatives" of the profit stream relative to the available capacity. They can be thought of (in value terms) as the marginal product of "not waiting"—along lines made familiar by the Austrian concepts of "waiting" and "periods of production." The parallel can perhaps be drawn a bit stronger by thinking in terms of a construction program. With $n = 5$, the enlargement is worthless if it first materializes in this period. Accelerating the program by one period—say, at premium or bonus rates—would be worth up to $t_4^* = \$15$. If the date when additional space is available can be moved up to period 3, it is worth $T_3^* = t_3^* + t_4^* + t_5^* = \$25$. Availability in still earlier periods adds nothing further, since cash rather than capacity is the effective constraint for this business in periods 1 and 2. The marginal cost of "not waiting" would therefore be the extra construction cost incurred adjusted for the marginal cost of funds, as measured by the relevant W^*'s or V^*'s.

Tracing through the v_j^*'s is somewhat more involved, so that their further analysis is best reserved for later sections. The following general characterization will, for the moment, suffice. From the earlier discussion of W_1^* as a "discount factor" it is clear that W_1^* can be expressed as

$$W_k^* = (1 + r_k)(1 + r_{k+1}) \ldots \times (1 + r_{n-1})(1 + r_n), \quad (13)$$

where r_k is the marginal productive rate of return (optimum incremental yield rate) for period k. From equation (13) and the definition of W^* it also follows that

$$\frac{W_k^*}{W_{k+1}^*} = 1 + r_k. \quad (13a)$$

But $v_k^* = r_k W_{k+1}^*$ and $V_k^* \equiv W_k^* - 1$, so that

$$v_k^* = r_k W_{k+1}^* = r_k(1 + V_{k+1}^*). \quad (14)$$

The lower-case evaluator, v_k^*, is therefore the product of two terms: (i) the marginal productive rate of return on funds for that period and (ii) the further accumulation made possible by their continued reinvestment in subsequent periods. With the precaution that W_{k+1}^* and V_{k+1}^*, like v_k^* itself, are constant only for a certain range of funds, it may be said that v_k^* represents the compound rate of accumulation of an additional dollar invested in that period and maintained in the business up to the horizon.

IX. EVALUATING TRADE CREDIT AS A SOURCE OF FUNDS

A simple extension of the previous model makes it possible to examine the effects of trade credit. Figure 5 presents the essential features when suppliers are willing to extend credit to the firm with a one-period lag. The schema simply extends that of Figure 2, with a new column of triangles (on the left) and new variables $x_1', x_2', \ldots, x_n'$ and costs $-c_1', -c_2', \ldots, -c_n'$ associated with these opportunities.

Such credit opportunities may involve

[51] It is possible also to think of the firm's capacity as deteriorating over time and, by cumulating in reverse, to interpret the t^*'s as maintenance evaluators. This topic will be dealt with in later papers.

penalties (such as loss of discounts) as compared with prompt payment, so that, in general, $c'_j \geq c_j$. The purpose of the present discussion is, however, to illustrate how the dual evaluators may be brought into play even when such premiums are absent. By assuming, therefore, that $c'_j = c_j$, for $j = 1, 2, \ldots, n$, it will be possible (i) to simplify the discussion and (ii) continue with the data of Table 1 for the remainder of this section.

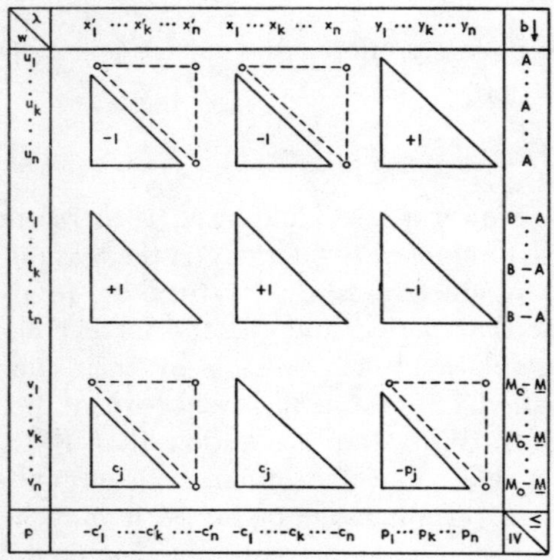

FIG. 5.—Schema for trade credit

Table 2 shows an optimum program returning (accrued) profits of $7,450 = $14,200 − $6,750, as may be calculated from the details shown under the heading "Income and Expense." In addition to physical details shown to the left of the "Income and Expense" columns, certain elements of "Financial Position" are shown on its right in order to facilitate tracing the cash and credit positions. Finally, the values for the dual evaluators are shown in the last three columns.

New values are now secured for T_1^* and U_1^*, but V_1^* remains at the same level as in Figure 2. Cash position remains binding in period 1. Extension

TABLE 2

DIRECT AND DUAL OPTIMUM FOR TRADE CREDIT MODEL
(Data from Table 1 and Details from Fig. 4)

Period	Price ($/Ton)		Purchases (Tons)		Sales (Tons)	Income and Expense ($)		Financial Position (Close of [$] Period)			Dual Variables ($/Unit)		
								Cash	Credit Position				
	p_j	c_j	Credit x'_j	Cash x_j	y_j	Expenditures	Receipts	Cash on Hand	Accounts Receivable	Accounts Payable*	t_k	u_k	v_k
1	20	25	...	20	...	500	.....	500	.....	.....	.	.	.
2	35	25	125	...	120	3,125	4,200	500	4,200	3,125	5	10	2/5
3	30	25	82	43	125	3,125	3,750	500	3,750	2,050	10	5	...
4	25	35	...	...	...	.....	.....	2,200	.....	.....	15	.	...
5	50	45	...	...	125	.....	6,250	2,200	6,250	.....	0	50	...
Total	..	..	207	63	370	6,750	14,200	8,450	.....	.....	$T_1 = 30$	$U_1 = 65$	$V_1 = 2/5$

* Exclusive of any accounts outstanding for the initial inventory.

of trade credit provides no assistance in this period, since sales are not effected until period 2 and cash is not realized until period 3. Starting in period 2, however, the opportunities provided by trade credit become apparent, and new purchases and sales are executed which could not previously be utilized.

The difference in program profits between Figure 2 and Table 2 indicates that it would have been worth the firm's while to have paid up to $625 for these credit facilities. This is justified, however, only if such payment can be withheld until the close of business. Suppose, however, that it cannot. The cumulative marginal yield on funds, $V_1^* = 2/5$, must then be considered. An easy application of preceding concepts then gives

$$CW_1^* = \Delta\pi = \$625 \,, \qquad (15)$$

or $C = \$446.43$ as the present cash equivalent of such a final period payment.

Of course, it is not customary to pay for this kind of credit directly. The funds may, if desired, be thought of rather as a "deposit" left with suppliers or (following the more usual custom) as an additional working-capital requirement imposed on the firm as a condition precedent to receiving such credit extensions. In either case, the issue is one of accounting for the "cost"—$178.57 = $625 − $446.43—of this further restriction.

Suppose, therefore, that an additional $446.43 of the firm's funds is impounded by one device or the other and consider once more the program of Table 2. This new stipulation requires the firm to contract its period 1 purchases by 17.857 units, thus reducing its period 2 profit accrual (and total net realization) by the indicated $178.57. This, therefore, is the cost of such a reservation of funds. The "capital equivalent" of trade credit extended at the beginning of business is therefore $446.43, which accumulates to $625 by the end.

X. BORROWING AND LENDING MODELS

It is possible to extend these imputation procedures in a variety of ways. Distributed lags on payments to vendors can be introduced to evaluate these opportunities, and distributed lags on receivables, if inserted, can be used to impute their carrying cost. Evaluation of "stretching" and like phenomena can thereby be encompassed in the analysis.

By means of the devices indicated in [5], it is possible to encompass multiple commodity considerations and varying prices as well. Some interest attaches, of course, to such extensions from the point of view both of realism and of theoretical clarification. In the interests of brevity, however, these extensions will be avoided. Attention will be directed, instead to opportunities associated with borrowing and lending so as to place the examples of this paper in better perspective against standard applications of capital and interest theory.

Suppose the firm has unlimited power to borrow and lend at constant (and equal) rates of interest. This approximates the assumption of perfect capital markets and makes it possible to restrict attention to a single type of security.[52] Specifically, it will be assumed that the firm can make contracts to borrow or lend at given interest rates for a term equal to the time remaining up to the horizon. With principal and interest thus assumed repayable only at the end of the planning period, it is possible to simplify matters. Interest and income (on lending) can then be handled in the

[52] See [27].

functional without introducing additional constraints.[53]

For this purpose let the new variables

$$\begin{aligned} m_j &= \text{amount to be borrowed in period } j = 1, 2, \ldots, n\,, \\ n_j &= \text{amount to be lent in period } j = 1, 2, \ldots, n\,, \end{aligned} \qquad (16)$$

be introduced into the problem in order that the amounts to be borrowed and loaned can be simultaneously ascertained with the program of purchases and sales. Then the terms

$$-\sum_{j=1}^{n} m_j\,[\,(1+d_j)^{n+1-j}-1\,] + \sum_{j=1}^{n} n_j\,[\,(1+d_j)^{n+1-j}-1\,]\,, \qquad (17)$$

where d_j = the given rate of interest prevailing in period j, can be adjoined to the functional of the direct problem—see equation (2a)—in order to allow for the interest cost and income associated with borrowing the amounts m_j and lending the amounts n_j.[54] Since financial position is also affected, it is necessary to replace equation (8) by the following expressions:

$$\sum_{j=1}^{i} c_j x_j - \sum_{j=1}^{i-1} p_j y_j - \sum_{j=1}^{i} m_j + \sum_{j=1}^{i} n_j \le \bar{M}\,. \qquad (18)$$

The assumption that all loans and borrowings are repaid only at the end of period n makes it unnecessary to insert the accumulation factors used in (17). It is unnecessary, also, to introduce new constraints.

Figure 6 presents the schema. The data of Table 1 will continue to serve for illustration, when supplemented by the data of Table 3. These numbers have been chosen with $e_j \cong 1/16$ to approximate a constant interest rate of $6\frac{2}{3}$ per cent.

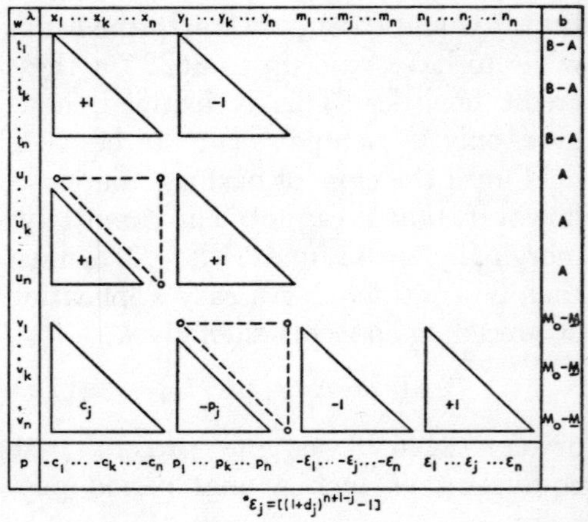

FIG. 6.—Schema for borrowing and lending

TABLE 3

$(1+e_1)^5-1=1/3$
$(1+e_2)^4-1=1/4$
$(1+e_3)^3-1=1/5$
$(1+e_4)^2-1=1/8$
$(1+e_5)\;-1=1/16$

Inserting these values and the information contained in Table 1, the optimum program is derived in Table 4. Net operating income[55] has now risen to $7,500 compared with the $6,825 total profit under the conditions of Figure 3. However, the borrowing necessary to

[53] Under the assumption of unlimited borrowing and lending nothing important appears to be lost by this approach. The interest drain (per period) would then simply lead the firm to borrow compensating amounts without affecting the dual evaluators. Of course, when capital is rationed, this proposition is no longer valid.

[54] Under these assumptions an equivalent functional could, of course, be defined in terms of "discounted" profits. It is simpler, however, to state the analysis in the same form as in preceding cases. It will then be seen that the V^*'s are directly related to the external (borrowing and lending) rates under the indicated assumptions..

[5] See n. 39 above.

finance this higher level of operations entails an interest expense of, approximately, \$822.92, which is, in part, recouped by lending to return \$718.75. When the net interest charges of \$104.17 are deducted, the level of total profits becomes \$7,395.83 for an increment of \$570.83 compared to the case (Fig. 3) when these opportunities were absent.

From a theoretical standpoint the important fact about the assumption of umlimited borrowing and lending power is that it effectively eliminates the cash constraint and therefore transfers the entire effect of financial considerations to the functional. On this assumption the purchases and sales are determined entirely by the pattern of prices, the interest rate, and the technological constraints.[56]

The matter may also be stated in another way which leads directly to an interpretation of the dual evaluators v_k^*. Having another dollar available in any period would simply lead the firm either to reduce its scheduled borrowing or to increase its scheduled lending.[57] This may be validated by scrutinizing the values V_k^* as $k = 1, 2, \ldots, 5$ in succession. Reading from Table 4, it is found that $V_1^* = 1/3$ the same as $(1 + e_1)^5 - 1$ in Table 3. Also $V_2^* = 1/4$, the same as $(1 + e_2)^4 - 1$, and so on. In short, the V_k^*'s now correspond to the market earning and borrowing rates in successive periods. Hence any such value, V_k^*, corresponds to the compound accumulated earnings (or savings) possible from having an extra dollar available in period k and continuing this investment, plus the earnings thereon in the business of buying, selling, lending, and borrowing.

TABLE 4

OPTIMUM PROGRAM: BORROWING AND LENDING

			DIRECT PROBLEM					DUAL PROBLEM		
			Purchases (Tons)	Sales (Tons)	Borrowing ($)	Lending ($)	Cumulative Net Borrowing ($)			
PERIOD	c_j	p_j	x_j	y_j	m_j	n_j		t_k	u_k	v_k
1.......	25	20	25	0	125	0	125	26/3	0	1/12
2.......	25	35	125	125	3,125	0	3,250	5/2	43/4	1/20
3.......	25	30	125	125	0	1,250	2,000	75/8	15/4	3/40
4.......	35	25	0	0	0	3,750	−1,750	85/8	0	1/16
5.......	45	50	0	125	0	0	−1,750	0	50	1/16
Total	..	..	...	...	.....	.....	....	31 1/6	64 1/2	1/3

By equations (11) and (14) it follows that

$$v_k^* = V_k^* - V_{k+1}^* = r_k W_{k+1}^* , \quad (19)$$

where (in this case) r_k is the market rate of interest. Translating the present example into analytic terms,

$$v_j^* = [(1+r)^{n+1-j} - 1] - [(1+r)^{n-j} - 1] = r(1+r)^{n-j} . \quad (20)$$

Thus $v_1^* = V_1^* - V_2^* = 1/3 - 1/4 = 1/12$ represents, in this case, the *earnings*

[56] It is perhaps worthwhile to stress again that this disappearance of financial considerations is a consequence of the assumption of perfect capital markets. Whenever capital rationing is effectively present, the cash-flow consequences of financing arrangements will have an influence on production (and investment) decisions.

[57] It follows from this that parametric programming over values of $(M_0 - \underline{M})$ will not lead to a tracing-out of the productive opportunity locus such as that of Figure 4*B*. Instead, given any vector of interest rates, we obtain only one "point" on that function, namely, the point at which the marginal productive rates of return of each period are equal to the interest rates of the periods. The entire function, if there were any use for it, could be generated by dropping the borrowing and lending vectors and repeating the procedure used to obtain Figure 4*B*.

on the earnings at the constant market rate, r, after the loan is liquidated at the end of the period.

These borrowing and lending contracts at constant market rates of interest can be used for still further clarification. Consider, for example, the evaluators T_k^* and t_k^*. The value of T_1^* has risen from \$25 per unit (Fig. 3) to \$31 1/6 per unit (Table 4).[58] Also, $t_k^* > 0$ in all periods save the last, where the selling constraint effectively eliminates the value of this facility. Hence the introduction of these borrowing and lending opportunities not only increases the value of this facility but also tends to even out the value fluctuations across the periods.

It may be noted that, although the value of T_1^* in Table 4 exceeds its correspond in Figure 3, this is not true for all T_k^*. Thus $T_4^* = \$85/8$ is less than its corresponding level, \$15, in Figure 3. This reduction occurs because using this facility in period 4 for a period 5 sale now adjusts for a non-zero accumulated interest cost. That is, the correct cost calculation is

$$p_5 - c_4(1+r)^2 = \$50 - \frac{\$35 \times 9}{8}$$
$$= \frac{\$400 - \$315}{8} = \frac{\$85}{8}.$$

Although an extra unit of warehouse capacity which is available for the last two periods still permits a \$15 increment to profit, it is necessary also to consider the accumulated interest cost associated with this transaction. The correct evaluation is therefore automatically supplied by T_4^* in Table 4, and like remarks apply to the remaining values T_k^*. It should occasion no surprise, therefore, that all values save T_1^* are reduced in passing from Figure 3 to Table 4.[59]

It is interesting also to trace through the effects on the values t_k^* and to do so in a manner which is different from the one used in Section VI. Consider, therefore, the formula

$$t_1^* = p_2(1+z)^3 - c_1(1+z)^5. \quad (21)$$

It is desired now to find that rate of interest; z, which would lead the firm to abandon the period 1 purchase and the period 2 sale. When this occurs, the "slack" associated with the first buying constraint will be in the "basis," and the value $t_1^* = 26/3$ will be replaced by $\hat{t}_1^* = 0$. It therefore follows that

$$z = 2\sqrt{\frac{p_2}{c_1}} - 1, \quad (22)$$

or $z = 28$ per cent[60] is this rate. Corresponding critical levels may be established for the other values t_k^*.

XI. SOME POSSIBLE FURTHER EXTENSIONS

The preceding examples are only selected (simple) illustrations of ways in which the incremental (opportunity cost)[61] yield factors made available from

[58] In order to ascertain the corresponding present value see equation (12).

[59] The matter may be summarized by saying that loosening the financial constraints sets up two opposing forces relative to this capacity. Easing of the restrictions on borrowing makes the facility more productive. Easing of the restrictions on lending raises the opportunity cost of the co-operating resources and thus tends to lower its net marginal productivity.

[60] More exactly, $(28 + \eta)$ per cent, $\eta > 0$.

[61] Any use of interest for judging investment opportunities is, of course, an opportunity cost valuation. Usually, but not necessarily (cf. [23], chap. xvii), it is a "money cost." That is, it is a measure of the income which must be foregone by absorbing otherwise available funds in the proposed alternative. The principle of opportunity cost (strictly interpreted) therefore requires that these yields be calculated incrementally and at the highest rates which can be secured from possible alternatives. This is true whether formulas based on the simpler $(1+r)^n$ or the more general

$$\prod_{j=1}^{n}(1+r_j) = (1+r_1) \times (1+r_2)\ldots(1+r\ )$$

are used.

the dual can be used. The model can be extended to embrace multiple commodities and facilities, inside and outside investment opportunities at various rates (along with conditional lending),[62] and other standard features of financial analysis.[63] Moreover, as already noted, there is no reason why such financial constraints cannot be incorporated in any linear programming problem. Finally, the activity analysis constructs of Koopmans [24] have been shown to be capable of reformulation (and complete solution) by means of linear programming,[64] so that, at least in principle, these constructs can be extended to economy-wide models for exploring, say, funds and income flows between various economic sectors, networks of transactions between banks and business firms (along with "terms of trade"), etc.

Exactly how (or whether) these possibilities can be used depends, of course, on the nature of the problem confronted. But it should be noted that most problems may be formulated in a variety of ways. In this paper the strategy has centered largely on evaluations within limited realms of variations,[65] but this is not the only possible approach. It is possible, for example, to commence instead with a given asset mixture simply as a preliminary to studying other possibilities. The additional data generated by the calculations can then be used to examine proposed changes in asset mix and volume without requiring that the calculations be initiated anew for each such proposed mixture. Indeed, if desired, the problem may be parameterized, and a sequence of tableaus can then be generated by allowing the parameters—A, B, etc.—to vary according to prescribed rules.[66] This will provide the corresponding optimal program for each range of parameter variations. It will also supply the dual evaluators. Thus, by relatively simple comparisons for the cost of each such asset mix, it should be possible to secure a basis for choice.

The use of a limited and fixed horizon (apparent throughout the models studied) appears to be a defect which these programming approaches share with alternatives that have been suggested. But, on further analysis,[67] it turns out that mathematical methods may also be brought to bear on this problem in ways which provide optimal rules for fixing horizon and subhorizon dates by reference to the available parameters.

The size of the problems that may be encountered in actual applications also needs to be considered. The possible use of model types (and approximations thereto) has already been suggested as one possible way of pushing back these boundaries. Supplemented by electronic computer aids (now available), these boundaries may be pushed back even further, especially as special codes (now in process of preparation by commerical computer firms) become available.

It must be remembered, too, that computer designs are in rapid evolution. Moreover, properly oriented business research can (at least conceivably) help to accelerate this evolution in particular

[62] E.g., working capital, dividends, and reduced opportunities for further borrowing (or credit).

[63] Including tax considerations, obsolescence phenomena, etc.

[64] See [6].

[65] E.g., on the "constant pattern" assumption.

[66] Cf. [18] for a method which covers all possible mixes. Usually, however, only "efficient-point programs" will be of interest. The parameterization methods described in [6] may then be used to restrict examinations to this subset of possibilities.

[67] These results are being readied for release in a research report being prepared in collaboration with J. Dreze.

directions. For example, it may be possible to design a "financial module" (analogue or digital) as part of a sequence of "moludes"[68] in a larger machine. A summary presentation is given in the Appendix to illustrate how such research might proceed by reference (only) to the relatively simple cases covered in this paper.

APPENDIX

One approach would be to separate the business into two interrelated parts, according to whether funds flows or physical flows are being viewed for transaction analysis purposes. To commence the desired analytical decomposition, let

$$\begin{aligned} \mathcal{C}_j &= c_j x_j \\ \mathcal{P}_j &= p_j y_j \, . \end{aligned} \tag{23}$$

Then the model of, say, Figure 2 becomes

$$\max. - \sum_{j=1}^{n} \mathcal{C}_j + \sum_{j=1}^{n} \mathcal{P}_j$$

subject to

$$\begin{aligned} &\sum_{j=1}^{i} x_j - \sum_{j=1}^{i} y_j && \leq B - A \\ &\qquad \sum_{j=1}^{i} \mathcal{C}_j - \sum_{j=1}^{i-1} \mathcal{P}_j && \leq \bar{M} \\ &- \sum_{j=1}^{i-1} x_j + \sum_{j=1}^{i} y_j && \leq A \\ &- c_j x_j \quad + \mathcal{C}_j && = 0 \\ &\qquad - p_j y_j \quad - \mathcal{P}_j && = 0 \end{aligned} \tag{24}$$

with $i, j = 1, 2, \ldots, n$.

The diagram of Figure 7 may be compared with Figure 2 to see what resulted from this transformation. The first pair of triangles in Figure 7 represent physical transactions into and out of the warehouse. The next pair represent transactions into and out of the firm's net cash balance. The third pair of triangles are also physical and appear directly under the first pair because of inventory interrelations.

The diagonals directly below the triangles now provide the rest of this "double-entry" system. $\mathcal{C}_j$, for any j, brings the firm closer to its cash limit, but, at an exchange of $-c_j$ per unit, it creates x_j which (i) relaxes the sales constraint (third pair of triangles) and (ii) tightens storage (first pair of triangles). Conversely, any y_j relaxes the constraints (starting on the diagonal) for the first pair of triangles, tightens those for the third pair, and, at the rate p_r, relaxes the cash condition one period later. In short, $-c_j$ and p_r are the rates at which cash is converted to goods, while $-1/c_j$ and $1/p_r$ are the rates at which goods are converted to cash in any transactions between the business, which is thus sectorized. Thus the echelons, at the bottom of Figure 7, serve to relate the two parts of the business (physical and funds) at the indicated exchange rates.

It is now desired to carry these transformations one stage further in order to secure a network analogue. Consider, therefore, the period 1 transactions. All sales must be made from inventory and all purchases from initial cash. Therefore, let

$$\begin{aligned} g_1 &= A - y_1 = \text{goods on hand after sale}\,, \\ \mathcal{R}_1 &= \bar{M} - c_1 x_1 = \text{cash available after purchase}\,. \end{aligned} \tag{25a}$$

Next define

$$\begin{aligned} h_1 &= g_1 + x_1 = \text{goods available for second-period sales}\,, \\ \mathcal{F}_2 &= \mathcal{R}_1 + p_1 y_1 = \text{funds available for second-period purchases}\,, \end{aligned} \tag{25b}$$

so that

$$g_2 = h_1 - y_2 \, . \tag{25c}$$

As is also readily seen, non-negativity is retained along with $h_1 \leq B$.

Continuing in this manner, the following equations emerge:

$$\begin{aligned} h_j &= x_j + g_j \\ \mathcal{F}_j &= c_j x_j + \mathcal{R}_j \end{aligned} \tag{26a}$$

[68] This term is borrowed from the field of electronic computer design. A modular design may be thought of as a sequence of submachines (modular units) co-ordinated into one larger unit where each of the modules is designed to handle particular problems with specialized efficiency.

and, also,

$$\mathcal{F}_{j+1} = p_j y_j + \mathcal{R}_j$$
$$h_{j-1} = y_j + g_j\ , \qquad (26b)$$

with all variables constrained to be nonnegative and $h_j \leq B, j = 1, 2, \ldots, n$.

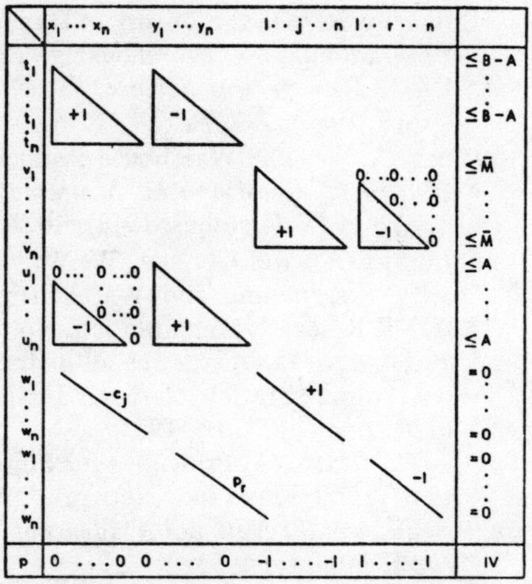

FIG. 7.—Model of Figure 2 separated into physical and funds flows.

With these transformations the functional becomes

$$\sum_{j=1}^{n} (\mathcal{F}_{j+1} - \mathcal{R}_j) - \bar{M} + \mathcal{R}_1$$
$$- \sum_{j=2}^{n} (\mathcal{F}_j - \mathcal{R}_j) = \mathcal{F}_{n+1} - \bar{M}\ . \qquad (27a)$$

The storage constraints are reduced to

$$\sum_{j=1}^{i} (h_j - g_j) - A + g_1$$
$$- \sum_{j=2}^{i} (h_{j-1} - g_j) \leq B - A\ , \qquad (27b)$$

or

$$h_i \leq B$$

for $i = 1, 2, \ldots, n$. The sales constraints, in turn, become

$$- \sum_{j=1}^{i-1} (h_j - g_j) + A - g_1$$
$$+ \sum_{j=2}^{i} (h_{j-1} - g_j) \leq A\ , \qquad (27c)$$

or, simply, $g_i \geq 0$. The financial constraints are similarly reduced to

$$\bar{M} - \mathcal{R}_1 + \sum_{j=2}^{i} (\mathcal{F}_j - \mathcal{R}_j)$$
$$- \sum_{j=1}^{i-1} (\mathcal{F}_{j+1} - \mathcal{R}_j) \leq \bar{M}\ , \qquad (27d)$$

or $\mathcal{R}_i \geq 0$.

Hence the originally stated problem is replaced by

$$\max.\ \mathcal{F}_{n+1}$$

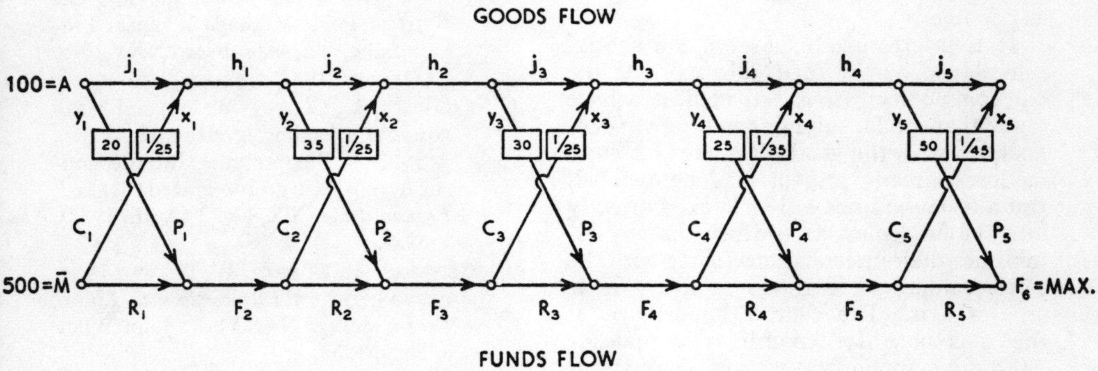

FIG. 8.—Warehouse—funds-flow network

NOTE: All values $h \leq B$, the gross warehouse capacity.

SOURCE: A. Charnes and W. W. Cooper, "The Use of Model Types in Some OR Applications to Business Planning" (two lectures in a series sponsored and published by the University of Michigan Seminar on Operations Research, October, 1957).

subject to

$$h_i \leq B \ ,$$

with

$$\begin{aligned} x_i + g_i - h_i &= 0 \\ c_i x_i + \mathcal{R}_i - \mathcal{F}_i &= 0 \\ p_i y_i + \mathcal{R}_i - \mathcal{F}_{i+1} &= 0 \\ y_i + g_i - h_{i-1} &= 0 \end{aligned} \qquad (28)$$

and

$$\begin{aligned} y_1 + g_1 &= A \\ c_1 x_1 + \mathcal{R}_1 &= \bar{M} \ , \end{aligned}$$

where $h_i, g_i, x_i, y_i, \mathcal{F}_i, \mathcal{R}_i \geq 0$, $i = 1, 2, \ldots, n$.

These transformations convert Figure 7 into Figure 8, which may be viewed as a directed graph, as shown by the arrows. There is a goods-flow and a funds-flow axis, each oriented in the same direction and connected as shown.

Alternatively, this figure may be viewed as a capacitated[69] network. The sources (e.g., of electrical current) are the initial inventory and (net) cash balance. The currents along these two similarly oriented branches are connected by the arrows moving across the diagram with the boxes containing current amplifiers and deamplifiers. The value at the final sink, distinguished as $\mathcal{F}_6$, is to be made a maximum. That is, values y and x, from and to the goods flow, or values $\mathcal{C}$ and $\mathcal{P}$, from and to the funds flow, are to be determined so that the current flowing into $\mathcal{F}_6$ will be as great as possible.

It is interesting to observe the central role played by the funds-flow axis. As the one commodity case is extended, it will be found that (under suitable conditions) direct hookups with the goods-flow axes for commodities already present may be avoided. But all commodities will be hooked directly into the funds-flow axis, which thereby establishes their interrelations (along with the corresponding yield rates) at every node on this axis. The central importance of this axis both for co-ordination and for alternative (opportunity) cost evaluations is thus brought out in a clear and striking manner. It is conjectured that these (funds-flow) connections will be found in any model type for which incremental yield evaluations are required for financial planning purposes.

[69] Because of the condition $h \leq B$ noted at the bottom of Fig. 8.

BIBLIOGRAPHY

[1] BELLMAN, R. "On the Theory of Dynamic Programming—a Warehousing Problem," *Management Science*, II, No. 3 (April, 1956), 272–75.

[2] CAHN, A. S. "The Warehouse Problem," *Bulletin of the American Mathematical Society*, LIV (October, 1948), 1073–80.

[3] CHARNES, A., and COOPER, W. W. "Duality, Regrouping and Warehousing." (ONR Research Memorandum No. 19.) Pittsburgh: Graduate School of Industrial Administration, Carnegie Institute of Technology, June, 1954.

[4] ———. "Extremal Principles for Simulation Traffic Flows in a Network," *Proceedings of the National Academy of Sciences*, January, 1958.

[5] ———. "Generalizations of the Warehousing Model," *Operational Research Quarterly*, IV (December, 1955), 131–72.

[6] ———. "Management Models and Industrial Applications of Linear Programming," *Management Science*, IV, No. 2 (October, 1957), 38–91.

[7] ———. "Non-linear Network Flows and Convex Programming over Incidence Matrices," *Logistics Research Quarterly*, V, No. 2 (June, 1958).

[8] ———. "Nonlinear Power of Adjacent Extreme Point Methods in Linear Programming," *Econometrica*, XXV, No. 1 (January, 1957), 132–53.

[9] CHARNES, A., COOPER, W. W., and MELLON, B. "Blending Aviation Gasolines: A Study in Programming Interdependent Activities in an Integrated Oil Co.," *Econometrica*, XX, No. 2 (April, 1952), 135–59.

[10] CHARNES, A., COOPER, W. W., and HENDERSON, A. *An Introduction to Linear Programming*. New York: John Wiley & Sons, 1953.

[11] CHARNES, A., COOPER, W. W., and SYMONDS, G. H. "Cost Horizons and Certainty Equivalents: An Approach to Stochastic Programming of Heating

Oil," *Management Science*, IV, No. 3 (April, 1958), 235–63.

[12] CHARNES, A., COOPER, W. W., and MILLER, M. "Dyadic Programs and Subdual Methods." Lafayette: Purdue University Research Project for Methodological Aspects of Management Science, 1957.

[13] CHARNES, A., and LEMKE, C. E. "A Modified Simplex Method for Control of Round-Off Error in Linear Programming," *Proceedings, Association for Computing Machinery, Pittsburgh Meeting, May, 1952.*

[14] COOPER, W. W. "Research on the Business Firm—Discussion," *American Economic Review, Papers and Proceedings of the 67th Annual Meeting*, XLV, No. 2 (May, 1955), 559–64.

[15] ———. "Revisions to the Theory of the Firm," *American Economic Review*, XXXIX, No. 6 (December, 1949), 1204–22.

[16] DEAN, JOEL. *Capital Budgeting*. New York: Columbia University Press, 1951.

[17] DORFMAN, R., SAMUELSON, PAUL A., and SOLOW, R. M. *Linear Programming and Economic Analysis*. New York: McGraw-Hill Book Co., 1958.

[18] GASS, S. I., and SAATY, T. L. "The Computational Algorithm for the Parametric Objective Function," *Logistics Research Quarterly*, II, Nos. 1 and 2 (March and June, 1955), 39–45.

[19] GARVIN, W. W., CRANDELL, H. W., JOHN, J. B., and SKELLMAN, R. A. "Applications of Linear Programming in the Oil Industry," *Management Science*, III, No. 4 (July, 1957), 407–30.

[20] HART, A. G. *Anticipations, Uncertainty, and Dynamic Planning*. ("Studies in Business Administration," Vol. XI, No. 1.) Chicago: University of Chicago Press, 1940.

[21] HILL, HORACE, G., JR. *A New Method for Computing the Rate of Return on Capital Expenditure*. Berwyn, Pa.: Horace G. Hill, 1953.

[22] HIRSHLEIFER, JACK. "On the Theory of Optimal Investment Decision," *Journal of Political Economy*, LXVI, No. 4 (June, 1958), 329–52.

[23] KEYNES, J. M. *The General Theory of Employment, Interest and Money*. New York: Harcourt, Brace & Co., 1939.

[24] KOOPMANS, T. C. (ed.). *Activity Analysis of Production and Allocation*. (Cowles Commission for Research in Economics, Monograph No. 13.) New York: John Wiley & Sons, 1951.

(1) DANTZIG, G. B. "Maximization of a Linear Function of Variables Subject to Linear Inequalities"

(2) GALE, D., KUHN, H. W., and TUCKER, A. W. "Linear Programming and the Theory of Games"

(3) KOOPMANS, T. C., and REITER, S. "A Model of Transportation"

[25] LEMKE, C. E. "The Dual Method of Solving the Linear Programming Problem," *Naval Research Logistics Quarterly*, I, No. 1 (March, 1954), 36–47.

[26] LORIE, J. H., and SAVAGE, L. J. "Three Problems in Capital Rationing," *Journal of Business*, XXVIII, No. 4 (October, 1955), 229–39.

[27] MODIGLIANI, FRANCO, and MILLER, MERTON H. "The Cost of Capital, Corporation Finance and the Theory of Investment," *American Economic Review*, XLVII, No. 3 (June, 1958), 261–97.

[28] PRAGER, W. "On Warehousing Problems," *Operations Research*, V, No. 4 (August, 1957), 504–12.

[29] SOLOMON, E. "The Arithmetic of Capital-budgeting Decisions," *Journal of Business*, XXIX, No. 2 (April, 1956), 124–29.

V
Special Aspects of Capital Measurement

RESIDUAL VALUES IN INVESTMENT ANALYSIS

GORDON SHILLINGLAW*

THE possibility of substantial end-of-life capital value is frequently overlooked in the appraisal of the internal investment proposals. A number of factors may help to explain this omission: (1) economic life is frequently so long and ultimate dollar realization so far away that these future values have very little effect on present investment decisions; (2) the probable residual value is so low that it can safely be ignored; (3) the available data do not provide an adequate base for forecasting; and (4) the future is so uncertain that changing conditions may wipe out whatever values now seem probable. The purpose of this article is to examine these propositions and to see how residual values can affect the investment worth of capital expenditure proposals.

THE NATURE OF RESIDUAL VALUE

Residual values are of many kinds. They include everything that produces or retains a cash or opportunity-cost value at the time the physical facilities contemplated in the investment proposal are retired, replaced, or relegated to stand-by status. They are usually positive in amount, but sometimes they may be negative (e.g., end-of-life product warranty liability). Thus the term is much broader in scope than the meaning usually attached to the phrase "salvage value."

One area in which residual values can have a great effect on investment worth is in the purchase of negotiable securities. Substantial premiums paid for "growth" stocks reflect not only a rising stream of future earnings and dividends per share but a conviction that future market prices will be higher than today's prices as a direct result of this earnings growth.[1]

Residual value also has great importance in real estate investments. The value of land may in some instances rise sufficiently to justify relatively low incremental earnings during the project's life. The extreme case of this kind is unimproved property bought purely on speculation with no plan for immediate use. Lease-back arrangements often carry relatively low interest charges, partly because the lessor forecasts an increase in the value of the land included in the lease-back package.

Resale values of used buildings and machinery—what is usually thought of as "salvage value"—are another source of residual value. So is the value of repair parts and fittings for the retired facilities. Another source of value that is sometimes overlooked, usually because its original cost is sometimes not included in the initial investment outlay, is the firm's investment in working capital—inventories, receivables, and the like. For many companies, net working capital takes up the largest part of invested capital; whether working-capital investments will retain residual value can be extreme-

* Consulting associate, Joel Dean Associates.

[1] If the shape and duration of future growth were precisely foreseeable, today's price would, in a perfect market, exceed the price of stocks of comparable risk by the present value of the future growth; any capital gain would be equal to the cost of capital tied up.

ly important in the appraisal of many kinds of investment proposals.

Residual values also include intangibles, the "good will" that can be built up with the aid of the facilities under review. Thus a young enterprise, considering the desirability of expanding its product line, must look beyond the period of economic usefulness of any particular aggregation of steel, bricks, and mortar to determine the true value of the proposal. This "good-will value" represents the discounted value at any future date of cash receipts net of cash outlays still to come. One way that this could be taken into consideration would be to project the investment timetable through several generations of equipment, in order to make a complete evaluation of future growth and stability of earnings. For practical purposes, however, it is generally simpler and no less accurate to make rough estimates of future "going-concern" value which can be used either to modify the estimated rate of return or to modify the risk factors, which must be appraised in connection with projects of borderline acceptability.

Yet another source of residual value derives from peculiarities of the tax laws. During periods when excess profits taxes are in force, it is not uncommon to see unprofitable firms bought up at relatively high prices, reflecting low base-period earnings, while other more successful companies go for lower prices because they have nothing to offer but good earnings prospects. Of more direct relevance is the capital loss that can be taken for tax purposes when a piece of equipment or a building is sold or scrapped before the end of its IRS-approved writeoff period. Capital losses for tax purposes can produce tax credits that are just as much a part of a project's cash flow as are the direct proceeds from the sale of the facilities themselves.

It is important to recognize that it is not necessary that all these values be represented by actual cash sales. Inventories and receivables should be valued at their cash value at normal turnover rates at the end of the facilities' useful life, even though there is no intention to liquidate them at that time. Conversely, if end-of-life inventories are expected to be unsalable (e.g., short-term "novelty" items), their residual value should be stated at actual market value (which may be zero) and not at cost.[2]

In the same vein, retired facilities need not be sold to give rise to a residual value in the investment-worth calculation. It may be that the company will decide to put the facilities on stand-by or retain them in the hope of speculative gain. This is a separate decision, independent of either the original investment decision or the later decision to withdraw the facilities from active service. What matters for investment decisions is cash value at the end of economic life, regardless of whether or not the facilities are actually sold.[3]

Thus many factors can contribute to residual value; but, if residual value does not influence materially the investment worth of a capital project, there is no practical gain to be had from measuring it. The next section attempts to answer the question as to when it is worth while to estimate residual value.

[2] Here again values should be stated after adjusting for the tax credit from the writeoff of unsalable merchandise.

[3] Under certain circumstances the opportunity value of facilities in stand-by service may be greater than their market value. This would occur if market values were low (perhaps reflecting substantial transfer costs associated with dismantling and removing the facilities) and if the property could be used to handle peak loads at lower cost than the next best alternative. In such circumstances the residual value assigned to the facilities should be measured by this opportunity value rather than by market value.

EFFECT OF RESIDUAL VALUE ON RATE OF RETURN

It is an open question whether investment worth should be appraised in terms of rate of return or whether, instead, each project should be evaluated on the basis of the present worth of its net cash flow discounted at the company's cost of capital.[4] The analysis of residual values is made by the discounted-cash-flow method.

Table 1 summarizes the rate-of-return calculation for a project whose economic life is expected to be ten years, with no end-of-life cash resale value. The initial cash outlay is $1,000, and the pretax cash earnings are $200 a year for ten years. Double-declining-balance depreciation is

TABLE 1

RATE OF RETURN CALCULATION: 10-YEAR LIFE, 10-YEAR TAX WRITEOFF, ZERO END-OF-LIFE RESALE VALUE

(a) Year	(b) Pretax Cash Flow	(c) Tax Writeoff*	(d) Tax at 50 Per Cent†	(e) After-Tax Cash Flow‡	(f) Present Worth at 9 Per Cent§
0	−$1,000	......	......	−$1,000	−$1,000
0– 1	200	$ 200	......	200	191
1– 2	200	160	$ 20	180	157
2– 3	200	128	36	164	131
3– 4	200	102	49	151	110
4– 5	200	82	59	141	94
5– 6	200	66	67	133	81
6– 7	200	52	74	126	70
7– 8	200	42	79	121	62
8– 9	200	34	83	117	55
9–10	200	27	87	113	48
10	....	107	− 54	54	22
Total	+$1,000	$1,000	$ 500	+$ 500	+$ 21

* Double-rate, declining-balance method.

† 50 per cent of (col. *b* − col. *c*).

‡ Column *b* − col. *d*.

§ Discount factors based on continuous compounding.

Source: Joel Dean Associates.

more conveniently carried out in terms of rate of return. Consequently, the illustrations that follow are drawn up in terms of the effect of residual value on rate of return.

The most accurate method of calculating rate of return is the discounted-cash-flow method. Under this approach, the rate of return is defined as that rate of interest which discounts the cash outlays and cash receipts associated with a project to a present worth of zero.[5] The rate-of-return calculations that follow are used in this illustration as in those that follow. For simplicity, a 50 per cent tax rate is assumed. For this project the residual value is provided by the tax write-off of the undepreciated balance of original cost at the end of ten years.

At a 9 per cent discount rate, the present worth of the stream of after-tax net cash receipts projected for this proposal

[4] For one viewpoint see the article by Lorie and Savage in this issue of the *Journal*.

[5] For an exposition of the discounted-cash-flow method see Joel Dean, "Better Management of Capital Expenditures through Research," *Journal of Finance*, May, 1953, pp. 119–28; and Horace G. Hill, Jr., "A New Method of Computing Rate of Return on Capital Expenditures," published privately in 1953.

is +\$21. Discounting at 10 per cent (not shown on the table) indicates a present worth of −\$17. The true rate of return is thus somewhere between 9 and 10 per cent, or approximately 9.5 per cent. The residual value produced by the \$54 end-of-life tax credit did not have much effect on rate of return. Its \$22 present worth at 9 per cent raised the rate of return from 9 to 9.5 per cent (without the residual value, the present worth of the total income and outlay stream would be −\$1, indicating that 9 per cent would be the appropriate rate of discount for this project).

This picture is changed if \$500 of the initial cash outlay is for land which cannot be depreciated for tax purposes. In this case, residual value has a sizable impact on rate of return. For example, if the land can be sold for \$500 at the end of ten years, the residual value is \$527 (\$500 for the resale value of the land and \$27 tax credit for the writeoff of the remaining book value of the depreciating facilities). The rate of return is 9.9 per cent. But if the land has a zero end-of-life resale value, the residual value is limited to a \$277 tax credit on a \$544 writeoff, and the rate of return is only 7.7 per cent.

Resale values in depreciating facilities can also be important. Turning back to the illustration in Table 1, if it is expected that the depreciating facilities can be sold for \$500 at the end of ten years, the residual value will be \$402 (\$500 less a 25 per cent capital gains tax on the difference between \$500 and the \$107 undepreciated balance of original cost). This will push the rate of return up to 12.3 per cent.

Several provisional inferences can be drawn from this series of illustrations. First, if tax depreciation is kept in line with actual depreciation as to both economic life and cash residual value before taxes, salvage or resale values do not have large effects on rate of return. Thus in the second illustration the rate of return is only four-tenths of 1 per cent higher than in the first example (9.9 per cent versus 9.5 per cent).

Second, when tax depreciation is not in accord with the economic realities, the residual value can have a relatively great effect on rate of return even for projects with a life as long as ten years. Thus the absence of residual value in land (or inventories) in the third illustration reduced rate of return from 9.9 per cent to 7.7 per cent.

Third, the residual value represented by tax credits can be highly significant. If the company were unable to write off the undepreciated balance of \$554 in the third example, the rate of return would be reduced still further, to approximately 5 per cent. This point is frequently overlooked, particularly by those who advocate before-tax calculations of rate of return. For projects within range of the border line of minimum acceptable profitability, the residual value represented by the end-of-life tax credit can swing the balance. Another, and perhaps more traditional, way to say this is that the timing of tax writeoffs over a project's life can affect the value of the project in ways that a before-tax analysis cannot reflect.

These tentative inferences can be amplified and qualified by a second series of illustrations. Table 2 shows the rate of return calculation for a project with \$1,000 initial outlay, no salvage value, a ten-year life for tax purposes, and cash earnings of \$400 a year for ten years. The rate of return on this project is 24.0 per cent. The only residual value is represented by the \$54 tax credit, which has virtually no effect on rate of return.

This illustration is introduced to demonstrate the impact of residual values at high discount rates. Varying the assumption as to residual value in Table 2 has relatively little effect on rate of return. For example, if half of the $1,000 outlay is for land and if the land is expected to have a $500 cash resale value at the end of ten years, the rate of return is not increased but is reduced to 21.7 per cent. The $527 after-tax residual value in this example has little effect on rate of return. If the facilities have zero end-of-life resale value, the rate of return will be cut only by nine-tenths of 1 per cent, to 20.8 per cent. (And if there is no end-of-life tax credit, the rate of return in this no-resale-value case will be reduced another full percentage point, to 19.8 per cent.)

As this second series of cases shows, tax policy may have a greater impact on rate of return than resale value can make. In the illustration sketched in Table 2, if (*a*) there is a cash resale value of $500, (*b*) tax depreciation is calculated on the full $1,000 initial outlay, and (*c*) a 25 per cent capital gains tax is applicable to end-of-life resale value, the rate of return is boosted from 24 to 25.2 per cent. Most of this rise is attributable to the greater after-tax residual value. But if we compare this case with the second illustration in this series, in which depreciation allowances took a $500 cash liquidation value into account, we find a spread of 3.5 percentage points (25.2 instead of 21.7 per cent). The relative increase in rate of return is 16.1 per cent (3.5 per cent/21.7 per cent). This is substantial but much less than the comparable increase in the first series of examples. At those lower discount rates the discrepancy between tax depreciation and real depreciation raised the rate of return from 9.9 to 12.3 per cent, a relative increase of 24.2 per cent.

This second set of illustrations is instructive. First, it reinforces the earlier conclusion that if depreciation writeoffs are in line with the loss in value of the initial outlay, the residual value has a

TABLE 2

RATE OF RETURN CALCULATION: 10-YEAR LIFE, 10-YEAR TAX WRITEOFF, ZERO END-OF-LIFE RESALE VALUE

(*a*) Year	(*b*) Pretax Cash Flow	(*c*) Tax Writeoff*	(*d*) Tax at 50 Per Cent†	(*e*) After-Tax Cash Flow‡	(*f*) Present Worth at 24 Per Cent§
0..........	−$1,000	......	....	−$1,000	−$1,000
0– 1.......	400	$ 200	$ 100	300	267
1– 2.......	400	160	120	280	196
2– 3.......	400	128	136	264	145
3– 4.......	400	102	149	251	109
4– 5.......	400	82	159	241	82
5– 6.......	400	66	167	233	62
6– 7.......	400	52	174	226	48
7– 8.......	400	42	179	221	37
8– 9.......	400	34	183	217	28
9–10.......	400	27	187	213	22
10..........	....	107	− 54	54	5
Total...	+$3,000	$1,000	$1,500	+$1,500	+$ 1

* Double-rate, declining-balance method.

† 50 per cent of (col. *b* − col. *c*).

‡ Column *b* − col. *d*.

§ Discount factors based on continuous compounding.

Source: Joel Dean Associates.

relatively small effect on rate of return. Second, when tax writeoff and real depreciation are kept in line, a greater residual value actually reduces the rate of return in the high-earnings-rate brackets. This apparent paradox reflects the fact that near-year tax writeoffs have a greater, value than distant residual values when effective rates of discount are high. Third, as was demonstrated in the preceding paragraphs, disparities between tax writeoff and real depreciation are less important at high rates of discount than when earnings rates are low.

Residual values have their greatest impact on the rate of return when economic life is short. This point may be self-apparent, but a third series of illustrations will demonstrate it more clearly. Since it has already been shown that the residual value has a relatively greater impact at low discount rates, the following examples have been developed in terms of high rates of return.

Table 3 presents an illustration similar to that shown in Table 2, but with a five-year economic life and a five-year tax writeoff at double-declining-balance rates.

TABLE 3

RATE-OF-RETURN CALCULATION: 5-YEAR LIFE, 5-YEAR TAX WRITEOFF, ZERO END-OF-LIFE RESALE VALUE

(a) Year	(b) Pretax Cash Flow	(c) Tax Writeoff*	(d) Tax at 50 Per Cent†	(e) After-Tax Cash Flow‡	(f) Present Worth at 19 Per Cent§
0	−$1,000	......	......	−$1,000	−$1,000
0–1	400	$ 400	......	400	364
1–2	400	240	$ 80	320	241
2–3	400	144	128	272	169
3–4	400	86	157	243	125
4–5	400	52	174	226	96
5	....	78	− 39	39	15
Total	+$1,000	$1,000	$ 500	+$ 500	+$ 10

* Double-rate, declining-balance method.
† 50 per cent of (col. *b* − col. *c*).
‡ Column *b* − col. *d*.
§ Discount factors based on continuous compounding.
Source: Joel Dean Associates.

The rate of return on this project is 19.6 per cent. The end-of-life tax credit contributes approximately one percentage point to this rate of return. If, on the other hand, a resale value of $500 taxable at a 25 per cent capital gains rate is expected in this proposal, the rate of return will be 25.4 per cent, an increase of 5.8 percentage points due to resale value.

These two calculations assume that the full initial outlay is depreciable at the five-year rate. If half the outlay is for land (or inventory), only $500 will be depreciable. If it is expected that the property can be sold for $500 at the end of five years, the rate of return is 19.8 per cent. This is not much different from the 19.6 per cent rate of return estimated in Table 3, on the basis of zero resale value but full depreciation base. The increased residual value is just about offset by the slower tax writeoff. But when tax writeoff is predicated upon an assumption of end-of-life resale value, the probability of realizing residual values has a very great effect on a project's profitability. If the projected $500 resale value fails to materialize, the rate of return will be reduced from 19.8 to 15.4 per cent. And if there is no end-of-life tax credit, the rate of return is reduced further, to 9.3 per cent. Thus not only the tangible but also the intangible component of residual value is important when economic life is short.

This list of illustrations could be expanded by changing the assumptions as to salvage value, economic life, tax life, and/or annual earnings. But the preceding examples are sufficient to support the following propositions:

1. If tax writeoff is in line with the lifetime decline in the resale value of the original investment, residual values have little effect on rate of return.

2. If these two variables are not in line, residual values can have a major influence on the investment decision, provided that economic life is short and/or the minimum cutoff rate is low.

3. When economic life is long (e.g., ten years or longer) and the company's minimum cutoff rate is high (e.g., 20 per cent or higher), the effect of the residual value on the investment decision is likely to be limited to borderline projects.

4. When economic life is short and/or when the minimum cutoff rate is low, residual values will have a broader range of influence, and estimates should be made.

5. Intangible residual values, i.e., end-of-life tax credits, are just as significant in investment decisions as intangibles and affect the rate of return in just the same manner.

6. When the minimum cutoff rate is high and economic life is long, the rate and level of the tax writeoff has a far greater impact on investment worth than is made by residual value.

ESTIMATING RESIDUAL VALUES

There are circumstances in which it is not very important whether or not estimates of residual value are made, as the preceding section indicates. Too often, however, in situations in which residual values can influence the investment decision, estimates are not made. The reason frequently advanced for this omission is that adequate data are not available.

It is true that the routine reporting systems in most companies do not produce a flow of data in readily usable form. It is also true that many estimates cannot be based completely on data that are produced as a by-product of the normal historical record of transactions. But this does not mean that the estimates should not be made or that satisfactory estimates cannot be made. Although it is generally not feasible to achieve precision in the estimates, great precision is not necessary; because of the effect of time on present values, fairly substantial error ranges in the estimates of residual value generally can be tolerated.

The estimates of residual value must be forward-looking. To the extent that historical data can be used, their relevance to the future must be evaluated. The estimating problem will vary, depending on the nature of the value to be predicted. Estimates of end-of-life tax credits are usually the easiest; they require knowledge of tax writeoff rates and assumptions as to future tax rates.

Past accounting records are generally most useful in estimating the resale values of plant and equipment. Each retirement of a piece of equipment gives rise to a set of information relative to resale price and removal and/or dismantling cost. The flow of this information can be systematized at little expense, to lay the foundation for future estimates. Assets can be grouped according to the nature of the resale market and the flow of information on resale transactions channeled so as to provide the basis for future estimates for assets of each type. For many types of equipment—motor vehicles, for example—information from public or quasi-public sources can be processed to provide an adequate estimation base. Appraisal companies can also be called upon to provide useful information. In the normal course of their business, these firms frequently act as collection agencies for market-value data, and in some instances appraisal companies have been willing to generalize salvage-value relationships on the basis of prior experience. Alternatively, salvage-value curves can be derived from special surveys.

Residual values of working capital investments seldom present great difficulties of estimation. The major problem arises in connection with inventories. The normal expectation is that inventories will continue to have value at the end of the economic life of the physical property contemplated in the investment proposal. Parts inventories, stocks of slow-moving items, perishable materials, and style merchandise can occasion end-of-life losses if they cannot be utilized by replacement facilities or by other activities of the firm. In general, it would be expected that any such losses would be minimized by gradual liquidation in the later stages of the project's life. Most of the substantial inventory losses that will occur cannot be predicted far in advance; if they could be predicted, the company would generally take action to forestall them.

Land values pose a special problem. A customary assumption is that residual values will remain constant through time and that ultimate realization will equal the initial outlay for land. Many real estate investment firms and long-term lessors have made substantial profits, disproving this assumption. Changes in local conditions, water supply, use of contiguous property, traffic patterns, etc., can raise or lower land values substantially.

This means that the residual value of land must be estimated on a case-by-case basis. This requires specific forecasting, a task for which past records of local property values may be of little relevance. But, as in any forecasting problem, some prediction must be made. When the value of the land involved is small, the end may not justify the expense of the forecast, but when the outlays are substantial relative to a company's resources, an ostrich-like "tomorrow will be the same as today" appraisal of residual values can be costly. Inadequate forecasting can saddle the company with obsolete real estate, or it may cause the company to pass up chances to locate in areas of growing industrial concentration and increasing land values. Petroleum marketers and food chains generally have highly organized real estate analysis programs.

It has been argued that investment analysis should ignore these trends in property values, on the ground that this is speculation and therefore not part of "normal" operations. But speculation cannot be avoided; it can only be evaluated. Any investment is a speculation; the risk and chance for gain may be less in one aspect of the proposal and greater in another, but they are always present. The earnings on an investment outlay are provided by a stream of net cash receipts which is made up of a number of different kinds of outlays and receipts. Anything that is likely to affect that stream must be evaluated in a realistic analysis of the proposal. All parts of the stream are relevant; to eliminate consideration of any one part can produce a distorted view of the value of the stream as a whole.

THE ROLE OF "CONSERVATISM"

In answer to the preceding arguments, an alleged need for "conservatism" is sometimes advanced as a justification for ignoring or sharply discounting future residual values. The reasoning underlying this position is that, since the future is so uncertain, the prudent investor should assume that changes in the economic environment will wipe out whatever residual values now seem likely to materialize. In its crudest form, this argument is that in a dynamic economy it is impossible to predict the future and that the only way to avoid mistakes is to predict the worst. (Carried to its logical extreme, this argument would mean that no investment should ever be made unless it is accompanied simultaneously by instantaneous net cash receipts equal to or greater than the investment outlay.)

There is a certain merit in this argument. Every estimate is subject to a range of error. It may be desirable to apply a greater discount for risk to distant receipts than to near-term realizations. And it is true that this brand of "conservatism" may prevent the company from making some investments that would prove unprofitable in the long run.

But the profits that are lost by a policy of "conservatism" in investment analysis, though hidden, are likely to be even greater than the losses that this policy avoids. These foregone profits do not appear directly on the income statement, but they are real losses nevertheless.

A realistic investment analysis should evaluate the probabilities of profit or loss. If the estimates are soundly made, the overestimates should be balanced by the underestimates. If it is always assumed that residual value is zero, many projects that would prove profitable will not be undertaken. The chance of profit must be evaluated along with the risk of loss; if the chance of profit is undervalued, profits will be lower than they could be.

The policy of ignoring residual values is not truly a conservative policy. A true conservatism aims to maintain and increase the value of the concern. It requires a clear-headed appraisal of risks and a willingness to go forward whenever the chance of gain appears to outweigh the risk of loss. A minimum cutoff rate based on cost of capital already contains an allowance for risk. To compound this by ignoring residual values is unnecessarily restrictive on capital expenditures.[6] A wise conservatism is to evaluate the future; a false conservatism is to ignore it.

CONCLUSIONS

Residual values should be assigned their rightful place in investment analysis. They stem from many sources and may even be negative. In some circumstances they will have such a small effect on the profitability of capital outlays that they can be ignored safely. In others, the acceptability of the project will be clearly visible without any appraisal of residual value. But residual values can be of importance to the investment decision, and, when they are, they should be estimated.

When the minimum acceptable rate of return is low or when economic life is short or when tax writeoff appears to be out of line with economic realities, the potential value of a capital outlay can be

[6] George Terborgh makes essentially this same point in his book, *Dynamic Equipment Policy* (New York: McGraw-Hill, 1949), chap. xii and pp. 167–68.

influenced strongly by the probable amount of future residual values. In such circumstances it is better to forecast residual value explicitly on the basis of the best available information than to ignore it or to make the implicit assumption that the future will be just like the present or the immediate past.

For many kinds of residual values, it is possible to adapt the record-keeping system to provide a sound basis for future estimates. Frequently, the forecast of residual values will be a by-product of forecasts of other aspects of investment worth. In some instances, whenever the size of the outlay and potential impact of residual values warrant, special-purpose studies may be necessary to provide the necessary information base. The important thing is to decide whether residual values can sway the investment decision; if they can, ways can generally be found to derive estimates of adequate accuracy and relevance.

PROFIT ANALYSIS FOR ABANDONMENT DECISIONS

GORDON SHILLINGLAW*

A DECISION to abandon an activity as no longer sufficiently profitable to justify expenditure of time, energy, and funds is sufficiently important in most companies to require top-management action. Yet the methods used to generate the information on which this decision is to be based are frequently poorly adapted to the task. In one company the method then in use indicated that the facilities serving a particular region of the country were losing money, and one top executive suggested that these facilities be abandoned. The situation was analyzed using another method, which indicated that the facilities were sufficiently profitable to warrant not only continued operation but an extensive rehabilitation program.

In a recent article a vice-president of one of the leading chemical companies emphasized the need for constant vigilance against the unprofitable activity and advocated a vigorous program of analysis to weed out facilities, product lines, and other activities that act as a drag on the other operations of the company.[1] He mentioned two alternative methods of approach to abandonment decisions. The first of these is the cash-return method, under which the abandonment decision is based on a comparison of some minimum rate of return with the rate-of-return relationship between cash earnings and recoverable capital investment. The second approach, which might be called the book-return method, contrasts net book return on net book investment with some minimum rate of return. The purpose of this paper is to contrast these two approaches and to outline how a disposal analysis might most accurately be carried out.

THE BOOK-RETURN METHOD

The book-return method is based on the presumption that a figure analogous to company-wide net profit can be computed in a meaningful way for most subunits or activities within the company. It also assumes that a net book-investment figure can be calculated for each of these subunits or activities, so that a rate of return can be derived as a ratio between the two. Under these assumptions it is possible to say that sales of product line A are so much, its expenses are so much, and the net profit is the difference between the two. This net profit, expressed as a percentage of the net book investment devoted to product line A, is the rate of return of that product line. This rate of return is then compared with a desired rate of return for this activity. If it falls short of this standard, then the activity is considered a likely candidate for disposal, unless someone can present a convincing argument that conditions are likely to improve sufficiently to push the rate of return above the desired level.

This, baldly stated, is the book-return method. Not all who subscribe to this method would agree with this description in every detail. Some would use gross book investment rather than net book investment. Some would agree up to the point at which the rate-of-return com-

* Assistant professor, School of Industrial Management, Massachusetts Institute of Technology. The writer wishes to acknowledge the helpful comments of Harry V. Roberts, Jr.

[1] T. Crawley Davis, "The Accountant and the Profitability of Productive Facilities," *N.A.C.A. Bulletin*, XXXVII, No. 5 (January, 1956), 648–56, esp. pp. 653–55.

parison is made but would regard a rate-of-return deficiency merely as a signal for an analysis by the cash-earnings method. These people really belong in the other camp, so their objections need not deter us. Others would say that no disposal decision is ever made on the basis of one year's performance and that trends and earnings projections must be introduced into the abandonment decision. To this objection we must also agree, although decisions are in fact often, and perhaps mistakenly, made on the basis of historical data alone. But this merely means that rate of return is computed as the ratio of estimated future net earnings to present net book investment—the measurement concept is essentially unchanged.

Others would object that rate-of-return criteria are not binding and that the company may be willing to support an operation or product line that yields less than standard return for a long period of time because other considerations make it desirable to do so. While this is doubtless true, it applies with equal force to both approaches and therefore cannot be regarded as a distinguishing feature of the book-return approach. The hallmark of this method is a reliance on the investment and earnings values prepared as an integral by-product of the company's daily accounting process and routine performance reports.

CASH-RETURN METHOD

Under the second approach the earnings of an activity are defined as the cash revenues (or their equivalent) that would be lost by discontinuation less the cash expenses (or their equivalent) that would be avoided thereby. The investment base is calculated by finding the net disposal value of the investment that would be released by abandonment. What could plant and equipment be sold for? What reduction in inventories, receivables and cash, net of current payables, could be achieved? What extraordinary expenses (such as severance pay) would be incurred, as an offset to liquidation value, if abandonment were decided upon? What immediate effect would liquidation have on income taxes?

Rate of return, under this approach, can be computed in either of two ways: by dividing indicated cash earnings by recoverable investment or by projecting the stream of cash earnings into the future and calculating a discounted cash-flow rate of return. Because both methods of calculation are based on the same concepts of earnings and investment, they will be lumped together at this stage of the presentation.

There are minor variations in this method, but the essential features remain. The distinguishing characteristics of the cash-return approach are that it works exclusively with increments—what will be different if the decision is made one way instead of the other—and that these increments are measured in terms of their effects on cash or its equivalent.

EVALUATION OF METHODS

Abandonment decisions are not always made solely on the basis of profitability. But seldom is it possible to arrive intelligently at these decisions without reliable information relating to the profitability of the activity being studied. The first problem, then, is to examine the two principal alternative approaches to profitability measurement for this purpose to determine which will provide a more reliable indication of activity profitability.

Presumably, the company's principal objective in measuring the profitability of abandonment is to find out whether the company as a whole will be better or worse off for discontinuing the activity in question. Therefore, the principal criterion for choosing between book return and cash return is their relative ability to provide information in this form. On this ground the cash-return method is clearly superior to the book-return method.

The main reason underlying this conclusion is to be found by examining how the book-return figures are developed. The book-return formula consists of a fraction in which the numerator is net earnings and the denominator is net (or, sometimes, gross) book investment. The investment denominator is found by adding the book values of facilities assigned to the activity to the book values of inventories and other working capital. There may be some difficulty in identifying particular assets with particular activities, particularly with respect to cash, receivables, and payables which are handled through a central accounting office for the company as a whole, but this identification problem applies in large measure to the cash-return approach as well.

To calculate the earnings numerator of the book-return formula, however, major problems arise. First, the total loss in sales volume might be greater or less than the sales volume of the activity in question. This means that sales revenue of the division or product line may be a poor indicator of the potential revenue loss or that product-line expenses may be unrepresentative of the potential expense saving through abandonment. One Midwest processor found that he could abandon a branch plant serving one sales territory with only a minor loss in sales and a considerably greater reduction in out-of-pocket expenses. In other words, abandonment of this plant did not completely eliminate its revenues and expenses; it merely reduced them by varying degrees and transferred them to other operating units of the company. True, a net profit figure could probably be calculated in such a way as to avoid this pitfall, but, if this were done, the figure could no longer be a routine by-product of the day-by-day accounting process, which is the basis for most net profit statements.

A second earnings measurement problem is even more of a barrier to satisfactory utilization of the book-return method. Almost every activity unit in a multi-activity firm shares directly or indirectly with other activity units the services of certain input factors. The costs of these shared services are called "common" costs or "joint" costs.[2] Costs may be common to two or more time periods (original cost of fixed assets), two or more divisions (top-management salaries), two or more plant departments (plant-management costs), two or more products (joint raw-material costs), two or more units of the same product (set-up costs), and so forth.

This multiplicity of common costs poses a serious problem of identification, namely, how to associate a given portion of common costs with individual benefit-sharing units. For purposes of profit determination and inventory valuation, most cost-accounting systems provide for a series of allocations of common costs to the various manufacturing and/or selling units and, in the case of costs originating in or assigned to manufacturing units, then proceed to make further assignments of costs to individual products or jobs. The defect in this procedure for analysis purposes is that it assumes a degree of relationship between cost and activity that does not exist. If a cost is common to two or more activities, any allocation which spreads the entire cost to the activities affected is bound to be ar-

[2] The distinction between common and joint costs is not relevant to this discussion, and the two terms are used synonymously here.

bitrary. This means that the net profit of the individual activity is loaded with expenses that will not be avoided if the activity is abandoned.[3]

For example, even if the activity is an entire division, its monthly expense sheet will ordinarily carry a number of items that will not be reduced in any real sense by the decision to abandon. The first, and perhaps the most obvious, of these items is the allocated share of central office overhead. Whereas it is probably true that abandonment of a unit as large as a division will permit reductions in central office expense, the reduction increasing as the time horizon of projection is lengthened, some of these expenses are fixed in total and will not be changed at all. Others are partially fixed and, although they will change in some degree, will not change in the proportion assumed by their allocation to the division.

Depreciation is another major item of expense on the usual division income statement that cannot necessarily be avoided in full by abandonment. True, abandonment of a facility and disposal of its capital equipment will reduce reported charges for depreciation. But book depreciation is not intended to, and seldom does, equal the decline in economic values that accompanies retention of an asset. For disposal decisions the depreciation that matters is the loss in resale value that will result from retaining the asset in its present use for a given length of time. Recorded amortization of original cost is unlikely to be very close to this decline in value in any given year or period shorter than the full ownership life of the asset. To deduct book depreciation from division revenues as part of division expenses is to provide a misleading estimate of avoidable profit. Under most circumstances this will produce an understatement of avoidable profit, but not necessarily so.[4]

Other items on the division's income statement might likewise be cited as illustrations of the poor fit of reported book profit to the expected profit change which is the relevant dimension in the abandonment decision, but they are not crucial to the proof of the issue. The list of exceptions is even greater when intra-divisional activities, such as product lines, departments, branches, or sales territories, are the subject of the abandonment analysis, mainly because allocations of fixed and joint costs bulk larger in income statements drawn up on these bases.

The pure fact of the matter is that the routine periodic income statements generated by most accounting and reporting systems are not geared to analysis of the profitability of abandonment. Among other things, they are designed to provide information for the company's financial reports to stockholders and other outsiders, for internal performance evaluation, for management motivation, for cost control, and possibly for other uses such as pricing policy. But all these uses presume a going concern. They take it for granted that the activity is to be continued, and the information is generated with this as a guiding principle.

[3] Association of common costs with units of activity on an avoidability criterion very likely would prove unworkable. Costs that could be avoided if a plant were to close down, for example, are of an entirely different order from the costs that could be avoided if a single product manufactured within that plant were to be discontinued. This is a case in which the whole is greater than the sum of its parts, in that many costs that are not avoidable with respect to individual products may very well be avoidable with respect to the plant as a whole.

[4] Some studies have indicated that, following a substantial value decline in the first few years of an asset's life, age has relatively little influence on the price at which an asset may be sold. For this reason it is frequently safe to assume that no real savings in depreciation can be made if the facility is abandoned, but the analyst should be careful to watch for exceptions to this rule.

This going-concern principle, however, does not govern the abandonment analysis. Under at least one of the alternatives under consideration the activity will not be a going concern; it will be abandoned. And it is perhaps a reluctance to part with the going-concern precept that causes some to reject the cash-return method or, if they accept it, to insist that book return must also enter into the analysis. One writer, after concluding that book return is generally superior to cash return, states: "Therefore, if a given situation calls for a cash earnings and recoverable capital presentation, it seems imperative that this be placed in juxtaposition to the normal accounting evaluation in such manner as to permit appropriate remarks upon the validity of each for the specific purposes under consideration."[5] It should be mentioned that this same writer in the very next paragraph is sufficiently impressed by at least one aspect of the cash-return method to advocate elimination of book depreciation charges from the expenses assigned to the activity under investigation.

Although the author of the above quotation does not present his reasons for preferring some version of book return (modified in the direction of cash return by elimination of book depreciation charges), he may be troubled, as many others are, by the fear that the cash-return method will regard all joint costs as being unaffected by the abandonment decision. This error would tend to overstate division profits, thus making it difficult to present any kind of an effective case for discontinuance of product lines, abandonment of plants or divisions, or withdrawal from individual sales territories. (On these grounds it is perhaps surprising that more activity managers, faced with potential abandonment of their units, are not more vigorous champions of the cash-return approach.)

[5] Davis, *op. cit.*, p. 655.

But this error is not an inherent part of the cash-return method. If the analyst falls into this trap, the obvious solution is to educate him or dispense with his services rather than fall back on the conceptually incorrect net-return method. The reason is that many joint costs (and by this is meant joint with respect to the activity under analysis and other activities within the company—costs that are joint among several sales territories, for example, may not necessarily be joint with respect to the division of which these territories are a part) are not fixed in total and therefore will change with a change in the scope or nature of the various activities to which they are common. To assume non-variability, without investigation, is just as great an error as to assume full variability, which is essentially the assumption under which the net book-return approach operates.

Another possible explanation for the allegiance that many swear to book return is that many companies feel that they are operating at the margin of managerial capacity. Thus they reason that, if a particular product or plant or division or territory is retained, acquisition of another potential product or plant or division or territory must be denied or delayed. Therefore, in order to justify its place in the sun, the existing activity must cover not only an adequate return in excess of its avoidable costs but also a certain "share" of joint costs and possibly depreciation on its specialized facilities as well.

Even if the assumption of managerial capacity limitations is granted, this argument cannot stand. The crucial question is whether the displacing activity can contribute a greater return on incremental investment than the existing activity can contribute on the recoverable investment in facilities it requires. Future decline in the value of new facilities is relevant to this choice; book depreciation on existing facilities is not. Furthermore, it is the recoverable portion of the existing investment that should enter into the return calculation, not its book value. Thus, if it is not a question of limited managerial capacity but rather limited financial resources, it is recoverable value, not book value, of existing assets that can be realized and used to finance the new activity.

Searching even deeper in an attempt to explain support given the book-return method, there is another misconception about the cash-return method that may contribute part of the explanation. An activity that produces a low or negative book profit while showing a cash return high enough to justify its continuation may remain a potential avenue for internal capital expenditures. If depreciation is to be ignored in the abandonment decision, the argument runs, what is there to prevent additional money being poured into this activity for additional or replacement plant, equipment, and working capital? (The phrase "pouring money down a rathole" generally enters into this argument.) This is a real danger, but the solution does not lie in adoption of the book-return method. Rather, the answer is to adopt a sound program of top-management control of capital expenditures, one aspect of which is to require a specified minimum rate of return not only on the incremental investment outlay but also on the recoverable value of the existing investment as well. A capital-rationing test of this kind can prevent major misdirections of the company's investable funds into unprofitable activities. This means that the activity will be retained either until denial of prop-up capital outlays reduces its profitability to the abandonment level or until a renovation investment program can be devised that will meet the stringent capital-rationing test mentioned above. This is not a program of pouring money into ratholes; it is a rational means of insuring that the company's money will be put where it can be most profitably used.

One final point should be considered. Application of the cash-return method requires a certain amount of data collection and interpretation that can be eliminated if the book-return method is used. Allocations of common costs are made periodically as part of the routine accounting process for other purposes. This generally means that net profit figures can be obtained fairly easily for any large unit of activity. Particularly if the activity is an organizational unit, such as a product division or manufacturing plant, much of the information underlying net profit is obtained as a by-product of the normal operation of the accounting system. And even if the activity is nonorganizational—a product line, for example—most cost-accounting systems permit isolation of the identifiable costs and assignment of overheads by standard overhead rates.

In short, measurement for the book-return approach is simple, because this approach uses measurements already being collected for other purposes. The cash-return method, in contrast, requires special analysis of the cost and investment information. In a sense, however, the information required is simpler than that needed for the book-return method, in that many of the usual accounting allocations of common costs need not be made. But the effort required is usually greater because few accounting systems are so set up that estimates of avoidable costs and revenues can be derived as routine by-products of the customary accounting records.

The smaller amount of effort required for the book-return approach, however, is not an important advantage. Abandonment analyses are not made every month or even every year. The amount of additional analytical and clerical expense is ordinarily small in comparison with the importance of the decision. The significant fact is that the cash-return method provides data of greater relevance to the abandonment decision than does the book-return method.

MEASURING CASH RETURN

Application of the cash-return method presents a number of conceptual and practical problems of measurement. Some of these can be resolved easily; the solutions for others may have to be approximate. The nature of the company's accounting system will affect the ease with which the calculations can be made. In order to provide a framework for discussion of some of these measurement problems, it will be helpful to restate the basic outline of the cash-return method. Briefly, then, the cash earnings that will be lost if the activity is discontinued are expressed as a rate of return on the disposable value of the assets that will be released if the decision is made to abandon the activity. The rate of return is then compared with a minimum rate of return established by company policy, normally the same rate used as a cut-off for new capital-outlay proposals. If the indicated rate of return is lower than the standard, abandonment is indicated unless other considerations lead management to accept a substandard return in this activity.[6]

Although it is conceivable that the cash-return measure might be estimated on the basis of experience in the most recent year or in a period of several recent years, the most logical approach is to project this earnings experience forward into the future with whatever modifications that forecasting insight may suggest. The earnings that will be lost are future earnings, not past earnings, and a calculation based exclusively on the past is unlikely to provide as accurate an indication of profitability as a calculation based on forecasts of future earnings, provided that forecasts are intelligently made and are not simply ill-considered extrapolations of poorly defined historical trends. Furthermore, the use of projections permits management to look beyond the next succeeding year. It can consider earnings trends, and, particularly if some discounted cash-flow method of rate-of-return calculation is in use, it can allow for these trends in the cash-return calculation. This discounted cash-flow method has been described elsewhere,[7] and its evaluation need not be repeated here. The question now is how the estimates of cash earnings and recoverable investment should be made.

ESTIMATING REVENUE EFFECTS

The first problem is to determine how much revenue would be lost. Indicated revenues of the activity under consideration provide a starting point, but they do not ordinarily provide a full answer. First, in many instances it is possible for other activities to pick up part of the revenues now accruing to the disposal candidate. One product line may be a partial substitute for another—dropping one basic paint formulation might lead

[6] One variant of the cash-return method is to compare the "present value" of future cash earnings with the recoverable investment value of the facilities. This variant is discussed below.

[7] See, e.g., John M. Schultz, "The Investor's Method of Computing Rate of Return as Applied to Replacement Valuation," in *Tested Approaches to Capital Equipment Replacement* (American Management Association Special Report No. 1 [New York: A.M.A., 1954]), pp. 43–52; and Joel Dean, "Better Management of Capital Expenditures through Research," *Journal of Finance*, VIII, No. 2 (May, 1953), 119–28.

some customers for that formulation to switch to another formulation marketed by the same company rather than to change suppliers.

Closing one plant may not mean loss of revenue if all production can be absorbed by other plants. Closing a local branch office or distribution center may lose some customers (in one instance, the product being highly perishable, the estimated loss ran as high as 80 per cent), but it may be possible to retain substantial portions of the market by reaching out from other branches.

On the other side of the coin, abandonment of one activity may start a small chain reaction that will reduce revenues of other activities. One product line may be partially complementary to another—paints and thinners, to continue the same example, might bear such a relationship that reduction in the sale of a given line of paints might also reduce the sale of thinners. In this kind of situation the revenue loss is greater than the revenues indicated by the activity's income statement. These indirect effects may not be important in all cases, but they should always be investigated.

Reported revenues may be misleading in another way. The revenues assigned to one plant, for example, might include revenues from products transferred to other plants in the company's structure. If these products are transferred at prices that approximate market prices, this revenue loss can be interpreted just like any other revenue loss.[8] But if some other transfer-price system is in use, such as standard cost plus 10 per cent, then further adjustment must be made to allow for the fact that abandonment of this plant will require other plants in the system to purchase materials outside at prices differing from those "paid" in the past. In other words, transfer prices must be readjusted to approximate market, and this should be done before the indirect effects of substitutability and complementarity are allowed for.

In some analyses this transfer-price question will be crucial. To illustrate the need for market-based transfer prices for disposal analysis, assume that a company has two divisions. Division A manufactures its product and delivers it to Division B, which processes it further and then sells it to outsiders. First assuming that the transfer price is based on average actual cost plus 10 per cent, the income statements might look like this:

	Division A	Division B	Total
Revenues	$110	$200	$200
Expenses:			
Materials	40	110	40
Processing	60	30	90
Profit	$ 10	$ 60	$ 70

At first glance it would appear that abandoning Division A would reduce company profits by only $10. But assume that the end product of Division A can be purchased in the market for $130. In this case the company's profit, if it ceases to operate Division A, will be, not $70 or $60, but $40 ($200 revenues minus $130 materials and $30 processing). Thus the effect of abandonment is $30 in lost profits, not $10.

Adjustment of the division income statements to a market-based transfer price system will give this correct result:

	Division A	Division B	Total
Revenues	$130	$200	$200
Expenses:			
Materials	40	130	40
Processing	60	30	90
Profit	$ 30	$ 40	$ 70

[8] Several excellent articles on transfer pricing have appeared recently, the latest being Jack Hirshleifer, "On the Economics of Transfer Pricing," *Journal of Business*, XXIX, No. 3 (July, 1956), 172–84. Professor Hirshleifer objects to market-based transfer prices under certain circumstances, but his excellently presented argument relates primarily to current output decisions and not to the abandonment problem.

Seldom will the entire output of one activity be absorbed by another. The less intracompany transfers there are, the less troublesome will be the transfer-price problem. But, to the extent that transfers do occur, departure from market will distort reported profit and require the analyst to adjust the data in preparing his estimates of profitability.

ESTIMATING COST EFFECTS

Abandonment of some activities will not affect total company revenues, but abandonment always influences cost in one way or another. The costs that will be avoided if an activity is abandoned differ according to the nature of the activity. Plant abandonment eliminates all the variable factory costs at that factory plus a good deal of the factory's fixed costs, plus perhaps some costs outside the factory. Discontinuation of a product line, on the other hand, may reduce only variable manufacturing costs plus a small amount of factory supervision, or it might conceivably have no effect on factory costs whatsoever (purchased product line) but might instead permit a great reduction in company selling costs through discontinuance of a separate sales force. One small company, with twenty million dollars in annual revenues, has three separate sales forces for its three product lines. Discontinuance of any one of those product lines would permit elimination of the entire sales force, right up to the product sales manager. Discontinuance of the weakest of the three product lines, however, would have virtually no effect on any non-selling costs except direct labor and direct materials used in its manufacture, whereas discontinuance of the company's major line would permit a substantial reduction in factory supervision and office clerical staff.

These differences are usually obvious in any abandonment analysis, and the analyst need observe only a few relatively simple rules to make sure that he will stay on the right track. A reduction in volume reduces direct (variable) manufacturing costs. This reduction may be offset, in whole or in part, by increases elsewhere if production is shifted from an abandoned plant to another or if lost volume in one product line is picked up by increased volume in another. On the other hand, if there is a complementary relationship between two or more products, the volume loss will be greater than the volume of the product to be discontinued, and the direct manufacturing costs of complementary products will also be reduced.

Product-line complementarity or substitutability may also influence the reduction in fixed costs that will accompany abandonment. Even apart from this, however, if complete product independence exists or if output cannot be shifted to other plants, "fixed" manufacturing costs may be reduced, but almost never can they be entirely eliminated. Even complete abandonment of a plant may not "save" all its fixed costs. The problem of depreciation has already been discussed. The depreciation cost that is relevant to the abandonment decision is the probable future decline in net disposal value of the facilities. But there are other division costs that may not respond completely to abandonment. Many division costs, such as product engineering, motive power, and maintenance, represent services provided by other units of the company. The "consuming" divisions are frequently charged on the basis of the average cost of providing these services to all units of the company. Average cost covers up the fact that the costs of these service operations are partly fixed and partly variable with respect to the operations of any one division, and abandonment of one division is unlikely to produce a proportionate reduction in these costs.

Time-sheet distributions of the activities of executives, salesmen, and office personnel may likewise be misleading. The fact that the sales manager now spends one-third of his time on a given product line does not necessarily mean that one-third of his salary can be avoided by dropping the line. What *is* relevant is what the sales manager can do with the time that will be freed by dropping the line. If he can take on work now being performed by others, then some real cost reduction may result. Looking at this from another viewpoint, there is an "opportunity cost" of the sales manager's time. This cost may be the cost of performing tasks now delegated to others, or it may be the added profit on added sales of other lines that might be obtained if the sales manager were free to rechannel his efforts.

A similar line of reasoning applies to time breakdowns on salesmen's time sheets. Dropping a line may permit reorganization of the sales force to operate with fewer salesmen, but frequently the salesman handles more than one product line per call, and most of the time devoted to the call will be required whether he handles this additional line or not. In most cases the truth will lie somewhere between a complete proportional reduction in the sales force and no reduction at all, because, even if each salesman saves only a few minutes per call, these few minutes, multiplied by the total number of calls made, may add up to a substantial increase in sales-force availability.

Office clerical time is perhaps more likely to be variable with respect to the volume of activity, but here again there are many fixed components of expense. Abandonment of a product line may reduce the number of lines per invoice, but it does not reduce the fixed costs associated with preparing the invoice. The volume of purchases may be reduced, but this may merely reflect a reduction in the size of the average purchase. A good analysis will attempt to determine the degree of variability in these costs, as well as in the costs of storage, insurance, transportation, shipping, receiving, and the various other enabling activities of the firm. It may be possible to estimate the degree of variability by means of time studies or statistical cost analyses, although the limitations inherent in these methods should be recognized.[9]

The analyst's problem is frequently made more difficult by the lack of a good system for functional classification of costs. Cost elements are accumulated in heterogeneous accounts, so that it is frequently well-nigh impossible to determine how abandonment or disposal will affect the level of cost. The practice of successive distributions of overhead costs from account to account often makes it difficult to estimate cost effects without first reconstructing the entire flow of information through the accounts. For example, in one company, by no means unique in this respect, "service department" costs were first accumulated in a series of departmental accounts, then "distributed" in total among a number of manufacturing departments, and then applied to individual product groups by means of a burden rate. Some of these product groups were then used as raw materials in the manufacture of other products. In attempting to evaluate the

[9] See, e.g., R. H. Couse, "Business Organization and the Accountant," in *Studies in Costing*, ed. David Solomons (London: Sweet & Maxwell, 1952), p. 145; a pioneer work in statistical cost analysis was Joel Dean's *Statistical Determination of Costs, with Special Reference to Marginal Costs* (Chicago: University of Chicago Press, 1936).

effects of abandoning one of these final product groups, it was necessary to unscramble the successive distributions and allocations underlying the cost figures of the product group being studied. Frequently the effort involved in this kind of detective work cannot be justified by the additional accuracy it will produce, in which case approximations will have to be made, based on logical assumptions as to the content of the accounting information.

ESTIMATING INVESTMENT COMMITMENT

The third element in estimating cash return is the amount of investment associated with the activity under investigation. It is in this area that errors are perhaps most frequently made. Book values of plant and equipment and of inventories are seldom truly relevant to the analysis. What matters is the disposable value of the assets involved. This is the amount of cash that is tied up by a decision to continue the activity; therefore, this is the true measure of the investment in facilities. As in any other capital-expenditure decision, the key figure is the expected earnings related to the free cash or its equivalent that must be invested to produce these earnings. A decision not to abandon is just the same as a decision to invest the recoverable value of the investment in the activity concerned.

The first step in this stage of the analysis is to estimate the probable market value of the "fixed" assets. (If the activity is such that it can be disposed of as a going concern, including fixed assets, inventories, good will, sales organization, etc., it is the market value of this composite that should be estimated, except in the case in which the total market value of the components exceeds the market value of the going concern.) This can be done roughly by appraisal or by seeking tentative bids from prospective purchasers, depending on the nature of the assets involved and the market situation. One of the large oil companies goes so far as to place service stations or station sites on the market to get estimates. If these bids are high enough to reduce the rate of return on the bid value to less than the company's demanded rate of return, the station or site is sold; if the bid is lower than this, the facilities are retained. If the bid is rejected, the company feels that it has lost nothing and has gained some valuable information. If the bid is accepted, the company is better off financially.

Particularly if the assets are to be sold piecemeal, however, the process of obtaining market bids may be too costly or cumbersome, and appraisals may become the basis for estimation. In either case, it is important to find out at least roughly what the property will bring if it is disposed of.

Cash and receivables less payables can usually be entered at their book values, but inventories may be another question. Particularly if LIFO inventory valuation is used, book values of inventories are likely to depart materially from their disposal value. Replacement cost is probably closest to the probable realization price of discontinued inventories, but the availability of a firm market is essential to the ready realization of replacement value. If the market is weak, or if a temporary market shortage exists, replacement cost may be a poor approximation to disposal value.

One other aspect of investment amount should be recognized. Although continued operation of the activity will not necessarily require immediate investment in new fixed assets, a decision to continue operations frequently commits the company to make such investments.

When this is true, these amounts should be entered at installed cost to the company. When these additional outlays will occur at dates removed in time from the abandonment decision, they should be discounted to find their "present value," or, if the discounted cash-flow method of computing rate of return is used, they should be entered at the appropriate points in the timetable of receipts and outlays.[10]

The preferable approach to disposal analysis, as in other types of capital-expenditure analysis, is to state all items after taxes. If the after-tax basis is followed, both the investment amount and the future earnings estimates must be adjusted for the expected impact of income taxes. In this calculation book values and book depreciation enter in, because they have a significant effect on the amount of taxes paid. Thus, if a plant has a book value of two million dollars and a disposal value of one million dollars, there will be a capital loss that may result in a tax credit. This tax credit should enter into the calculation of the recoverable investment amount.

SUMMARIZING THE DATA

Once the earnings and investment data have been gathered, they must be related to each other and to the company's standard of minimum acceptable performance.

Under one method for doing this, all future sums, both future cash earnings and future investment outlays associated with continuation of the activity, are discounted to a present value at a discount rate equal to the company's minimum acceptable rate of return on investment. This discounted sum then becomes a "refusal price." If the value of the investment, computed in the manner just described, is less than this refusal price, the facilities should be retained and the activity continued. If investment value exceeds refusal price, the facilities should be sold.

This is simply another way of saying that, if continued operation is worth more to the company than it could get by selling facilities, the activity should not be abandoned. What the operation is "worth" to the company is indicated by the stream of future earnings that it will produce, discounted at cost of capital or other minimum cut-off rate. If this "worth" exceeds recoverable investment value, it means that the future earnings stream will produce a rate of return on that recoverable investment value which is in excess of the minimum rate of return demanded by the company.

Although this method is conceptually simpler than the discounted cash-flow method of computing rate of return, it suffers from lack of familiarity. Although cash-flow rate-of-return estimates cannot be said to be universally known, it is a smaller jump from the traditional average return on book value to cash-flow rate of return than it is from conventional methods to present worth.

The discounted cash-flow method defines rate of return as that interest rate which, when used to discount future receipts and outlays to present value, will produce a present value of future receipts and earnings equal to the present recoverable value of the investment. This method is equivalent to the more popular method of expressing average annual earnings as a percentage of recoverable investment value, provided that two con-

[10] For a discussion of the present-value computation see Friedrich and Vera Lutz, *The Theory of Investment of the Firm* (Princeton, N.J.: Princeton University Press, 1951); present-value calculations are also at the heart of the "MAPI formula," originally presented in George Terborgh's *Dynamic Equipment Policy* (New York: McGraw-Hill Book Co., 1949).

ditions are met: (*a*) the future earnings stream is constant from year to year and extends indefinitely into the future at this constant level and (*b*) there will be no future decline in recoverable investment value. If these conditions are not met, the discounted cash-flow method provides a more sensitive mechanism for recording and evaluating variations in the timing of cash flows.[11]

Once rate of return has been computed, by the method selected, it can then be compared with the company's minimum acceptable rate of return. This minimum rate may be determined with reference to an estimate of the company's cost of capital; it indicates the minimum return that management believes can be tolerated without worsening the financial position of creditors and owners. The abandonment decision can then be made in terms of how well the indicated rate of return stacks up against the minimum rate.

These two methods of handling the earnings and investment data will generally lead to the same decision unless the time pattern of the stream of cash flows is highly unusual. Although the present-value method is conceptually superior (and in fact easier to compute), it is difficult to believe that any great damage will be done in most circumstances if the discounted cash-flow rate-of-return method is adopted.[12]

[11] The discounting method is compared with the annual average method in Joel Dean's article, "Measuring the Productivity of Capital," *Harvard Business Review*, XXXIII, No. 2 (January–February, 1954), 120–30.

CONCLUSIONS

The principles set forth here are not new. Even the discounting technique, which is an important but not a crucial aspect of the plan, has been in common use for centuries. The principles of increments and cash values have been formally recognized in economics since the nineteenth century, if not earlier. And the idea of different costs for different purposes is now so well established that it is an accepted part of the cost-accounting code.[13] Although the cash-return approach to abandonment analysis is not universally followed, a number of companies have used it with a high degree of effectiveness. In one company alone its application led to the abandonment and sale of one plant at an annual saving of more than one million dollars and to the retention and rejuvenation of another facility at another sizable increase in earnings. In both these instances the average book-return method would have led to diametrically opposite decisions. But the method deserves more widespread application. The plan outlined above should provide a framework to guide management in adopting and applying sound review and appraisal of existing activities with the purpose of improving the over-all profitability of the company as a whole.

[12] For a presentation of the merits of the present-value method see James H. Lorie and Leonard J. Savage, "Three Problems in Rationing Capital," *Journal of Business*, XXVIII, No. 4 (October, 1955), 236–39.

[13] See, e.g., "The Uses and Classifications of Costs" (Research Series No. 7), *N.A.C.A. Bulletin*, XXVII, No. 18 (May 15, 1946), 937–52.

CAPITAL EXPENDITURE MANAGEMENT

HORACE G. HILL, JR.*

PROFESSIONAL economists and financial officers of corporations have written and talked a great deal in recent years about the formidable analytical problems of capital budgeting. There has been, it seems to me, a dearth of adequate discussion of the administrative problems which must be solved successfully before any analytical system can be useful in its business context. This paper is an effort to indicate what some of these administrative problems are and what solutions to them might be. The expository device which is used is to present the "life history" of an investment proposal from its inception to its final disposition. This "life history" is an idealized one in that it presents the stages that a proposal should go through in a corporation where the members of management, from the directors to the foremen, are imbued with a spirit of stewardship in investing the owners' money.

THE LIFE HISTORY OF AN INVESTMENT PROPOSAL

1. CONCEPTION

The untapped profit potentialities in any business appear to be innumerable. A manager or supervisor working in this fertile field will frequently be struck with a new idea if he has even a normal degree of imagination. If he also has a fair modicum of common sense and some basic training in the analysis of capital projects, he can subject his idea to his own screening process to see whether it will bear critical scrutiny. His personal study, aided by the opinions of any of his associates in whom he has confided, will either point out some glaring oversight or erroneous assumption, or it will convince him that he has an idea with some merit. At this point many ideas which had appeared plausible will be properly consigned to oblivion by the men who conceived them, but the survivors will deserve further attention.

2. FORMALIZATION

The incipient project will now be fitted into the adopted form which will state precisely what its author proposes to do, how much money or other asset values will be spent or fixed, when these outlays will be made, when the project will become operative, what economic life may be reasonably expected, what net receipts will be returned to the treasury during each of the first five years of operation, what net receipts may be expected in subsequent five-year periods, and what ultimate recovery of cash or other asset values should result at the close of the project's economic life. Every one of these questions has a bearing on the worth of the project. Anyone requesting the privilege of investing some of the stockholders' money should be able to provide forthright answers and be prepared to be judged by their dependability. The first recording of these data in black and white on a concise form may convince the applicant that his project is not financially sound, and he may decide

* Senior associate, Joel Dean Associates.

not to submit it. However, if it continues to depict an attractive investment opportunity, he will be glad to acknowledge authorship and to work for its approval.

3. CO-ORDINATION

The project is going to need a sponsor who is recognized in top management circles. The Board will have determined the policy of controlling capital expenditures, and it will have delegated the administration of this policy to its chief executive officer, the president. He in turn will have elected to delegate specified limits of approval authority to his major department heads, on whom he has also placed the responsibility for personally endorsing even those projects which are beyond their limit of authority. He will have named these same department heads as the individuals from whom he will expect to receive a realistic capital-expenditure budget. This places the department head in a key position in these matters, with considerable authority and responsibility, and the applicant from down the line will take his project to the head of his department.

The first question raised by the department head will be whether any other department needs to be consulted. A simple labor-saving or fuel-saving scheme will generally involve no other part of the company. An increase in manufacturing capacity might present problems of procuring raw material or disposing of additional finished product. Upgrading a product might flood a market and bring no increase in revenue. Improved means of transportation might entail major changes in receiving facilities at many points. Countless possible complications could be listed which might affect the total cost of the project to the whole company or the incremental increase in expense or revenue. After this review and any conferences which it might entail, the project will emerge in the pattern of a company proposal.

4. EVALUATION

The author of the project will have prepared his data in the generally desired form and may have made his own calculation of the expected rate of return before submitting it to his superior. The department head will now wish to verify the soundness of all the assumptions made as to volumes, prices, and time periods. These are the factors which determine the project value and any undue optimism in any one of them can lead to a disastrous investment. The department head will know that his endorsement will mean that he has adopted the project as his own from this point and he will logically insist on being convinced that the basic data are reasonable.

Points which will require the greatest care while checking the project data are whether all prices are current market values and whether the claimed net revenue is limited to the incremental portion which the project will produce but which could not be procured without making the proposed investment. These principles are broad but essential. New problems of application will appear constantly with the endless variety of projects competing for available funds, but fair evaluations will result from strict adherence to these logical rules.

The department head will probably have a member of his own staff qualified to translate the outlay and income data into a rate of return comparable with the company cost of capital, or he might ask the president's staff to perform this function. This step may involve nothing more than a check of the calculation made by the author, but it will supply an important part of the label attached to the project and there should be no question as to its dependability.

5. CAPITAL BUDGET REQUEST

When the department head is satisfied that the project compares favorably with the standard of desirability which he is following, he will adopt it as his own, and give it a place in his capital-expenditure budget. The frequency and the time coverage of these budgets will be determined by top management, and this may be anywhere between the extremes of budgeting every thirty days for the single month ahead or budgeting every year for five years ahead.

The value of the long-range forecast as a control device for the Board is obvious if it can be prepared realistically. Such industries as telephone, power, gas, railroads, and some others will find it quite practical if based on proper studies of the factors which influence the demand for service. Any company will do well if it makes every effort to perfect a system of preparing a reasonable long-range forecast. A few attempts will not be wasted time, even though they may not prove to be reliable guides, as they will require some serious consideration of what probably lies ahead.

The short-range capital budget, which will generally cover a year and may provide for quarterly revision, will be the first chapter of the long-range forecast, will have unquestioned value to top management in its control program, and will arouse the active interest of operating management at all levels. The department head, with a new project which he is prepared to sponsor, will want his project specifically included in the adopted budget. His recommended list will be submitted to the budget director for coordination with requests from other departments and consideration by the Budget Committee.

In order to avoid presenting a heterogeneous mass of projects to the Budget Committee, the budget director will perform two preliminary steps. He will satisfy himself that the requests will not create an unbalanced operating situation if they should be approved, and he will arrange the projects in priority order according to their calculated rates of return. While he is engaged in this work of co-ordination, the financial officers will make their current estimate of the average cost of capital to the company over the next few years and the minimum rate of return which they believe should be acceptable to management, and they will also procure the best available forecasts of the cash position during the coming year. Then the way will be open for the Budget Committee to proceed with its consideration of the requests.

6. CAPITAL BUDGET FORMATION

The Budget Committee will undertake the reconciliation of the financial and the operating aims of management in the light of policies determined by the Board. This will require top-level personnel, with the president generally serving as chairman. He will probably find a small committee more satisfactory to serve with him, such as two operating executives and two financial officers, which might be the treasurer and the budget director.

The Budget Committee's function in reviewing the capital budget will be to report to the Board on any significant features of the plan which may be clearly indicated or implied, such as: points of accelerated expansion, changes in course, acquisitions of new business enterprises, rate of return on total capital outlay for the year, total for which no profit justification can be made, probable effect on dividend payments, and most likely source of needed funds.

At this stage the Budget Committee will be helping the Board to reach final policy decisions in several important fields, but it will not attempt to examine the merits of the individual projects which compose the aggregate request. The Committee will conclude its report with recommendations.

7. CAPITAL BUDGET APPROVAL

Consideration of the capital budget by the Board will give this top-level body its opportunity to examine the aims of the operating management, see how well they can be met by the ingenuity of the financial management, and agree upon a program which should work out to the best interest of the owners. Adoption of new policies may be involved, and the directors will want to take ample time to explore the capital budget thoroughly before giving it the stamp of their approval or ordering its modification along specified lines.

When the Board has satisfied itself that it has the best program, it will adopt the budget and delegate the subsequent administration to the president, with or without qualifying limitations. The president will establish the procedure to be followed in procuring the actual authorization of a specific project and the further delegation of his approval authority which he may choose to make. He will want particularly strict approval requirements for projects which were not included in the budget. The exact plan of delegated approval authority will be determined by the characteristics of the president and his subordinates and by the extent to which he can depend upon teamwork instead of police work to accomplish his purpose of capital management.

8. PROJECT JUSTIFICATION

With the adoption of the capital-expenditure budget by the Board, the way will be clear for the department head to push his particular project into the foreground for action. The adoption of the budget was an expression of agreement with various policies, but was not an approval to proceed immediately with every project included in its rather complex composition. Such specific approval will now be in order, however, and the department head will instruct the author of the project to prepare the justification in a concise and convincing form as the preliminary step.

The justification data which were used for budget purposes will be the basis of this work. Considerable amplification and refinement will be needed to produce a record which will bear critical analysis, which will be filed as the expressed judgment of the project's sponsors, and which will be checked against performance at intervals during the project's operating life. The budget director will be available for any needed assistance.

9. APPLICATION FOR AUTHORIZATION

When the justification data have been accumulated and arranged to the satisfaction of the department head, he will prepare the standard application form and transmit it to the budget director for final scrutiny and further routing. The signature of the department head will be required in all cases, and this may be final approval or merely endorsement for higher-level approval, depending upon the project involved and schedule of delegated authority established by the president. Each higher level will have the power to approve or reject certain categories of projects and to endorse or withhold endorsement in other categories where the final word will be spoken by a yet higher authority. When due consideration leads to any adverse action by an approving or endorsing authority, he will attach an explanation for the absence of his signature.

10. UNBUDGETED PROJECT

When an unforeseen project of great desirability appears between regular budget intervals, there will be some plan for giving it prompt consideration, although this may vary from year to year, depending upon the conditions in which the budget was adopted. For instance, if the Board has pared the budget to the maximum which should be spend in the current period, it will expect the president to insist on deleting some less attractive plans in order to make financial room for the new project. Or the Board might be willing to consider a revision of the budget to embrace a larger program. The time of adopting the budget and delegating its administration to the president will be the time for the Board to declare its current policy in regard to unbudgeted projects.

11. AUTHORIZATION

When the highest required signature is affixed to the application, it will become an authorization. It will clear through the budget director and immediately receive its identifying account number from the accounting department. Copies of the authorization will be distributed to all interested parties so that all charges will be properly routed. The project will now be out in the open with a tangible individuality.

12. CAPITAL EXPENDITURE

Progress reports on the outlay of funds will be available at the close of each accounting period which will generally be monthly. The department head, the budget director, or any other interested member of management will be able to compare the actual use of funds with the rate of expenditure which was forecast in the justification. As the work approaches the end it will be possible to see whether the authorized amount will be sufficient or will require a supplementary request, which would involve another application and approval. The final statement of the initial cost of the project will provide the first formal check on the validity of its claim to a place in the budget.

13. AUTHORIZATION CLOSING

Top management will find that the completion of the work described in the project authorization should be immediately followed by closing the authorization account. Open authorizations will always exert a magnetic drawing power for the costs of many minor jobs of dubious value which some operating supervisors want to perform without charging them against their current expenses or attempting to justify them as bona fide capital expenditures. If the president will designate the budget director or the chief engineer, or any staff officer who will know what he is doing, as the one who should tell the accounting department to close the account, much confusion will be avoided.

14. PROJECT PERFORMANCE

After a project has been in operation for a reasonable time, it will be desirable to see whether it is performing in accordance with its forecast. The original justification data will provide the yardstick for any selected year and the actual experience may be adjusted for prices or labor rates which were not predicted. Such tests at the close of the first and the fifth year will be particularly enlightening, as the early life is most important, but later checks will also be of value. The budget director should be constantly working with the accounting department and with the various department heads to determine the reliability of the justifications previously presented, and any means of improving them.

15. ABANDONMENT

Every project will reach a point at which it will be unable to make the required rate of return on its liquidation value. The department head who has absorbed the profit concept of his responsibilities will frequently take stock of his facilities to see which ones should be sold or even abandoned. This time may come before its estimated economic life has been reached, but the current facts and the new look at the future should govern. Inertia, pride, and sentiment will produce plenty of reasons for freezing capital funds in an investment which has ceased to be high grade. Eternal vigilance and cold-blooded financial analysis will always be needed at every step, including the much neglected housecleaning.

ADMINISTRATIVE ORGANIZATION IN CAPITAL BUDGETING

FRANK E. NORTON*

INVESTMENT decisions are inherently more complicated and less subject to rule-of-thumb treatment than are most of the decisions of a business firm relating to day-to-day operations. They relate to the "long run" rather than the "short run," and a mistake with respect to them is less easily rectified than in the case of more routine decisions. For the most part they are unique in some significant sense, in that no two investment decisions ever involve exactly the same circumstances. Business judgment of a high order is involved, because they are long-run decisions which deal with an uncertain future environment about which knowledge is imperfect. To an important extent the "art" of business management rests in the ability of the businessman to formulate, on the average, expectations about this uncertain future which are basically correct, as attested by realized results. The role of the businessman is one of making decisions; act he must, but unfortunately he can never have sufficient information to serve as a basis of such action.

The success with which firms make correct investment decisions is dependent upon how well they are organized to meet the challenging situation remarked upon. This involves the details of administrative organization and procedure as well as the application of appropriate economic criteria. The latter are applied to investment opportunities by the personnel of the firm within the framework established by the former.

This paper gives attention to what the widely scattered literature has to offer pertaining to administrative organization and procedures in connection with capital budgeting. Much of the literature consulted was found in technical journals or bulletins written by persons actively engaged in business operations, and, presumably, the procedures described by these industry representatives and surveyed here depict actual capital-budgeting practices.

INITIATION, SCREENING, AND APPROVAL OF CAPITAL-EXPENDITURE PROPOSALS

As is well known, there are a number of stages in the formulation of an explicit capital budget. The initiation of proposals for capital expenditures constitutes the first. Such proposals may initially encompass everything from minor suggestions or ideas to major capital projects involving elaborate engineering studies. There is an increasing recognition of the fact that projects should originate in many ways—beginning with the "suggestion system" in order to utilize the ingenuity of workers.[1] The most work-

* School of Business Administration, University of California, Los Angeles. I am indebted to Arthur Montgomery and Stuart Newmark for assistance in connection with this study and wish to acknowledge assistance provided by the Bureau of Business and Economic Research of the University of California. My colleague, Professor J. Fred Weston, has offered helpful comments regarding this paper.

[1] Charles H. Gleason, "An Organized Profit Improvement Program," *National Association of Cost Accountants Bulletin*, No. 32 (October, 1950), pp. 123–31; P. M. Chiuminatto, "Control of Capital Expenditures—Planning and Follow Through," *National Association of Cost Accountants Bulletin*, No. 30 (April, 1949), pp. 885–92.

able suggestions for removal of bottlenecks and consequent capital expenditures relating thereto come from workmen and foremen.[2] Likewise, industrial engineers and plant staff are apt to develop useful ideas in the course of their daily work.[3] While each department may make recommendations for general improvements, recommendations for the acquisition of cost-saving equipment ordinarily originates with the plant engineers.[4] Where investment projects are of such a nature as to involve a more or less elaborate technical analysis, initiation of proposals is usually made by the production engineers.[5] This is particularly true with respect to investment in the electric-power industry.[6] There is a tendency to provide for initiation of proposals on a regional basis where the firm conducts operations in widely scattered geographic regions.[7] Moreover, in the case of firms with a number of product lines, the administrative basis for originating and reviewing investment proposals is by individual product.[8]

Initial approval of capital-expenditure proposals rests at different levels in the firm, depending primarily upon the amount of such expenditure. Minor expenditures amounting to such a figure as $1,500 or less may be approved by the factory manager,[9] engineering department,[10] or the president of a division.[11] Larger projects are frequently sent to the engineering department for review and screening and then to a high operating executive for his final approval.[12] The comptroller[13] and sometimes the treasurer[14] are responsible for the consolidation of the various specific projects proposed into an over-all proposal of capital expenditures. Final authority on approval of capital expenditures usually rests with the chief executives and the board of directors.[15] Sometimes the executive committee is involved.[16] Usually the board of directors passes on the capital budget as a whole, for all preliminary

[2] Charles Belknap, "When We Expand," *Factory Management and Maintenance*, XCVIII (May, 1940), 52 f.

[3] Gleason, *op. cit.*

[4] Dale Purves, "Meet Mr. Budget," *Factory Management and Maintenance*, C (January, 1942), 99; Richard J. Hanwell, "Controlling Plant and Equipment Costs," *Corporate Treasurer's and Controller's Handbook*, ed. Lillian Doris (New York: Prentice-Hall, 1950), pp. 277–308.

[5] Allen H. Ottman, "Developing and Installing a Budget Program," *Corporate Treasurer's Handbook*, ed. Lillian Doris (New York: Prentice-Hall, 1950), pp. 97–135; John F. Gaither, "Fixed Asset Procedure from Requisition to Retirement," *National Association of Cost Accountants Bulletin*, No. 31 (December, 1949), pp. 447–54; John W. Watson, "Budgeting Capital Expenditures for an Oil Company," *National Association of Cost Accountants Bulletin*, No. 23 (October, 1941), pp. 207–20.

[6] Michael Gort, "The Planning of Investment: A Study of Capital Budgeting in the Electric Power Industry. I," *Journal of Business*, XXIV (April, 1951), 79–95.

[7] Chester E. Weger, "Financial Budgeting Technique," *Handbook of Business Administration*, ed. W. J. Donald (New York: McGraw-Hill Book Co., 1931), pp. 340–47; Henry McGrew, "A Case Study in the Budgeting of Airline Revenue, Expense, and Capital Outlay," *National Association of Cost Accountants Bulletin*, No. 30 (March, 1949), pp. 833–47.

[8] American Management Association, *A Program of Financial Planning and Controls: The Monsanto Chemical Company* ("Financial Management Series," No. 103 [New York: The Association, 1953]).

[9] Wesley L. Baie, Jr., "Control of Expenditures for Plant Additions and Improvements," *National Association of Cost Accountants Bulletin*, No. 32 (October, 1950), pp. 195–99.

[10] *Ibid.*

[11] Theodore Lang, *Cost Accountant's Handbook* (New York: Ronald Press Co., 1948), p. 1169.

[12] Baie, *op. cit.*

[13] Hanwell, *op. cit.*; Controllership Foundation, *Business Forecasting: A Survey of Business Practices and Methods* (New York, 1950).

[14] Weger, *op. cit.*

[15] Hanwell, *op. cit.*

[16] American Management Association, *op. cit.*; Chiuminatto, *op. cit.*

screening has been accomplished before this stage is reached.[17] Unfortunately, we find that too often in current practice top operating officers and the board of directors are involved in passing on individual projects even of a minor sort.[18] The accounting department approves all requisitions for the purchase of capital equipment.[19]

THE PLANNING HORIZON AND CAPITAL BUDGETING

Capital budgeting as a form of budgeting has lagged well behind general budgeting both in theory and in practice. This is importantly attributable to the fact that capital budgets involve forecasts about a more extended future than do current operating budgets. Even though capital budgets may be made annually, they involve a much longer planning horizon. This is true because of the very durability of capital assets. The expected productivity to be derived from such assets extends over a substantial period of the future. Thus long-run forecasts concerning an uncertain future are called for. Joel Dean has remarked that capital budgeting has remained largely "dream stuff" because of this inability of business firms to make long-run forecasts.[20]

Until the last decade and a half, true capital budgeting was largely restricted to public utilities. Because of the stability of their sales, they were able to forecast the demand for their services. In most cases, the demand for their services possessed an upward secular trend and exhibited a low sensitivity to changes in gross national product. No market-share problems were involved, and substitution relations were seldom significant. For the vast majority of business firms, however, sales forecasting was particularly precarious because of the inability to forecast the general level of business activity. Since most firms were faced with demand that is highly sensitive to changes in gross national product, an error in the estimation of future business conditions was certain to lead to a large discrepancy between expected and realized sales volume. Capital-expenditure plans based upon such shaky forecasts of sales volume were of little value. The result was that capital expenditures were frequently based on *ad hoc* circumstances—current lack of productive capacity, need for lowering current costs, and similar immediate considerations. No continuous attention was given to the planning of investment. Capital expenditures were made mostly when there was an obvious immediate need for them and when funds were available. There was a serious tendency to gear investment decisions primarily to the current and immediate past environmental conditions.

Important advances have been made in sales forecasting in the postwar years. Economic analysis has been brought to bear on the problem of analyzing the market for the products of an individual firm.[21] Significant progress has also been made in the forecasting of general business conditions upon which most sales forecasts rest.[22] This has made possible the extension of capital budgeting to a

[17] Hans J. Lang, "Managing Capital Invested in Buildings, Plant, and Equipment," *Business Finance Handbook* (New York: Prentice-Hall, 1953), pp. 393–424.

[18] "How and Why Industry Spends," *Businessweek*, August 12, 1950, pp. 31–32.

[19] Gaither, *op. cit.*

[20] Joel Dean, *Managerial Economics* (New York: Prentice-Hall, Inc., 1951), p. 159, n. 5.

[21] *Ibid.*; see especially chap. iv and the important studies in empirical demand analysis therein cited.

[22] See, e.g., the contributions by various authors on forecasting in *Journal of Business*, XXVII (January, 1954), 1–106.

much wider range of firms than those falling in the public utility classification. Such budgeting is likely to be feasible where firms with established markets exist. However, it remains true that capital budgets have to be flexible because of our inability to make long-run forecasts of general business conditions.

For the reasons previously indicated, the longest planning horizon with respect to capital expenditures is to be found in the public utility field. An analysis of the market for their services and corresponding productive capacity requirements for five to ten years into the future is common.[23] For example, the American Telephone and Telegraph Company makes tentative forecasts of sales ten years in advance.[24] Beyond this, an attempt may be made to get some notion of the potential demand for services up to twenty years.[25] As a matter of fact, a whole series of horizons is utilized. The shorter ones are, of course, characterized by a higher degree of clarity.[26] An annual capital budget is employed in the majority of such firms.[27]

Outside the public utility field, the capital-expenditures planning horizon must, of necessity, be much shorter. It is the view of many, however, that business firms have not organized their affairs as well as they might with respect to such planning. Continuous and systematic study and the formulation of budgets are found far less often in the area of capital expenditures than in the area of general-operations budgeting. In the cases where formal capital budgeting is undertaken, annual capital budgets with quarterly breakdowns are frequently found.[28] The forecasting of general business conditions and sales volume extends up to about five years.[29] Sometimes five-year moving forecasts are maintained.[30] Occasionally, a planning committee exists which has as part of its functions the formulation of future capital requirements.[31]

Very little is known as to how rigid investment plans are with respect to changes in current sales volume, current profits, and other relevant business variables. One study found that capital budgets were subject to frequent and unscheduled revisions, especially with respect to unexpected changes in profits and working-capital positions.[32] There is also some evidence that the planning horizon tends to contract during periods of declining demand.[33]

[23] H. H. Scoff, "Financial Planning—Long Term Forecasting," in *Corporate Treasurer's and Controller's Handbook*, ed. Lillian Doris (New York: Prentice-Hall, Inc., 1950), pp. 53–94; D. W. Peterson, "Control of Construction Expenditures," *American Gas Association Proceedings, 1949* (New York: American Gas Association, Inc., 1949), pp. 204–7.

[24] Theodore Lang, *op. cit.*, p. 1231.

[25] Gort, *op. cit.*, pp. 79–95.

[26] *Ibid.*

[27] *Ibid.*; Russels G. Houck, "Budgetary Review of Plant Additions in a Public Utility," *National Association of Cost Accountants Bulletin*, No. 30 (November, 1948), pp. 251–56.

[28] T. W. Leland, "Economy Studies in Replacement Decision," *National Association of Cost Accountants Bulletin*, No. 32 (April, 1951), pp. 930–39. Controllership Foundation, *op. cit.*; McGrew, *op. cit.*

[29] Louis W. Jaeger, "Long-Range Forecasts of Operations," *Management Review*, XXXVI (January, 1947), 42–44.

[30] Scoff, *op. cit.*

[31] S. Payson Hall, "Eyes on the Next Decade—Forward Planning Procedure," *National Association of Cost Accountants Bulletin*, No. 30 (December, 1948), pp. 375–80.

[32] Walter Heller, "The Anatomy of Investment Decisions," *Harvard Business Review*, XXIX (March, 1951), 95–103.

[33] Michael Gort, "The Planning of Investment: A Study of Capital Budgeting in the Electric Power Industry. II," *Journal of Business*, XXIV (July, 1951), 181–203.

CONCLUSIONS

The survey of the literature purporting to describe existing administrative organization and procedures with respect to capital budgeting would seem to suggest that much remains to be done by way of developing systematic capital-budgeting practices. It is important to recognize that optimal decision-making in this area presupposes not only the application of appropriate economic criteria but also an administrative and procedural framework within which they may be implemented. To date, more progress has been made with respect to the former than the latter. The current status of the subject is such that we need a more thorough knowledge of prevailing practices as a basis for the formulation of tentative hypotheses concerning the most effective administrative structure and its procedural counterpart.

HAS MAPI A PLACE IN A COMPREHENSIVE SYSTEM OF CAPITAL CONTROLS?

JOEL DEAN* AND WINFIELD SMITH†

I. INTRODUCTION

OUR purpose in this article is to determine whether and how the MAPI system for evaluating equipment-replacement proposals can be fitted into a comprehensive program of capital-expenditure controls.[1] The MAPI system has been persuasively advocated and widely adopted. Now, however, many firms are going on to explore the feasibility of a unified, consistent, capital-controls program covering the firm's investment expenditures for all purposes, not merely the replacement investments that were the original concern of the MAPI system. As a result, there is a need for a systematic investigation of the way in which the MAPI method measures the productivity of capital as compared with measurement by the discounted-cash-flow method (including both the rate-of-return and the present-worth variants). This comparison leads to a discussion of the possibilities for modifying and adapting the MAPI method to make it usable for nonreplacement proposals or of translating MAPI measurements of capital productivity into terms that are comparable with measurements of investment worth that are used in the discounted-cash-flow systems.

The central problem of capital budgeting is the choice of a criterion of capital productivity to measure the value of individual investment proposals. Most well-managed companies study many more capital-investment proposals each year than they can finance internally. The company's major capital-budgeting problem is to pick the best set of proposals that can be had with available funds, preferably by the use of an index of investment-worth that is easy to apply and correct in its measurements. The MAPI system offers an index for one such purpose. Section II of this article describes the system and its relationship to conventional measures of capital value; Section III examines the possibilities for integrating the MAPI system into a company-wide capital-budgeting program; and Section IV considers and evaluates the MAPI system as the sole basis for a capital-budgeting program.

In this article we are concerned with only one of the problems of measuring the productivity of capital, namely, the choice of a logical device for selecting, arranging, and evaluating data. We shall avoid, where possible, the problems of estimating and forecasting those technical and economic events that will follow acceptance or rejection of a particular investment proposal.

* Joel Dean Associates and professor of business economics, Columbia University.

† Joel Dean Associates.

[1] The MAPI system discussed in this article is the system devised by the Machinery and Allied Products Institute and presented in George Terborgh, *Dynamic Equipment Policy* (New York: McGraw-Hill Book Co., 1949). One variant of the system is described more briefly in *MAPI Replacement Manual* (New York: MAPI, 1950).

II. COMPARISON OF THE MAPI AND DISCOUNTED-CASH-FLOW SYSTEMS

A. DESCRIPTION OF THE MAPI SYSTEM

As presented in *Dynamic Equipment Policy*, the MAPI system deals almost exclusively with the equipment-replacement problem, that is, the problem of choosing among alternative ways of doing a given job. Although its originators have made little attempt to develop it into a general capital-budgeting device, the MAPI system can be adapted for use in other types of investment proposals and, with some modifications, could be used as the single basis for capital budgeting throughout the firm. It is here discussed in this more general context, in which the term "replacement" is broadened to cover any investment for which there is an alternative.

The MAPI system gives yes-no answers to the question of whether to make a replacement now and points to the best of the alternative replacement plans without quantifying in conventional terms the advantage of one plan over another. The implication is that each proposal passing the primary test of "good versus not good" should be bought. For this and other reasons MAPI may be classified as a present-worth test for use in "nonrationing" situations.[2] The MAPI system expresses the relative value of an investment proposal in terms of its "adverse minimum" (A.M.). The A.M. of a replacement proposal measures the average annual opportunity cost of the proposal. The total opportunity cost of using a piece of equipment is equal to the sum of two component costs: (1) One component is the time-adjusted cost of acquiring the equipment. In the case of new equipment, this is equal to original acquisition costs *plus* the present value of future capital additions *less* the present value of end-of-life salvage value. In the case of existing equipment it is the cost of retaining the equipment, which is equal to its present salvage value. (2) The second component is what is called the "operating inferiority" of the piece of equipment. This is equal to the present value of the stream of estimated annual operating cost disadvantages from using the equipment under consideration instead of an annual succession of newer and better alternatives. Because acceptance of the presently proposed equipment precludes, for a time, the use of future improved models, the sacrifice of future economies is counted as a cost of the present proposal.

This total opportunity cost is expressed as a level annual cost extending over the equipment's estimated life. However, the value of this annual cost varies with the length of life that is assumed. This is so because the capital-cost component will fall when these costs are spread over a longer period. On the other hand, annual operating inferiority costs will rise with the length of life assumed. There is one assumed length of service life which will yield a minimum value for the sum of these two costs. This minimum value is the "adverse minimum" of a given piece of equipment. In the MAPI system the choice is made

[2] This classification follows that developed in Joel Dean, "Capital Budgeting and the Firm's Demand for Capital," *Zeitschrift für Ökonometrie*, December, 1951, pp. 3–23, and set forth more clearly in the Lorie-Savage article elsewhere in this issue. A nonrationing situation is one in which the firm obtains sufficient funds to enable it to accept all proposals which beat its cost of money, i.e., which have positive present worth when their cash flows are discounted at the firm's cost of capital. We are adopting this convenient term provisionally, even though we are aware that further analysis may show that the contrasted "rationing" situations are rare or even formally impossible.

between two mutually exclusive proposals by first computing the A.M. of each and selecting the alternative which has the lower A.M.[3]

The operating-cost inferiority of a given investment is presumed to grow from year to year, for three reasons: (1) operating costs of the investment will rise as equipment wears down, loses precision, and requires more maintenance; (2) first-year operating costs of future new equipment will decrease with improvements in technology; and (3) the output available from future machinery will be better adapted to future demand and hence will be more valuable than the future output of currently available equipment. Thus, as the life-estimate for the investment is increased, the present value of operating inferiority rises, and the lifetime flat annuity equivalent to this present value also rises.

The present value of capital costs is also larger for longer life-estimates,[4] since salvage value is falling and is being more heavily discounted to present value. However, the time pattern of these costs is usually such that the lifetime flat annuity equivalent to their present value is smaller for longer life-estimates. Hence, as the life-estimate is increased, the declining capital cost and rising operating inferiority aspects of the investment proposal offset each other, with the result that, for some estimated life, there is a minimum lifetime flat annuity, which is the A.M.

It should be noted that there are two fundamental assumptions underlying the MAPI system of A.M.'s. The first is that the operating-cost inferiority gradient for presently available equipment will be constant over the life of such equipment; and the second is that future replacement equipment will have the same A.M. as presently available equipment. These assumptions are essential to the validity of the MAPI system and are discussed further below.

B. DESCRIPTION OF THE DISCOUNTED-CASH-FLOW APPROACH

The discounted-cash-flow approach has two main variants: one measures the rate of return by finding for each project that discounting rate which makes the present value of the stream of net receipts just equal to the present value of the outlay stream. The second variant discounts cash flows of all projects at a uniform rate, usually the company's cost of capital, and develops a ranking index by relating the resulting present worth to the project's outlays. The main features of the discounted-cash-flow approach have been described elsewhere,[5] so we shall merely summarize them here.

For both variants, the economic forecasts of cost, revenue, and tax behavior over the life of the proposed investment are first arranged in a period-by-period timetable of net cash flows, reaching as far as necessary into the future and showing for each year their net after-tax impact on the company's cash receipts and payments. This time series makes no distinction between capitalized outlays

[3] Where there are several alternatives, comparisons can be made among pairs of alternatives and the best alternative chosen through a process of successive eliminations.

[4] Except for owned equipment with no present salvage value.

[5] Joel Dean, *Capital Budgeting* (New York: Columbia University Press, 1951); "Better Management of Capital Expenditures through Research," *Journal of Finance*, VIII, No. 2 (May, 1953), 119–28; and "Measuring the Productivity of Capital," *Harvard Business Review*, XXXII, No. 1 (January–February, 1954), 120–30; Horace G. Hill, Jr., "A New Method of Computing Rate-of-Return on Capital Expenditures"; and James Lorie and L. J. Savage, "Three Problems in Rationing Capital," in this issue.

and current operating transactions except in so far as these affect corporate income taxes. These net cash flows are then discounted to yield either a measure of rate of return or of present value, which then becomes the criterion for accepting or rejecting the proposal and for comparing it with other proposals.

C. TRANSLATION OF MAPI TO DISCOUNTED CASH FLOWS

By itself an A.M. is not the kind of variable that is found in economic analysis of capital-expenditure policy, where attention is focused on differences in time patterns of cash outlays and receipts in production. The A.M. is not a measure of cash flows or of differences in cash flows between one plan and another, except by extraordinary coincidence. As reflected in the A.M., each year's cost of a plan is measured relative not to the costs of a reasonably alternative plan but rather to the first-year costs of the best new method then available for doing the job, regardless of whether a switch might be made that year to the new method.[6] Hence an important question in appraising the MAPI system and integrating it with other systems is the relationships of the A.M.'s in MAPI to present worth or rate of return of an investment.

In the MAPI system it is not the level of a single A.M. that matters but rather the difference in level of a pair of competitive A.M.'s. The meaning of these differences is stated most simply by an example: Assume that plan S has an A.M. of $500 over an optimal life of 7 years, and competitive plan T has an A.M. of $300 for a life of 10 years. Then compute the present worth of a 7-year steady annuity of $200 per year, where 7 years is the life of plan S and $200 is the excess of S's A.M. over T's A.M.[7] At a 15 per cent discount rate, the present worth would be $867. This present worth is equal to the total present worth, as conventionally computed, of plan T as an alternative to plan S. That is, if total outlays and receipts in plan S, taken as far into the future as possible, are discounted to a net present worth of receipts less costs, and if T's cash flows are similarly discounted to net present worth, the excess of T's present worth over S's present worth is equal to the $867, the present worth of the 7-year $200 annuity. In brief, the present value of the difference in A.M.'s over the shorter of the two economic lives measures the total capital value of one plan as an alternative to the other.[8] This straightforward relationship between A.M.'s and present values is the basis for translating MAPI measurements into a more general capital-budgeting system based on discounted-cash-flow present-worth estimates.

This relationship depends for its validity upon the accuracy of MAPI's pair of underlying assumptions, namely (1) that operating costs and obsolescence inferiority costs rise at a constant rate over time during the life of the proposed investment and (2) that the A.M.'s of future replacement possibilities are the same as for this year's proposal. These assumptions must in fact be tightened

[6] The extraordinary coincidence by which the A.M. might measure cash flows would occur when the obsolescence factors reflected in the operating inferiority act upon prices and/or sales in such a way as to cut back cash earnings in just the manner described by the inferiority gradient. In the MAPI system, use of the best new plans as cost benchmarks is not intended to imply that cash earnings will take such a course.

[7] The discount rate in the present-worth calculation is the rate used in computing the two A.M.'s.

[8] The equality holds for any estimates of economic life, not only those for which the A.M.'s are actually minimum. But, in general, only the optimal life-estimates are relevant.

somewhat for the simple present-value relationship to hold. The assumption of constant cost gradients must be extended to cover the indefinite future beyond the life of the proposal, and the assumption of constant future A.M.'s must be replaced by the almost equivalent assumption that investment prices and economic life-estimates will be constant for all future replacements. Without this new pair of assumptions—e.g., if exponential time trends of obsolescence costs are assumed—the simple relation of A.M. differences and present-worth differences breaks down, and it is not possible in any general way to convert the one into the other or to put an economic interpretation on the A.M.

It is the peculiar nature of MAPI's A.M. computation that makes these assumptions so critical. The obsolescence gradients incorporated in the A.M. do not represent cash flows as such during the life of the investment. Their relevance to the problem lies in their effect on operating costs of future investments that are to be replacements of this year's investment. And in cases where the two basic assumptions in the computation are valid, the manner in which obsolescence is brought into the differences between A.M.'s is the correct statement of the effect of obsolescence on the cost behavior of future investments. It is a correct statement, that is, when and only when the obsolescence rate is constant through time and when prices and life are neutralized by being held constant.

The relationship just discussed provides a link not only to present-worth measurement but to the measurement of rate of return as well. There are no new concepts involved here beyond those in the A.M.—present-worth relationship. The rate of return of a proposal is the discount rate that reduces the present value of the future stream of receipts to equality with the present value of total costs in the investment. It follows directly that investment rate of return in the MAPI system is the rate at which the computed A.M. for the proposal is equal to the A.M. of its alternative.[9]

D. MAJOR DIFFERENCES BETWEEN MAPI AND DISCOUNTED CASH FLOW

The most general difference between these two systems is in the nature and quantity of the required input data. In its most abbreviated form, the MAPI system requires that only three variables be estimated: (1) first-year amount of operating-cost inferiority for the defending equipment, (2) investment amount for the new equipment, and (3) an inferiority gradient applicable to both. No externally derived estimate of economic life is needed. (However, an estimate of service life can be used in MAPI as an alternative to the gradient estimate. *Dynamic Equipment Policy* leans heavily toward the use of gradients, and the *MAPI Replacement Manual* uses an estimate of service life to the exclusion of the gradient.) The discounted-cash-flow approach, in contrast, generally deals with more variables and hence seems to call for more data, including an explicit estimate of economic life.

It would, however, be very surprising if these two systems showed real differences in their requirements for data to solve a particular problem. Both are merely devices for making logical judgments about facts rather than substitutes for facts. The amount of basic information required for a decision is determined

[9] This discounted rate of return for a proposal is the one that must be put into the calculation of the challenger's A.M. in order to make it equal the A.M. of the defender.

by the problem, not by the nature of the "logic machine," although two such machines may require that this information be fed to them in different forms.

The basic difference between the two systems is not in the amount of data that is needed but rather in the amount of data that is free to vary from problem to problem. Under MAPI the two simplifying assumptions that are its principal contribution replace an explicit estimate of the timetable of costs, revenues, and tax effects, because under MAPI these are expressed as one simple linear time series. More specifically, there are four ways in which the systems differ: (1) the way in which corporate income tax effects are allowed for, (2) the way in which the time shape of costs and revenues is allowed for, (3) the way in which cash costs and opportunity costs are introduced and reflected, and (4) the way in which economic life is estimated and used.

1. *Corporate income taxes.*—The discounted-cash-flow system in both its variants emphasizes the importance of taking into account the impact of federal income taxes on any investment decision. This is because the impact is large and is not, as some have supposed, uniform in its effect upon the profitability of different projects. Especially under the new depreciation provisions, but also in the distinction between expensed and capitalized outlays, tax effects are not uniformly distributed over time. And it is the essence of the contribution of a discounting system to recognize and accurately take into account differences in time shape.

Published expositions of the MAPI system do not attempt to take income taxes into account beyond the use of a discount rate reflecting after-tax earnings requirements. This omission may be for simplification, but it makes a lot of difference. Partial allowance for income tax could be built into the MAPI system through the initial inferiority and by tax deflation of expensable portions of the investment amount. However, tax effects stemming from accelerated amortization or either of the new tax-depreciation plans could only be approximated by this suggested modification. Modifying the earnings standard (discount rate) for taxes is desirable and uncommon. But this blanket adjustment does not do the full job of differentiating among projects on the basis of their after-tax rate of return.

2. *Timetable versus gradient.*—Tax effects are only one of the large number of cost and revenue flows which have irregular time shapes and which can affect the investment worth of projects importantly and differently. The explicit timetable of net cash flows that characterizes any discounted-cash-flow system is displaced in the MAPI system by (1) a first-year operating-cost inferiority estimate, (2) a gradient or annual change in this inferiority, and (3) an initial investment. The combination of this gradient with the estimate of first-year inferiority projects a timetable of a simple and special sort. A similar simplification of forecasting can be used in the cash-flow method, but the latter is not confined to this simplification. While linear projections of future costs and revenues by means of a simple formula have not proved particularly realistic, they are likely to be more correct for key factors in the replacement investment than for other types of capital proposals.

3. *Cash and opportunity costs.*—The discounted-cash-flow approach is confined to after-tax flows of cash or cash equivalents. Cash equivalents include opportunity costs that are relevant, esti-

mated at pertinent market values. Opportunity costs, in general, refer to gains foregone by the proposed course of action. Both systems make use of opportunity costs in many places. For example, in estimating the amount of the investment, the cash-equivalent disposal value of the old equipment rather than its book value is used by both. The MAPI system, however, introduces opportunity costs in a way that is not matched by the cash-flow system. The inferiority gradient represents the opportunity costs of not replacing the present or proposed investment at each of a series of successive future dates. The discounted-cash-flow method deals with this problem of obsolescence directly by an explicit estimate of economic life.

4. *Economic life.*—Forecasting economic life, though difficult, must be done to evaluate any proposed capital investment, replacement or otherwise. One of MAPI's attractive features, heavily stressed in *Dynamic Equipment Policy*, is that it avoids the need for an explicit estimate of economic life. This simplification is achieved by taking the analysis one step backward and incorporating in the MAPI method the basic determinants of future economic life, gradients of technological advance, rising repair costs, and the assumption that the yet unborn machines will have the same adverse minima as present machines.

If these are, in fact, the determinants of a correct estimate of an economic life, then going back to them does not produce a better or easier forecast than if the life-estimate were made separately and inserted explicitly. If the real determinants of economic life cannot be correctly represented by these linear gradients, then this solution is not just a desirable simplification of the projection process, it is instead an incorrect simplification.

The alternative is to estimate economic life separately and to introduce it explicitly into the calculation. Some have thought that this means that the forecast must be determined by historical service life, even where the facts indicate that past service life was incorrect or will not hold in the future. In fact, no such constraint is necessary. Economic life can be forecasted separately by any means that seems likely to produce acceptable results. Where desirable, an approach analogous to discounted cash flows can be used to take correct account of the timing and amounts of all relevant future revenues, outlays, and opportunity costs.

The simplification of a linear gradient can also be used in such a cash-flow timetable approach to forecasting economic life. But this simplification is not forced upon the user, and whenever the future behavior of repair costs, capital wastage, taxes, and operating costs does not seem likely to be linear, more realistic projections can conveniently be used.

E. ILLUSTRATION OF RELATIONSHIPS

The following hypothetical case study demonstrates with numbers the major points discussed previously. Since the relationship between the MAPI system and cash-flow discounting holds only when the two MAPI assumptions hold, these assumptions are used in the first part of this illustration.

The case to be studied is a proposal to mechanize an operation now carried out by hand. This is a replacement proposal in the general sense, but it brings out certain questions not found in the usual problems of replacing machinery with newer machinery. Two forms of the problem are discussed. In the first form, there is an assumption that earnings of the machine, relative to hand operation, will be constant over the years (setting aside in this problem the possible effects of price and wage variations). Such will be the case if either (1) the level of operations stays constant into the indefinite future or (2) the operation utilizes the full capacity of the new machine from the very beginning. In the second form of the problem, the level of activity for the machine is assumed to vary from year to year.

1. *Constant-earnings case.*—The relevant data in the problem are shown in the accompanying table. The cost sav-

Cost of machine............	\$5,000
Cost savings relative to hand operation................	\$2,000 per year
Expected life of machine.....	10 years
Final salvage value..........	None
Company's cost of capital....	10 per cent

ings in the case take into account all the effects of making the investment as compared with not making it. For example, they reflect added income taxes on earnings *less* the tax savings from allowable depreciation charges. Similarly, the cost of the machine is net of tax savings in the current year because of the investment amounts that can be expensed against current income.

To give the estimated life as ten years is equivalent to saying that the machine's inferiority gradient is about \$130 per year. If the machine is replaced in ten years, it is because its operating inferiority relative to then available machines has cumulated to such an amount that the present value of earnings from replacement will just equal the cost of a replacement machine. If future machines cost \$5,000 and have the same inferiority gradient as the present machine, this gradient for a ten-year life works out to be \$130.[10]

The value of this investment proposal in terms of discounted cash flows depends on what the alternative to investment is taken to be. The usual alternative in such cases is to make a similar investment next year. Measured against this possibility, the cash flows in the problem are a \$2,000 income for one year and a deficiency of \$130 per year (relative to next year's machine) for nine following years, followed by similar cycles of replacement outlays giving one year of earnings and nine of losses, and so on into the future. The net present worth of such a stream (earnings *less* losses) amounts to \$639, and the rate of return is 33 per cent.[11]

Another alternative that could be used as a basis for measuring earnings is the possibility of continuing the hand operation for ten years, the full life of the machine. The present worth of the investment in this case is somewhere between \$4,320 and \$7,300, depending on the amount of deterioration (as opposed to obsolescence) in the inferiority gradi-

[10] This value and most others mentioned in this section are computed for year-end payments discounted once per year at the stated discount rate. While continuous discounting of continuous flows gives more realistic estimates, the convention of discrete payments is used here to make the discounted-cash-flow results comparable with the results of the MAPI formulas, which reflect discrete discounting.

[11] Under the MAPI assumptions, the present worth can be computed fairly simply as the present worth of \$2,000 for one year *less* the capital cost for one year and a ten-year annuity of the \$130 annual losses. That is, it is

$$2{,}000\,(1+r)^{-1} - 5{,}000\,[1-(1+r)^{-1}]$$
$$-\,130\,(1+r)^{-1}\left[\frac{1-(1-r)^{-10}}{r}\right].$$

This simplified computation results from the interrelationships that exist under the MAPI assumptions between the price of the machine, its age, and its inferiority gradient. To demonstrate these relations would take more space than is warranted in this discussion.

ent. This is not usually an important alternative in this kind of problem.

In terms of the MAPI system, the value of the investment is measured by computing adverse minima for the machine and for the hand operation. Since this is a no-salvage investment, we can apply the short-cut MAPI formulas presented in chapter vii of *Dynamic Equipment Policy*.[12] Given a life-estimate of ten years, it is possible to compute the adverse minimum for the new machine as

$$c\left(\frac{2n-1}{n^2}+\frac{i}{1.4}\right),$$

where c is the cost of the machine, n is its economic life, and i the cost of capital.

This formula yields an estimate of $1,307 for the A.M. of the new machine. This is a reasonable approximation to the true A.M. (i.e., as computed by discounting rather than by the short-cut formula), which is $1,297. The A.M. for the hand operation to be replaced is $2,000, the operating-cost advantage of using the machine.

In the MAPI system, the fact that the challenger's A.M. of $1,297 is less than the $2,000 A.M. for the hand operation indicates that the machine should be bought. In this discussion, the point to be noted (see Sec. IIC) is that the difference between the two A.M.'s—$703 in the full computation—is equal to a payment one year hence having a present worth of $639. And $639, as noted, is the present worth computed directly by discounting cash flows for the investment as an alternative to replacement next year.[13]

The MAPI formula produces a reasonably good estimate of the present worth of the investment in this case, but it is somewhat wider of the mark in estimating rate of return. Rate of return can be estimated from the short-cut formula by setting the expression equal to $2,000, the A.M. for handwork, and solving for i. The resulting rate of return is 29 per cent, compared to the 33 per cent computed by discounting cash flows.

The MAPI formulas can also be used to compute the present worth of the investment as an alternative to ten years of handwork. This is done by computing the present worth of a ten-year annuity of the difference between the two A.M.'s. However, the A.M. for handwork over ten years is greater than for one year if there is an obsolescence component in the inferiority gradient. For example, if the gradient is all obsolescence, this A.M. is $2,483 for ten years, as against the $2,000 for one year, and the ten-year annuity of the difference in A.M.'s has a present worth of $7,300, as in the corresponding discounted-cash-flow computation mentioned previously. When the gradient represents only deterioration, the handwork A.M. stays at $2,000, and the ten-year annuity of A.M. differences has a present worth of $4,320—again as in the discounted-cash-flow computation.

The MAPI computations are thus related closely to discounted cash flows and give workable estimates, for this problem, of present worth and rate of return by use of the life-estimate short-cut

[12] These short-cut formulas simplify the computation of adverse minima by substituting for the full discounting procedure the sum of (1) the life-average of accumulated inferiority gradient, (2) a straight-line depreciation charge for one year, and (3) a one-year interest charge on the average investment (estimated as half of the original investment cost).

[13] The short-cut formula yields an A.M. difference of $693 or an estimated present worth of $630 for the investment proposal. The alternative short-cut formula, using the gradient rather than the life-estimate, gives an A.M. of $1,326, an A.M. difference of $674 ,with a present worth of $612. It should be noted that the proposal's present worth computed by continuous discounting of continuous cash flows is $711 rather than $639 (see n. 10).

formula. (The short-cut gradient formula works less well here.) In this problem, however, it was assumed that production on the machine was to be at a constant level. We turn now to the case where output is expected to change over the machine's life.

2. *Variable-earnings case.*—Two situations are considered here, one in which output is expected to rise steadily over a few years until it reaches some level, and another where output declines steadily for a period. For each of the situations, only the alternative of investment next year is considered. The investment proposal considered is the same as in the preceding discussion—a $5,000 machine to replace a hand operation, saving $2,000 in operating costs in the first year.

a) *Increasing output.*—If production is expected to rise over the years, the cost savings relative to handwork will also rise above the $2,000 first-year level. Assume that the future output plateau, perhaps the machine's capacity, is at a level where, if new, it would save $3,200 over handwork. At the same time that output is rising, the inferiority gradient is also rising, and what was a $130 gradient at the $2,000 output level is $208 at the $3,200 level. That is, whereas in the former problem, a machine bought next year would earn $130 per year more than this year's machine, in this case next year's machine will ultimately be earning $208 more than the current prospect. Thus the cash-flow stream for this proposal represents one year with $2,000 earnings followed by a series of years with rising losses (relative to next year's machine), reaching a final level of $208 per year.

The effect of the rising gradient is to shorten the expected life of the new machine (provided that machine prices stay constant), since its cumulated inferiority relative to new machines will be higher at any point than in the preceding problem. In this case the optimum life becomes about eight years rather than the previous ten years.

The discounted-cash-flow value of this proposal depends on the rate at which output increases. If it takes eight years to reach the top output level, it has a present worth of about $500 and a rate of return of about 29 per cent. If output reaches the top level in the second year, the investment's present worth is only $250, and the return is 16 per cent. In either case the optimum life is about eight years.

The MAPI short-cut formulas turn out to be insensitive to this sort of problem. If we apply the service-life formula used in the preceding problem and estimate service life at eight years, the A.M. for the new machine is estimated at $1,525, the difference between the two A.M.'s is $475, and the present worth of the proposal is $432. This can be considered a relevant estimate for the case in which maximum output is not reached until the last year of machine life. But the case in which maximum output is achieved in the second year also has an eight-year life and thus gets the same present-worth estimate from the MAPI service-life formula. The formula thus cannot distinguish between two different cases that have the same machine cost, first-year earnings, and estimated life.[14]

[14] The case is somewhat different for the short-cut gradient formula for the A.M.:

$$\sqrt{2cg} + \frac{ic - g}{2}.$$

This formula will yield the correct present worth, provided that the correct weighted average gradient (*g* in the formula) is fed into it. But this only transforms the problem into one of estimating the gradient. Using the first-year gradient—$130—gives the same present worth, $611, as in the constant-

b) Decreasing output.—Assume, finally, that output is decreasing in the operation in question and will eventually reach a level at which the present machine, if new, could save only $800 over handwork. In this case the gradient decreases from $130 to a final level of $52, and the optimum service life of the machine would be about eighteen years.

Here the present worth of investment now compared with investment next year is higher than when output is rising. If the $800 earnings level is reached in the seventh year, for example, the present worth of the investment is $480 as computed by discounting cash flows.

Again, as in the case of increasing output, the MAPI formulas are essentially insensitive to the changing earnings stream. The service-life formula gives a present worth of $1,000, applicable to any cash-flow stream, resulting in an eighteen-year optimum life for a $5,000 investment. The gradient formula is again useless without a proper average estimate of the gradient.

The difficulty in both the increasing- and the decreasing-output cases is that we have not adhered to the basic MAPI assumptions. Specifically, the inferiority gradient has not held constant but rather has varied with changes in production.

The assumption of constant gradients is presented in *Dynamic Equipment Policy* as the most reasonable assumption to make in the face of uncertainty about the future. And under conditions of constant output, a constant gradient is indeed a reasonable and frequently adopted assumption. When output varies, however, constancy in gradients requires extraordinary relationships between the affairs of an individual company, on the one hand, and deterioration and technological advance, on the other.[15] Since such relationships cannot reasonably be expected in the general case, it is evident that underlying the assumption of a constant gradient is a further general assumption that output is to be constant into the future.

However, for the case of constant output, constant inferiority gradients, and constant prices of future machines, which is the case illustrated in the first part of this section, it appears that there are workable relationships between the MAPI short-cut formulas and cash-flow-discounting techniques that allow estimating discounted cash flows by the MAPI system.[16]

III. INTEGRATION OF MAPI WITH DISCOUNTED-CASH-FLOW SYSTEM

The relationships between MAPI and discounted-cash-flow systems have now been explored on a technical level. With this background we can evaluate the usefulness of the MAPI system. First, in this section we shall examine problems of integrating MAPI with a discounted-cash-flow system of capital controls. Next, in Section IV, we shall appraise MAPI as a possible universal index of capital productivity and instrument of capital budgeting. The problem in inte-

earnings problem, whereas the maximum present worth in this problem is $500. The final gradient of $208 gives a present worth of $375, which is somewhere between the real minimum and maximum. We are at sea trying to fit a gradient to this problem.

[15] One case in which gradients can be assumed constant is the situation in which output is presumed to be a linear function of time, either increasing or decreasing, into the infinite future.

[16] It can be shown algebraically that under the explicit and implicit MAPI assumptions the relationships are exact as between the full MAPI computations and discounted cash flows. The demonstration is too long to include here, but the equality is suggested by the results in the first part of this section.

grating MAPI into broader capital-budgeting systems is to make sure that replacement proposals measured by the MAPI method are placed on the same financial footing as proposals measured by discounted-cash-flow methods, so that one type will not be favored over the other.

Ultimately, all investments are competitive with one another, since all draw on the same pool of investable funds. Replacement investments are not an exception to this rule; by not making a replacement, funds are released for other purposes. If the best use is to be made of the money available, replacements, as well as investments for additions, modernization, new products, research, promotion, etc., must all be subjected to the same test, or at least to tests that impose the same standards on all competing investments. Investment funds are, wasted and profits are sacrificed if a particular class of investment is judged by a method that is more tolerant than those used elsewhere.[17]

A. INTEGRATION WITH PRESENT WORTH

The analysis in Section II indicated the basic relationship between MAPI and a present-worth system. For the most common replacement problem, in which the alternatives are replacement now or replacement next year, we have already shown that the difference in A.M.'s is the value of the replacement proposal as of a year from now. In order to bring these differences into a company-wide capital budgeting process, it is necessary only to multiply them by the proper one-year discount factor, reflecting the company's cost of capital.[18] Some additional work is needed if the alternative to replacement now is replacement several years hence (e.g., when a large rehabilitation expenditure now will extend the life of the present machine for several years); it is then necessary to compute the present value of the annuity of A.M. differences.

B. INTEGRATION WITH RATE OF RETURN

It was shown in a preceding section that, in the more abbreviated forms of the MAPI system, the equations can be used to approximate the investment rate of return on the proposed replacement. These rates of return can then be used to determine whether this replacement is justified in the light of the firm's over-all investment needs and sources of funds, through the standard rate-of-return-rationing procedure.

While this is technically possible, there is little to be gained by it except when the MAPI assumptions are exceptionally plausible. Some algebra is involved, and this multiplies rapidly if it is desired to introduce salvage values or other variations into the calculations. There are alternative procedures for calculating rate of return directly, which are more flexible, no more complicated, and equally accurate.[19]

IV. MAPI AS THE SOLE INDEX OF CAPITAL PRODUCTIVITY

MAPI has not, to our knowledge, been used as an all-purpose device for measuring and ranking the investment worth of

[17] The possibility of a double standard of investment acceptability is, of course, not eliminated by the company-wide use of a single method for evaluating investments; the method may still be applied inconsistently. This possibility is greatly increased, however, when dissimilar indexes of investment worth are used, especially if these criteria are used blindly and without formal evaluation and comparison. A capital-budgeting plan which allocated a fixed sum of money (e.g., equal to depreciation) to replacement investments and the remainder to other types of investment would be a system with a dual standard.

[18] The intricacies of comparing present-worth measurements in a capital-budgeting system are discussed by Lorie and Savage in their article elsewhere in this issue.

[19] See Joel Dean, *Capital Budgeting*, chap. vi.

all types of proposals, that is, doing the full capital-budgeting job. Although its proponents have occasionally referred to its potential versatility, they have not, as far as we know, provided explicit solutions for the problems of modification and adaptation that must be solved to achieve this claimed versatility. What follows, then, is a brief consideration of its usefulness in this function.

The distinctive trait of a pure replacement investment is that only the *method* of doing the job is at issue. The profitability of the proposed replacement investment turns on a comparison of the old method with the proposed new equipment. This trait simplifies profitability measurement. Future changes in receipts can be neglected because the continuance, volume, and scope of the operation are not at issue, only the method of performing it. The analysis can be confined to a comparison of forecasts of the relevant future costs of the old and the new methods.

This distinction between replacements and other types of investment is convenient for practical analysis, but it is not a necessary distinction in the measurement of earnings. Earnings from a conventional equipment-replacement investment arise from differences in costs and receipts between the present mode of operation and the proposed alternative mode of operation. The fact that receipts are unaffected and hence can be ignored in replacement investments permits handy simplification but is not a basic conceptual difference.

Thus, the essence of analysis of any investment problem is a comparison of alternatives. An expansion investment requires a comparison of the receipts and costs of expanded volume with the alternative of continuing with the capacity limits of the present facilities. Similarly, a product-improvement or new-product investment requires a comparison of the proposal against the alternative of continuing without the contemplated change. And in all types of investment the alternatives are usually multiple, e.g., expanding next year, the following year, or never.

To modify MAPI to apply to these nonreplacement investments it is necessary to include a measure of differential receipts omitted in the replacement-investment simplification. The earnings from an expansion investment, for example, are the determinants of the A.M. for the no-expansion plan, since they are the opportunity costs, the foregone gains, of not expanding. But adapting the data so as to use the MAPI method for nonreplacement investments requires ingenuity and skill and a full understanding of the analysis that lies behind the short-cut formulas. For example, when a new-product investment this year will give a better long-run market position than the same investment delayed a year, the analysis becomes intricate.

Examination of the ways in which the MAPI method must be modified for use in appraising nonreplacement capital proposals reveals three shortcomings as a universal capital-budgeting device.

The first is that it takes a virtuoso to apply the MAPI method to these other types of investments. It is necessary to translate the relevant economic and financial estimates into a new and esoteric set of concepts and terms. This translation involves setting up pseudo-comparisons with alternatives and must be ingeniously manufactured. Moreover, the terms in which the results of these comparisons are stated, namely, comparative adverse minimums, are not easily and plausibly verbalized and do not have much meaning for most executives, who are accustomed to think in financial terms of the relationship of earnings (or savings) to capital tied up.

A second deficiency is that the two basic MAPI assumptions impose serious constraints on its flexibility for appraising the typically diverse investment proposals of a large corporation. These two assumptions are (1) a linear gradient of change in the net effect of obsolescence, rising repair costs, quality deterioration, revenues, income taxes, etc., and (2) an identical adverse minimum for successive generations of replacements. They are unduly restrictive for most nonreplacement investments and even for some replacement investments, especially those with complex outlay and receipt streams or where pure replacement is combined with expansion, product improvement, and combining or splitting of processing steps.

In the third place, serious administrative difficulties would be encountered in a large corporation if MAPI were used as a universal index of investment worth. Profit-center decentralization accentuates these difficulties, because the process of originating, refining, reviewing, and approving capital proposals under decentralized operations involves so many people at different levels of responsibility and specialization.

The problems of education and communication in capital budgeting require a yardstick of project worth which (1) is easy to compute and apply, (2) is versatile and handily adaptable to all types of investment proposals, (3) bears a recognizable relationship to familiar concepts of financial merit, and (4) measures financial worth correctly. In its present form, the MAPI system seems to have serious shortcomings, compared with its alternative, in meeting these administrative specifications.

SOME COMMENTS ON THE DEAN-SMITH ARTICLE ON THE MAPI FORMULA

GEORGE TERBORGH*

I SHOULD like to offer a few comments on the interesting article by Joel Dean and Winfield Smith in this *Journal* (XXVIII [October, 1955], 261–74), entitled "Has MAPI a Place in a Comprehensive System of Capital Controls?"

The article makes two principal points: (1) the MAPI formula is not a universally applicable device for appraising the merits of investment proposals; (2) it does not provide a means for ranking proposals analyzed by its use with proposals analyzed by the so-called "discounted-cash-flow" method. Let me make a few observations on these points, followed by a brief comment on the development work on the MAPI formula now under way.

THE QUESTION OF UNIVERSALITY

The first contention can be quickly disposed of. No knowledgeable person has ever claimed universality of application of the MAPI formula. It was conceived and presented as a *replacement* formula (the term "replacement" being broadly construed to include mixed replacement-improvement-expansion situations), its main purpose being to indicate the proper *timing* of re-equipment decisions. It was offered as an improvement over the primitive rules of thumb so widely employed in American industry to make these decisions. As such, it has proved very useful, as evidenced by the extent of its employment.

Essentially, it provides a quick test of current replaceability on the basis of a prefabricated structure of assumptions and projections into which the analyst can insert the necessary stipulations and estimates for the case in hand (the amount of the investment, the income tax rate, the interest rate, the service life, the terminal salvage ratio, etc.). It is an elaborate gadget to simplify an otherwise almost insoluble problem. But it has never been endowed with universality, least of all by its sponsors, who have repeatedly cautioned against its overuse even in the special area of replacement analysis for which it was designed.

I can summarize the position of the institute by quoting the final paragraph of the *MAPI Replacement Manual:*

> The foregoing examples cover, obviously, a considerable range of replacement problems. They indicate, by the same token, the wide usefulness of the MAPI formula. We do not wish to close, however, without reiterating that we make no claim for its universal applicability. While the standard assumptions underlying the formula yield a generally reasonable pattern of projections for most cases, they do not do so for all. As we have been at pains to emphasize, our procedure offers only a useful tool in aid of judgment. We believe that if applied with discrimination it will yield, by and large and on the average, a substantially correct timing of replacement decisions.

In undertaking to disprove what has never been claimed for the formula, Messrs. Dean and Smith have merely demolished a straw man of their own creation.

* Research director, Machinery and Allied Products Institute.

THE RANKING PROBLEM

The second point is more interesting. It is said, first of all (p. 262), that the MAPI formula is designed for "non-rationing" situations in which sufficient capital funds are at hand to permit all indicated replacements to be made but that it does not quantify "in conventional terms" the advantage of one proposal over another.

If by "conventional terms" is meant rate-of-return or present-worth comparisons, the statement is technically correct; but it must not be inferred that the formula provides no procedure for ranking replacement proposals in the order of urgency or advantage. It does provide such a procedure. The "next-year gain from replacement" is stated in each case as a percentage of the required investment, and competing proposals are ranked in the order of these percentages.[1]

A more substantial contention, however, is that this ranking procedure for MAPI formula replacement analyses is not comparable to, and cannot be integrated with, rate-of-return or excess-present-worth rankings derived by the so-called "discounted-cash-flow" method.

My first observation is that MAPI rankings cannot be expected to jibe with both the rate-of-return *and* the excess-present-worth rankings because the two are incompatible with each other—notwithstanding the fact that the authors of the article appear to regard them as interchangeable.[2] I can illustrate by an oversimplified example, so contrived that the two rankings are precisely reversed. We have, let us say, four investment proposals, A, B, C, and D, which promise "gross earnings" of $1,000 a year for 5, 10, 15, and 20 years, respectively.[3] They are purchased to yield rates of return of 20, 18, 17, and 16 per cent. The "cost of capital" employed in the present-worth computations is 10 per cent. We then have the data given in Table 1.

TABLE 1

Investment Proposal	Amount of Investment	Present Worth of Earnings at Cost of Capital	Excess Present Worth as Per Cent of Investment	Rate of Return	Ranking: Excess Present Worth	Ranking: Rate of Return
A.	$2,991	$3,791	26.8	20	1	4
B.	4,494	6,145	36.7	18	2	3
C.	5,324	7,606	42.9	17	3	2
D.	5,929	8,514	43.6	16	4	1

Since the two Dean-Smith rankings are incompatible, perhaps further discussion should be suspended until we are told to which of them the MAPI ranking is expected to conform. It cannot conform to both.

We are involved here in a matter so complex and technical that an adequate discussion would run far beyond the limits of a brief rejoinder, which I do not intend to transgress. At the risk of being completely cryptic. I can only say that

[1] *MAPI Replacement Manual* (Chicago: MAPI, 1950), pp. 44, 45.

[2] See also another article by J. H. Lorie and L. J. Savage, "Three Problems in Rationing Capital," *Journal of Business*, XXVIII (October, 1955), 229–39. Here the potential incompatibility of the two ranking procedures is recognized, but it is assumed to occur only with exceptional, or freak, patterns of "gross earnings."

[3] A level annuity is an improbable pattern for earnings but will do for illustrative purposes. A similar reversal of rankings can be obtained with declining annuities.

MAPI rankings can be integrated with excess-present-worth rankings, but not with rate-of-return rankings. The method of integration is not, however, the one suggested in the Dean-Smith article.

DEVELOPMENT PROJECT

I alluded at the outset to the development work on the MAPI formula now under way. The reference is to a research project aimed at widening the applicability and improving the intelligibility of the formula. I shall not attempt to touch here on all aspects of the project but may refer to a few which bear on criticisms of the present formula in the Dean-Smith article.

Choice of projection patterns.—At present there is available only one projection for the accumulation of deterioration and obsolescence on the proposed installation. This assumes a constant rate of accumulation. There is no reason, however, why other patterns cannot be provided, thus giving the analyst a range of choice. For example, the projected accumulation rate can be more rapid in the early years of service than later, or slower at first and then faster. With a choice of projection patterns, the analyst can select the one that seems most appropriate for the proposed equipment and can achieve a better "fit" than when he has only one pattern for all cases. We expect to offer such a choice.

Precise income tax adjustments.—The present formula allows for the income tax by an appropriate "loading" of the interest rate. The result is approximative rather than exact, with deviations depending on the method of depreciation used for tax purposes. For straight-line, declining-balance, and sum-of-digits depreciation, these deviations are surprisingly small, but in the case of 5-year amortization they become substantial. One object of the development project is to provide an exact tax adjustment for the particular method of tax depreciation specified.

Precise adjustment for capital mix.—This improvement is closely related to the one just described. The present formula allows for the differing income tax effects of debt and equity capital by varying the tax "loading" of the interest rate. Here again the result is only approximately correct, and we propose to supply an exact solution for any specified debt-equity ratio.

Generalization.—As already stated, the present formula was conceived primarily as a device for timing replacements. There is no reason, however, why the basic theory of the formula cannot be applied in the analysis of completely new projects, and we are hopeful that the reformulation now under way will provide a useful guide for that purpose also. Incidentally, this reformulation will facilitate the comparison of new-project and replacement proposals in the preparation of capital budgets.

I have no illusion that an improved MAPI formula—or, indeed, any other—can solve the capital-investment problems of management. Many of these problems are so complex they defy formula solutions. Nevertheless, a good formula, intelligently applied, can be a valuable aid to judgment. This is all that has ever been claimed for the present MAPI formula and is, I hope, all that ever will be claimed for the improved version now in preparation.

VI

Discount Tables

TABLE 1

COMPOUND DISCOUNT $P = (1+R)^{-N}$

PRESENT VALUE OF ONE DOLLAR DUE AT THE END OF N YEARS

N	1%	2%	3%	4%	5%	6%	7%	8%	9%	10%	N
01	.99010	.98039	.97007	.96154	.95238	.94340	.93458	.92593	.91743	.90909	01
02	.98030	.96117	.94260	.92456	.90703	.89000	.87344	.85734	.84168	.82645	02
03	.97059	.94232	.91514	.88900	.86384	.83962	.81630	.79383	.77218	.75131	03
04	.96098	.92385	.88849	.85480	.82270	.79209	.76290	.73503	.70843	.68301	04
05	.95147	.90573	.86261	.82193	.78353	.74726	.71299	.68058	.64993	.62092	05
06	.94204	.88797	.83748	.79031	.74622	.70496	.66634	.63017	.59627	.56447	06
07	.93272	.87056	.81309	.75992	.71068	.66506	.62275	.58349	.54703	.51316	07
08	.92348	.85349	.78941	.73069	.67684	.62741	.58201	.54027	.50187	.46651	08
09	.91434	.83675	.76642	.70259	.64461	.59190	.54393	.50025	.46043	.42410	09
10	.90529	.82035	.74409	.67556	.61391	.55839	.50835	.46319	.42241	.38554	10
11	.89632	.80426	.72242	.64958	.58468	.52679	.47509	.42888	.38753	.35049	11
12	.88745	.78849	.70138	.62460	.55684	.49697	.44401	.39711	.35553	.31863	12
13	.87866	.77303	.68095	.60057	.53032	.46884	.41496	.36770	.32618	.28966	13
14	.86996	.75787	.66112	.57747	.50507	.44230	.38782	.34046	.29925	.26333	14
15	.86135	.74301	.64186	.55526	.48102	.41726	.36245	.31524	.27454	.23939	15
16	.85282	.72845	.62317	.53391	.45811	.39365	.33873	.29189	.25187	.21763	16
17	.84438	.71416	.60502	.51337	.43630	.37136	.31657	.27027	.23107	.19784	17
18	.83602	.70016	.58739	.49363	.41552	.35034	.29586	.25025	.21199	.17986	18
19	.82774	.68643	.57029	.47464	.39573	.33051	.27651	.23171	.19449	.16351	19
20	.81954	.67297	.55367	.45639	.37689	.31180	.25842	.21455	.17843	.14864	20
21	.81143	.65978	.53755	.43883	.35894	.29415	.24151	.19866	.16370	.13513	21
22	.80340	.64684	.52189	.42195	.34185	.27750	.22571	.18394	.15018	.12285	22
23	.79544	.63416	.50669	.40573	.32557	.26180	.21095	.17031	.13778	.11168	23
24	.78757	.62172	.49193	.39012	.31007	.24698	.19715	.15770	.12640	.10153	24
25	.77977	.60953	.47760	.37512	.29530	.23300	.18425	.14602	.11597	.09230	25

TABLE 1

PRESENT VALUE OF ONE DOLLAR DUE AT THE END OF N YEARS

N	11%	12%	13%	14%	15%	16%	17%	18%	19%	20%	N
01	.90090	.89286	.88496	.87719	.86957	.86207	.85470	.84746	.84034	.83333	01
02	.81162	.79719	.78315	.76947	.75614	.74316	.73051	.71818	.70616	.69444	02
03	.73119	.71178	.69305	.67497	.65752	.64066	.62437	.60863	.59342	.57870	03
04	.65873	.63552	.61332	.59208	.57175	.55229	.53365	.51579	.49867	.48225	04
05	.59345	.56743	.54276	.51937	.49718	.47611	.45611	.43711	.41905	.40188	05
06	.53464	.50663	.48032	.45559	.43233	.41044	.38984	.37043	.35214	.33490	06
07	.48166	.45235	.42506	.39964	.37594	.35383	.33320	.31392	.29592	.27908	07
08	.43393	.40388	.37616	.35056	.32690	.30503	.28478	.26604	.24867	.23257	08
09	.39092	.36061	.33288	.30751	.28426	.26295	.24340	.22546	.20897	.19381	09
10	.35218	.32197	.29459	.26974	.24718	.22668	.20804	.19106	.17560	.16151	10
11	.31728	.28748	.26070	.23662	.21494	.19542	.17781	.16192	.14756	.13459	11
12	.28584	.25667	.23071	.20756	.18691	.16846	.15197	.13722	.12400	.11216	12
13	.25751	.22917	.20416	.18207	.16253	.14523	.12989	.11629	.10420	.09346	13
14	.23199	.20462	.18068	.15971	.14133	.12520	.11102	.09855	.08757	.07789	14
15	.20900	.18270	.15989	.14010	.12289	.10793	.09489	.08352	.07359	.06491	15
16	.18829	.16312	.14150	.12289	.10686	.09304	.08110	.07078	.06184	.05409	16
17	.16963	.14564	.12522	.10780	.09293	.08021	.06932	.05998	.05196	.04507	17
18	.15282	.13004	.11081	.09456	.08080	.06914	.05925	.05083	.04367	.03756	18
19	.13768	.11611	.09806	.08295	.07026	.05961	.05064	.04308	.03669	.03130	19
20	.12403	.10367	.08678	.07276	.06110	.05139	.04328	.03651	.03084	.02608	20
21	.11174	.09256	.07680	.06383	.05313	.04430	.03699	.03094	.02591	.02174	21
22	.10067	.08264	.06796	.05599	.04620	.03819	.03162	.02622	.02178	.01811	22
23	.09069	.07379	.06014	.04911	.04017	.03292	.02702	.02222	.01830	.01509	23
24	.08170	.06588	.05322	.04308	.03493	.02838	.02310	.01883	.01538	.01258	24
25	.07361	.05882	.04710	.03779	.03038	.02447	.01974	.01596	.01292	.01048	25

TABLE 1

PRESENT VALUE OF ONE DOLLAR DUE AT THE END OF N YEARS

N	21%	22%	23%	24%	25%	26%	27%	28%	29%	30%	N
01	.82645	.81967	.81301	.80645	.80000	.79365	.78740	.78125	.77519	.76923	01
02	.68301	.67186	.66098	.65036	.64000	.62988	.62000	.61035	.60093	.59172	02
03	.56447	.55071	.53738	.52449	.51200	.49991	.48819	.47684	.46583	.45517	03
04	.46651	.45140	.43690	.42297	.40960	.39675	.38440	.37253	.36111	.35013	04
05	.38554	.37000	.35520	.34111	.32768	.31488	.30268	.29104	.27993	.26933	05
06	.31863	.30328	.28878	.27509	.26214	.24991	.23833	.22737	.21700	.20718	06
07	.26333	.24859	.23478	.22184	.20972	.19834	.18766	.17764	.16822	.15937	07
08	.21763	.20376	.19088	.17891	.16777	.15741	.14776	.13878	.13040	.12259	08
09	.17986	.16702	.15519	.14428	.13422	.12493	.11635	.10842	.10109	.09430	09
10	.14864	.13690	.12617	.11635	.10737	.09915	.09161	.08470	.07836	.07254	10
11	.12285	.11221	.10258	.09383	.08590	.07869	.07214	.06617	.06075	.05580	11
12	.10153	.09198	.08339	.07567	.06872	.06245	.05680	.05170	.04709	.04292	12
13	.08391	.07539	.06780	.06103	.05498	.04957	.04472	.04039	.03650	.03302	13
14	.06934	.06180	.05512	.04921	.04398	.03934	.03522	.03155	.02830	.02540	14
15	.05731	.05065	.04481	.03969	.03518	.03122	.02773	.02465	.02194	.01954	15
16	.04736	.04152	.03643	.03201	.02815	.02478	.02183	.01926	.01700	.01503	16
17	.03914	.03403	.02962	.02581	.02252	.01967	.01719	.01505	.01318	.01156	17
18	.03235	.02789	.02408	.02082	.01801	.01561	.01354	.01175	.01022	.00889	18
19	.02673	.02286	.01958	.01679	.01441	.01239	.01066	.00918	.00792	.00684	19
20	.02209	.01874	.01592	.01354	.01153	.00983	.00839	.00717	.00614	.00526	20
21	.01826	.01536	.01294	.01092	.00922	.00780	.00661	.00561	.00476	.00405	21
22	.01509	.01259	.01052	.00880	.00738	.00619	.00520	.00438	.00369	.00311	22
23	.01247	.01032	.00855	.00710	.00590	.00491	.00410	.00342	.00286	.00239	23
24	.01031	.00846	.00695	.00573	.00472	.00390	.00323	.00267	.00222	.00184	24
25	.00852	.00693	.00565	.00462	.00378	.00310	.00254	.00209	.00172	.00142	25

TABLE 1

PRESENT VALUE OF ONE DOLLAR DUE AT THE END OF N YEARS

N	31%	32%	33%	34%	35%	36%	37%	38%	39%	40%	N
01	.76336	.75758	.75188	.74627	.74074	.73529	.72993	.72464	.71942	.71429	01
02	.58272	.57392	.56532	.55692	.54870	.54066	.53279	.52510	.51757	.51020	02
03	.44482	.43479	.42505	.41561	.40644	.39754	.38890	.38051	.37235	.36443	03
04	.33956	.32939	.31959	.31016	.30107	.29231	.28387	.27573	.26788	.26031	04
05	.25920	.24953	.24029	.23146	.22301	.21493	.20720	.19980	.19272	.18593	05
06	.19787	.18904	.18067	.17273	.16520	.15804	.15124	.14479	.13865	.13281	06
07	.15104	.14321	.13584	.12890	.12237	.11621	.11040	.10492	.09975	.09486	07
08	.11530	.10849	.10214	.09620	.09064	.08545	.08058	.07603	.07176	.06776	08
09	.08802	.08219	.07680	.07179	.06714	.06283	.05882	.05509	.05163	.04840	09
10	.06719	.06227	.05774	.05357	.04973	.04620	.04293	.03992	.03714	.03457	10
11	.05129	.04717	.04341	.03998	.03684	.03397	.03134	.02893	.02672	.02469	11
12	.03915	.03574	.03264	.02984	.02729	.02498	.02287	.02096	.01922	.01764	12
13	.02989	.02707	.02454	.02227	.02021	.01837	.01670	.01519	.01383	.01260	13
14	.02281	.02051	.01845	.01662	.01497	.01350	.01219	.01101	.00995	.00900	14
15	.01742	.01554	.01387	.01240	.01109	.00993	.00890	.00798	.00716	.00643	15
16	.01329	.01177	.01043	.00925	.00822	.00730	.00649	.00578	.00515	.00459	16
17	.01015	.00892	.00784	.00691	.00609	.00537	.00474	.00419	.00370	.00328	17
18	.00775	.00676	.00590	.00515	.00451	.00395	.00346	.00304	.00267	.00234	18
19	.00591	.00512	.00443	.00385	.00334	.00290	.00253	.00220	.00192	.00167	19
20	.00451	.00388	.00333	.00287	.00247	.00213	.00184	.00159	.00138	.00120	20
21	.00345	.00294	.00251	.00214	.00183	.00157	.00135	.00115	.00099	.00085	21
22	.00263	.00223	.00188	.00160	.00136	.00115	.00098	.00084	.00071	.00061	22
23	.00201	.00169	.00142	.00119	.00101	.00085	.00072	.00061	.00051	.00044	23
24	.00153	.00128	.00107	.00089	.00074	.00062	.00052	.00044	.00037	.00031	24
25	.00117	.00097	.00080	.00066	.00055	.00046	.00038	.00032	.00027	.00022	25

TABLE 2

PRESENT VALUE OF ONE DOLLAR PER YEAR. N YEARS AT R%

Year	1%	.2%	3%	4%	5%	6%	7%	8%	9%	10%	Year
1	.9901	.9804	.9709	.9615	.9524	.9434	.9346	.9259	.9174	.9091	1
2	1.9704	1.9416	1.9135	1.8861	1.8594	1.8334	1.8080	1.7833	1.7591	1.7355	2
3	2.9410	2.8839	2.8286	2.7751	2.7232	2.6730	2.6243	2.5771	2.5313	2.4868	3
4	3.9020	3.8077	3.7171	3.6299	3.5459	3.4651	3.3872	3.3121	3.2397	3.1699	4
5	4.8535	4.7134	4.5797	4.4518	4.3295	4.2123	4.1002	3.9927	3.8896	3.7908	5
6	5.7955	5.6014	5.4172	5.2421	5.0757	4.9173	4.7665	4.6229	4.4859	4.3553	6
7	6.7282	6.4720	6.2302	6.0020	5.7863	5.5824	5.3893	5.2064	5.0329	4.8684	7
8	7.6517	7.3254	7.0196	6.7327	6.4632	6.2098	5.9713	5.7466	5.5348	5.3349	8
9	8.5661	8.1622	7.7861	7.4353	7.1078	6.8017	6.5152	6.2469	5.9852	5.7590	9
10	9.4714	8.9825	8.5302	8.1109	7.7217	7.3601	7.0236	6.7101	6.4176	6.1446	10
11	10.3677	9.7868	9.2526	8.7604	8.3064	7.8868	7.4987	7.1389	6.8052	6.4951	11
12	11.2552	10.5753	9.9539	9.3850	8.8632	8.3838	7.9427	7.5361	7.1607	6.8137	12
13	12.1338	11.3483	10.6349	9.9856	9.3935	8.8527	8.3576	7.9038	7.4869	7.1034	13
14	13.0038	12.1062	11.2960	10.5631	9.8986	9.2950	8.7454	8.2442	7.7861	7.3667	14
15	13.8651	12.8492	11.9379	11.1183	10.3796	9.7122	9.1079	8.5595	8.0607	7.6061	15
16	14.7180	13.5777	12.5610	11.6522	10.8377	10.1059	9.4466	8.8514	8.3125	7.8237	16
17	15.5624	14.2918	13.1660	12.1656	11.2740	10.4772	9.7632	9.1216	8.5436	8.0215	17
18	16.3984	14.9920	13.7534	12.6592	11.6895	10.8276	10.0591	9.3719	8.7556	8.2014	18
19	17.2261	15.6784	14.3237	13.1339	12.0853	11.1581	10.3356	9.6036	8.9501	8.3649	19
20	18.0457	16.3514	14.8774	13.5903	12.4622	11.4699	10.5940	9.8181	9.1285	8.5136	20
21	18.8571	17.0111	15.4149	14.0291	12.8211	11.7640	10.8355	10.0168	9.2922	8.6487	21
22	19.6605	17.6580	15.9368	14.4511	13.1630	12.0416	11.0612	10.2007	9.4424	8.7715	22
23	20.4559	18.2921	16.4435	14.8568	13.4885	12.3033	11.2722	10.3710	9.5802	8.8832	23
24	21.2435	18.9139	16.9355	15.2469	13.7986	12.5503	11.4693	10.5287	9.7066	8.9847	24
25	22.0233	19.5234	17.4131	15.6220	14.0939	12.7833	11.6536	10.6748	9.8226	9.0770	25

TABLE 2

PRESENT VALUE OF ONE DOLLAR PER YEAR. N YEARS AT R%

Year	11%	12%	13%	14%	15%	16%	17%	18%	19%	20%	Year
1	.9009	.8929	.8850	.3772	.8696	.8621	.8547	.8475	.8403	.8333	1
2	1.7125	1.6901	1.6681	1.6467	1.6257	1.6052	1.5852	1.5656	1.5465	1.5278	2
3	2.4437	2.4018	2.3612	2.3216	2.2832	2.2459	2.2096	2.1743	2.1399	2.1065	3
4	3.1024	3.0373	2.9745	2.9137	2.8550	2.7982	2.7432	2.6901	2.6386	2.5887	4
5	3.6959	3.6048	3.5172	3.4331	3.3522	3.2743	3.1993	3.1272	3.0576	2.9906	5
6	4.2305	4.1114	3.9976	3.8887	3.7845	3.6847	3.5892	3.4976	3.4098	3.3255	6
7	4.7122	4.5638	4.4226	4.2883	4.1604	4.0386	3.9224	3.8115	3.7057	3.6046	7
8	5.1461	4.9676	4.7988	4.6389	4.4873	4.3436	4.2072	4.0776	3.9544	3.8372	8
9	5.5370	5.3282	5.1317	4.9464	4.7716	4.6065	4.4506	4.3030	4.1633	4.0310	9
10	5.8892	5.6502	5.4262	5.2161	5.0188	4.8332	4.6586	4.4941	4.3389	4.1925	10
11	6.2065	5.9377	5.6869	5.4527	5.2337	5.0286	4.8364	4.6560	4.4865	4.3271	11
12	6.4924	6.1944	5.9176	5.6603	5.4206	5.1971	4.9884	4.7932	4.6105	4.4392	12
13	6.7499	6.4235	6.1218	5.8424	5.5831	5.3423	5.1183	4.9095	4.7147	4.5327	13
14	6.9819	6.6282	6.3025	6.0021	5.7245	5.4675	5.2293	5.0081	4.8023	4.6106	14
15	7.1909	6.8109	6.4624	6.1422	5.8474	5.5755	5.3242	5.0916	4.8759	4.6755	15
16	7.3792	6.9740	6.6039	6.2651	5.9542	5.6685	5.4053	5.1624	4.9377	4.7296	16
17	7.5488	7.1196	6.7291	6.3729	6.0472	5.7487	5.4746	5.2223	4.9897	4.7746	17
18	7.7016	7.2497	6.8399	6.4674	6.1280	5.8178	5.5339	5.2732	5.0333	4.8122	18
19	7.8393	7.3658	6.9380	6.5504	6.1982	5.8775	5.5845	5.3162	5.0700	4.8435	19
20	7.9633	7.4694	7.0248	6.6231	6.2593	5.9288	5.6278	5.3527	5.1009	4.8696	20
21	8.0751	7.5620	7.1016	6.6870	6.3125	5.9731	5.6648	5.3837	5.1268	4.8913	21
22	8.1757	7.6446	7.1695	6.7429	6.3587	6.0113	5.6964	5.4099	5.1486	4.9094	22
23	8.2664	7.7184	7.2297	6.7921	6.3988	6.0442	5.7234	5.4321	5.1668	4.9245	23
24	8.3481	7.7843	7.2829	6.8351	6.4338	6.0726	5.7465	5.4509	5.1822	4.9371	24
25	8.4217	7.8431	7.3300	6.8729	6.4641	6.0971	5.7662	5.4669	5.1951	4.9476	25

TABLE 2

PRESENT VALUE OF ONE DOLLAR PER YEAR. N YEARS AT R%

ear	21%	22%	23%	24%	25%	26%	27%	28%	29%	30%	Year
1	.8264	.8197	.8130	.8065	.8000	.7937	.7874	.7813	.7752	.7692	1
2	1.5095	1.4915	1.4740	1.4568	1.4400	1.4235	1.4074	1.3916	1.3761	1.3609	2
3	2.0739	2.0422	2.0114	1.9813	1.9520	1.9234	1.8956	1.8684	1.8420	1.8161	3
4	2.5404	2.4936	2.4483	2.4043	2.3616	2.3202	2.2800	2.2410	2.2031	2.1662	4
5	2.9260	2.8636	2.8035	2.7454	2.6893	2.6351	2.5827	2.5320	2.4830	2.4356	5
6	3.2446	3.1669	3.0923	3.0205	2.9514	2.8850	2.8210	2.7594	2.7000	2.6427	6
7	3.5079	3.4155	3.3270	3.2423	3.1611	3.0833	3.0087	2.9370	2.8682	2.8021	7
8	3.7256	3.6193	3.5179	3.4212	3.3289	3.2407	3.1564	3.0758	2.9986	2.9247	8
9	3.9054	3.7863	3.6731	3.5655	3.4631	3.3657	3.2728	3.1842	3.0997	3.0190	9
10	4.0541	3.9232	3.7993	3.6819	3.5705	3.4648	3.3644	3.2689	3.1781	3.0915	10
11	4.1769	4.0354	3.9018	3.7757	3.6564	3.5435	3.4365	3.3351	3.2388	3.1473	11
12	4.2785	4.1274	3.9852	3.8514	3.7251	3.6060	3.4933	3.3868	3.2859	3.1903	12
13	4.3624	4.2028	4.0530	3.9124	3.7801	3.6555	3.6381	3.4272	3.3224	3.2233	13
14	4.4317	4.2646	4.1082	3.9616	3.8241	3.6949	3.5733	3.4587	3.3507	3.2487	14
15	4.4890	4.3152	4.1530	4.0013	3.8593	3.7261	3.6010	3.4834	3.3726	3.2682	15
16	4.5364	4.3567	4.1894	4.0333	3.8874	3.7509	3.6228	3.5026	3.3896	3.2832	16
17	4.5755	4.3908	4.2190	4.0591	3.9099	3.7705	3.6400	3.5177	3.4028	3.2948	17
18	4.6079	4.4187	4.2431	4.0799	3.9279	3.7861	3.6536	3.5294	3.4130	3.3037	18
19	4.6346	4.4415	4.2627	4.0967	3.9424	3.7985	3.6642	3.5386	3.4210	3.3105	19
20	4.6567	4.4603	4.2786	4.1103	3.9539	3.8083	3.6726	3.5458	3.4271	3.3158	20
21	4.6750	4.4756	4.2916	4.1212	3.9631	3.8161	3.6792	3.5514	3.4319	3.3198	21
22	4.6900	4.4882	4.3021	4.1300	3.9705	3.8223	3.6844	3.5558	3.4356	3.3230	22
23	4.7025	4.4985	4.3106	4.1371	3.9764	3.8273	3.6885	3.5592	3.4384	3.3254	23
24	4.7128	4.5070	4.3176	4.1428	3.9811	3.8312	3.6918	3.5619	3.4406	3.3272	24
25	4.7213	4.5139	4.3232	4.1474	3.9849	3.8342	3.6943	3.5640	3.4423	3.3286	25

TABLE 2

PRESENT VALUE OF ONE DOLLAR PER YEAR. N YEARS AT R%

Year	31%	32%	33%	34%	35%	36%	37%	38%	39%	40%	Year
1	.7634	.7576	.7519	.7463	.7407	.7353	.7299	.7246	.7194	.7143	1
2	1.3461	1.3315	1.3172	1.3032	1.2894	1.2760	1.2627	1.2497	1.2370	1.2245	2
3	1.7909	1.7663	1.7423	1.7188	1.6959	1.6735	1.6516	1.6302	1.6093	1.5889	3
4	2.1305	2.0957	2.0618	2.0290	1.9969	1.9658	1.9355	1.9060	1.8772	1.8492	4
5	2.3897	2.3452	2.3021	2.2604	2.2200	2.1807	2.1427	2.1058	2.0699	2.9352	5
6	2.5875	2.5342	2.4828	2.4331	2.3852	2.3388	2.2939	2.2506	2.2086	2.1680	6
7	2.7386	2.6775	2.6187	2.5620	2.5075	2.4550	2.4043	2.3555	2.3083	2.2628	7
8	2.8539	2.7860	2.7208	2.6582	2.5982	2.5404	2.4849	2.4315	2.3801	2.3306	8
9	2.9419	2.8681	2.7976	2.7300	2.6653	2.6033	2.5437	2.4866	2.4317	2.3790	9
10	3.0091	2.9304	2.8553	2.7836	2.7150	2.6495	2.5867	2.5265	2.4689	2.4136	10
11	3.0604	2.9776	2.8987	2.8236	2.7519	2.6834	2.6180	2.5555	2.4956	2.4383	11
12	3.0995	3.0133	2.9314	2.8534	2.7792	2.7084	2.6409	2.5764	2.5148	2.4559	12
13	3.1294	3.0404	2.9559	2.8757	2.7994	2.7268	2.6576	2.5916	2.5286	2.4685	13
14	3.1522	3.0609	2.9744	2.8923	2.8144	2.7403	2.6698	2.6026	2.5386	2.4775	14
15	3.1696	3.0764	2.9883	2.9047	2.8255	2.7502	2.6787	2.6106	2.5457	2.4839	15
16	3.1829	3.0882	2.9987	2.9140	2.8337	2.7575	2.6852	2.6164	2.5509	2.4885	16
17	3.1931	3.0971	3.0065	2.9209	2.8398	2.7629	2.6899	2.6206	2.5546	2.4918	17
18	3.2008	3.1039	3.0124	2.9260	2.8443	2.7668	2.6934	2.6236	2.5573	2.4941	18
19	3.2067	3.1090	3.0169	2.9299	2.8476	2.7697	2.6959	2.6258	2.5592	2.4958	19
20	3.2112	3.1129	3.0202	2.9327	2.8501	2.7718	2.6977	2.6274	2.5606	2.4970	20
21	3.2147	3.1158	3.0227	2.9349	2.8519	2.7734	2.6991	2.6285	2.5616	2.4979	21
22	3.2173	3.1180	3.0246	2.9365	2.8533	2.7746	2.7000	2.6294	2.5623	2.4985	22
23	3.2193	3.1197	3.0260	2.9377	2.8543	2.7754	2.7008	2.6300	2.5628	2.4989	23
24	3.2209	3.1210	3.0271	2.9386	2.8550	2.7760	2.7013	2.6304	2.5632	2.4992	24
25	3.2220	3.1220	3.0279	2.9392	2.8556	2.7765	2.7017	2.6307	2.5634	2.4994	25

TABLE 3

DIFFERENCE BETWEEN CONTINUOUS (C) AND ANNUAL (A) DISCOUNTING INTERVALS

PRESENT VALUE OF ONE DOLLAR DUE AT THE END OF N YEARS

	5 per cent		10 per cent		15 per cent		20 per cent	
N	C	A	C	A	C	A	C	A
01	.9512	.9524	.9048	.9091	.8607	.8696	.8187	.8333
05	.7788	.7835	.6065	.6209	.4724	.4972	.3679	.4019
10	.6065	.6139	.3679	.3855	.2231	.2472	.1353	.1615
15	.4724	.4810	.2231	.2394	.1054	.1229	.0498	.0649
20	.3679	.3769	.1353	.1486	.0498	.0611	.0183	.0261
25	.2865	.2953	.0821	.0923	.0235	.0304	.0067	.0105

VII
Classified Bibliography

Classified Bibliography

This bibliography is classified under six general headings:

I. General Works

II. The Measurement of Investment Worth

III. The Technical Apparatus of Capital Decisions

IV. The Cost of Capital

V. Equipment Replacement, Leasing, and Abandonment

VI. Procedures and Policies

Items marked with an asterisk (*) are included in this volume.

I. *General Works*

Anthony, R., *Management Accounting,* Ch. 17 and 18, R. D. Irwin Inc., Homewood, 1956.

Boulding, Kenneth E., *Economic Analysis,* rev. ed., pp. 782-830, Harper and Brothers, New York, 1948.

Dean, Joel, *Capital Budgeting,* Columbia University Press, New York, 1951.

Dean, Joel, *Managerial Economics,* Ch. 10, Prentice-Hall, New York, 1951.

Fisher, Irving, *The Nature of Capital and Income,* MacMillan Company, London, 1906.

Fisher, Irving, *The Theory of Interest,* MacMillan Company, New York, 1930.

Hunt, Williams, and Donaldson, *Basic Business Finance,* Ch. 16 and 17, R. D. Irwin, Inc., Homewood, 1958.

Lutz, Friedrick and Vera Lutz, *Theory of Investment of the Firm,* Princeton University, Princeton, 1951.

Spencer, M. H. and L. Siegelman, *Managerial Economics,* Ch. 10 and 11, R. D. Irwin, Inc., Homewood, 1959.

II. *The Measurement of Investment Worth*

*Alchian, A. A., "The Rate of Interest, Fisher's Rate of Return over Cost, and Keynes' Internal Rate of Return," *American Economic Review,* Dec., 1955.

Bierman, H. and S. Smidt, "Capital Budgeting and the Problem of Reinvesting Cash Proceeds," *Journal of Business,* Oct., 1957.

Dean, Joel, "Better Management of Capital Expenditures through Research," *Journal of Finance,* May, 1953.

Dean, Joel, "Break-even Analysis and the Measurement of Capital Productivity," *Advanced Management,* April, 1955.

Dean, Joel, "Capital Expenditure and Return on Investment," *Annals of the National Society of Business Budgeting,* 1953.

Dean, Joel, "Capital Rationing and the Firm's Demand for Capital," *Zeitschrift fur Oekonometrie,* 1951.

*Dean, Joel, "Measuring the Productivity of Capital," *Harvard Business Review,* Jan.-Feb., 1954.

Dean, Joel, "Profitability Indexes for Capital Investment," *The Controller,* Feb., 1958.

Dean, Joel, "Using the Capital Budgeting System," *Commercial Car Journal,* 1948.

Fagley, W. L. and G. W. Blum, "Calculate Payout Time for Your Capital Investment," *Chemical Engineering,* July, 1950.

*Gordon, M. J., "The Payoff Period and the Rate of Profit," *Journal of Business,* Oct., 1955.

Grant, E. L., *Principles of Engineering Economy,* Ronald Press, New York, 1950.

Griswold, John A., "More for your Capital Dollar: Finding the Realistic Rate of Return," Amos Tuck School of Business Administration, Dartmouth College, 1957.

Happel, J., "New Approach to Payout Calculations," *Chemical Engineering,* Oct., 1951.

Happel, J., "The Venture Worth Method for Economic Balances in Chemical Engineering," *Chemical Engineering Progress,* Dec., 1955.

Heller, Walter W., "The Anatomy of Investment Decisions," *Harvard Business Review,* March, 1951.

*Hill, Horace, "A New Method of Computing the Rate of Return on Capital Expenditures," Phil. Society of Business Budgeting, 1953.

Jelen, F. G., "Technology Review," *Chemical En-*

gineering, April, 1956.

Kamsky, L., "Cost Analysis for Improved Return on Investment," N.A.C.A. Bulletin, July, 1955.

Keynes, J. M., *The General Theory of Employment, Interest, and Money,* Ch. 11, MacMillan and Company, London 1936.

*Lorie, J. and L. J. Savage, "Three Problems in Capital Rationing," *Journal of Business,* Oct., 1955.

McLean, John G., "How to Evaluate New Capital Investments," *Harvard Business Review,* Nov.-Dec., 1958.

*Renshaw, E., "A Note on the Arithmetic of Capital Budgeting Decisions," *Journal of Business,* July, 1957.

Reul, R. I., "Newest Way to Figure Payoff," *factory Management and Maintenance,* Oct., 1955.

Rohleder, G. V., "Evaluating Investments by the Discounted Cash Flow Method," *World Oil,* Sept., 1955.

*Robinson, Romney, "Interest—Return over Costs or Internal Rate: Comment," *American Economic Review,* Dec., 1956.

Scheuble, P. A., Jr., "How to Figure Equipment Replacement," *Harvard Business Review,* Sept.-Oct., 1955.

Schweyer, H. E., *Process Engineering Economics,* Ch. 1, 2 and 7, McGraw-Hill Book Company, New York, 1955.

*Shillinglaw, G., "Residual Values in Investment Analysis," *Journal of Business,* Oct., 1955.

*Solomon, Ezra, "The Arithmetic of Capital Budgeting Decisions," *Journal of Business,* April, 1956.

Weaver, J. B. and R. J. Reilly, "Interest Rate of Return for Capital Expenditure Valuation," *Chemical Engineering Progress,* Oct., 1956.

Winn, F. W., "How to Invest Your Capital for Profits," *Petroleum Refiner,* July, 1956.

III. *The Technical Apparatus of Capital Decisions*

Bennion, Edward G., "Capital Budgeting and Game Theory," *Harvard Business Review,* Nov.-Dec., 1956.

*Charnes, A., W. W. Cooper, and M. H. Miller, "Application of Linear Programming to Financial Budgeting and the Costing of Funds," *Journal of Business,* Jan., 1959.

Dean, Joel, and Associates, *Interest Tables for Determining Rate of Return by the Discounted Cash Flow Method,* (From 0-100%), Joel Dean Associates, New York.

Fetter, R. B. and T. P. Goodman, "An Equipment Investment Analog," *Operations Research,* Oct., 1957.

*Hirshleifer, J., "On the Theory of Optimal Investment Decision," *Journal of Political Economy,* Aug., 1958.

Knight, F. H., "Interest," Encyclopedia of the Social Sciences, Macmillan Company, New York, 1937.

Todhunter, R., *The Institute of Actuaries' Textbook on Compound Interest and Annuities Certain,* 4th ed. rev., Cambridge, England, 1937.

Williams, K. P., *The Mathematical Theory of Finance,* rev. ed., Macmillan Company, New York, 1948.

Williams, J. B., *The Theory of Investment Values,* Harvard Univ. Press, Cambridge, Massachusetts, 1938.

IV. *The Cost of Capital*

Allen, F. B., "Does Going Into Debt Lower the 'Cost of Capital'?", *Analysts Journal,* August, 1954.

Dean, Joel, "The Present Cost of Investing in the Company's Future," *Planning Ahead for Profits,* American Management Association, 1958.

Dobrovolsky, S. P., "Economics of Corporate Internal and External Financing," *Journal of Finance,* March, 1958.

Durand, David, "Growth Stocks and the Petersburg Paradox," *Journal of Finance,* Sept., 1957.

*Durand, D., "The Cost of Capital in an Imperfect Market: A Reply to Modigliani and Miller," *American Economic Review,* Sept., 1959.

*Durand, D., "The Cost of Debt and Equity Funds for Business," in *Conference on Research in Business Finance,* National Bureau of Economic Research, New York, 1952.

Foster, Louis O., "Corporate Debt and the Stockholder," Amos Tuck School of Business Administration, Dartmouth College, 1956.

Gordon, M. J., "Dividends, Earnings, and Stock Prices," *Review of Economics and Statistics,* May, 1959.

*Gordon, M. J. and Eli Shapiro, "Capital Equipment Analysis: The Required Rate of Profit," *Management Science,* Oct., 1956.

Hunt, P. and Williams, "Liquigas, Inc." in *Case Problems in Finance,* rev. ed. pp. 193-196, R. D. Irwin, Inc., Homewood, 1955.

McGraw-Hill, "How and Why Industry Modernizes," *Business Week,* Special Report, Sept. 27, 1958.

*Modigliani, F. and M. H. Miller, "The Cost of Capital, Corporation Finance, and the Theory of Investment," *American Economic Review,* June, 1958.

Modigliani, F. and Morton Zeman, "The Effect of the Availability of Funds and the Terms thereof on Business Investment," in *Conference on Research in Business Finance,* National Bureau of Economic Research, New York, 1952.

*Roberts, H. V., "Current Problems in the Economics of Capital Budgeting," *Journal of Business,* Jan., 1957.

Smith, D. T., *Effects of Taxation on Corporate Financial Policy,* Harvard University, Boston, 1953.

*Solomon, Ezra, "Measuring a Company's Cost of Capital," *Journal of Business,* Oct., 1955.

Soule, Roland P., "Trends in the Cost of Capital," *Harvard Business Review,* March-April, 1953.

Thatcher, L. W., "Cost-of-Capital Techniques Employed in Determining the Rate of Return for Public Utilities," *Land Economics,* May, 1954.

V. *Equipment Replacement, Leasing, and Abandonment*

Alchian, A. A., "Economic Replacement Policy," Rand Corporation, Special Report No. R-224, 1952.

American Management Association, *Capital Equipment Replacement,* Special Report No. 1, American Management Association, New York, 1954.

Anthony, R. N. and S. Schwartz, *Office Equipment —Buy or Rent?,* Management Analysis Center, Inc., Boston, 1957.

Anthony, R. N., *Shoe Machinery—Buy or Lease?,* National Shoe Manufacturers Association, 1955.

Bellman, R., "Equipment Replacement Policy," *Journal of Industrial Applied Mathematics,* Sept., 1955.

*Dean, J. and W. Smith, "Has MAPI a Place in a Comprehensive System of Capital Controls?," *Journal of Business,* Oct. 1955, (Discussion: G. Terbough, April, 1956).

Griesinger, Frank K., "Pros and Cons of Leasing Equipment," *Harvard Business Review,* March-April, 1955.

Jelen, F. C., "Replacement Analysis by Capitalized Costs," *Chemical Engineering,* August, 1955.

Karush, William, "On a Class of Minimum-Cost Problems," *Management Science,* Vol. 4, pp. 136-153, The Institute of Management Science, Baltimore, 1958.

Orensteen, R. B., "Topics on MAPI Formula," *Journal of Industrial Engineering,* Nov.-Dec., 1956.

MAPI Replacement Manual, *Machinery and Allied Products Institute,* Washington, D. C., 1950.

Schwan, H. T., "Replacement of Machinery and Equipment," *Industrial Engineering Handbook,* McGraw-Hill, New York, 1956.

*Shillinglaw, G., "Profit Analysis for Abandonment Decisions," *Journal of Business,* Jan., 1957.

Smith, Vernon L., "Economic Equipment Policies: An Evaluation," *Management Science,* Oct., 1958.

Terborgh, George, *Business Investment Analysis,* Machinery and Allied Products Institute, Washington, D. C., 1958.

Terborgh, George, *Dynamic Equipment Policy,* McGraw-Hill, New York, 1949.

*Terborgh, George, "Some Comments on the Dean-Smith Article on the MAPI Formula," *Journal of Business,* April, 1956.

Treynor, J. L. and R. F. Vancil, *Machine Tool Leasing,* Management Analysis Center, Inc., Boston, 1956.

VI. *Procedures and Policies*

Bishop, A. N., Jr., "Practical Budgeting of Capital Expenditures," *N.A.C.A. Bulletin,* Dec., 1956.

Dean, Shillinglaw, Wipfler, and Hill, *Modern Management of Capital Expenditures,* Financial Management Services #105, American Management Association, New York, 1953.

Eisner, Robert, "Determinants of Capital Expenditures—An Interview Study," Bureau of Economics and Business Research, University of Illinois, 1956.

Frank, G. W., "Let's Develop Return-on-Investment Consciousness," *N.A.C.A. Bulletin,* Oct., 1956.

Gort, M., "Planning of Investment: A Study of Capital Budgeting in the Electric Power Industry," *Journal of Business,* April, 1951.

Heiser, H. C., "Justifying Capital Expenditures—Before and After," *N.A.C.A. Bulletin,* Sept., 1956.

*Hill, Horace, "Capital Expenditure Management," *Journal of Business,* Oct., 1955.

Kempster, J. H., "How We Project Our Capital Needs," *N.A.C.A. Bulletin,* May, 1956.

Kutvirt, O., "Departmentalization of Return-on-Investment," *N.A.C.A. Bulletin,* Oct., 1956.

Lindsey, D. N., "Problems in Analysis of Return on Investment," *N.A.C.A. Bulletin,* Feb., 1956.

Livingston, W. G., "Clarifying Return-on-Investment Determination," *N.A.C.A. Bulletin,* Oct., 1956.

Matthews, John B., Jr., "How to Administer Capital Spending," *Harvard Business Review,* March-April, 1959.

Mettler, F. L., "Before-the-Fact Control of Capital Outlay," *N.A.A. Bulletin,* June, 1951.

National Bureau of Economic Research, *Conference of Regularization of Business Investment,* Princeton University Press, Princeton, 1954.

*Norton, F. E., "Administrative Organization in Capital Budgeting," *Journal of Business,* Oct., 1955.

Peirce, J. L., "The Budget Comes of Age," *Harvard Business Review,* May, 1954.

Platt, D. R., "Capital Expenditure Analysis Procedure," *Advanced Management,* Oct., 1957.

Wagner, H. R., "The Appropriation Request—An Instrument for Control of Capital Charges," *Chemical Engineering Progress,* pp. 402-4, Oct., 1956.

Smith, D. T., Effects of Taxation on Corporate Financial Policy, Harvard University, Boston, 1952.

Solomon, Ezra, "Measuring a Company's Cost of Capital," Journal of Business, [illegible]

[illegible], "[illegible] to the Cost of Capital," [illegible] Review, March, [illegible]

Witmer, F. W., "[illegible] Financial [illegible] the [illegible] Public Utilities," Land Economics, Aug., 1954.

V. Equipment Replacement, Leasing, and Acquisition

Alchian, A. A., "Economic Replacement Policy," Rand Corporation Study, Report No. [illegible]

American Institute of Accountants, [illegible] Accounting Research Bulletin No. [illegible], American Institute [illegible], New York, [illegible]

Anderson, R. N., [illegible] Management Analysis Corp., Inc., [illegible]

[illegible], [illegible] Machinery and Allied Products Institute, [illegible]

[illegible], Journal of Accounting, [illegible]

[illegible], "[illegible] Comprehensive System of [illegible] Control," Journal of Engineering, [illegible]

[illegible], "[illegible] Equipment," Harvard Business Review, March-April, [illegible]

[illegible], "[illegible] Capitalized [illegible]," Applied Engineering, August, 1955.

[illegible], "[illegible] Case of Machine [illegible]," [illegible] Management Series No. [illegible]

[illegible], "[illegible] of MAPI Formula," Journal of Industrial Engineering, [illegible]

MAPI Replacement Manual, Machinery and Allied Products Institute, Washington, D.C., 1950.

[illegible], "The Replacement of [illegible]," Engineering [illegible] Handbook, McGraw-Hill, New York, 1956.

[illegible], "[illegible] MAPI [illegible]," Journal of Business, Jan., 1957.

[illegible], "[illegible] Evaluation," Management Series [illegible]

[illegible], Machinery and Allied Products Institute, Washington, D.C., 1958.

[illegible], Harvard Business Review, [illegible]

McGraw-Hill, New York, 1949.

[illegible], "[illegible] on the [illegible] Attack on the MAPI Formula," Journal of Business, [illegible]

[illegible] and [illegible], Machine Tool [illegible] Management Analysis Corp., Inc., Boston, [illegible]

VI. Inventories and [illegible]

[illegible], "[illegible] Inventory of Capital [illegible]," [illegible], Dec., 1956.

[illegible], [illegible] of Capital Expenditures, American Management Association, New York, [illegible]

[illegible], Robert, "The Determination of Capital Expenditures," [illegible] and Business Review, University of Illinois, 1957.

Clark, [illegible], "[illegible] Return on [illegible]," [illegible] Bulletin, Dec., 1956.

[illegible], "[illegible] A Study of [illegible] Budgeting in the Electric Power Industry," Journal of Business, April, 1955.

[illegible], "[illegible] Capital [illegible] Before and After," [illegible]

[illegible], "Capital Expenditure Management," Journal of Business, Oct., 1957.

[illegible], "[illegible] Our Capital [illegible]," [illegible], May, [illegible]

[illegible], "[illegible] Return on [illegible]," [illegible] Bulletin, Oct., 1956.

[illegible], "[illegible]," [illegible] Bulletin, [illegible]

[illegible], "[illegible]," [illegible] Bulletin, [illegible]

[illegible], John G., "[illegible] Capital [illegible]," Harvard Business Review, [illegible]

[illegible], "[illegible] Control of Capital [illegible]," [illegible] Bulletin, June, [illegible]

National [illegible] of [illegible] Conference, [illegible]

[illegible], "[illegible] in Capital [illegible]," Journal of Business, Oct., [illegible]

[illegible], "[illegible]," Harvard Business Review, May, [illegible]

[illegible], "[illegible] Comprehensive Analysis [illegible]," [illegible] Management, Oct., [illegible]

[illegible], "[illegible] Control of Capital [illegible]," [illegible] Engineering, [illegible]